# Lecture Notes
# in Economics and
# Mathematical Systems

Managing Editors: M. Beckmann and H. P. Künzi

Operations Research

171

## G. F. Newell

## Approximate Behavior
## of Tandem Queues

Springer-Verlag
Berlin Heidelberg New York 1979

**Author**

Gordon F. Newell
Institute of Transportation Studies
University of California
Berkeley, CA 94720/USA

AMS Subject Classifications (1980): 60 K 25, 90 B 22, 90-02

ISBN 3-540-09552-7 Springer-Verlag Berlin Heidelberg New York
ISBN 0-387-09552-7 Springer-Verlag New York Heidelberg Berlin

Library of Congress Cataloging in Publication Data
Newell, Gordon Frank, 1925-
Approximate behavior of tandem queues.
(Lecture notes in economics and mathematical systems ; 171 : Operations research)
    Bibliography: p.
    Includes index.
1. Queuing theory. I. Title. II. Series: Lecture notes in economics and mathematical
systems ; 171.T57.9.N486 519.8'2 79-20953
ISBN 0-387-09552-7

© by Springer-Verlag Berlin Heidelberg 1979
Printed in Germany

Printing and binding: Beltz Offsetdruck, Hemsbach/Bergstr.
2142/3140-543210

## Preface

The following monograph deals with the approximate stochastic behavior
of a system consisting of a sequence of servers in series with finite storage
between consecutive servers. The methods employ deterministic queueing and
diffusion approximations which are valid under conditions in which the storages
and the queue lengths are typically large compared with 1. One can disregard
the fact that the customer counts must be integer valued and treat the queue
as if it were a (stochastic) continuous fluid. In these approximations, it
is not necessary to describe the detailed probability distribution of service
times; it suffices simply to specify the rate of service and the variance rate
(the variance of the number served per unit time).

Specifically, customers are considered to originate from an infinite
reservoir. They first pass through a server with service rate $\mu_0$ , variance rate $\Delta_0$ , into a storage of finite capacity $c_1$ . They then pass
through a server with service rate $\mu_1$ , variance rate $\Delta_1$ , into a storage
of capacity $c_2$ , etc., until finally, after passing through an nth server,
they go into an infinite reservoir (disappear). If any jth storage become
full $j = 1, 2, \ldots , n$ , the service at the j-1th server is interrupted
and, of course, if a jth storage becomes empty the jth server is interrupted; otherwise, services work at their maximum rate.

Equivalently one could have a system of servers 1, 2, . . . , n fed
by an arrival process of rate $\mu_0$ , variance rate $\Delta_0$ . If the storage $c_1$
is full, the arrival process is considered either to be interrupted or to
throw any excess arrivals that cannot enter the full storage out of the system
("lost call") or back into the infinite source.

The properties of the system are described in terms of the random vector $D_0(t)$, $D_1(t)$, ..., $D_n(t)$; in which $D_j(t)$ is the cumulative number of customers to pass the jth server by time $t$ starting from some initial state at time $0$.

Chapter I first describes the general formulation of the problem. The deterministic approximation $(\Delta_j = 0)$ is then analysed leading to an explicit evaluation of the $D_j(t)$ starting from an arbitrary initial state and for arbitrary choices of the $\mu_j$ and $n$. For sufficiently large $t$, all servers will serve at the rate $\mu = \min \mu_j$ of the "bottleneck." For $\Delta_j > 0$, the stochastic properties of the $D_j(t)$ are described in terms of their time-dependent joint probability density. This probability density is shown to satisfy (approximately) a diffusion equation in $n+1$ space variables plus time. The density must, in addition, satisfy certain boundary conditions when one or more of the storages is either empty or full. Various general properties of the system of equations, such as overall service rate, marginal queue length distributions, etc., are described. Subsequent chapters will deal with solutions of the equations in whatever special cases one can obtain solutions in some manageable form.

Chapter II will deal with the case $n = 1$, a single queue. The analysis is for arbitrary choices of the $\mu_0$, $\Delta_0$, $c_1$, $\mu_1$, $\Delta_1$ and describes the time-dependent behavior of the joint distribution of $D_0(t)$, $D_1(t)$ from an arbitrary initial state. In contrast with previous treatments of a single server system, this analysis describes both the input and the output or equivalently the queue length and the output. In particular, the results give an explicit formula for the equilibrium service rate $\mu$ and the equilibrium variance rate of the output as a function of the storage capacity $c_1$ (and the $\mu_0$, $\Delta_0$, $\mu_1$, $\Delta_1$).

v

Chapters III and IV will deal with equilibrium queue distributions for
$n = 2$ in the special cases $\mu_0 = \mu_1 = \mu_2$, but arbitrary $c_1$, $c_2$, $\Delta_0$, $\Delta_1$,
and $\Delta_2$. The joint probability density of the two queue lengths satisfies
a diffusion equation inside a rectangle (sides $c_1$, $c_2$) in a two-dimensional
space, but a linear transformation of coordinates will map the equilibrium
distribution into a solution of Laplace's equation in a parallelogram (subject to an unconventional type of boundary condition). These equations are
solved through a series of conformal mappings which eventually yield a solution in parametric form. Chapter III describes the formal solution. Chapter
IV gives numerical evaluations of the marginal queue length distributions and
the dependence of service rate $\mu$ upon $c_1$ and $c_2$ (and $\Delta_0$, $\Delta_1$, $\Delta_2$).

Chapter V deals with the time-dependent properties of the joint probability distributions of the cumulative departures $D_0(t)$, $D_1(t)$, $D_2(t)$ past
servers 0, 1, and 2 for a two-server system with infinite storage ($c_1 = c_2 = \infty$)
and equal variance coefficients $\Delta_0 = \Delta_1 = \Delta_2$. It gives general solutions for
this joint distribution starting from any initial state $D_0(0)$, $D_1(0)$, $D_2(0)$
or initial distribtuion of states. This is derived by image methods, but the
solution requires multiple reflections over several boundaries and gives a
rather unwieldy formula containing six terms, each of which involves some
multiple integrals. Although the methods used can be generalized to more
servers, the conclusion of this chapter is little more than "it can be done."
The general results seem to be too clumsy to be of much practical use.

Chapters VI and VII employ Laplace Transform and techniques similar
to the Wiener-Hopf factorization to derive the joint equilibrium queue
distribution for the two-server system with very large ($\infty$) storages $c_1$,
$c_2$ but general service rates $\mu_0$, $\mu_1$, $\mu_2$ and variance coefficients

$\Delta_0$, $\Delta_1$, $\Delta_2$ . Chapter VI discusses the case $\mu_0 < \mu_1$ , $\mu_2$ , i.e., an input rate $\mu_0$ less than the service rates of servers 1 and 2. The joint distribution of $Q_1$, $Q_2$ and particularly the marginal distribution of $Q_2$ are analyzed in some detail for the special case $\Delta_0 = \Delta_2 = 0$ , $\Delta_1 > 0$ (regular input, regular server at 2). Properties of the queue distribution for general $\Delta_j$ are described but explicit solutions are obtained only for a few other special choices of the $\Delta_j$ , including $\Delta_1 = 0$ , $\Delta_0$, $\Delta_2 > 0$; $\Delta_0 = \Delta_1$, $\Delta_2 > 0$; and $\Delta_0 = 0$ , $\Delta_1 = \Delta_2$ . Comparisons are made between the distributions of $Q_2$ for $\mu_0 < \mu_1$, $\mu_2$ and corresponding systems from Chapters III, IV with $c_1 < \infty$ , $c_2 = \infty$ , $\mu_0 = \mu_1 = \mu_2$ but with the $c_1$ chosen so that the input rate to server 2 in the latter system is equal to the $\mu_0$ of the former.

Chapter VII deals with the case of arbitrarily large $c_1$, $c_2$ but $\mu_1 < \mu_0$, $\mu_2$, i.e., server 1 is a bottleneck. One is concerned here with the joint distribution of the number of vacant storage spaces $Q_1' = c_1 - Q_1$ upstream of server 1 and the queue $Q_2$ downstream. The marginal distributions of $Q_1'$ and $Q_2$ for $c_1$, $c_2 \to \infty$ are known to be exponential (for arbitrary $\mu_0$, $\mu_2 > \mu_1$ and $\Delta_j$'s) so the main emphasis is on the statistical dependences between $Q_1'$, $Q_2$, particularly the asymptotic properties for large $Q_1'$, $Q_2$ . These distributions are then used to estimate the effect of finite but large values of $c_1$ and $c_2$ . The main conclusion is that the reductions in the overall service rate due to finite $c_1$ and to finite $c_2$ are nearly additive.

Chapters III, IV, VI, and VII all deal with equilibrium queue distributions for a system with an input server followed by two other servers in tandem. The queues $Q_1$, $Q_2$ behind servers 1 and 2 depend upon the service rates $\mu_0$, $\mu_1$, $\mu_2$, variance rates $\Delta_0$, $\Delta_1$, $\Delta_2$ and the storages

$c_1$ , $c_2$ .  No practical analytic method was found for evaluating these distributions accurately if $c_1$ , $c_2$ are finite and the $\mu_j$ are different. Chapters III, IV deal with $\mu_0 = \mu_1 = \mu_2$ and $c_1$ , $c_2 < \infty$ giving special attention to the analytic singularities at corners of the state space, and the blocking effects.  Chapters VI and VII deal with $\mu_0 \neq \mu_1 \neq \mu_2$ but $c_1 = c_2 = \infty$ , giving special attention to the effect of different $\mu_j$ on the shape of the queue distribution.  By comparing the effects of different $\mu_j$ and the effects of finite $c_1$ , $c_2$ , one can, however, infer how the queue distributions vary qualitatively with all the parameters.  This is probably all that one would want from an analytic formulation anyway, since, for any specific choice of the parameters, one could evaluate the distribution by simulation.

Chapter VIII, Epilogue, is a commentary on how one can (usually) analyze a real tandem queueing system with many servers by identifying a critical server or a critical pair of interacting servers with finite storage.  There is also a discussion of where the problem now stands and what techniques are likely to produce further advances.

The research described in this monograph was supported in part by the National Science Foundation under a series of grants entitled, "Application of Mathematics to Transportation Studies."  The work was done over a time span from 1974 to 1978 and was previously distributed as Research Report UCB-ITS-RR-78-3 and UCB-ITS-RR-77-19.  The typing of the manuscript was done by Inta Vodopals.

Contents

# I. General Theory

**1.** <u>Introduction.</u> Most of the literature relating to the analysis of tandem
queues (or more general queueing systems) is limited to the rare situation
in which a Poisson arrival stream to one service facility generates a
Poisson output stream, which, in turn becomes a Poisson arrival stream
for other servers. Furthermore, most of this literature is concerned only
with equilibrium queue distributions.[1-3] Many attempts have been made
to determine stochastic properties of the output process for more general
service systems,[4] but the detailed probability structure of the output
is usually so complicated that, even if one knew it, one could not make
much progress in analysing any subsequent queues for which this might be
the input.

Since there is not much likelihood of anyone making much progress in
the exact analysis of non-Poisson or non-stationary queueing systems, we
shall attempt here to use deterministic and diffusion approximations.
Some crude answers to practical problems are better than no answers.

The general type of system with which we will deal is that shown
schematically in Fig. I-1. In the conventional formulation of tandem
queues, one usually postulates a given (constant) arrival rate to a first
server. If the first server has a finite storage (waiting room) of capacity $c_1$, and the storage is full, a newly arriving customer will leave
the system (lost call in telephone traffic). For reasons of symmetry,
however, it will be more convenient here to imagine an equivalent system
which is fed by an infinite reservoir of customers passing through a
(hypothetical) server having a service rate $\mu_0$ (this service rate corresponds to the arrival rate in the more common interpretation, where it

2

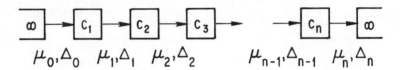

Fig. I-1. Schematic representation of the flow of customers through a tandem queueing system. Server $j$ has service rate $\mu_j$ , variance rate $\Delta_j$ , and storage capacity $c_j$ .

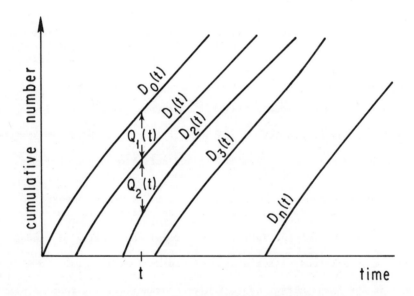

Fig. I-2. $D_j(t)$ represents the cumulative number of number of customers to leave server $j$ by time $t$ . $Q_j(t)$ is the queue length at the $j$th server.

is also usually designated as $\lambda$). If the storage $c_1$ is full, the server

0 is now described as being "blocked," or, equivalently, it may serve a

customer but then throw him back into the infinite reservoir or out of the

system.

Any subsequent server $j$ will serve customers at a rate $\mu_j$ pro-

vided it (a) has customers waiting to be served and (b) is not blocked by

a full storage $c_{j+1}$. If a customer is blocked he remains in the queue

from which he was blocked.

If initially we had an empty system and we let

$$D_j(t) = \text{cumulative number of customers to depart from server } j \text{ by time } t \text{ , } j = 0, 1, \ldots, n \text{ ,}$$

$$Q_j(t) = D_{j-1}(t) - D_j(t) = \begin{array}{l}\text{queue waiting at the} \\ \text{jth server,}\end{array} \qquad (1.1)$$

(for $j = 0$ , we may define $D_{-1}(t) = +\infty$), then the $D_j(t)$ must satisfy

the constraints

$$D_{j-1}(t) \geq D_j(t) \text{ , } \quad \begin{array}{l}\text{(non-negative queue before server } j) \\ j = 1, 2, \ldots, n\end{array} \qquad (1.2)$$

and

$$D_{j+1}(t) + c_{j+1} \leq D_j(t) \text{ , } \quad \begin{array}{l}\text{(maximum queue of } c_{j+1} \text{ after} \\ \text{server } j) \, j = 0, 1, 2, \ldots, n-1. \end{array} \quad (1.3)$$

Since we will be using deterministic or diffusion approximations, it

will be unnecessary to specify the detailed probability structure of the

processes $D_j(t)$ . We do assume that, for any time $\tau$ large compared with

a mean service time but short compared with any other relevant time con-

stants (busy periods, relaxation times, etc.) associated with the system,

during which time the jth server is constantly busy,

$$E\{D_j(t + \tau) - D_j(t)\}/\tau = \mu_j , \qquad (1.4)$$

and

$$\mathrm{Var}\{D_j(t + \tau) - D_j(t)\}/\tau \simeq \Delta_j . \qquad (1.5)$$

The $\mu_j$ and $\Delta_j$ are assumed to be independent of both $t$ and $\tau$. The variance to mean ratio, $\Delta_j/\mu_j$ is expected to be comparable with 1 (for exponentially distributed service times they are exactly 1).

As in the treatment of the diffusion approximations for a single queue, we disregard the discrete nature of the customer counts. All storages $c_j$ are assumed to be large compared with 1 and the $D_j(t)$ are treated as if they were continuous random variables (a stochastic fluid), having a joint probability density at time $t$

$$f(x_0, x_1, \ldots, x_n; t) dx_0 dx_1 \ldots dx_n = P\{x_j < D_j(t) < x_j + dx_j,$$

$$j = 0, \ldots, n\} . \qquad (1.6)$$

The $dx_j$ are, of course, not really infinitesimal intervals; they must actually be at least 1. In fact, for integer $x_j$, $f$ has the interpretation of being approximately the discrete probability associated with the state $x_0, x_1, \ldots, x_n$ (i.e. $dx_j = 1$). The $f(\cdot)$ is assumed also be vary slowly on a scale of $x_j$ of order 1.

Whereas, for a single queue, the diffusion approximation applies only for "heavy traffic," $\mu_0/\mu_1 > 1$ or $1 - \mu_0/\mu_1 \ll 1$ (traffic intensity greater than 1 or close to 1), we would expect the corresponding approximations to apply to multiple-server systems if all queues are (almost always) large compared with 1. Actually it suffices, for most purposes, to assume only that some queue is large. Although the diffusion approximation will

give relatively inaccurate estimates of short queues (expected queue of
order 1 or less), these inaccuracies in the estimates of the short queue
will not seriously affect the estimates of those queues which are large.
If some queue is large, we do not usually care about the actual size of the
short queues.

2. Graphical Representations and Deterministic Approximation. Whereas in
deterministic queueing models for tandem queues, it is fairly common
practice to work with the cumulative arrival and departure curves $D_j(t)$
and to analyse the behavior of the system by means of graphical construc-
tions,[5] people who deal with stochastic models (particularly with constant service rates $\mu_j$) usually work directly with the queue lengths
(1.1). The reason for this, no doubt, is that queue lengths remain finite
(with probability 1) for $t \to \infty$ if $\mu_0 < \mu_j$ for all $j > 0$, whereas
the cumulative arrivals grow approximately linearly with $t$.

We will deal here mostly with the random functions $D_j(t)$ rather
than the $Q_j(t)$. The advantage of this is that some iterative structure
is more elegantly displayed in terms of the $D_j(t)$. For example, the
behavior of the curve $D_j(t)$, while the jth server is busy, is independent of the behavior of any other server, and, furthermore, the jth server
sees an input process $D_{j-1}(t)$, and acts upon it, independent of how the
process $D_{j-1}(t)$ was generated. Some of these simple structural features
are not displayed as conveniently in terms of queue lengths alone. That
the curves $D_j(t)$ are unbounded is a relatively minor inconvenience.

One can picture the evolution of the system by drawing possible
realizations of the $D_j(t)$ as in Fig. I-2. The stochastic properties can
be visualized by comparison of many "typical" other realizations. For

each such realization, the constraint (1.2) implies that the curve $D_j(t)$ must remain below (or to the right) of $D_{j-1}(t)$, whereas (1.3) implies that the vertical separation must be less than the appropriate $c_j$ at all times. On such a diagram the queue lengths are represented as the vertical heights between the curves. If the queue discipline is FIFO, the horizontal distances between the curves represent the waiting times.

In the deterministic approximation, we, in effect, assume that $\Delta_j =$ for all $j$, i.e., the jth server, when busy, serves at exactly a rate $\mu_j$. All curves $D_j(t)$ are piecewise linear. The evolution of the system is uniquely defined starting from any initial state

$$D_j(t_0) = y_j \quad \text{at time } t_0 , \quad j = 0, 1, \ldots, n . \quad (2.1)$$

It is not a priori obvious how small $\Delta_j$ must be in order that we can approximate a system with $\Delta_j > 0$ by one with $\Delta_j = 0$ because we have, as yet, no scale for deciding when $\Delta_j$ is "small." Furthermore the accuracy of results depends upon what the question was. In any case, one should use the deterministic approximations at least to classify various types of situations. It is, in many cases, intuitively obvious what types of situations are well described by the deterministic approxima tions and which are not. The most obvious question for which the deter- ministic approximation gives too crude an answer is: what is the equilib- rium queue length? If an equilibrium exists, the deterministic approxima- tion will say that the equilibrium jth queue is either 0 or $c_j$.

Formally the deterministic behavior of any $D_j(t)$ starting from an initial state $y_j$ at time $t_0$ is described by the equations

$$D_j(t) = \min\{y_j + \mu_j(t - t_0) , \ D_{j-1}(t) , \ D_{j+1}(t) + c_{j+1}\} , \quad (2.2)$$

or by iteration

$$D_j(t) = \min\{y_k + \mu_k(t - t_0), \quad 0 \le k \le j ;$$

$$y_k + \mu_k(t - t_0) + \sum_{m=j+1}^{k} c_m, \quad j+1 \le k \le n\} .$$

(2.3)

Thus $D_j(t)$ , if constrained, is constrained either by an "upstream bottleneck" which restricts the input and forces the queue to zero, or by a "downstream bottleneck" which causes a queue to back up filling all storages between the jth server and the bottleneck. Unfortunately, which constraint applies may vary from time to time.

One can always construct graphs of $D_j(t)$ iteratively in time. Starting from some unconstrained state, one draws curves of $y_j + \mu_j(t - t_0)$ for each j , extending them in time until a constraint is violated. One then follows the curve along the constraint until one hits another constraint, etc.

Fig. I-3 illustrates some of the typical types of complications one can encounter. Serve 1 is fast and serves its queue quickly. At point 1 the queue vanishes and $D_1(t)$ must follow $D_0(t)$ for awhile. Server 2 is slower, however, and it builds up a queue which blocks server 1 at point 2 causing the queue behind server 1 to reform again. Server 3 is slower yet. At point 3 its storage becomes full and retards server 2, at a time when the storage behind server 2 is already full. This causes the queue behind server 1 to grow faster at point 3'. Finally at point 4, server 0 is blocked by the queue which has backed up from server 3 through 2 and 1.

Server 4 is a fast server and fills the storage behind server 5 at

8

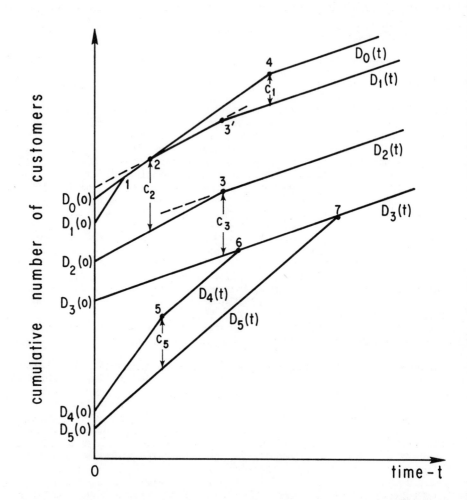

Fig. I-3.  Graphical representation of the evolution of the
$D_j(t)$  from the deterministic approximation.

point 5, but at point 6 it has served all its queue and can serve only at the rate of server 3. This causes the full storage behind server 5 to decrease until it becomes empty at point 7.

As a prelude to an attempt to treat the stochastic problem, the point we wish to make here is that a complete solution of the stochastic problem, even if it could be derived, would be too complicated to be of any practical use. One must decide what problems are worth doing.

As a practical matter, in the deterministic approximation it would be difficult to achieve an arbitrary initial state from natural causes. It is, for example, difficult to imagine how one could have generated spontaneously a queue behind server 1 in Fig. I-3 if that is a fast server. Most states which evolve naturally are those which could be created from a state with zero queues. On the other hand, in the treatment of the stochastic problem one must recognize that any state can be reached with non-zero probability. Having reached any particular state, the average evolution from that state is similar to what the deterministic approximation predicts, at least for short times.

There is an alternative way of constructing Fig. I-3 which tends to produce iteratively various parts of the graph more or less in order of their importance. Consider first the server $j_1$ with the smallest $\mu_j$ (in Fig. I-3, it is $j_1 = 3$). Clearly this server will never be interrupted (in the deterministic approximation), and therefore

$$D_{j_1}(t) = \mu_{j_1} + \mu_{j_1}(t - t_0) .$$

This server will be the eventual bottleneck for all new arrivals. It ultimately causes all storages behind it to fill and all queues downstream to vanish.

Consider next the server $j_2$ with the second smallest $\mu_j$ . It can be influenced only by $j_1$ . If $j_2 < j_1$ , $D_{j_2}(t)$ will have one and only one slope change, when all storages between $j_2$ and $j_1$ are full (server in Fig. I-3. If $j_2 > j_1$ (as for server 5), $D_{j_2}(t)$ will again have only one slope change, namely when all queues between $j_1$ and $j_2$ have disappeared. Actually the servers with $j < j_1$ behave independent of those with $j > j_1$ so that the slowest server with $j > j_1$ (or with $j < j_1$) is influenced only by server $j_1$ regardless of whether or not it is the second slowest.

If $j_2 < j_1$ then any server $j$ with $j < j_2$ behaves independent of any server with $j_2 < j < j_1$ or with $j > j_1$ . The slowest server in each of these ranges of $j$ has a $D_j(t)$ with at most two slope changes (such as server 4 of Fig. I-3). The iteration of this is quite straight-forward but the curves become more complex with each step. Server 1 of Fig. I-3 , for example, has a $D_1(t)$ with four slope changes by virtue of $\mu_1 > \mu_0 > \mu_2 > \mu_3$.

Clearly, in the treatment of the stochastic behavior, one will be mostly interested in effects which may influence the operation of the principal bottleneck.

Particularly for the analysis of the stochastic behavior of only a few servers, it is convenient also to use another type of graphical representation. We could imagine a realization as a single curve $(D_0(t)$, $D_1(t)$, ..., $D_n(t)$, t) in an (n + 2)-dimensional space $(x_0, x_1, ..., t)$ or as a curve $(D_0(t), D_1(t), ..., D_n(t))$ in an (n+1)-dimensional space, with time represented as a parameter along the curve.

Fig. I-4 shows $(D_0(t) , D_1(t))$ as a curve in the space $(x_0 , x_1)$. The condition $D_0(t) \geq D_1(t)$ means that the curve $(D_0(t) , D_1(t))$ must stay in the half-plane $x_0 \geq x_1$; the condition $D_1(t) + c_1 \geq D_0(t)$ means that it must stay above the line $x_1 + c_1 = x_0$. Of course, it becomes more difficult to "visualize" such a curve as the dimension of the space increases, but the set of contraints (1.2), (1.3) imply that the curve $(D_1(t) , \ldots , D_n(t))$ is confined to a region between various hyperplanes which form a cylindrical parallelogram with axis in the $(1, 1 , \ldots , 1)$ direction.

The connection between the various pictures is that Fig. I-2 (or I-3), and I-4, respectively, are projections of the curve $(D_0(t) , D_1(t) , \ldots , D_n(t),t)$ in the $(n + 2)$-dimensional space onto the $(x_j , t)$ planes, and the $(x_0 , x_1 , \ldots , x_n)$ space. A realization of the process in Fig. I-2 is a set of $n + 1$ curves, but in Fig I-4 it is just one curve. The constraints in Fig. I-2 are limiting relations among the curves but in Fig. I-4 it is a geometrical boundary.

The probability density (1.6) should be pictured as a function on the complete $(n + 2)$-dimensional space or as an evolving family of functions in the $(x_0 , x_1 , \ldots , x_n)$ space. The marginal probability densities of the $D_j(t)$ individually can, of course, be pictured as functions on the $x$, $t$ space of Fig. I-2.

3. <u>Motion of Holes</u>. If we consider the storage $j$ to contain $c_j$ locations which may either be occupied or empty, then a queue of $Q_j(t)$ occupied positions can also be interpreted as

$$Q_j'(t) \equiv c_j - Q_j(t) \tag{3.1}$$

12

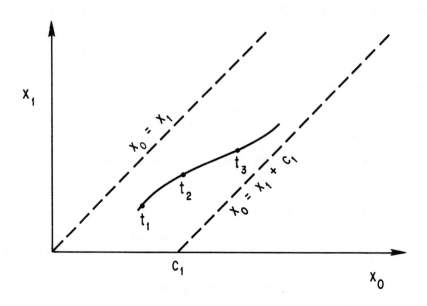

Fig. I-4.  Evolution of the vector $D_0(t)$, $D_1(t)$ in an $(x_0, x_1)$-space.  The dashed lines are boundaries for the trajectory.

empty positions. Sometimes it is more convenient to follow the empty positions or holes than the customers. Each time a customer is served by the
jth server, he leaves the jth storage and enters the j+1th storage; equivalently a hole leaves the j+1th storage and enters the jth. For the system
as a whole, customers moving through servers 0, 1, ..., n can be interpreted
as holes moving through servers n, n-1, ..., 0, in the reverse order.

In defining the $D_j(t)$ , it was assumed that at time 0 we started
with an empty system. We can, however, create any arbitrary state at
time $t_0 > 0$ by injecting into the system however many customers are
needed to create the desired state. Thus, if we want queue lengths $Q_j(t_0)$
at time $t_0$ and $D_n(t_0) = 0$ (we start the customer count from the first
customer to leave the system after time $t_0$ ), then we must choose

$$y_{n-1} \equiv D_{n-1}(t_0) = Q_n(t_0)$$

$$y_{n-2} \equiv D_{n-2}(t_0) = Q_n(t_0) + Q_{n-1}(t_0) \qquad (3.2)$$

$$y_j = D_j(t_0) = Q_n(t_0) + \cdots + Q_{j+1}(t_0) .$$

If we wished to follow the motion of the holes, it would be natural
to start from an initial state with no holes, and then, if necessary,
inject holes into the system (through servers n, n-1, ...) to create any
other state at time $t_0$ .

Starting from a state with no holes $(Q_j(0) = c_j)$, let

$$D_j'(t) \equiv \text{cumulative number of holes to pass} \atop \text{server j by time } t , j = 0, 1, \ldots, n . \qquad (3.3)$$

The initial state of no holes corresponds to a state

$$D_j(0) \;=\; c_n + c_{n-1} + \cdots + c_{j+1} \qquad\qquad j = 0, 1, \cdots, n-1$$

$$D_n(0) \;=\; 0 \;.$$

Subsequently, the number of customers to pass server $j$ must be equal to the number of holes to pass $j$, i.e.,

$$D_j(t) - D_j(0) \;=\; D_j'(t) - D_j'(0) \;=\; D_j'(t)$$

thus the $D_j'(t)$ and $D_j(t)$ are related through

$$D_j'(t) \;=\; D_j(t) - (c_n + c_{n-1} + \cdots + c_{j+1}) \;, \qquad\qquad (3.4)$$

i.e., each $D_j'(t)$ is a vertical translation of $D_j(t)$.

Equations (3.4) and (3.1) imply that

$$Q_j'(t) \;=\; D_j'(t) - D_{j-1}'(t) \qquad\qquad (3.5)$$

as the counterpart of (1.1).

The above mappings have certain mathematical uses and also some con-
ceptual advantages. From the mathematical point of view, there is no
difference between objects which are physically identified as "holes" and
objects physically identified as "customers." If we have described the
evolution of the $D_j(t)$ for a system with parameters $\mu_0$, $\Delta_0$, $\mu_1$, $\Delta_1$, $\cdots$
$\mu_n$, $\Delta_n$ and initial state $y_0$, $\cdots$, $y_{n-1}$ ($y_n = 0$); we have also described
the evolution of the holes, i.e., the corresponding $D_j'(t)$ from initial
states $y_0'$, $\cdots$, $y_{n-1}'$ ($y_n' = 0$). But if we reinterpret "holes" as "custome

the $D_j'(t)$ also describe the evolution of another (hypothetical) tandem

queueing system with parameters $\mu_n$, $\Delta_n$, $\mu_{n-1}$, $\Delta_{n-1}$, $\cdots$, $\mu_0$, $\Delta_0$ and

storage capacities $c_{n-1}$, $\cdots$, $c_1$ . Thus each solution of a tandem queueing

problem also solves a second problem. We shall see later that this is par-

ticularly helpful in analysing systems for which the image problem is iden-

tical to the original problem, i.e., $\mu_j = \mu_{n-j}$, $\Delta_j = \Delta_{n-j}$, and $c_j = c_{n-j}$.

Conceptually, there are certain advantages in following the holes

rather than the customers upstream from a bottleneck. Since the storages

will eventually become nearly full upstream from the bottleneck, it is

often easier to count the small number of holes rather than the possibly

large number of full spaces.

Fig. I-5 illustrates the $D_j'(t)$ corresponding to the $D_j(t)$ of

Fig. I-3. Each $D_j'(t)$ is simply a translation of the corresponding $D_j(t)$

such that $D_j'(t) \geq D_{j-1}'(t)$ (whereas $D_j(t) < D_{j-1}(t)$). Every point,

1, 2, - - of Fig. I-3 where $D_j(t) = D_{j-1}(t)$ (the lines meet), maps into a

point where $D_j'(t) - D_{j-1}'(t) = c_j$ , and conversely each $D_j'(t) = D_{j-1}'(t)$

corresponds to $D_{j-1}(t) - D_j(t) = c_j$ .

The geometrical representation in the $(x_0, x_1, \cdots, x_n)$ space perhaps

shows more clearly the relation between the $D_j(t)$ and $D_j'(t)$ . Both

$D_j(t)$ and $D_j'(t)$ must stay within a cylindrical parallelogram with axis

along the $(1, 1, 1 - -)$ direction. The two cylinders are similar and

simply translations of each other.

4. Diffusion Equation. Suppose now that $\Delta_j > 0$ for all $j$ . If at time $t_0$

we know that the system is in a state

$$(D_0(t_0), D_1(t_0), \cdots, D_n(t_0)) = (y_0, y_1, \cdots, y_n) \qquad (4.1)$$

16

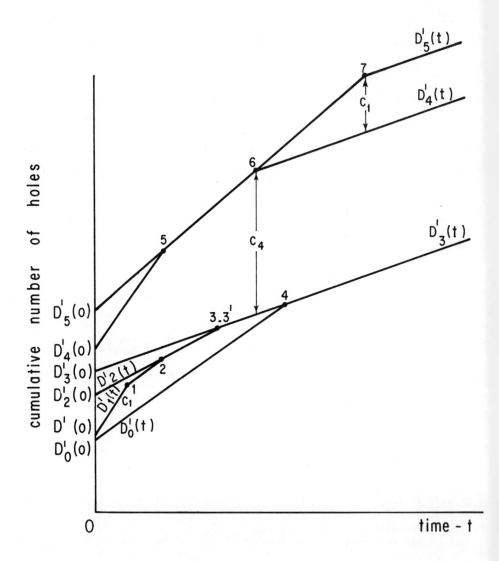

Fig. I-5. Graphical representation of the motion of holes for the system shown in figure I-3.

which is not on or too near any of the boundaries corresponding to a queue length of 0 or $c_j$ , then, until such time when the system can reach one of the boundaries, changes in the $D_j(t)$ are assumed to be statistically independent and approximately normally distributed with mean and variance growing linearly with $t - t_0$ in accordance with (1.4) and (1.5). Thus, for $t - t_0$ sufficiently small that there is a negligible probability for $D_j(t)$ to have reached a boundary, but sufficiently large as to contain several service times as implied by (1.5), the probability density (1.6) is approximately

$$f(x_0,x_1,\ldots,x_n;t) = \prod_{j=0}^{n} \frac{\exp\left\{\dfrac{-[x_j - y_j - \mu_j(t - t_0)]^2}{2\Delta_j\,(t - t_0)}\right\}}{(2\pi)^{1/2}[\Delta_j\,(t - t_0)]^{1/2}} . \qquad (4.2)$$

Equation (4.2) is a solution of the diffusion equation

$$\frac{\partial f}{\partial t} = \sum_{j=0}^{n} (-\mu_j \frac{\partial f}{\partial x_j} + \frac{\Delta_j}{2} \frac{\partial^2 f}{\partial x_j^2}) \qquad (4.3)$$

over the region

$$x_{j-1} > x_j , \quad x_j + c_j > x_{j-1} , \quad j = 1, 2, \ldots, n \qquad (4.4)$$

except possibly near the boundary of (4.4). Although (4.2) is not valid after the system has had time to reach any of the boundaries, it does describe the conditional probability density for "transition" from points $y_0, \ldots, y_n$ to $x_0, \ldots, x_n$ , for any $(y_0, \ldots, y_n)$ inside the region (4.4) and any time $t_0$ . In particular it still describes the transitions even after the system has reached a boundary and been "reflected" back in the interior of (4.4) so as to create a new initial state $(y_0, \ldots, y_n)$ a a new initial time $t_0$ . The f will at all times satisfy (4.3) inside the region (4.4).

Our problem is first to determine an appropriate set of boundary conditions for (4.3), and then determine solutions of (4.3) which satisfy the boundary conditions. If we wish to obtain the complete time-dependent solution of (4.3) starting from an initial state (4.1), we may further specify that the solution behaves like (4.2) for sufficiently small $t - t_0$ .

If it were not for the condition (4.4) we could integrate both sides of (4.3) with respect to any $x_k$ from $-\infty$ to $+\infty$ and obtain another diffusion equation for the marginal probability density of the remaining variables. Even with condition (4.4), we can integrate both sides of (4.3) with respect to $x_k$ up to the boundary and obtain a new diffusion equation, but with some boundary terms.

If we let $f^{(k)}$ denote the marginal joint probability density of the $D_j(t)$ , $j = 1, \ldots, n, j \neq k$ , then

$$f^{(k)} \equiv \int_{\max(x_{k+1}, x_{k-1}-c_{k+1})}^{\min(x_{k-1}, x_{k+1}+c_{k+1})} dx_k \, f(x_0, x_1, \ldots, x_k, \ldots, x_n; t) \qquad k = 0, 1, \ldots, n \qquad (4.5)$$

in which, for the end cases $k = 0$ or $n$ , we define $x_{-1} = +\infty$ , $x_{-1} - c_0 = -\infty$ , $x_{n+1} + c_{n+1} = +\infty$ , and $x_{n+1} = -\infty$ . Integration of (4.3) with respect to $x_k$ over the range of (4.5) gives

$$\frac{\partial f^{(k)}}{\partial t} = \sum_{\substack{j=0 \\ j \neq k}}^{n} \left[ -\mu_j \frac{\partial f^{(k)}}{\partial x_j} + \frac{\Delta_j}{2} \frac{\partial^2 f^{(k)}}{\partial x_j^2} \right] + B_+^{(k)} - B_-^{(k)} , \qquad (4.6)$$

with

$$B_+^{(k)} = \begin{cases} (-\mu_k + \mu_{k+1})f + \dfrac{(\Delta_k - \Delta_{k+1})}{2} \dfrac{\partial f}{\partial x_k} - \Delta_{k+1} \dfrac{\partial f}{\partial x_{k+1}} \\[4pt] \quad \text{at } x_k = x_{k+1} + c_{k+1} \text{ if } x_{k+1} + c_{k+1} < x_{k-1} \\[12pt] (-\mu_k + \mu_{k-1})f + \dfrac{(\Delta_k - \Delta_{k-1})}{2} \dfrac{\partial f}{\partial x_k} - \Delta_{k-1} \dfrac{\partial f}{\partial x_{k-1}} \\[4pt] \quad \text{at } x_k = x_{k-1} \text{ if } x_{k+1} + c_{k+1} > x_{k-1} \end{cases} \tag{4.6a}$$

and

$$B_-^{(k)} = \begin{cases} (-\mu_k + \mu_{k+1})f + \dfrac{(\Delta_k - \Delta_{k+1})}{2} \dfrac{\partial f}{\partial x_k} - \Delta_{k+1} \dfrac{\partial f}{\partial x_{k+1}} \\[4pt] \quad \text{at } x_k = x_{k+1} \text{ if } x_{k+1} > x_{k-1} - c_k \\[12pt] (-\mu_k + \mu_{k-1})f + \dfrac{(\Delta_k - \Delta_{k-1})}{2} \dfrac{\partial f}{\partial x_k} - \Delta_{k-1} \dfrac{\partial f}{\partial x_{k-1}} \\[4pt] \quad \text{at } x_k = x_{k-1} - c_k \text{ if } x_{k+1} < x_{k-1} - c_k. \end{cases} \tag{4.6b}$$

Equations (4.3) and (4.6) describe how $f$ and $f^{(k)}$ change with $t$ starting from any arbitrary distribution $f$ at time $t_0$. We could choose an initial $f$ so that all the above boundary terms of (4.6) vanish, at least temporarily, by virtue of not having the state near any boundary, i.e., $f$ vanishes at and near all boundaries. We could also allow the initial state to be close to any one boundary so that all boundary terms vanish except those associated with the one boundary of interest. Thus we can investigate the meaning of each boundary term individually.

Suppose that we allow $D_k(t)$ to be near $D_{k+1} + c_{k+1}$, but no othe

$D_j(t)$ is near a boundary. The consequence of this is that the kth serve

might be interrupted for lack of storage in $c_{k+1}$. This, in itself, wi

have no immediate effect upon the behavior of any server except the kth.

Thus the probability density $f^{(k)}$ of all $D_j(t)$ except the kth will,

temporarily at least, behave as if there were no such interruption. The

$f^{(k)}$ will evolve like the corresponding marginal distribution of (4.2) a

satisfy a diffusion equation with no boundary term generated by condition

at $x_k = x_{k+1} + c_{k+1}$. We conclude that the first boundary term above

must vanish, i.e.,

$$(-\mu_k + \mu_{k+1})f + \frac{(\Delta_k - \Delta_{k+1})}{2} \frac{\partial f}{\partial x_k} - \Delta_{k+1} \frac{\partial f}{\partial x_{k+1}} = 0 \qquad (4.$$

$$\text{at } x_k = x_{k+1} + c_{k+1}.$$

Similarly, if we allow $D_k(t)$ to be close to $D_{k-1}(t)$, but no

other $D_j(t)$ is near a boundary, the kth server may be interrupted for

lack of customers. This also will have no immediate effect upon the

evolution of $f^{(k)}$. Thus we conclude that the next boundary term above

also vanishes, i.e.,

$$(-\mu_k + \mu_{k-1})f + \frac{(\Delta_k - \Delta_{k-1})}{2} \frac{\partial f}{\partial x_k} - \Delta_{k-1} \frac{\partial f}{\partial x_{k-1}} = 0 \qquad (4.8$$

$$\text{at } x_k = x_{k-1}.$$

If, on the other hand, $D_k(t)$ is near $D_{k+1}(t)$, the (k+1)th

server may be interrupted, or if $D_k(t)$ is near $D_{k+1}(t) - c_k$, the (k - 1)th server may be interrupted. Either of these would be expected to affect the behavior of $f^{(k)}$ . The boundary terms of $B_-^{(k)}$ , therefore, do not necessarily vanish.

Our immediate purpose here is not to obtain equations for the marginal distributions (which do not, in general, determine their own future behavior), it is to establish boundary conditions for the original diffusion equation (4.3). Although the boundary conditions (4.7) and (4.8) specify a condition at every point on the bounding surfaces, they are not of the type usually associated with diffusion equations (as they arise in physics, for example) and do not define a "well-posed" problem. We need still other boundary conditions at edges.

If we substitute (4.7) with k replaced by k - 1 , and (4.8), with k replaced by k + 1 , into $B_-^{(k)}$ , we can simplify it to

$$
B_-^{(k)} = \begin{cases} -\dfrac{(\Delta_k + \Delta_{k+1})}{2} \left( \dfrac{\partial f}{\partial x_k} + \dfrac{\partial f}{\partial x_{k+1}} \right) \\ \qquad \text{at } x_k = x_{k+1} \text{ if } x_{k+1} > x_{k-1} - c_k \\ -\dfrac{(\Delta_k + \Delta_{k-1})}{2} \left( \dfrac{\partial f}{\partial x_k} + \dfrac{\partial f}{\partial x_{k-1}} \right) \\ \qquad \text{at } x_k = x_{k-1} - c_k \text{ if } x_{k+1} < x_{k-1} - c_k . \end{cases} \qquad (4.9)
$$

In (4.9), $\partial f/\partial x_k + \partial f/\partial x_{k+1}$ means

$$
\left( \frac{\partial}{\partial x_k} + \frac{\partial}{\partial x_{k+1}} \right) f(x_1, \ldots, x_k, x_{k+1}, \ldots, x_n ; t)
$$

evaluated at $x_k = x_{k+1}$ , which can also be written as

$$\frac{\partial}{\partial x_{k+1}} f(x_1, \ldots, x_{k-1}, x_{k+1}, x_{k+1}, x_{k+2}, \ldots, x_n; t) ,$$

the derivative of $f$ tangential to the boundary $x_k = x_{k+1}$ . Correspondingly,

$$B_-^{(k)} = \begin{cases} -\dfrac{(\Delta_k + \Delta_{k+1})}{2} \dfrac{\partial}{\partial x_{k+1}} f(x_1, \ldots, x_{k-1}, x_{k+1}, x_{k+1}, x_{k+2}, \ldots; t) \\ \qquad\qquad \text{if } x_{k+1} + c_k > x_{k-1} \\[2ex] -\dfrac{(\Delta_k + \Delta_{k-1})}{2} \dfrac{\partial}{\partial x_{k-1}} f(x_1, \ldots, x_{k-1}, x_{k-1} - c_k, x_{k+1}, x_{k+2}, \ldots \\ \qquad\qquad \text{if } x_{k+1} + c_k < x_{k-1} . \end{cases} \qquad (4.$$

If, in (4.6), we can think of the terms $-\mu_{k+1} \partial f^{(k)}/\partial x_{k+1}$ and $-\mu_k \partial f^{(k)}/\partial x_{k-1}$ as representing "drift terms" in the diffusion associated with service rates $\mu_{k+1}$ and $\mu_{k-1}$ , respectively, it is natural also to identify the terms of (4.9a), which involve corresponding derivatives of $f$ at the boundaries, as the drag on the motion of $D_{k+1}$ when the kth server is interrupted for lack of a queue, and the drag on the motion of $D_{k-1}$ when the k-1th server is interrupted for lack of storage.

If, continuing the procedure of (4.5), (4.6), we let

$$f^{(k,k+1)} = \int_{\max(x_{k+2}, x_{k-1} - c_k - c_{k+1})}^{\min(x_{k-1}, x_{k+2} + c_{k+2})} f^{(k)}(x_0, \ldots, x_n; t) \, dx_{k+1} = \int_{\max(x_{k+2}, x_{k-1} - c_k)}^{\min(x_{k-1}, x_{k+2} + c_{k+1} + c_{k+2})} f^{(k+1)}(x_0, \ldots, x_n; t) \, dx_k \qquad (4.1$$

be the marginal joint probability density of the $D_j(t)$ , $j \neq k, k+1$ , then by integration of (4.6), we can obtain an equation of the form

$$\frac{\partial f}{\partial t}^{(k,k+1)} = \sum_{\substack{j=0 \\ j \neq k,k+1}}^{n} \left( -\mu_j \frac{\partial f}{\partial x_j}^{(k,k+1)} + \frac{\Delta_j}{2} \frac{\partial^2 f}{\partial x_j^2}^{(k,k+1)} \right) + B_+^{(k,k+1)} - B_-^{(k,k+1)}$$

$$(4.11)$$

in which $B_+^{(k,k+1)}$ is a surface term from the upper limits of integration and $B_-^{(k,k+1)}$ from the lower limits.

The upper limits, analogous to the effects in (4.6), describe consequences of servers $k$ and/or $k + 1$ serving so many customers as to either dissipate the queue of customers upstream or fill the storage downstream, while possibly interfering with each other. None of these are supposed to affect the behavior of $f^{(k,k+1)}$; in particular it should not have any immediate effect on the behavior of $D_{k-1}(t)$ or $D_{k+2}(t)$. We should, therefore, expect $B_+^{(k,k+1)}$ to vanish, if it does not do so already as a consequence of the previous boundary conditions (4.7) and (4.8). The lower limit terms $B_-^{(k,k+1)}$ describe the consequences of servers $k$ and/or $k + 1$ serving too few customers so as to fill the upstream storage or cause the downstream queue for $k + 2$ to vanish. Either of these may influence the behavior of $f^{(k,k+1)}$. Therefore, the terms of $B_-^{(k,k+1)}$ need not vanish.

A "formal" integration of (4.6) to determine $B_+^{(k,k+1)}$ and $B_-^{(k,k+1)}$ is straightforward, but somewhat tedious because, already with just two servers $k$ and $k + 1$, there are several bounding surfaces to consider and even more edges. In deriving an expression for $B_+^{(k,k+1)}$, one will use (4.7) or (4.8) along any of the bounding surfaces; they will contribute nothing to $B_+^{(k,k+1)}$, but there will be some terms coming from the edges. Also the integration of (4.9a) will contribute some edge terms.

One can show that $B_+^{(k,k+1)}$ contains edge terms

$$\frac{1}{2} (\Delta_k - \Delta_{k+2}) \ f(x_0,\ldots,x_n;t) \quad \text{at } x_k = x_{k+1} + c_{k+1}$$

$$x_{k+1} = x_{k+2} + c_{k+2} \tag{4.11a}$$

$$\frac{1}{2} (\Delta_k - \Delta_{k-1}) \ f(x_0,\ldots,x_n;t) \quad \text{at } x_{k-1} = x_k = x_{k+1} \tag{4.11b}$$

and

$$\frac{1}{2} (\Delta_{k-1} + \Delta_{k+1}) \ f(x_0,\ldots,x_n;t) \quad \text{at } x_{k-1} = x_k, \quad x_k = x_{k+1}+c_{k+1} \ .$$

$$\tag{4.11c}$$

Since $D_k(t)$ , $D_{k+1}(t)$ could be near any of the edges described in (4.11a, b or c), while all other $D_j(t)$ are interior to the region (4.4), and since, under these conditions, the other $D_j(t)$ should satisfy a diffusion equation with no terms from the $B_+^{(k,k+1)}$, we might expect that each of the above terms should vanish, by the same reasoning as used for (4.7) and (4.8).

Unfortunately the "formal" methods of integration described above yield some false results. The methods are based upon an assumption that f and various partial derivatives are continuous at the bounding surfaces and edges. One would not ordinarily challenge these assumptions, because the diffusion equation generally tends to smear irregularities. There is indeed no reason to question the validity of (4.7) and (4.8) along the surfaces but these conditions applied to each of two intersecting surfaces generates some non-analytic behavior of f at the edges. We will have some specific illustrations of this later, but one can see where in the above arguments the difficulties originate.

Equation (4.7) was based upon the argument that, if the storage $c_{k+1}$ becomes full, this should not affect the immediate behavior of the

$D_j(t)$, $j \neq k$ ; $f^{(k)}$ should satisfy a diffusion equation <u>provided</u> that

these other $D_j(t)$ are not also near boundaries. If $D_k(t)$ were near

$D_{k+1}(t) + c_{k+1}$ and also near $D_{k-1}(t)$ simultaneously, then server k

would be interrupted both because of the lack of storage and lack of

customers. This, in itself, would have no immediate effect upon the behav-

ior of $D_{k-1}(t)$ or $D_{k+1}(t)$ . There is no obvious reason why (4.7) and

(4.8) should not be valid at the edge $x_{k-1} = x_k = x_{k+1} + c_{k+1}$ .

If, however, storage $c_k$ is full when $D_k(t)$ hits $D_{k+1}(t) + c_{k+1}$ ,

the interruption of server k will, in general, affect the immediate

behavior of $D_{k-1}(t)$ . The $(k-1)$th server sees a full storage which is

feeding another full storage. Consequently, the condition (4.7) is not

necessarily valid at the edge $x_{k-1} = x_k + c_k$ , $x_k = x_{k+1} + c_{k+1}$ . Sim-

ilarly if there is no queue at server $k + 1$ when $D_k(t)$ meets $D_{k-1}(t)$ ,

the interruption of service at k will, in general, affect the behavior

of $D_{k+1}(t)$ . Condition (4.8) is not necessarily valid at the edge

$x_{k-1} = x_k = x_{k+1}$ .

Since we expect some peculiar behavior of f near the corners of

(4.11a,b), we have reason to doubt the validity of the formal procedures

which led to these edge terms. Whether or not one need impose any bound-

ary conditions at these edges is unclear at the moment. We can expect the

solution of the diffusion equation to have singularities at these edges

but we shall not attempt to analyse this now. There are also other types

of edges not in (4.11a, b, c), for example, $x_{k-1} = x_k + c_k$ (storage $c_k$

full) and $x_k = x_{k+1}$ (storage $c_{k+1}$ empty) which are potential places

for non-analytic behavior of f .

The goal of the above analysis of the edges was to establish conditions

at the edge (4.11c). At this edge server k is interrupted both for lack

of customers and lack of storage. We have no reason to question the
validity of the above integrations at this edge and, consequently, conclude
that (if $\Delta_{k-1} + \Delta_{k+1} > 0$)

$$f(x_1, \ldots, x_n; t) = 0 \qquad \text{at} \quad x_{k-1} = x_k = x_{k+1} + c_{k+1} \, . \qquad (4.$$

It is intuitively plausible that (4.12) should be true. When storage
$c_{k+1}$ is full, fluctuations in service at the $(k + 1)$th server, in effect,
cause the queue simply to back up over the kth server (although in the form
description it appears as a queue behind server k). If we could somehow
force the system into a state with an empty queue at k and a full storage
at k + 1 , a queue is likely to form very quickly at k if either the
kth or (k + 1)th server suffers a temporary slow fluctuation in service.
If there is an abnormally high rate for leaving this state, the probability
of finding the system in this state must be very small.

To define a "well-posed problem," (4.12) is a necessary subsidiary
condition to (4.3), (4.7), and (4.8). One can imagine hypothetical systems
which satisfy (4.3), (4.7), and (4.8) but which, when they reach the state
(4.12), would receive a boost in service from server k + 1 sending excess
customers downstream of k + 1 instead of upstream from k . Presumably
(4.12) would not hold for such systems and their evolution would also be
quite different. It is also clear that (4.3), (4.7), and (4.8) alone do
not necessarily define a unique solution. In the special case $\mu_j = \mu_0$
for all j , the boundary conditions (4.7), (4.8) involve only derivatives
of f but not f itself. Consequently if one had one solution f of
(4.3), (4.7), (4.8), f plus any constant would also be a solution.
Condition (4.12) at least rules out this possible source of non-uniqueness.

For the moment, we accept "on faith" that the system of equations (4.3), (4.7), (4.8), (4.12) along with the initial conditions (4.1), (4.2) defines a well-posed problem. Since these equations describe $f$ as a function of the initial state, independent of the history prior to time $t_0$, the diffusion approximation approximates the process $(D_0(t), \ldots, D_n(t))$ by a Markov process (whether this is exactly true or not). The above $f$ describes the transition probabilities from $(y_0, \ldots, y_n)$ at time $t_0$ to $(x_0, \ldots, x_n)$ at time $t$ which, along with the Markov property, gives a complete description of the stochastic behavior of the system.

Our goal is to obtain some explicit solutions for relatively simple special cases or at least some properties of solutions, not to settle convergence questions. If one must resort to numerical methods to solve the diffusion equation, one might as well have solved the original queueing problem by numerical methods. Most numerical methods would approximate the diffusion equation by finite difference equations which would be essentially equivalent to going back to some (perhaps hypothetical) exact queueing problem with discrete states.

5. Queue Length Distribution. It was stated previously that a representation of the behavior of the system in terms of the $D_j(t)$ was, for reasons of symmetry, simpler than a representation in terms of queue lengths. It is possible, of course, to describe the evolution in terms of one cumulative arrival function, $D_0(t)$ for example, plus the queue lengths. If we let

$$Q_j(t) = D_{j-1}(t) - D_j(t) \qquad j = 1, 2, \ldots, n \qquad (5.1)$$

and $g(x_0, \ell_1, \ell_2, \ldots, \ell_n)$ be the joint probability density of $D_0(t)$, $Q_j(t)$, then

$$f(x_0, x_1, \ldots, x_n; t) = g(x_0, x_0 - x_1, x_1 - x_2, \ldots, x_{n-1} - x_n; t) . \quad (5$$

Substitution of this into the equations of section 4 gives the follow
ing equations for  g

$$\frac{\partial g}{\partial t} = -\mu_0 \frac{\partial g}{\partial x_0} + \frac{\Delta_0}{2} \frac{\partial^2 g}{\partial x_0^2} + \Delta_0 \frac{\partial^2 g}{\partial x_0 \partial \ell_1}$$

$$+ \sum_{j=1}^{n} [(-\mu_{j-1} + \mu_j) \frac{\partial g}{\partial \ell_j} + \frac{(\Delta_{j-1} + \Delta_j)}{2} \frac{\partial^2 g}{\partial \ell_j^2}] \qquad (5.3)$$

$$- \sum_{j=1}^{n-1} \Delta_j \frac{\partial^2 g}{\partial \ell_j \partial \ell_{j+1}} \qquad\qquad \text{for } 0 < \ell_j < c_j ,$$

subject to the boundary conditions

$$(-\mu_0 + \mu_1)g + \frac{(\Delta_0 - \Delta_1)}{2} \frac{\partial g}{\partial x_0} + \frac{(\Delta_0 + \Delta_1)}{2} \frac{\partial g}{\partial \ell_1} - \Delta_1 \frac{\partial g}{\partial \ell_2} = 0 ,$$

$$\text{for } \ell_1 = c_1 , \qquad (5.4a)$$

$$(-\mu_{k-1} + \mu_k)g - \frac{(\Delta_{k-1} - \Delta_k)}{2} \frac{\partial g}{\partial \ell_{k-1}} + \frac{(\Delta_{k-1} + \Delta_k)}{2} \frac{\partial g}{\partial \ell_k} - \Delta_k \frac{\partial g}{\partial \ell_{k+1}} = 0 ,$$

$$\text{for } \ell_k = c_k , \quad 2 \le k \le n - 1 , \quad (5.4b)$$

$$(-\mu_{n-1} + \mu_n)g - \frac{(\Delta_{n-1} - \Delta_n)}{2} \frac{\partial g}{\partial \ell_{n-1}} + \frac{(\Delta_{n-1} + \Delta_n)}{2} \frac{\partial g}{\partial \ell_n} = 0 ,$$

$$\text{for } \ell_n = c_n , \qquad (5.4c)$$

$$(-\mu_0 + \mu_1)g + \frac{(\Delta_0 - \Delta_1)}{2}\frac{\partial g}{\partial \ell_2} + \frac{(\Delta_0 + \Delta_1)}{2}\frac{\partial g}{\partial \ell_1} + \Delta_0\frac{\partial g}{\partial x_0} = 0 ,$$

$$\text{for } \ell_1 = 0 , \quad (5.4d)$$

$$(-\mu_{k-1} + \mu_k)g + \frac{(\Delta_{k-1} - \Delta_k)}{2}\frac{\partial g}{\partial \ell_{k+1}} + \frac{(\Delta_{k-1} + \Delta_k)}{2}\frac{\partial g}{\partial \ell_k} - \Delta_{k-1}\frac{\partial g}{\partial \ell_{k-1}} = 0 ,$$

$$\text{for } \ell_k = 0 , \quad 2 \le k \le n - 1 , \quad (5.4e)$$

$$(-\mu_{n-1} + \mu_n)g + \frac{(\Delta_{n-1} + \Delta_n)}{2}\frac{\partial g}{\partial \ell_n} - \Delta_{n-1}\frac{\partial g}{\partial \ell_{n-1}} = 0 ,$$

$$\text{for } \ell_n = 0 , \quad (5.4f)$$

$$g = 0 , \quad \text{for} \quad x_0 = \pm \infty , \quad\quad\quad (5.4g)$$

$$g = 0 , \quad \text{for} \quad \ell_k = 0, \ \ell_{k+1} = c_{k+1} , \ 1 \le k \le n - 1 . \quad (5.4h)$$

Clearly, the explicit form of the differential equation and the boundary conditions appear more complex than those for $f$. In particular (5.3) contains some cross derivatives $\partial^2/\partial\ell_j\partial\ell_{j+1}$, which are rather unpleasant, and most boundary conditions contain three derivative terms. On the other hand, we have simplified the region of motion to a rectangular cylinder $0 \le \ell_j \le c_j$, $-\infty < x_0 < +\infty$.

That there is no boundary on the $x_0$ means that we can integrate with respect to $x_0$ and obtain a diffusion for the joint marginal distribution of the $Q_j(t)$ alone. If we let

$$g^*(\ell_1,\ell_2,\ldots,\ell_n;t) \equiv \int_{-\infty}^{+\infty} dx_0 \ g(x_0,\ell_1,\ldots,\ell_n;t), \quad (5.5)$$

then integration of (5.3) and (5.4) with respect to $x_0$ gives

$$\frac{\partial g^*}{\partial t} = \sum_{j=1}^{n} \left[ (-\mu_{j-1} + \mu_j) \frac{\partial g^*}{\partial \ell_j} + \frac{(\Delta_{j-1} + \Delta_j)}{2} \frac{\partial^2 g^*}{\partial \ell_j^2} \right]$$

$$- \sum_{j=1}^{n-1} \Delta_j \frac{\partial^2 g^*}{\partial \ell_j \partial \ell_{j+1}} \quad , \quad \text{for } 0 < \ell_j < c_j \quad , \tag{5.6}$$

subject to the boundary conditions

$$(-\mu_0 + \mu_1) g^* + \frac{(\Delta_0 + \Delta_1)}{2} \frac{\partial g^*}{\partial \ell_1} - \Delta_1 \frac{\partial g^*}{\partial \ell_2} = 0 , \text{ for } \ell_1 = c_1 , \quad (5$$

$$(-\mu_{k-1} + \mu_k) g^* - \frac{(\Delta_{k-1} - \Delta_k)}{2} \frac{\partial g^*}{\partial \ell_{k-1}} + \frac{(\Delta_{k-1} + \Delta_k)}{2} \frac{\partial g^*}{\partial \ell_k} - \Delta_k \frac{\partial g^*}{\partial \ell_{k+1}} =$$

$$\text{for } \ell_k = c_k , \quad 2 \le k \le n - 1 , \tag{5.7b}$$

$$(-\mu_{n-1} + \mu_n) g^* - \frac{(\Delta_{n-1} - \Delta_n)}{2} \frac{\partial g^*}{\partial \ell_{n-1}} + \frac{(\Delta_{n-1} + \Delta_n)}{2} \frac{\partial g^*}{\partial \ell_n} = 0 ,$$

$$\text{for } \ell_n = c_n , \tag{5.7c}$$

$$(-\mu_0 + \mu_1) g^* + \frac{(\Delta_0 - \Delta_1)}{2} \frac{\partial g^*}{\partial \ell_2} + \frac{(\Delta_0 + \Delta_1)}{2} \frac{\partial g^*}{\partial \ell_1} = 0 ,$$

$$\text{for } \ell_1 = 0 , \tag{5.7d}$$

$$(-\mu_{k-1} + \mu_k) g^* + \frac{(\Delta_{k-1} - \Delta_k)}{2} \frac{\partial g^*}{\partial \ell_{k+1}} + \frac{(\Delta_{k-1} + \Delta_k)}{2} \frac{\partial g^*}{\partial \ell_k} - \Delta_{k-1} \frac{\partial g^*}{\partial \ell_{k-1}} =$$

$$\text{for } \ell_k = 0 , \quad 2 \le k \le n - 1 , \tag{5.7e}$$

$$(-\mu_{n-1} + \mu_n)\, g^* + \frac{(\Delta_{n-1} + \Delta_n)}{2} \frac{\partial g^*}{\partial \ell_n} - \Delta_{n-1} \frac{\partial g^*}{\partial \ell_{n-1}} = 0 ,$$

$$\text{for } \ell_n = 0 , \qquad (5.7\text{f})$$

$$g^* = 0 \quad \text{for} \quad \ell_k = 0 , \quad \ell_{k+1} = c_{k+1} , \quad 1 \le k \le n - 1 . \qquad (5.7\text{g})$$

Although this system of equations still appears rather complicated, the number of space variables has been reduced from $n + 1$ to $n$, and the region is a rectangular one $0 < \ell_j < c_j$. That such a system of equations exists at all implies that the set of $Q_j(t)$ themselves define (approximately) a Markov process. Although the general solution of these equations will be too complicated to be of any practical use, one can see the possibility of solving some special cases, for small $n$, particularly if some of the $\Delta_j$ are zero (regular service) or some $\Delta_j = \Delta_{j-1}$ (which bears some relation to the fact that Poisson arrivals and exponential service times lead to some simplications in exact problems), or some of the servers have the same rate $\mu_{k-1} = \mu_k$. One should also keep in mind that, in most practical problems, one need analyse the stochastic properties of only certain critical parts of the system, particularly any queues which would affect the behavior of the bottleneck.

6. Soft Boundaries. We saw in the last two sections that the boundary conditions for the diffusion equation are rather complicated and perhaps even questionable. If one tries to continue the formal integration of the diffusion equation with respect to three, four, etc., variables (generalizing (4.10)) in an attempt to verify the conservation equation

32

$$\frac{\partial}{\partial t} \int \cdots \int dx_1 \cdots dx_n \, f(x_1, x_2, \ldots, x_n; t) = 0 , \qquad (6.1)$$

which one will then use as a basis for normalizing the probability density f ;

$$\int \cdots \int dx_1 \cdots dx_n \, f(x_1, x_2, \ldots, x_n; t) = 1 , \qquad (6.2)$$

one encounters further complications at other edges due to the non-analytic behavior of f near edges.

To avoid some of these problems, it is possible to formulate the problem in another way, which is actually more accurate than the above. One can eliminate the boundary conditions at the expense of making the diffusion equation more complicated (and almost impossible to solve explicitly.

Suppose that each server is considered to be a multiple-channel server; server j has $n_j$ channels. In counting customers for a multiple-channel service system, it is customary to count also the customers in service (which we have neglected in previous sections because, by implication, the number of customers in service was negligible, 0 or 1, compared with the queue). Rather than do this, however, we will take as a reference state for $D_j(t)$ , a state for which the jth server has $n_j$ customers in service and none in queue. Thus, instead of the condition $D_{j-1}(t) > D_j(t)$ , the $D_j(t)$ would now satisfy $D_{j-1}(t) > D_j(t) - n_j$ , or $Q_j(t) \geq - n_j$ . A negative queue means that $-Q_j(t) > 0$ servers are idle.

We will also allow $Q_{j+1}(t)$ to exceed $c_{j+1}$ , but, when this happens, we interpret $Q_{j+1}(t) - c_{j+1}$ as the number of customers in the jth service who have completed service but had no place to go. They remain in the jth service but block the server from serving any new customers. Note that we still retain the symmetry of section 3 because a server is idle either if it has no customer or has a blocking customer.

Suppose now that $n_j \gg 1$ for all $j$, and each service channel has a service rate $\mu_j/n_j$. We will continue to disregard the discrete nature of the customers and, with $-Q_j(t)$ or $Q_{j+1} - c_{j+1}$ treated as continuous random variables, introduce a state dependent service rate for the jth server

$$\mu_j^* = \mu_j^*(x_{j-1}, x_j, x_{j+1})$$

$$= \mu_j[1 - |x_j - x_{j-1}|^+/n_j - |x_j - x_{j+1} - c_{j+1}|^+/n_j] \qquad (6.3)$$

with

$$|x_j - x_{j-1}|^+ \equiv \begin{cases} x_j - x_{j-1} & \text{if } x_j - x_{j-1} > 0 \\ \\ 0 & \text{if } x_j - x_{j-1} < 0 . \end{cases} \qquad (6.4)$$

Thus the service rate of the jth server is reduced by the fraction $-Q_j(t)/n_j$ if $Q_j(t) < 0$ plus $|Q_{j+1}(t) - c_{j+1}|/n_j$ if $Q_{j+1}(t) - c_{j+1} > 0$, the fraction of servers that are idle either for lack of customers or blocking customers.

The service rate (6.3) could become negative if $-Q_j(t) + Q_{j+1}(t) - c_{j+1} > n_j$, but this is somewhat academic. When $\mu_j^*$ becomes small compared with $\mu_j$, the jth server cuts off the source to the downstream queue and causes a queue to grow upstream. The probability that the system could ever reach states in which $\mu_j^*/\mu \ll 1$ would be negligible.

Although we have interpreted the $n_j$ as the number of channels, in

34

(6.4) they appear simply as another set of parameters to describe the system
(along with the $\mu_j$ , $\Delta_j$) . Equation (6.4) is well-defined even for non-
integer $n_j$ , even $n_j < 1$ . Indeed, we would expect that the results of
the previous sections would obtain from taking the limit $n_j \to 0$ or at
least $n_j/c_j \to 0$ , i.e., the service rate is drastically reduced if the
queue tries to become negative or cannot dispose of served customers.

We are not particularly interested here in how realistically (6.3) describes the detailed properties of the servers themselves. We will not worry
about whether the effective $\Delta_j$ is the same for $-Q_j(t) > 0$ as for $Q_j(t)$
etc.[6] These will all be minor refinements which have little effect upon
queue evolution in any situations in which one would want to use diffusion
approximations. Actually the following questions will describe the behavior
of the servers themselves quite accurately if the individual servers have
exponential service times.

For a state-dependent service rate (6.3), the diffusion equation (4.3)
is now replaced by

$$\frac{\partial f}{\partial t} = \sum_{j=0}^{n} \left[ -\frac{\partial}{\partial x_j}(\mu_j^* f) + \frac{\Delta_j}{2}\frac{\partial^2 f}{\partial x_j^2}\right] . \tag{6.5}$$

The $\mu_j^*$ must be placed inside the $\partial/\partial x_j$ ; it can be taken outside only
if it is independent of $x_j$[7] .

The boundary conditions for (6.5) are replaced by

$$f \to 0 , \text{ for } x_0 \to \pm\infty \quad \text{or} \quad x_{j-1} - x_j \to \pm\infty . \tag{6.6}$$

By allowing queue lengths to go to $\pm\infty$, we admit the possibility of negative service rates but we actually expect $f$ to become negligible by

the time $\mu_j^*/\mu$ becomes small. The new terms in $\mu_j^*$ should automatically force the system to do what the boundary conditions of section 4 were supposed to guarantee.

An immediate advantage of (6.5), (6.6) is that an integration of (6.5) over the entire space $x_1, \ldots, x_n$ will confirm the validity of (6.1). Each term on the right-hand side integrates out to a surface term where $f$ vanishes.

One can readily check that the solution of (6.5), (6.6) is consistent with the boundary conditions (4.7), (4.8) in the limit $n_j \to 0$, $j = 1, \ldots, n$. Consider, for example, the solution of (6.5) near the boundary $x_k = x_{k-1}$ of (4.8), particularly for $x_{k-1} < x_k$. If the coordinates $x_1, \ldots, x_n$ are not near an edge of the boundary, then the only term of (6.5) containing an $n_\ell$, is the term

$$\frac{\partial}{\partial x_k} \frac{\mu_k}{n_k} \left| x_k - x_{k-1} \right|^+ f \quad . \tag{6.7}$$

For $n_k \to 0$ and $x_k > x_{k-1}$, this large term must be cancelled by a large term from the second derivatives.

The solution $f$ must decrease very rapidly as $x_k - x_{k-1}$ becomes positive. From the form of (6.7) one can guess that $f$ should have the form

$$f(\ldots,x_{k-1},x_k,\ldots;t) = \exp\left[-n_k(x_k - x_{k-1})^2\right]f^*(\ldots,x_{k-1},x_k,\ldots) \tag{6.8}$$

for $x_k > x_{k-1}$, in which $f^*$ is a slowly varying (relative to $n_k^{-1}$) function that is smooth across the boundary $x_k = x_{k-1}$ and matches $f$ for $x_k < x_{k-1}$.

If one substitutes (6.8) into (6.5), one can easily verify that the dominant term of (6.7) will be cancelled by the second derivative terms of (6.5) if we choose

$$\eta_k = \mu_k n_k^{-1} (\Delta_k + \Delta_{k-1})^{-1} . \qquad (6.9)$$

The term of (6.5) in question is the term

$$\frac{\mu_k (x_k - x_{k-1})}{n_k} \frac{\partial f}{\partial x_k} = \frac{\mu_k^2 \, 2 \, (x_k - x_{k-1})^2}{n_k^2 (\Delta_k + \Delta_{k-1})} f^* \quad ,$$

which is actually of order $n_k^{-2}$ .

In addition to the terms of order $n_k^{-2}$ , the substitution of (6.8) into (6.5) generates a number of terms proportional to $n_k^{-1} (x_k - x_{k-1})$ . These terms will cancel provided that $f^*$ of (6.8) satisfies the conditions (4.8). Thus it would appear that a solution of (6.5), (6.6) would automatically satisfy the condition (4.8) for $n_k \to 0$ at the boundary $x_k = x_{k-1}$ . Similarly one can show that the boundary condition (4.7) results from (6.5) in the limit $n_k \to 0$ .

Unfortunately the solution of (6.5) in the vicinity of the edges is much more difficult, even the asymptotic solution for $n_k \to 0$ . Despite the fact that f will show various non-analytic behavior near the edges for $n_k \to 0$ , we can still exploit certain properties of (6.5) if we postulate that the total probability near edges is negligible compared with that near the boundary surfaces.

7. <u>Moments</u>. Suppose that $Z(x_0, x_1, \ldots, x_n)$ is any twice differentiable function of $x_0, \ldots, x_n$ for which

$$E\{Z(D_0(t), D_1(t), \ldots, D_n(t))\} \equiv \int \cdots \int dx_0 \cdots dx_n \, f(x_0, x_1, \ldots, x_n; t)$$

$$\text{(7.1)}$$

$$\cdot \; Z(x_0, x_1, \ldots, x_n)$$

exists. If we multiply (6.5) by $Z$, integrate over the space $(x_0, \ldots, x_n)$, perform an integration by parts, and use the boundary conditions (6.6), we conclude that

$$\frac{d}{dt} E\{Z(D_0(t), \ldots, D_n(t))\} = \int \cdots \int dx_0 \cdots dx_n \, f(x_0, x_1, \ldots, x_n; t)$$

$$\cdot \sum_{j=0}^{n} [\mu_j^* \frac{\partial Z}{\partial x_j} + \frac{\Delta_j}{2} \frac{\partial^2 Z}{\partial x_j^2}]$$

$$= \sum_{j=0}^{n} E\{\mu_j^* \frac{\partial Z}{\partial x_j} + \frac{\Delta_j}{2} \frac{\partial^2 Z}{\partial x_j^2}\} . \qquad \text{(7.2)}$$

In particular, for $Z(x_0, \ldots, x_n) = x_k$ , we have

$$\frac{d}{dt} E\{D_k(t)\} = E\{\mu_k^*(D_{k-1}(t), D_k(t), D_{k+1}(t))\} ,$$

which simply says that the expected rate of change of $D_k(t)$ is the expected service rate of the kth server. Substitution of (6.3) now gives

38

$$\frac{d}{dt} E\{D_k(t)\} = \mu_k - \frac{\mu_k}{n_k} \int \cdots \int dx_0 \cdots dx_n |x_k - x_{k-1}|^+ f(x_0, \ldots, x_n;t)$$

$$- \frac{\mu_k}{n_k} \int \cdots \int dx_0 \cdots dx_n |x_k - x_{k+1} - c_{k+1}|^+ f(x_0,\ldots,x_n;t)$$

For $n_j \to 0$ , we can substitute (6.8) into the first integral and the corresponding expression in the second integral, and integrate the $x_k$ variable. This leads to a form

$$\frac{d}{dt} E\{D_k(t)\} = \mu_k - \frac{(\Delta_k + \Delta_{k-1})}{2} g_k^*(0;t) - \frac{(\Delta_k + \Delta_{k+1})}{2} g_{k+1}^*(c_{k+1};t) , \quad (7$$

in which $g_k^*(\ell_k;t)$ is the marginal probability density of $Q_k(t)$ ,

$$g_k^*(\ell_k;t) = \int_0 \cdots \int \prod_{\substack{j \\ j \neq k}}^{c_j} d\ell_j \, g^*(\ell_1, \ldots, \ell_n;t) ,$$

$$(7.5)$$

$$g_0^*(\ell_0;t) \equiv 0 , \qquad g_{n+1}^*(\ell_{n+1};t) \equiv 0 .$$

The service rate of the kth server is thus decreased whenever $Q_k(t) = 0$ or $Q_{k+1}(t) = c_{k+1}$ , the average decrease being proportional to the probability densities for the queues being empty or full.

Although we have not yet determined the probability density of queue lengths, we do expect that the queue distributions will approach some equilibrium distribution for $t \to \infty$ ,

$$g^*(\ell_1, \ell_2, \ldots, \ell_n;t) \to g^*(\ell_1, \ldots, \ell_n) ,$$

$$(7.6)$$

$$g_k^*(\ell_k;t) \to g_k^*(\ell_k) , \qquad \text{for } t \to \infty .$$

This means, from (7.4), that $dE\{D_k(t)\}/dt$ has a limit for $t \to \infty$; there is an equilibrium service rate and, consequently, $E\{D_k(t)\}$ grows asymptotically linearly with $t$.

Since

$$\frac{dE\{D_{k-1}(t)\}}{dt} - \frac{dE\{D_k(t)\}}{dt} = \frac{dE\{Q_k(t)\}}{dt} \to 0 ,$$

it follows that,

$$\frac{dE\{D_k(t)\}}{dt} \to \mu , \qquad \text{for } t \to \infty \qquad (7.7)$$

is independent of $k$,

$$\mu = \mu_k - \frac{(\Delta_k + \Delta_{k-1})}{2} g_k^*(0) - \frac{(\Delta_k + \Delta_{k+1})}{2} g_{k+1}^*(c_{k+1}) , \quad (7.8)$$

$$k = 0, 1, \ldots, n .$$

That this is the same for all $k$ imposes conditions on the, as yet unknown, $g_k^*(\ell_k)$. These conditions will, in fact, be used later as further boundary conditions in the $g^*(\ell_1, \ldots, \ell_n)$.

One of the primary objectives in the analysis of stochastic properties of tandem queues is to evaluate the $\mu$. The most important practical question is: to what extent do the finite storages $c_j$ reduce the equilibrium service rate $\mu$ relative to that given by deterministic approximation, $\min_j \mu_j$? Unfortunately there does not appear to be any "short-cut" method of evaluating the $\mu$ without evaluating the complete joint distribution of all the queues.

If one is interested in fluctuations in the number of customers serve,
one may wish also to evaluate variances and covariances of the $D_k(t)$ , o
at least their rates of growth

$$\frac{d}{dt} \, \text{cov}[D_j(t), D_k(t)] = \frac{d}{dt} \, E\{D_j(t) \, D_k(t)\} - \frac{d}{dt} \, E\{D_j(t)\}E\{D_k(t)\}. \qquad (7$$

If we substitute $Z(x_0, \ldots, x_n) = x_j \, x_k$ in (7.2), we obtain

$$\frac{d}{dt} \, E\{D_k^2(t)\} = \Delta_k + 2E\{\mu_k^* \, D_k(t)\} , \qquad (7.10a)$$

$$\frac{d}{dt} \, E\{D_j(t) D_k(t)\} = E\{\mu_j^* D_k(t) + \mu_k^* D_j(t)\} , \quad j \neq k . \qquad (7.10b)$$

Since,

$$\frac{d}{dt} \, E\{D_j(t)\}E\{D_k(t)\} = E\{D_j(t)\}E\{\mu_k^*\} + E\{D_k(t)\} E\{\mu_j^*\}$$

we can write

$$\frac{d}{dt} \, \text{Var}\{D_k(t)\} = \Delta_k + 2 \, \text{cov}\{\mu_k^*, \, D_k(t)\} ,$$

$$\qquad (7.11)$$

$$\frac{d}{dt} \, \text{cov} \, \{D_j(t), \, D_k(t)\} = \text{cov}\{\mu_j^*, \, D_k(t)\} + \text{cov}\{\mu_k^*, \, D_j(t)\} .$$

We can also replace $\mu_k^*$ by $\mu_k^* - \mu_k$ in these formulas so that

$$\frac{d}{dt} \, \text{Var}\{D_k(t)\} = \Delta_k + 2E\{(\mu_k^* - \mu_k)D_k(t)\} - 2E\{D_k(t)\}E\{\mu_k^* - \mu_k\} .$$

Since $\mu_k^* - \mu_k = 0$ except for $x_k > x_{k-1}$ or $x_k > x_{k+1} + c_{k+1}$ ,
the integrations associated with the expectations are confined to these
ranges. If we again let $n_j \to 0$ and use (6.8), (7.11) gives

$$\frac{d}{dt} \text{Var}\{D_k(t)\} = \Delta_k - (\Delta_k + \Delta_{k-1})g_k^*(0;t)[E\{D_k(t)|Q_k(t) = 0\} - E\{D_k(t)\}]$$

$$- (\Delta_k + \Delta_{k+1})g_{k+1}^*(c_{k+1};t)[E\{D_k(t)|Q_{k+1}(t) = c_{k+1}\}$$

(7.12)

$$- E\{D_k(t)\}].$$

If all $c_j$ are finite, one would expect the difference between the conditional expectation $E\{D_k(t)|Q_k(t) = 0\}$ and $E\{D_k(t)\}$ to approach a finite limit for $t \to \infty$. Consequently, $d\text{Var}\{D_k(t)\}/dt$ should have a limit, and $\{\text{Var } D_k(t)\}$ should grow linearly with $t$ for large $t$. Since

$$\frac{d}{dt} \text{Var}\{D_k(t)\} = \frac{d}{dt} \text{Var}\{D_{k+1} + Q_{k+1}(t)\},$$

$$= \frac{d}{dt}[\text{Var}\{D_{k+1}(t)\} + 2\text{cov}\{Q_{k+1}(t),D_{k+1}(t)\} + \text{Var}\{Q_{k+1}(t)\}],$$

we also expect, for $t \to \infty$, that $Q_{k+1}(t)$ should have a limit distribution and that

$$\frac{d}{dt} \text{Var}\{D_k(t)\} \to \frac{d}{dt} \text{Var}\{D_{k+1}(t)\} \to \Delta$$

(7.13)

with $\Delta$ independent of $k$.

The situation here is analogous to that of $\mu$ in (7.8). For $t \to \infty$, the right hand side of (7.12) should approach a limit $\Delta$ which is the same for all servers, but there is no quick way to determine what that limit is. Next to $\mu$, the $\Delta$ is perhaps the second most important measure of overall performance of the system.

In the following chapters, we will evaluate some of the quantities described above for special systems.

42

References - Chapter I

1.  R. R. P. Jackson, "Queueing Systems with Phase Type Service," Operational Res. Q. 5, 109-120 (1954).

2.  E. Reich, "Waiting Times When Queues Are in Tandem," Ann. Math. Stat. 28, 768-773 (1957).

3.  J. R. Jackson, "Networks of Waiting Lines," Opns. Res. 5, 518-521 (1957).

4.  D. J. Daley, "Notes on Queueing Output Processes," Mathematical Methods of Queueing Theory, Lecture Notes in Economics and Mathematical Systems #98, Springer-Verlag, 1974.

5.  G. F. Newell, Applications of Queueing Theory, Chapman & Hall, London, 1971.

6.  G. F. Newell, "Approximate Stochastic Behavior of n-server Service Systems with Large n," Lecture Notes in Economic and Mathematical Systems #87, Springer-Verlag, 1973.

7.  D. R. Cox and H. D. Miller, The Theory of Stochastic Processes, J. Wiley, New York, 1965.

## II. A Single Server

**1. Diffusion Equations.** In the formulation of I, even the system with a single server is non-trivial for we are concerned not just with the queue length at the first server but with the joint probability distribution of $D_0(t)$ and $D_1(t)$, or equivalently, the joint distribution of $D_0(t)$ or $D_1(t)$ and the queue length $D_0(t) - D_1(t)$ .

In this special case (I 4.3), (I 4.7), and (I 4.8) give

$$\frac{\partial f}{\partial t} = - \mu_0 \frac{\partial f}{\partial x_0} - \mu_1 \frac{\partial f}{\partial x_1} + \frac{\Delta_0}{2} \frac{\partial^2 f}{\partial x_0^2} + \frac{\Delta_1}{2} \frac{\partial^2 f}{\partial x_1^2} \tag{1.1}$$

with $x_0 > x_1$ and $x_1 + c_1 > x_0$

subject to the boundary conditions

$$(- \mu_0 + \mu_1) \, f \; + \; \frac{(\Delta_0 - \Delta_1)}{2} \frac{\partial f}{\partial x_0} - \Delta_1 \frac{\partial f}{\partial x_1} \; = \; 0 \quad \text{at } x_0 = x_1 + c_1 \tag{1.2a}$$

$$(- \mu_0 + \mu_1) \, f \; + \; \frac{(\Delta_0 - \Delta_1)}{2} \frac{\partial f}{\partial x_1} + \Delta_0 \frac{\partial f}{\partial x_0} \; = \; 0 \quad \text{at } x_0 = x_1 \tag{1.2b}$$

For $n = 1$ , there are no edge conditions corresponding to (I 4.12).

The solution of this system over the strip shown in figure I4 can be obtained either by image or transform methods, but both lead to rather cumbersome (infinite series) formulas. We will concentrate here on special properties.

The corresponding formulas for the distribution of $D_0(t)$ and $Q_1(t) = D_0(t) - D_1(t)$

$$f(x_0, x_1; t) \; = \; g(x_0, x_0 - x_1; t)$$

are, from (I 5.3), (I 5.4)

$$\frac{\partial g}{\partial t} = -\mu_0 \frac{\partial g}{\partial x_0} + \frac{\Delta_0}{2} \frac{\partial^2 g}{\partial x_0^2} + \Delta_0 \frac{\partial^2 g}{\partial x_0 \partial \ell_1} + (-\mu_0 + \mu_1)\frac{\partial g}{\partial \ell_1} + \frac{(\Delta_0 + \Delta_1)}{2} \frac{\partial^2 g}{\partial \ell_1^2}$$

subject to the boundary conditions

$$(-\mu_0 + \mu_1)g + \frac{(\Delta_0 - \Delta_1)}{2} \frac{\partial g}{\partial x_0} + \frac{(\Delta_0 + \Delta_1)}{2} \frac{\partial g}{\partial \ell_1} = 0 \quad \text{at } \ell_1 = c_1 \qquad (1.4a)$$

$$(-\mu_0 + \mu_1)g + \frac{(\Delta_0 + \Delta_1)}{2} \frac{\partial g}{\partial \ell_1} + \Delta_0 \frac{\partial g}{\partial x_0} = 0 \quad \text{at } \ell_1 = 0 . \qquad (1.4b)$$

The marginal distribution of the queue length satisfies (I 5.6)

$$\frac{\partial g^*}{\partial t} = (-\mu_0 + \mu_1) \frac{\partial g^*}{\partial \ell_1} + \frac{(\Delta_0 + \Delta_1)}{2} \frac{\partial^2 g^*}{\partial \ell_1^2} \qquad (1.5)$$

subject to (I 5.7)

$$(-\mu_0 + \mu_1) g^* + \frac{(\Delta_0 + \Delta_1)}{2} \frac{\partial g^*}{\partial \ell_1} = 0 \quad \text{at } \ell_1 = c_1 \text{ and } \ell_1 = 0 . \qquad (1.6)$$

2.  Queue Distribution. The one-dimensional system (1.5), (1.6) is obviously easier to solve than the complete system (1.1), (1.2) or (1.3), (1.4), so we will start with this rather classic problem.

If we integrate (1.5) with respect to $\ell_1$ from 0 to $c_1$ and apply the boundary conditions (1.6), we obtain the conservation equation

$$\frac{\partial}{\partial t} \{\int_0^{c_1} dz \, g^*(z;t)\} = 0 .$$

It is convenient, therefore, to work with the distribution function of queue length,

$$G^*(\ell_1;t) = \int_0^{\ell_1} dz\, g^*(z;t) , \qquad (2.1)$$

which satisfies the same equation

$$\frac{\partial G^*}{\partial t} = (-\mu_0 + \mu_1)\frac{\partial G^*}{\partial \ell_1} + \frac{(\Delta_0 + \Delta_1)}{2}\frac{\partial^2 G^*}{\partial \ell_1^2} , \qquad (2.2)$$

with

$$G^*(0;t) = 0 \quad \text{and} \quad G^*(c_1;t) = 1 \quad \text{for all } t . \qquad (2.3)$$

If $c_1 = \infty$, one can obtain a "closed form" solution of (2.2) and (2.3) by image methods starting from any initial queue $y_0 - y_1$ at time $0$

$$G^*(\ell_1;t) = \Phi\left\{\frac{\ell_1 - (y_0 - y_1) - (\mu_0 - \mu_1)\, t}{[(\Delta_0 + \Delta_1)\, t]^{1/2}}\right\}$$

$$- \exp(-\alpha_1\ell_1)\Phi\left\{\frac{-\ell_1 - (y_0 - y_1) - (\mu_0 - \mu_1)t}{[(\Delta_0 + \Delta_1)t]^{1/2}}\right\} , \qquad (2.4)$$

with

$$\alpha_1 = 2(-\mu_0 + \mu_1)/(\Delta_0 + \Delta_1) . \qquad (2.5)$$

The first term of (2.4) describes the "free diffusion" starting from the initial queue length; the second term represents the reflection from the boundary $\ell_1 = 0$ . If $\mu_0 > \mu_1$ (oversaturated system), the argument

of the $\Phi$ in the second term becomes negative and large as t becomes
sufficiently large; the second term goes to zero. The first term describes
the queue increasing at a mean rate $\mu_0 - \mu_1$ .

If, however, $\mu_0 < \mu_1$ (undersaturated) the arguments of both $\Phi$-functions become positive for sufficiently large t ; the $\Phi$-functions approach 1 and

$$G^*(\ell_1;t) \rightarrow 1 - \exp(-\alpha_1\ell_1) \qquad \text{for } t \rightarrow \infty, \quad c_1 = \infty .$$

This is, of course, the well-known heavy traffic exponential queue distribution.

For finite $c_1$ , one can not obtain a closed form solution for the
initial value problem. One can obtain an infinite series solution by successive reflections over the boundaries at $\ell_1 = 0$ and $\ell_1 = c_1$ . This
is an appropriate method to obtain the "short time" solution when the
queue distribution has barely had enough time to reach one boundary or
the other. For the long time behavior, however, it is more appropriate
to use "separation of variable" methods (Fourier series).

For $c_1 < \infty$, $G^*(\ell_1;t)$ will always approach an equilibrium for
$t \rightarrow \infty$

$$G^*(\ell_1;t) \rightarrow G^*(\ell_1) = \frac{1 - \exp(-\alpha_1\ell_1)}{1 - \exp(-\alpha_1 c_1)} . \qquad (2.6)$$

For $\mu_0 < \mu_1$ $(\alpha_1 > 0)$, the queue distribution tends to concentrate near
$\ell_1 = 0$, but for $\mu_0 > \mu_1$ $(\alpha_1 < 0)$, it concentrates near $\ell_1 = c_1$ . The
distribution (2.6) is the diffusion approximation to the "lost call"
queue distribution.

To obtain the transient solution for large but finite $t$, the simplest procedure is to work with the difference $G^*(\ell_1;t) - G^*(\ell_1)$ which also satisfies (2.2) but vanishes at both $\ell_1 = 0$ and $\ell_1 = c_1$. The distribution approaches equilibrium exponentially fast, with the dominant transient term having the form

$$G^*(\ell_1;t) - G^*(\ell_1) = A \sin(\pi\ell_1/c_1) \exp\left(-\frac{\alpha_1}{2}\ell_1\right)$$

$$\cdot \exp\left\{-\frac{(\Delta_0 + \Delta_1)}{2}\left[\left(\frac{\pi}{c_1}\right)^2 + \left(\frac{\alpha_1}{2}\right)^2\right]t\right\}$$

$$(2.7)$$

for some constant $A$. The "relaxation time" is

$$\left\{\frac{(\Delta_0 + \Delta_1)}{2}\left[\left(\frac{\pi}{c_1}\right)^2 + \left(\frac{\alpha_1}{2}\right)^2\right]\right\}^{-1}.$$

$$(2.8)$$

**3. Service Rates.** From (I 7.4), the service rates are given by

$$\frac{dE\{D_0(t)\}}{dt} = \mu_0 - \frac{1}{2}(\Delta_0 + \Delta_1) g^*(c_1;t),$$

$$(3.1a)$$

$$\frac{dE\{D_1(t)\}}{dt} = \mu_1 - \frac{1}{2}(\Delta_0 + \Delta_1) g^*(0;t),$$

$$(3.1b)$$

which can be evaluated directly in terms of the (marginal) queue length distribution described in section 2. As $g^*(\ell_1;t)$ approaches the equilib-queue distribution (2.6), the service rates approach a value (I 7.8)

$$\mu = \frac{dE\{D_0(t)\}}{dt} = \frac{dE\{D_1(t)\}}{dt} = \frac{(\mu_0 + \mu_1)}{2} - \frac{(-\mu_0 + \mu_1)}{2} \text{ctnh}\left(\frac{\alpha_1 c_1}{2}\right)$$

$$(3.2)$$

$$= \frac{(\mu_0 + \mu_1)}{2} - \frac{(\Delta_0 + \Delta_1)}{2c_1}\left[\frac{\alpha_1 c_1}{2} \text{ctnh}\left(\frac{\alpha_1 c_1}{2}\right)\right].$$

For sufficiently large storage capacity that $|\alpha_1 c_1| \gg 1$, the queue distribution is concentrated near either $\ell_1 = c_1$ or $\ell_1 = 0$, accordingly as $\mu_0 > \mu_1$ or $\mu_0 < \mu_1$, and (3.2) reduces to

$$\mu \simeq \min(\mu_0, \mu_1) \qquad \text{for } |\alpha_1 c_1| \gg 1 . \qquad (3.2a)$$

Since for $\mu_0 \neq \mu_1$, $\alpha_1 \to \infty$ if $\Delta_0 + \Delta_1 \to 0$, this limiting case also corresponds to the deterministic approximation; the overall service rate is that of the bottleneck. If, however, the service rates are nearly equal (or $\Delta_0 + \Delta_1$ is sufficiently large) that $|\alpha_1 c_1| \ll 1$, (3.2) reduces to

$$\mu \simeq \frac{\mu_0 + \mu_1}{2} - \frac{(\Delta_0 + \Delta_1)}{2c_1} \qquad \text{for } |\alpha_1 c_1| \ll 1 . \qquad (3.2b)$$

The expression (3.2) is of considerable practical value. If server is real, not just an artificial generator of an arrival process for server but the arrival rate to 0 exceeds $\mu$, the queue behind server 0 grows in time. Then (3.2) describes the service rate of the combined system of servers 0 and 1 with a finite storage $c_1$ between them.

Presumably, the cost of building or operating a service system is some increasing function of $\mu_0$, $\mu_1$, and $c_1$. If one wishes to design a system to serve a rush hour, the most efficient design will typically be the one which provides the largest $\mu$ for a given cost. From (3.2) one can see the relative influence of changes in the $\mu_0$, $\mu_1$, or $c_1$ (or $\Delta_0$ and $\Delta_1$).

Special cases of (3.2), particularly for exponentially distributed service times, can be derived exactly. The present result, however, shows at least approximately, how the service variances $\Delta_0$ and $\Delta_1$ affect the

The influence of a finite storage is frequently quite significant, particularly if the two servers are very similar. If $\mu_0 = \mu_1$ and $\Delta_0 = \Delta_1 = \mu_0$, as for exponentially distributed service times, the effect of a finite $c_1$ is to reduce the combined service rate by a factor $1 - 1/c_1$ relative to $c_1 = \infty$ ; a storage capacity of 10 will reduce the service rate by about 10%. Since rush hour delays are very sensitive to the value of $\mu$ , a 10% loss in service rate could be quite important.

<u>Longtime Behavior of the Joint Distributions.</u>  In the absence of any boundaries, $\ell_1 = 0$ or $\ell_1 = c_1$ , the distribution $f$ starting from some initial state $D_0(0) = y_0$ , $D_1(0) = y_1$ , would travel with a mean "velocity" $\mu_0$ horizontally and $\mu_1$ vertically in figure I4. It would spread with a variance $\Delta_0 t$ in the horizontal direction and $\Delta_1 t$ in the vertical direction, as described by (I 4.2). When the probability mass hits a boundary, it is reflected, but in a manner such as to interrupt the service (never to give extra service). This interruption has the effect of retarding the movement of $f$ , much like viscous drag will retard the movement of a fluid through a channel.

The boundary conditions (1.2) are not the usual "reflecting boundary" conditions, however, which specify a condition on the directional derivative of $f$ in a direction normal to the boundary. The derivatives in (1.2) are directional derivatives oblique to the boundary, not even the same direction at the two boundaries.

After a sufficiently long time, and many reflections from the boundaries, we expect the distribution $f$ to travel with some velocity in the $45^\circ$ direction of Fig. I-4, actually with the velocity $\mu$ in both the vertical and horizontal directions. The distribution is expected also to spread in the direction of motion, with a variance $\Delta t$ growing linearly with $t$ as in (I 7.13). Although the shape of $f$ in this direction should be similar to a normal distribution, it eventually becomes so spread that the derivative of $f$ in this direction becomes very small, compared with the derivative in the direction perpendicular to the boundaries.

In a direction normal to the boundaries (coordinate equal to the queue length), the distribution will bounce off the two boundaries. As becomes nearly constant, or actually slowly varying, in the direction of motion, we expect the distribution of queue length to approach the equilibrium distribution (2.6), for most values of $D_0(t)$ . In other words, $D_0(t)$ and $D_0(t) - D_1(t)$ should become "asymptotically independent."

It remains to be seen exactly how the above behavior emerges from (1.1) and (1.2). Even though the above statements may be true, one cannot simply disregard the statistical dependence between $D_0(t)$ and $Q_1(t)$ . What dependence that does exist gives rise to boundary drag on the motion of $D_0(t)$ and $D_1(t)$ .

In anticipation that $f$ and $g$ will behave as described above, for sufficiently large $t$ , one is inclined, as a first approximation to the longtime behavior of (1.3) and (1.4), to neglect $\partial g/\partial t$ and all derivati of $g$ with respect to $x_0$ . This leads to the approximate equations

$$(- \mu_0 + \mu_1) \frac{\partial g}{\partial \ell_1} + \frac{(\Delta_0 + \Delta_1)}{2} \frac{\partial^2 g}{\partial \ell_1^2} \simeq 0 \qquad (4.1)$$

with

$$(- \mu_0 + \mu_1)g + \frac{(\Delta_0 + \Delta_1)}{2} \frac{\partial g}{\partial \ell_1} \simeq 0 \quad \text{at} \quad \ell_1 = c_1 \text{ and } \ell_1 = 0 , \qquad (4.1a$$

the same equations as for $g^*$ , (1.5) and (1.6).

Although we have two boundary conditions on the second order differential equation (4.1), if one boundary condition is satisfied, the other is automatically also satisfied. The "general solution" of (4.1), (4.1a) is

$$g(x_0, \ell_1; t) \simeq A(x_0;t) \exp(-\alpha_1 \ell_1) \quad , \tag{4.1b}$$

with $A(x_0;t)$ some arbitrary positive function, which, however, is presumed to be slowly varying.

The exact solution of (1.3), (1.4) is not actually of the form (4.1b). If we substitute (4.1b) back into (1.3), (1.4) in an attempt to obtain an equation for $A(x_0;t)$ , we see that the boundary conditions (1.4) force $\partial A/\partial x_0 = 0$ . Then the differential equation (1.3), in turn, forces $\partial A/\partial t = 0$ . Thus $A(x_0;t)$ is a constant. But, if $A(x_0;t)$ is a constant, we cannot satisfy the normalization condition

$$\int_{-\infty}^{+\infty} dx_0 \int_0^{c_1} d\ell_1 \, g(x_0, \ell_1;t) = 1 ,$$

(except for $A = 0$).

The form (4.1b) is approximately correct, but to obtain a second approximation, one must proceed differently from the above. In a second approximation we might further anticipate that the form of $g$ is such that, if we go to a coordinate system traveling with the velocity $\mu$ , and let

$$\xi_0 = \frac{x_0 - \mu t}{L} , \quad \tau = t/T , \quad g^\dagger(\xi_0, \ell_1;\tau) = g(x_0, \ell_1;t) , \tag{4.2}$$

then there is a scaling of coordinates $L$ and $T$ , with $T$ of order $L^2$ , such that, for sufficiently large $t$, $g^\dagger$ approaches some limiting form

If we make the transformation of variables (4.2), then (1.3) and (1.4) give an equation for $g^\dagger$,

$$\frac{1}{T}\frac{\partial g^\dagger}{\partial \tau} = \frac{(-\mu_0 + \mu)}{L}\frac{\partial g^\dagger}{\partial \xi_0} + \frac{\Delta_0}{2L^2}\frac{\partial g^\dagger}{\partial \xi_0^2} + \frac{\Delta_0}{L}\frac{\partial^2 g^\dagger}{\partial \xi_0 \partial \ell_1}$$

$$- (\mu_0 + \mu_1)\frac{\partial g^\dagger}{\partial \ell_1} + \frac{(\Delta_0 + \Delta_1)}{2}\frac{\partial^2 g^\dagger}{\partial \ell_1^2} , \qquad (4.3)$$

subject to the boundary conditions

$$(-\mu_0 + \mu_1) g^\dagger + \frac{(\Delta_0 + \Delta_1)}{2}\frac{\partial g^\dagger}{\partial \ell_1} = -\frac{(\Delta_0 - \Delta_1)}{2L}\frac{\partial g^\dagger}{\partial \xi_0} \quad \text{at } \ell_1 = c_1 \quad (4$$

$$(-\mu_0 + \mu_1) g^\dagger + \frac{(\Delta_0 + \Delta_1)}{2}\frac{\partial g^\dagger}{\partial \ell_1} = -\frac{\Delta_0}{L}\frac{\partial g^\dagger}{\partial \xi_0} \quad \text{at } \ell_1 = 0 . \quad (4.3b)$$

Whereas the first approximation (4.1) corresponds to neglect of all terms of order $L^{-1}$, $L^{-2}$, and $T^{-1}$, we would expect in a second approximation to retain the terms of order $L^{-1}$ but neglect terms of order $L^{-2}$ and $T^{-1}$. Thus, we might next consider replacing (4.3) by

$$(-\mu_0 + \mu_1)\frac{\partial g^\dagger}{\partial \ell_1} + \frac{(\Delta_0 + \Delta_1)}{2}\frac{\partial^2 g^\dagger}{\partial \ell_1^2} \simeq -\frac{(-\mu_0 + \mu)}{L}\frac{\partial g^\dagger}{\partial \xi_0} - \frac{\Delta_0}{L}\frac{\partial^2 g^\dagger}{\partial \xi_0 \partial \ell_1} , \quad (4$$

subject to (4.3a), (4.3b).

The terms on the right-hand side of (4.4) and (4.3a,b) are small, of order $L^{-1}$. We will further estimate these terms by substituting the first approximation (4.1b) for $g^\dagger$. We can write the equations in the for

$$\frac{(\Delta_0 + \Delta_1)}{2} \frac{\partial}{\partial \ell_1} \exp(-\alpha_1 \ell_1) \frac{\partial}{\partial \ell_1} \exp(+\alpha_1 \ell_1) \ g^\dagger$$

$$\text{(4.5)}$$

$$\simeq \frac{1}{L} \frac{\partial}{\partial \ell_1} \left[ \frac{(-\mu_0 + \mu)}{\alpha_1} - \Delta_0 \right] \frac{\partial}{\partial \xi_0} A^\dagger(\xi_0; \tau) \exp(-\alpha_1 \ell_1)$$

subject to

$$\frac{(\Delta_0 + \Delta_1)}{2} \exp(-\alpha_1 \ell_1) \frac{\partial}{\partial \ell_1} \exp(+\alpha_1 \ell_1) \ g^\dagger$$

$$= \frac{-(\Delta_0 - \Delta_1)}{2L} \frac{\partial}{\partial \xi_0} A^\dagger(\xi_0; \tau) \exp(-\alpha_1 \ell_1) \quad \text{at } \ell_1 = c_1 \quad \text{(4.5a)}$$

$$= \frac{-\Delta_0}{L} \frac{\partial}{\partial \xi_0} A^\dagger(\xi_0; \tau) \quad\quad\quad \text{at } \ell_1 = 0 \quad\quad \text{(4.5b)}$$

in which $A^\dagger(\xi_0; \tau) = A(x_0; t)$ .

Equation (4.5) has been arranged so that both sides are derivatives with respect to $\ell_1$ . If we integrate (4.5) from $0$ to $\ell_1$ and use the boundary condition (4.5b) at $\ell_1 = 0$ , we obtain

$$\frac{(\Delta_0 + \Delta_1)}{2} \exp(-\alpha_1 \ell_1) \frac{\partial}{\partial \ell_1} \exp(+\alpha_1 \ell_1) g^\dagger$$

$$\text{(4.6)}$$

$$= \frac{1}{L} \left[ \frac{(-\mu_0 + \mu)}{\alpha_1} - \Delta_0 \right] \frac{\partial A^\dagger(\xi_0; \tau)}{\partial \xi_0} \exp(-\alpha_1 \ell_1) - \frac{(-\mu_0 + \mu)}{L \alpha_1} \frac{\partial A^\dagger(\xi_0; \tau)}{\partial \xi_0} .$$

We have not yet used the value of $\mu$ derived in (3.2). One can readily check, however, that the boundary condition (4.5a) will be satisfied by (4.6) if and only if $\mu$ satisfies (3.2). If we now substitute this value of $\mu$ into (4.6), it can be written in the form

$$\frac{\partial}{\partial \ell_1} \exp(\alpha_1 \ell_1) g^\dagger = -\frac{1}{L}\left[\frac{1}{\exp(\alpha_1 c_1) - 1} + \frac{2\,\Delta_0}{(\Delta_0 + \Delta_1)}\right]\frac{\partial A^\dagger(\xi_0;\tau)}{\partial \xi_0}$$

$$+ \frac{\exp(\alpha_1 \ell_1)}{L[\exp(\alpha_1 c_1) - 1]} \frac{\partial A^\dagger(\xi_0;\tau)}{\partial \xi_0} \quad .$$

Now we can integrate this with respect to $\ell_1$ to obtain the "solution"

$$g^\dagger(\xi_0,\ell_1;\tau) \simeq g^\dagger(\xi_0,0;\tau)\exp(-\alpha_1 \ell_1)$$

$$\tag{4.7}$$

$$+ \left\{-\frac{2\Delta_0 \alpha_1 \ell_1}{(\Delta_0 + \Delta_1)} + \frac{\exp(\alpha_1 \ell_1) - 1 - \alpha_1 \ell_1}{\exp(\alpha_1 c_1) - 1}\right\}\frac{\exp(-\alpha_1 \ell_1)}{\alpha_1 L}\frac{\partial g^\dagger(\xi_0,0;\tau)}{\partial \xi_0}$$

or, in terms of the original coordinates $x_0$ , $\ell_1$, $t$ ,

$$g(x_0,\ell_1;t) \simeq g(x_0,0;t)\exp(-\alpha_1 \ell_1)$$

$$\tag{4.8}$$

$$+ \left\{-\frac{2\Delta_0 \alpha_1 \ell_1}{\Delta_0 + \Delta_1} + \frac{\exp(\alpha_1 \ell_1) - 1 - \alpha_1 \ell_1}{\exp(\alpha_1 c_1) - 1}\right\}\frac{\exp(-\alpha_1 \ell_1)}{\alpha_1}\frac{\partial g(x_0,0;t)}{\partial x_0} \quad .$$

This still does not describe an explicit solution for $g(x_0,\ell; t)$; it only relates $g(x_0,\ell;t)$ to an as yet unknown function $g(x_0,0;t)$ , the probability density at zero queue. The first term is equivalent to (4.1b) and the second term gives a correction due to the drag at the boundaries. We cannot substitute this back into (4.3) to obtain an approximate equation for the $g(x_0,0;t)$ . We would need to add a term of order $L^{-2}$ to (4.7) to obtain a consistent set of equations. Nevertheless, we can extract from (4.7) or (4.8) most of the things we want to know about the longtime behavior.

Even though we have not actually evaluated the solution, we can anticipate that $g(x_0,0;t)$ has a shape similar to a normal distribution with a mean of approximately $\mu t$ and a variance approximately of the form $\Delta t$ (but an as yet unknown value of $\Delta$). For $x_0 \gtrsim \mu t$, $\partial g/\partial x_0$ should be negative, but for $x_0 \lesssim \mu t$, it should be positive. The second term of (4.7) describes a statistical dependence between the arrival process, $D_0(t)$, and the queue, $Q_1(t)$. The shape of the queue distribution deviates from the exponential form of the first term by a known function of $\ell_1$ multiplied by the $\partial g/\partial x_0$. Since the integral of the second term with respect to $x_0$ from $-\infty$ to $+\infty$ gives nothing, the second term does not contribute to the marginal queue distribution $g^*(\ell_1;t)$ which we know, from section 2, must approach the exponential distribution, for $t$ large compared with the relaxation time (2.8).

To illustrate the qualitative shape of the queue distribution, we might consider some special cases. If $|\alpha_1 c_1| \ll 1$, i.e., for $\mu_0$ sufficiently close to $\mu_1$, (4.8) simplifies to

$$g(x_0,\ell_1;t) \simeq g(x_0,0;t) + \ell_1\left(-\frac{2\Delta_0}{\Delta_0 + \Delta_1} + \frac{\ell_1}{2c_1}\right)\frac{\partial g(x_0,0;t)}{\partial x_0} \,. \qquad (4.9)$$

If we were to think of $g$ as representing the density of a diffusing fluid flowing through a channel, as in Fig. I-4 with the walls of the channel at $\ell_1 = 0$ and $\ell_1 = c_1$ causing a viscous drag, then the fluid would tend to move further down the channel for coordinates not too near the boundary. One way to describe (4.9) is to consider the contour lines of $g$. For some fixed $x_0$ and small $x_0^*$, the behavior of $g$ at points $x_0 + x_0^*$, $\ell_1$ is

$$g(x_0 + x_0^*, \ell_1; t) \simeq g(x_0 + x_0^*, 0; t) + \ell_1 \left[ \frac{-2 \, \Delta_0}{\Delta_0 + \Delta_1} + \frac{\ell_1}{2c_1} \right] \frac{\partial g}{\partial x_0}$$

$$\simeq g(x_0, 0; t) + \left[ x_0^* + \ell_1 \left( \frac{-2 \, \Delta_0}{\Delta_0 + \Delta_1} + \frac{\ell_1}{2c_1} \right) \right] \frac{\partial g}{\partial x_0} \ .$$

Starting from any point $x_0, 0$ where $g$ has the value $g(x_0, 0; t)$ , the contour line through this point is the curve

$$x_0^* + \ell_1 \left( -\frac{2 \, \Delta_0}{\Delta_0 + \Delta_1} + \frac{\ell_1}{2c_1} \right) = 0 \ , \tag{4.10}$$

which is independent of $\partial g/\partial x_0$, $g$, $t$, and, except for a translation of coordinates, also $x_0$ .

In terms of the original coordinates $x_0$, $x_1$, the contours (4.10) can also be represented by a family of parabolas

$$\left[ \frac{x_0 - x_1}{c_1} - \frac{1}{2} + \frac{\Delta_1 - \Delta_0}{\Delta_1 + \Delta_0} \right]^2 + \frac{x_0 + x_1}{c_1} = \text{const.} \tag{4.11}$$

with axis along the line

$$\frac{x_0 - x_1}{c_1} = \frac{1}{2} + \frac{\Delta_0 - \Delta_1}{\Delta_0 + \Delta_1} \ .$$

In particular, for $\Delta_0 = \Delta_1$ , the contour lines are symmetric about the line $\ell_1 = c_1/2$ as shown in Fig. II-1a. For $\Delta_0 = 0$ (regular arrivals to server 1), the axis is at $x_0 - x_1 = -c_1/2$ and (as can be inferred directly from (1.2b)), the contour lines are vertical at $x_0 = x_1$ (zero queue). For $\Delta_1 = 0$ (regular service at 1), the axis is at $x_0 - x_1 = 3c_1$

57

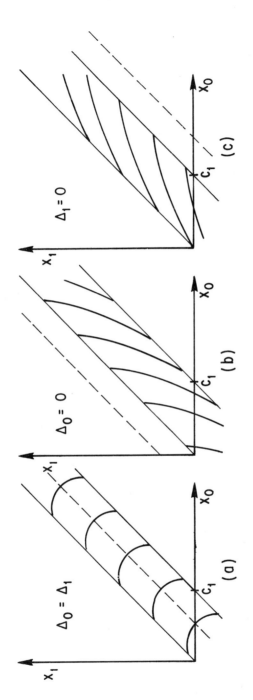

Fig. II-1.  Equal probability density contours for $\mu_0 = \mu_1$ .

58

as in Fig. II-1c, which is a reflection of Fig. II-1b over the line $x_0 - x_1$ $= c_1/2$ . This last symmetry between $\Delta_0 = 0$ or $\Delta_1 = 0$ follows the symmetry between customers and holes discussed in section I3.

These are contours of constant probability density, but we do not yet have labels of the density values for these contours. Obviously as $x_0, x_1$ increase along a $45^o$ direction, the density varies from 0 at $(- \infty, - \infty)$ to a maximum and back to 0 at $(+ \infty, + \infty)$. An interpretation of Fig. II-1 for example, is that, for relatively large values of $x_0, x_1$ where the density is decreasing with $x_0$ , there is a higher probability density near $\ell_1 = 0$ than at $\ell_1 = c_1$ . With $\Delta_0 = 0$ , any fluctuation in $D_0(t)$ , $D_1(t)$ must originate at server 1. That this server served more than the average number of customers, to send the state $(x_0, x_1)$ to high values, while the arrivals from server 0 remain regular, clearly would force the queue to be relatively short. Correspondingly, for relatively small values of $x_0, x_1$ , where the probability density is increasing with $x_0$ , there is a higher probability for a full storage than an empty one.

If $\mu_1 > \mu_0$ $(\mu_1 < \mu_0)$, the probability mass tends to concentrate near $\ell_1 = 0$ $(\ell_1 = c_1)$. Rather than describe the contours of $g$ as we did above for $\mu_0 = \mu_1$ , it is more advantageous to generalize these method by considering contours of

$$g(x_0, \ell_1; t) \exp(\alpha_1 \ell_1) = f(x_0, x_1; t) \exp(\alpha_1 \ell_1) , \qquad (4.12)$$

which also reduces to the above for $\alpha_1 = 0$ . Since the marginal distribution of queue length approaches the form $\exp(-\alpha_1 \ell_1)$ rather quickly for t larger than the time (2.8), the quantity (4.12) can be interpreted as an approximation to the conditional probability density of $D_0(t)$ given a queue length $Q_1(t) = \ell_1$ (except for a normalization factor $\alpha_1^{-1}[1-\exp(-\alpha_1 c$

According to (4.8), the quantity (4.12) should be approximately constant along contour lines

$$\frac{x_0 + x_1}{c_1} + 2\left\{(-\frac{1}{2} + \frac{\Delta_1 - \Delta_0}{\Delta_1 + \Delta_0})\frac{\ell_1}{c_1} + \frac{\exp(\alpha_1\ell_1) - 1 - \alpha_1\ell_1}{(\alpha_1 c_1)[\exp(\alpha_1 c_1) - 1]}\right\} = \text{const} \quad (4.13)$$

which reduce to (4.11) in the special case $\alpha_1 \to 0$ . Again these contours are independent of $t$ , and, except for a translation of coordinates, are independent of $g$ .

If, at the other extreme, $\alpha_1 > 0$ and $|\alpha_1 c_1| \gg 1$ , the terms of (4.13) involving the $\alpha_1$ can be neglected. The contours reduce to straight lines tangent at $\ell_1 = 0$ to the curves (4.11) shown in Fig. II-1a, b, c (or the corresponding figures for other values of $\Delta_1, \Delta_0$). Actually it is the boundary condition (1.2b) which determines the slope of the contour at $\ell_1 = 0$ . Condition (1.2b) is equivalent to

$$\left[\frac{(\Delta_0 - \Delta_1)}{2}\frac{\partial}{\partial x_1} + \Delta_0\frac{\partial}{\partial x_0}\right]f(x_0,x_1;t)\exp(\alpha_1\ell_1) = 0 , \quad \text{at} \ \ell_1 = 0 \quad (4.14b)$$

whereas (1.2a) is equivalent to

$$\left[\frac{(\Delta_0 - \Delta_1)}{2}\frac{\partial}{\partial x_0} - \Delta_1\frac{\partial}{\partial x_1}\right]f(x_0,x_1;t)\exp(\alpha_1\ell_1) = 0 , \quad \text{at} \ \ell_1 = c_1 \quad (4.14a)$$

and these conditions on $f \exp(\alpha_1\ell_1)$ are independent of $\mu_0$ and $\mu_1$ (or equivalently $\alpha_1$).

Condition (4.14b) can be interpreted as a statement that the derivative of $f \exp(\alpha_1\ell_1)$ vanishes in the direction of the vector $\Delta_0$, $(\Delta_0 - \Delta_1)/2$ in the $x_0, x_1$-plane, at the boundary $\ell_1 = 0$ , i.e., the contour lines have this direction. Similarly, the contour lines must be parallel to the vector $(\Delta_0 - \Delta_1)/2$, $-\Delta_1$ at $\ell_1 = c_1$ . These directions are independent of $\alpha_1$ .

The curvature of the contours in Fig. II-1 can be interpreted as being caused by the boundary drags at the two boundaries, which force different slopes for the contours at $\ell_1 = 0$ and $\ell_1 = c_1$ . If $\alpha_1 > 0$ and $|\alpha_1 c_1| \gg 1$ , the probability density is concentrated mostly near $\ell_1 = 0$ however, and there is not much drag from the boundary at $\ell_1 = c_1$ . Actually there is a "boundary layer effect" at $\ell_1 = c_1$ . The straight line limit of (4.13) will not satisfy (4.14a); for $|\alpha c_1| \gg 1$ , the slope of (4.13) changes rapidly as $\ell_1 \to c_1$ even though the contour itself remains close to the limiting line. Fig. II-2a,b,c shows the contours analogous to those of Fig. II-1a,b,c for $\alpha c_1 = 5$ .

For $\alpha_1 < 0$ and $|\alpha_1 c_1| \gg 1$ , the same type of effects occur but with the roles of the boundaries $\ell_1 = 0$ and $\ell_1 = c_1$ reversed; the probability mass is concentrated at the boundary $\ell_1 = c_1$ .

It was noted previously that for $t \to \infty$ , $D_0(t)$ and $Q_1(t)$ should become asymptotically independent; indeed this is the proper interpretation of the approximation (4.1b). In the second approximation, the second term of (4.7) or (4.8) described the form of the statistical dependence. T fact that (4.12) is constant along the contours (4.13) can, however, be interpreted to mean that, to this second approximation, the random variable $Q_1(t)$ is statistically independent of the random variable

$$\frac{2D_0(t) - Q_1(t)}{c_1} + 2\left\{\left[-\frac{1}{2} + \frac{\Delta_1 - \Delta_0}{\Delta_1 + \Delta_0}\right]\frac{Q_1(t)}{c_1} + \frac{\exp[\alpha_1 Q_1(t)] - 1 - \alpha_1 Q_1(t)}{\alpha_1 c_1[\exp(\alpha_1 c_1) - 1]}\right\} \qquad (4.$$

i.e., a random variable which labels the contour line (4.13). Since, for sufficiently large $t$, the standard deviation of $D_0(t)$ will be large

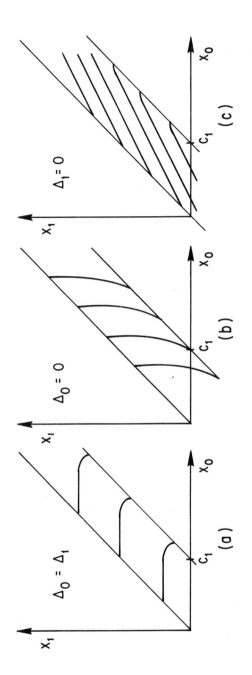

Fig. II-2. Equal probability density contours for $\mu_1 > \mu_0$.

compared with that of $Q_1(t)$, the random variable (4.15) is approximatel[y] equivalent to the random variable $D_0(t)$, or actually $2D_0(t)/c_1$. Thus the independence of $Q_1(t)$ and (4.15), in this second approximation, does not contradict the independence of $Q_1(t)$ and $D_0(t)$ in the first approx[imation]. imation.

In section 6 we will obtain a complete solution of the time-dependent joint distributions for $\alpha_1 c_1 \to \infty$. This will shed some light on the meaning of this approximate independence of $Q_1(t)$ and (4.15). We will also exploit this independence in section 5 to evaluate $\text{Var}\{D_0(t)\}$, but, at the moment, this is an interesting mathematical conclusion which has no obvious "physical interpretation."

Although we still have not found the $g(x_0,0;t)$ needed to evaluate (4.8) explicitly, we do have enough information to evaluate $\text{Var}\{D_0(t)\}$, which, in fact, one would need to calculate as a preliminary to any furthe[r] approximations extending the above methods.

5. <u>Service Variances.</u> In section 3 we determined the asymptotic (for $t \to \infty$) service rate $\mu$ from the asymptotic marginal queue distribution using (I 7.8). It is also of interest to estimate the variance of $D_0(t)$ and $D_1(t)$ as measures of the spread of the distribution in the $45°$ direction of the $(x_0,x_1)$ plane. This cannot be found directly from the asymptotic behavior of $f$ or $g$ as described in section 4 (nor could $\mu$) because we did not determine the shape of the distribution in the $45°$ direction nor the marginal distribution of $D_0(t)$. We can evaluate the variance in-directly, however, by combining the results of section 4 with those of section I7, particularly (I 7.12).

From (7.12) we have

$$\frac{d}{dt} \text{Var}\{D_0(t)\} = \Delta_0 - (\Delta_0 + \Delta_1) g_1^*(c_1;t) [E\{D_0(t)|Q_1(t) = c_1\} - E\{D_0(t)\}] \quad (5.1)$$

and

$$\frac{d}{dt} \text{Var}\{D_1(t)\} = \Delta_1 - (\Delta_0 + \Delta_1) g_1^*(0;t) [E\{D_1(t)|Q_1(t) = 0\} - E\{D_1(t)\}]. \quad (5.2)$$

For large $t$, $E\{D_0(t)\}$ is approximately $\mu t$. To a first approximation, (4.1b), $D_0(t)$ is asymptotically independent of $Q_1$; it appears as though the second terms of (5.1) and (5.2) will vanish because the conditional expectations of $D_0(t)$, $D_1(t)$ are equal to the unconditional expectations. They vanish, however, only to order $t$. To estimate the terms of order 1 (relative to $t$), we must use the second approximations of section 4.

In (5.1) or (5.2) we can express $D_0(t)$ or $D_1(t)$ as $c_1/2$ times the random variable (4.15) plus some function of $Q_1(t)$. Since, however, (4.15) is, to the second approximation, independent of $Q_1(t)$, its contribution to (5.1) and (5.2) will vanish, leaving only some expectations with respect to the distribution of $Q_1(t)$, namely

$$\frac{d}{dt} \text{Var}\{D_0(t)\} \simeq \Delta_0 - (\Delta_0 + \Delta_1) g_1^*(c_1;t) \Bigg[ c_1 - E\{Q_1(t)\}$$

$$- c_1 \left( \frac{\Delta_1 - \Delta_0}{\Delta_1 + \Delta_0} + \frac{\exp(\alpha_1 c_1) - 1 - \alpha_1 c_1}{\alpha_1 c_1 [\exp(\alpha_1 c_1) - 1]} \right)$$

$$+ c_1 E\left\{ \frac{(\Delta_1 - \Delta_0)}{(\Delta_1 + \Delta_0)} \frac{Q_1(t)}{c_1} + \frac{\exp[\alpha_1 Q_1(t)] - 1 - \alpha_1 Q_1(t)}{\alpha_1 c_1 [\exp(\alpha_1 c_1) - 1]} \right\} \Bigg]$$

$$(5.1a)$$

64

and

$$\frac{d}{dt} \text{Var}\{D_1(t)\} \simeq \Delta_1 - (\Delta_0 + \Delta_1) g_1^*(0;t) c_1 E \left\{ \frac{(\Delta_1 - \Delta_0)}{(\Delta_1 + \Delta_0)} \frac{Q_1(t)}{c_1} \right.$$

$$\left. + \frac{\exp[\alpha_1 Q_1(t)] - 1 - \alpha_1 Q_1(t)}{\alpha_1 c_1 [\exp(\alpha_1 c_1) - 1]} \right\} . \tag{5.2a}$$

For large $t$, we can also approximate the queue distribution $g_1^*(\ell_1;$ by its equilibrium distribution (2.6) and evaluate all expectations relative to this distribution. The integrations are all elementary (but somewhat tedious). The result is:

$$\frac{d}{dt} \text{Var}\{D_0(t)\} = \frac{d}{dt} \text{Var}\{D_1(t)\} \rightarrow \Delta$$

$$= \frac{[\sinh(\alpha_1 c_1) - \alpha_1 c_1][\Delta_0 \exp(\alpha_1 c_1/2) + \Delta_1 \exp(-\alpha_1 c_1/2)]}{4 \sinh^3(\alpha_1 c_1/2)}$$

$$\tag{5.3}$$

which reconfirms our earlier prediction that, for large $t$, $d\text{Var}\{D_k(t)\}/d$ should approach a limit $\Delta$ independent of $k$, (I 7.13).

From (5.3) we see that, for $\mu_0 < \mu_1$ and $c_1$ sufficiently large that $\alpha_1 c_1 \gg 1$,

$$\Delta \simeq \Delta_0 \tag{5.3a}$$

whereas, for $\mu_0 > \mu_1$ and $-\alpha_1 c_1 \gg 1$,

$$\Delta \simeq \Delta_1 . \tag{5.3b}$$

These are obvious checks of (5.3). In the former case, the source is hardly ever blocked by a full storage so that $D_0(t)$ has the usual normal distribution of the undisturbed service from $0$, with variance increasing like $\Delta_0 t$. In the latter case, the storage fills and the queue behind server 1 hardly ever vanishes. Therefore $D_1(t)$ grows at its un-interrupted rate having a normal distribution with variance increasing like $\Delta_1 t$.

In the limiting case $|\alpha_1 c_1| \ll 1$, i.e., for $\mu_0$ and $\mu_1$ suffi-ciently close,

$$\Delta \simeq (\Delta_0 + \Delta_1)/3 , \qquad (5.3c)$$

a rather surprising result perhaps, since, unlike the service rate $\mu$ in (3.2b), this does not depend upon the storage capacity $c_1$. For $\Delta_0 = \Delta_1$, (5.4c) becomes $2\Delta_0/3$; the drag from the two boundaries reduces the variance of the uninterrupted servers by a factor of 2/3. Although this is formally independent of $c_1$, it applies only for $|\alpha_1 c_1| \ll 1$. Thus the larger we take $c_1$, the nearer we must choose $\mu_0$ to $\mu_1$ (so that the queue distribution $g^*$ remains nearly constant). Also the larger we choose $c_1$, the longer it takes for the queue distribution to reach an equilibrium.

The expansion of (5.3) in powers of $(\alpha_1 c_1)$ converges rapidly even for $|\alpha_1 c_1| \simeq 1$. The first terms give

$$\Delta \simeq \frac{(\Delta_0 + \Delta_1)}{3}\left[1 + \left(\frac{\alpha_1 c_1}{2}\right)\left(\frac{\Delta_0 - \Delta_1}{\Delta_0 + \Delta_1}\right) + \frac{1}{5}\left(\frac{\alpha_1 c_1}{2}\right)^2 + \cdots\right] . \qquad (5.3d)$$

For $\Delta_0 = \Delta_1$, $\Delta$ increases quite slowly from its value $2\Delta_0/3$ for $(\alpha_1 c_1) = 0$ to $\Delta_0$ at $(\alpha_1 c_1) = \infty$.

Fig. II-3 shows some curves of $\Delta/(\Delta_0 + \Delta_1)$ vs $\alpha_1 c_1$ as described by (5.3), for various values of $\Delta_0/\Delta_1$. The curves all cross at $\alpha_1 c_1 = 0$ where, according to (5.3d), $\Delta/(\Delta_0 + \Delta_1) = 1/3$ for all $\Delta_0/\Delta_1$. For

66

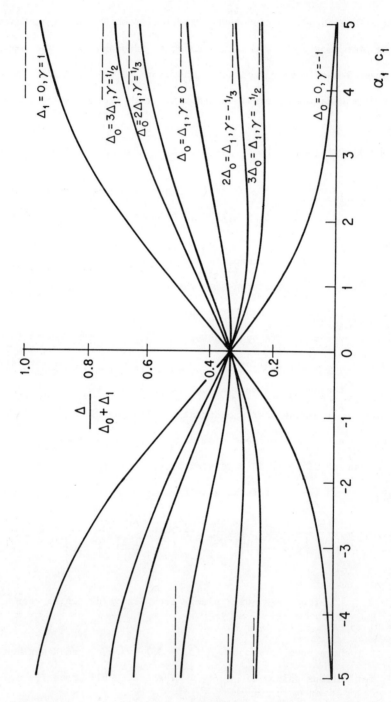

Fig. II-3. The longtime variance $\Delta$ as a function of the storage capacity $c_1$ for various ratios of server variance rates $\Delta_0/\Delta_1$.

$\alpha_1 c_1 \to + \infty$ , the curves approach $\Delta_0/(\Delta_0 + \Delta_1)$ , and, for $\alpha_1 c_1 \to - \infty$, they approach $\Delta_1/(\Delta_0 + \Delta_1)$ as given by (5.3a,b). For $\Delta_0 = \Delta_1$ , the curve has a minimum at $\alpha_1 c_1 = 0$ , i.e., for fixed $\Delta_0$ and $\Delta_1$ , $\Delta$ has a minimum with respect to the service rates $\mu_0$ and $\mu_1$ at $\mu_0 = \mu_1$ . Even for $\Delta_0 \neq \Delta_1$ , the curves display minima with respect to the service rates with a value of $\Delta$ which is less than the smaller of $\Delta_0$ and $\Delta_1$ .

6. <u>Image Solution $c_1 = \infty$.</u> The previous sections have dealt mostly with the behavior of f for large t , after the distribution has had time to "feel" both boundaries. If the system starts from the state $(D_0(t), D_1(t))$ $= (y_0, y_1)$ at time $t_0$ with $(y_0, y_1)$ not on a boundary, we also know the short time behavior prior to the time that the distribution feels either boundary. The intermediate time behavior becomes quite complicated as the distribution adjusts to the two boundaries. One can obtain formal solutions of (1.1),(1.2) but they are too complicated to be of much use. It is possible, however, to obtain relatively simple time-dependent solutions of (1.1) describing the effects of just one boundary.

If we let $c_1 = \infty$, the exact solution of (1.1),(1.2b) starting from the state $(y_0, y_1)$ at time $t_0$ is

$$f(x_0, x_1; t) = \frac{1}{2\pi (\Delta_0 \Delta_1)^{1/2} (t-t_0)} \exp\left\{ \frac{-[x_1 - y - \mu_1(t-t_0)]^2}{2 \Delta_1 (t-t_0)} - \frac{[x_0 - y_0 - \mu_0(t-t_0)]^2}{2\Delta_0(t - t_0)} \right\}$$

$$+ \frac{1}{2\pi (\Delta_0 \Delta_1)^{1/2} (t-t_0)} (\frac{\partial}{\partial x_1}) \exp[\alpha_1(x_1 - x_0)] \exp\left\{ - \frac{[x_0' - y_0 - \mu_0(t-t_0)]^2}{2 \Delta_0 (t - t_0)} \right\}$$

$$\cdot \int_0^\infty dz \, \exp\left\{ \frac{-[z + x_1' - y_1 - \mu_1(t - t_0)]^2}{2 \Delta_1 (t - t_0)} \right\} \qquad (6.1)$$

in which

$$
\begin{pmatrix} x_0' \\ x_1' \end{pmatrix} = \begin{pmatrix} -\gamma & 1 + \gamma \\ 1 - \gamma & \gamma \end{pmatrix} \begin{pmatrix} x_0 \\ x_1 \end{pmatrix}, \quad \gamma = \frac{\Delta_0 - \Delta_1}{\Delta_0 + \Delta_1} \tag{6.2}
$$

and the derivative $(\partial/\partial x_1)$ acts on the complete expression which follows it, with $x_0'$, $x_1'$ treated as functions of $x_0$, $x_1$ .

The method by which this was derived is not worth describing in detail. If one is clever enough to guess the solution, that is clearly the easiest way to find it. One can easily verify that this is the solution by just substituting it into (1.1),(1.2b). (Since I was not clever enough, I had to derive it the hard way.)

The first term of (6.1) is the obvious solution (I 4.2) that would exist in the absence of any boundaries; the second term comes from a boundary reflection. The method that was actually used to find the second term employed the following steps:

1. If we let $h(x_0, x_1; t)$ represent the left-hand side of (1.2b)

$$
h(x_0, x_1; t) = (-\mu_0 + \mu_1)f + \frac{(\Delta_0 - \Delta_1)}{2} \frac{\partial f}{\partial x_1} + \Delta_0 \frac{\partial f}{\partial x_0} , \tag{6.3}
$$

then $h$ also satisfies (1.1) but with the boundary condition $h(x_0, x_0; t) =$ If we knew $h$ , we could find $f$ by solving the first order partial differential equation (6.3). This involves an integration along a characteristic line; it is the origin of the $z$-integral in (6.1). It suffices, therefore, to determine an $h$ which satisfies (1.1), vanishes on the boundary $x_1 = x_0$ , and behaves initially like the $h$ generated by the first term of (6.1).

2. By going to a moving coordinate system $x_j - \mu_0 t$ , we can

eliminate the first derivative term $-\mu_0 \partial h/\partial x_0$ from (1.1).

3. We can rescale the $x_0, x_1, t$ so that the coefficients of the remaining four terms of (1.1) are $\pm 1$ or $\frac{1}{2}$ (as one wishes) but, in particular, so that the second derivative terms give the Laplacian of $h$, which is invariant to rotations. This non-orthogonal transformation of $(x_0, x_1)$, unfortunately, changes the slope of the boundary line $x_0 = x_1$ if $\Delta_0 \neq \Delta_1$.

4. By multiplying $h$ by an appropriate exponential in $x_1$, we can eliminate the other first derivative term $\partial h/\partial x_1$ from (1.1) at the expense of adding a term proportional to $h$ itself. The new differential equation, however, is now invariant to both rotations and reflections. This step is the source of the first exponential factor in the second term of (6.1), $\exp[\alpha_1(x_1-x_0)]$.

5. Finally, with a differential equation that is invariant to reflections across the boundary, and a boundary condition that the solution must vanish, one can generate a solution by image methods. From a known solution in the absence of the boundary conditions, one subtracts the image of that solution with respect to reflections across the boundary.

6. The above steps are now reversed to determine the corresponding solution f.

The above methods could be employed for more or less arbitrary coefficients of the terms in (1.2b). They do not exploit any special properties associated with the particular coefficients in question until, after some rather heavy algebra, one suddenly discovers that many cumbersome expressions cancel. There is, no doubt, a better way to derive (6.1) than the above. We are not concerned here, however, with what methods are most efficient; the techniques for solving such problems are all very classic. We are mostly interested in analysing properties of the solution itself.

Since, in the diffusion approximation, the process $(D_0(t), D_1(t))$ is a Markov process, the solution (6.1) gives a complete description of the probability structure of the process (for $c_1 = \infty$). The $f(x_0,x_1;t)$ for an arbitrary initial state $y_0,y_1$ at time $t_0$ is to be interpreted as the conditional density of $D_0(t),D_1(t)$ given $D_0(t_0) = y_0$, $D_1(t_0) = y_1$ from which all other probabilities can be derived.

It is fortunate that the solution (6.1) is as simple as it is, considering that it is a function of six variables $x_0,x_1,t,y_0,y_1,t_0$ and four parameters $\mu_0, \mu_1, \Delta_0$, and $\Delta_1$. Some of these variables, however, can appear only in certain combinations. Because of translational symmetry in time, $f$ depends upon $t$ and $t_0$ only through $t - t_0$. Without loss of generality we could therefore have chosen $t_0 = 0$.

Since we can choose to start our count of customers from any origin, provided we start the count of $D_0(t)$ and $D_1(t)$ with the same customer, the solution (4.1) must be invariant to translations in the (1,1) direction of the $(x_0, x_1)$ plane. Note that this translation also translates $x_0',x_1'$ by the same amount. Thus we could also arbitrarily choose $y_1 = 0$ so that $y_0$ becomes the initial queue behind the first service.

There are other symmetry relations mentioned above, in the solution method. By going to a moving coordinate system and rescaling the $x_0,y_0,t$ variables, we can reduce the differential equations to a "non-dimensional" form involving only one parameter $\gamma$. Altogether, we can reduce, by symmetry arguments, the original 10 variables and 4 parameters to 4 variables and 1 parameter.

In the following equations of this section, we will take $t_0 = 0$, but we choose not to exploit the other symmetries because this tends to obscure some of the notational symmetry of (6.1) relative to the interchange of indices 0 and 1.

To describe other properties of (6.1), it is convenient to work also with the quantity,

$$F_0(x_1, x_1; t) \equiv \frac{\partial}{\partial x_0} P\{D_0(t) < x_0, D_1(t) < x_1\} = \int_{-\infty}^{x_1} dz \; f(x_0, z; t) \; . \qquad (6.3)$$

An integration of (6.1) with respect to $x_1$ eliminates the $(\partial/\partial x_1)$ in the second term and gives (with $t_0 = 0$)

$$F_0(x_0, x_1; t) = \frac{1}{(2\pi\Delta_0 t)^{1/2}} \exp\left\{ - \frac{[x_0 - y_0 - \mu_0 t]^2}{2 \Delta_0 t} \right\} \; \Phi\left( \frac{x_1 - y_1 - \mu_1 t}{(\Delta_1 t)^{1/2}} \right)$$

$$\qquad (6.4)$$

$$+ \frac{1}{(2\pi\Delta_0 t)^{1/2}} \exp\left\{ \frac{-[x_0' - y_0 - \mu_0 t]^2}{2 \Delta_0 t} \right\} \exp[\alpha_1(x_1 - x_0)] \left\{ 1 - \Phi\left( \frac{x_1' - y_1 - \mu_1 t}{(\Delta_1 t)^{1/2}} \right) \right\}$$

which better displays a certain degree of symmetry between the two terms.

This $F_0(x_0, x_1; t)$ must also be a solution of the differential equation (1.1); the first term of (6.4) obviously is. The transformation (6.2) is the "reflection" across the boundary, but it is an oblique reflection. It maps the boundary $x_1 = x_0$ into itself and a line

$$x_1 = \frac{-(1 - \gamma)}{1 + \gamma} x_0 \qquad \text{or} \qquad \frac{x_1}{\Delta_1} = - \frac{x_0}{\Delta_0}$$

into its negative. Relative to (1.1) and (1.2b), this transformation has the special property that it leaves the second derivative terms of (1.1) unchanged and it leaves the boundary unchanged. The first derivative terms of (1.1) are changed by this mapping but the factor $\exp[\alpha_1(x_1 - x_0)]$ in the second terms of (6.1) or (6.4) compensate for this. One can readily check that this combination of multiplying a solution of (1.1) by an exponential factor and reflecting it, leads to another solution of (1.1).

It is actually the boundary condition (1.2b) that causes the complications which make it difficult just to guess at the solution. One can verify that (6.1) satisfies (1.2b) directly, but the boundary condition (1.2b) was actually derived in section I3 from a requirement that the marginal distribution of $D_0(t)$ be independent of what the first server does If we let $x_1 \rightarrow x_0$ in (6.4) then $(x_0', x_1') \rightarrow (x_0, x_1)$, the exponential factor of the second term goes to 1 and the $\Phi(\cdot)$ in the first and second terms cancel leaving

$$F_0(x_0,x_0;t) \;=\; \frac{1}{(2\pi\Delta_0 t)^{1/2}} \, \exp\left\{ - \frac{[x_0 - y_0 - \mu_0 t]^2}{2\,\Delta_0\,t} \right\} \tag{6.5}$$

as the marginal probability density of $D_0(t)$, which is indeed independent of the properties of server 1.

It is possible to form a schematic picture of what (6.4) means. Suppose, in the $(x_0,x_1)$ plane of Fig. II-4, we identify a point $y_0, y_1$ as the initial point of the distribution. In the absence of the boundary, the mean of the probability density moves along a line $(y_0 + \mu_0 t, \, y_1 + \mu_1 t)$ $t > 0$, of slope $\mu_1/\mu_0$, represented by the broken line. The figure shows the case $\mu_1 > \mu_0$ for which the distribution is moving toward the boundary, i.e., the broken line intersects the line $x_1 = x_0$ for $t > 0$.

As the distribution moves, it also spreads with a standard deviation $(\Delta_0 t)^{1/2}$ and $(\Delta_1 t)^{1/2}$ in the $x_0$ and $x_1$ directions, respectively. The distribution at five time points is illustrated in Fig. II-4 by the drawing, for each time point, of a single ellipse with axes $(\Delta_0 t)^{1/2}$ and $(\Delta_1 t)^{1/2}$ and center at $(y_0 + \mu_0 t, \, y_1 + \mu_1 t)$. This single curve for

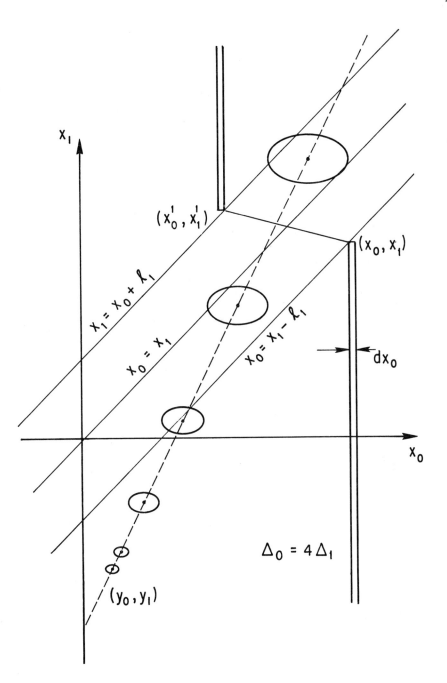

Fig. II-4.   Motion of the joint probability density.

fixed $t$ can be imagined to represent one contour of the function $f(x_0, x_$

corresponding to a value of $f$ which is $e^{-1/2}$ times its value at the

center. As the distribution spreads with increasing time, its amplitude a

the center decreases as $1/t$. In Fig. II-4, we have chosen $\Delta_0 > \Delta_1$ (act

ally $\Delta_0 = 4\Delta_1$) so that the major axis of the ellipse is in the $x_0$-directi

In (6.4), the first term times $dx_0$ can be interpreted as the proba-

bility (in the unreflected distribution) at time $t$ contained in a vertic

strip of width $dx_0$ extending from $(x_0, -\infty)$ to $(x_0, x_1)$, as shown in

Fig. II-4. The second term can be interpreted similarly as the probability

at time $t$ , again in the unreflected distribution contained in a vertica

strip of width $dx_0$ extending from $(x_0', x_1')$ to $(x_0', +\infty)$. The point $(x_0', x_1'$

is obtained by reflecting $(x_0, x_1)$ across the boundary line, along a line

of slope $-\Delta_1/\Delta_0$. The slope in the figure corresponds to $\Delta_0 < \Delta_1$; the

line tilts in the direction of the major axis of the ellipse. This second

term must also be multiplied by the exponential factor

$$\exp[-\alpha_1(x_0 - x_1)] \tag{6.6}$$

with exponent proportional to the queue length $\ell_1 = x_0 - x_1 = x_1' - x_0'$
at the point $(x_0, x_1)$.

The geometrical interpretation of (6.5) is that, for $x_1 = x_0$ , the

end points of the two vertical strips in Fig. II-4 coincide. Also (6.6)

has the value 1, and the integration becomes a single integral over the

unreflected distribution from $x_1 = -\infty$ to $x_1 = +\infty$ .

As a final check on (6.1), we can also evaluate the marginal distribu-

tion of queue length. The complimentary distribution of queue length,

$1 - G^*(\ell_1; t)$ of section 2, is

$$P\{D_0(t) - D_1(t) > \ell_1\} = \int_{-\infty}^{+\infty} dx_0 \int_{-\infty}^{x_0-\ell_1} dz \ f(x_0,z;t) = \int_{-\infty}^{+\infty} dx_0 \ F_0(x_0,x_0-\ell;t).$$

Geometrically, in Fig. II-4, it is the probability in the unreflected distribution below a line $x_1 = x_0 - \ell_1$, plus the exponential (6.6) times the probability above the line $x_1 = x_0 + \ell_1$. Note that the component of the reflection $(x_0,x_1) \to (x_0',x_1')$ parallel to the boundary has no effect on this region of integration. The integration of the unreflected distribution over these two half-planes leads immediately to the formula (2.4).

From (6.4) and (6.5), we can also evaluate the conditional distribution of the queue length, given $D_0(t)$

$$P\{Q_1(t) > \ell_1 | D_0(t) = x_0\} = F_0(x_0,x_0-\ell_1;t)/F_0(x_0,x_0;t) . \qquad (6.7)$$

After some rearranging of the exponents in the second term of (6.4), this can be written in the form

$$P\{Q_1(t) > \ell_1 | D_0(t) = x_0\} = \Phi\left(\frac{x_0 - \ell_1 - y_1 - \mu_1 t}{(\Delta_1 t)^{1/2}}\right) + \exp\left\{\frac{-2\ell_1[\mu_1 - (x_0-y_0)/t]}{(\Delta_0 + \Delta_1)}\right\}$$

$$\cdot \exp\left[\frac{-2\Delta_0\ell_1^2}{(\Delta_0+\Delta_1)^2 t}\right]\left\{1 - \Phi\left(\frac{x_0 - \gamma\ell_1 - y_1 - \mu_1 t}{(\Delta_1 t)^{1/2}}\right)\right\} . \qquad (6.7a)$$

The interesting feature of this formula is that it does not contain the mean arrival rate $\mu_0$ of customers to server 1. The reason for this is that server 1 acts on the customers it actually sees, not what it should see, on the average. What it actually sees, for given $x_0$, is $(x_0 - y_0)$ arrivals in time $t$ or an average arrival rate of $(x_0 - y_0)/t$.

The first term of (6.7a) describes the queue contribution from the unreflected distribution. With $x_0$ given, this term depends only upon the behavior of $D_1(t)$; that server 1 will serve so few customers that $D_1(t) < x_0 - \ell_1$. The $\Phi$-function of the second term describes part of the reflected distribution and has no simple interpretation. The first exponential factor of the second term, however, is similar to the equilibrium queue distribution $\exp(-\alpha_1\ell_1)$, except that the $\mu_0$ in $\alpha_1$, (2.5), is replaced by the actual arrival rate $(x_0-y_0)/t$.

If, for sufficiently large $t$, one could guarantee that server 0 would serve a number of customers $x_0 - y_0$, significantly different from $\mu_0 t$, the queue at server 1 would apparently try to reach the "equilibrium distribution" corresponding to the arrival rate $(x_0 - y_0)/t$. The second factor of this term, with exponent proportional to $\ell_1^2/t$, curtails the formation of the tail of the queue distribution. With $x_0$ fixed, server 1 of course, sees no fluctuation in the total number of arrivals in time $t$, only fluctuations in the number during subintervals of the time $t$. Consequently the queue will not form quite as readily as it would for an unconstrained mean arrival rate $(x_0 - y_0)/t$.

We have seen above that one can obtain reasonably compact formulas for the marginal distributions of $D_0(t)$ and $Q_1(t)$, the joint distribution of $Q_1(t)$ and $D_0(t)$, and the conditional distribution of $Q_1(t)$ given $D_0(t)$, but we have carefully avoided evaluation of the marginal distribution of $D_1(t)$, or discussion of the joint distribution of $D_1(t)$ and $Q_1(t)$, or conditional distributions given $D_1(t)$ or $Q_1(t)$. It is, of course, fairly straightforward, in principle, to evaluate any joint distributions one wishes from the probability density (6.1), but we have concentrated our attention only on those quantities which follow readily from the simpler expression (6.4). To evaluate other joint distributions or marginal distributions, it is typically necessary to expand the derivative $(\partial/\partial x_1)$ in (6.1) and then perhaps integrate with respect to some variable other than $x_1$. Although it is possible to carry out such integrations in terms of exponential functions, $\Phi$-functions, etc., one is likely to encounter expressions involving at least four terms, most of which are dificult to interpret. With formulas which involve so many variables, one must proceed in a very delicate fashion to avoid formulas which are a page long. We are indeed lucky to have a formula as simple as (6.4) which describes so many effects.

Whereas $D_0(t)$ and $Q_1(t)$ are each one dimensional diffusion processes by themselves, $D_1(t)$ is not. One may consider $D_0(t)$, $D_1(t)$, or $Q_1(t)$, $D_1(t)$ as a two-dimensional Markov process and evaluate the marginal distribution of $D_1(t)$ from (6.1) or (6.4), but this marginal distribution will not be of much value to us. If $D_1(t)$ is later to be considered as the input to a server 2 with $c_2 = \infty$, then, supposedly, it suffices, in describing the behavior of server 2, to know the stochastic properties of the process $D_1(t)$, independent of $D_0(t)$. Since $D_1(t)$ is not a Markov process, however, it is not sufficient merely to specify the marginal distribution of $D_1(t)$. In fact, this apparent independence of $D_0(t)$ cannot be exploited at all. If one attempts to treat the process $D_1(t)$ independent of $D_0(t)$, one must recognize that $D_1(t)$ is a semi-Markov process, and that one must keep track of either the process $D_0(t)$ or $Q_1(t)$ at the same time in order to describe the future evolution of $D_1(t)$. It is essential, therefore, that we understand the properties of the joint distributions (6.1) or (6.4) which do describe completely the stochastic properties of the process $D_1(t)$.

Since $D_0(t)$, $D_1(t)$ is a Markov process, we should interpret (6.1)

78

or (6.4) not only as the transient joint distribution at time $t$ starting from an arbitrary initial state $(y_0, y_1)$ at time $t_0 = 0$, but also as the transition probabilities for the Markov process.

7. __Longtime Behavior__ $c_1 = \infty$. If $\mu_0 < \mu_1$ as in Fig.II-4, so that server is undersaturated, there will be a time period during which both terms of the joint distribution (6.1) or (6.4), and of the queue distribution (2.4) are important. After the unreflected distribution has almost completely crossed the boundary, however, all $\Phi$-functions start to approach limiting values of either 0 or 1. The queue distribution, (2.4), approaches its exponential equilibrium distribution and (6.4) goes to

$$F_0(x_0, x_1; t) \to \frac{1}{(2\pi\Delta_0 t)^{1/2}} \exp\left\{\frac{-[x_0' - y_0 - \mu_0 t]^2}{2\,\Delta_0\,t}\right\} \exp[-\alpha_1(x_0 - x_1)],$$

(7.1)

$$F_0(x_0, x_0 - \ell_1; t) \to \frac{1}{(2\pi\Delta_0 t)^{1/2}} \exp\left\{\frac{-[x_0 - y_0 - \mu_0 t - (1+\gamma)\ell_1]^2}{2\,\Delta_0\,t}\right\} \exp(-\alpha_1 \ell_1).$$

For the queue distribution (2.4) to approach its equilibrium distribution, it is necessary, first, that the mean of the distribution reach the boundary, i.e.,

$$(\mu_1 - \mu_0)\, t \; > \; y_0 - y_1 \; , \tag{7.2a}$$

but then it is further necessary that, for $\ell_1$ comparable with the mean queue length, for example twice the mean, that

$$(\mu_1 - \mu_0) t \; > \; \ell_1 \; \sim \; 2/\alpha_1 \; = \; (\Delta_0 + \Delta_1)/(\mu_1 - \mu_0) \; ,$$

i.e.,

$$t \geq (\Delta_0 + \Delta_1)/(\mu_1 - \mu_0)^2 . \tag{7.2b}$$

This condition is necessary in order that the $\Phi$-function in the second term of (2.4) be negligible. This also guarantees that the ellipse of figure 4 has moved out so as to lie entirely above the line $x_1 = x_0 + \ell_1$ . These same conditions also guarantee that the $\Phi$-functions in (6.4) are negligible in the range of $x_0, x_1$ where the probability mass of (7.1) is located.

Equation (7.1) shows, first of all, that $Q_1(t)$ and the random variable

$$D_0(t) - (1 + \gamma)Q_1(t) = D_1(t) - \gamma Q_1(t) \tag{7.3}$$

are nearly statistically independent. For $c_1 \to \infty$, (7.3) is proportional to (4.15) which reconfirms some of the results of section 4. Unlike the deductions of section 4, however, we now have (for $c_1 = \infty$) the distribution of (7.3), which is the same as the marginal distribution of $D_0(t)$ itself.

The above independence, as applied to (7.1), can be interpreted as a special case of the fact that any set of joint normal random variables can be represented as linear combinations of a set of independent random variables. In (7.1), we can interpret $D_0(t)$ and $Q_1(t)$ to be joint normal. Usually this set of independent random variables is a mathematical convenience devoid of much physical interpretation. This is perhaps also true here except that in (6.7a), which approaches the limit

$$P\{Q_1(t) > \ell_1 | D_1(t) = x_0\} \simeq \exp\left\{\frac{-2\ell_1[\mu_1 - (x_0 - y_0)/t]}{(\Delta_0 + \Delta_1)}\right\} \exp\left[\frac{-2\Delta_0 \ell_1^2}{(\Delta_0 + \Delta_1)^2}\right],$$

we did give some rationale for the first factor.

Most of the above discussion has centered around the behavior for $\mu_1 > \mu_0$ which leads to the equilibrium queue distribution. For $\mu_1 \leq \mu_0$ one does not reach an equilibrium; for $\mu_0 \to \mu_1$ the time to reach equilibrium, as indicated in (7.2b), becomes infinite.

In the special case $\mu_0 = \mu_1$, (2.4) simplies to

$$G^*(\ell_1;t) = \Phi\left\{\frac{\ell_1 - (y_0 - y_1)}{[(\Delta_0 + \Delta_1)t]^{1/2}}\right\} - \Phi\left\{\frac{-\ell_1 - (y_0 - y_1)}{[(\Delta_0 + \Delta_1)t]^{1/2}}\right\} \tag{7.4}$$

which describes a simple "free diffusion" with reflection. For large $t$, $(\Delta_0 + \Delta_1)t \gg (y_0 - y_1)$, this becomes nearly independent of the initial state, $y_0 - y_1$

$$G^*(\ell_1;t) \to 2\,\Phi\left\{\frac{\ell_1}{[(\Delta_0 + \Delta_1)t]^{1/2}}\right\} - 1 \ . \tag{7.4a}$$

The mean queue grows like

$$E\{Q_1(t)\} \to [2(\Delta_0 + \Delta_1)t/\pi]^{1/2} , \tag{7.5}$$

proportional to $t^{1/2}$.

To choose $\mu_0 = \mu_1$ does not simplify the joint distribution (6.4) appreciably. There is a strong dependence between $Q_1(t)$ and $D_0(t)$ as indicated by the fact that (6.7a) does not contain $\mu_0$; consequently the choice of $\mu_0 = \mu_1$ has no effect upon the form of (6.7a).

If $\mu_0 > \mu_1$, server 1 is oversaturated and the queue will (eventuall) grow. In Fig. II-4, the broken line describing the motion of the means has slope less than 1, and the ellipses will eventually lie entirely in the region $x_1 < x_0$ . Obviously the first terms of (6.1) or (6.4) will be important at all times. The second terms represent a correction for the possibility that the queue will vanish and interrupt the service at 1. If this happens, it clearly must happen within a finite time before the mean queue has drifted too far away from the boundary. In Fig. II-4, the contribution to (6.4) from the vertical strip above the line $x_0 = x_1$ must diminish as the ellipses move further away from the boundary on the side $x_1 < x_0$ .

Once the queue has reached such a state, at a time $t_0 > 0$ , that it is virtually impossible for the queue ever to vanish again, the distribution will, thereafter, behave according to just the first term of (6.4), i.e., $D_0(t) - D_0(t_0)$ and $D_1(t) - D_1(t_0)$ will be normally distributed with means $\mu_j(t-t_0)$ and variances $\Delta_j(t-t_0)$, $j = 0, 1,$ independent of the values of $D_0(t), D_1(t_0)$ (provided they are sufficiently far from the boundary). Thus $D_0(t), D_1(t)$ can be represented as the sum of independent random vectors $D_0(t_0), D_1(t_0)$ and $D_0(t) - D_0(t_0), D_1(t) - D_1(t_0)$ .

The random vector $D_0(t_0), D_1(t_0)$ does not depend upon $t$ , but $D_j(t) - D_j(t_0)$ will become arbitrarily large for sufficiently large $t$. The (vector) central limit theorem implies that the sum of any random vector (with finite first and second moments) and an arbitrarily large independent normal random vector is itself approximately normal. Thus, for large $t$ , $D_0(t), D_1(t)$ must become approximately joint normal random variables with

$$E\{D_j(t)\} \simeq \mu_j t + [E\{D_j(t_0)\} - \mu_j t_0] \qquad (7.6a)$$

$$\text{Var}\{D_j(t)\} \simeq \Delta_j t + [\text{Var}\{D_j(t_0)\} - \Delta_j t_0] \qquad (7.6b)$$

$$\text{cov}\{D_0(t), D_1(t)\} \simeq \text{cov}\{D_0(t_0), D_1(t_0)\} . \qquad (7.6$$

The second terms of (7.6a) and (7.6b), and the value of (7.6c) do not depend upon $t$ . For large $t$ , the net effect of the boundary is simp) to cause a constant displacement of the means and covariances.

The presence of the boundary cannot affect the marginal distribution of $D_0(t)$ . For $j = 0$ , the second terms of (7.6a) and (7.6b) vanish. The effect of the boundary is to introduce only a constant (negative) dis placement of $E\{D_1(t)\}$ , a constant displacement of $\text{Var}\{D_1(t)\}$ , and a constant (positive) covariance. These, in turn, induce constant displace ments in the mean and variance of $Q_1(t)$ .

It is straightforward (but somewhat tedious) to evaluate the exact values of the moments (7.6) directly from (6.1). Alternatively, one can confirm the correctness of the above arguments and, at the same time, det mine the moments (7.6) by evaluating some asymptotic properties of (6.4) or (6.7a) for large $t$ .

In (6.7a), the first factor of the second term will, for the relevant range of $x_0$ values, be an increasing exponential in $\ell_1$ , but the [1 − factor will be decreasing in $\ell_1$ . To estimate the value of this second term one should use the asymptotic expansion of the $\Phi$-function

$$1 - \Phi(z) \simeq \frac{1}{(2\pi)^{1/2}} \exp(-z^2/2) \frac{1}{z} [1 - \frac{1}{z^2} + \cdots] \quad \text{for } z \gg 1 . \qquad (7$$

From this one can show, after some rearrangement of the exponential factor that

$$P\{Q_1(t) > \ell_1 \mid D_0(t) = x_0\} \simeq \Phi\left[\frac{x_0 - \ell_1 - y_1 - \mu_1 t}{(\Delta_1 t)^{1/2}}\right]$$

$$\text{(7.8)}$$

$$+ \frac{1}{(2\pi)^{1/2}} \exp\left\{\frac{-(x_0 - \ell_1 - y_1 - \mu_1 t)^2}{2\,\Delta_1\,t}\right\} \exp\left\{\frac{-2\ell_1(y_0 - y_1)}{(\Delta_0 + \Delta_1)t}\right\} \frac{1}{z}\left(1 - \frac{1}{z^2} + \cdots\right)$$

with

$$z = (x_0 - \gamma\ell_1 - y_1 - \mu_1 t)(\Delta_1 t)^{-1/2}$$

$$= |\alpha_1|(\Delta_1 t)^{1/2} + (x_0 - \ell_1 - y_1 - \mu_1 t)(\Delta_1 t)^{-1/2} \qquad \text{(7.8a)}$$

$$+ [\ell_1 - (\mu_0 - \mu_1)t]|\alpha_1|(\Delta_1 t)^{1/2}/(\mu_0 - \mu_1)t\,.$$

In the second term, we can also write in the second exponential

$$\frac{2\ell_1(y_0 - y_1)}{(\Delta_0 + \Delta_1)t} = \frac{2(\mu_0 - \mu_1)(y_0 - y_1)}{(\Delta_0 + \Delta_1)} + \frac{2[\ell_1 - (\mu_0 - \mu_1)t](y_0 - y_1)}{(\Delta_0 + \Delta_1)\,t}$$

$$= |\alpha_1|(y_0 - y_1) + \frac{[\ell_1 - (\mu_0 - \mu_1)t]|\alpha_1|(y_0 - y_1)}{(\mu_0 - \mu_1)\,t}\,. \qquad \text{(7.8b)}$$

A "large" $t$ is again to be interpreted to mean that (7.2b) is true. This condition contains $(\mu_1 - \mu_0)^2$ which is positive for both $\mu_1 < \mu_0$ and $\mu_1 > \mu_0$. Over the relevant part of the distribution, for large $t$, we expect that $x_0 - \ell_1 - y_1 - \mu_1 t$ in (7.8a) will be of order $(\Delta_1 t)^{1/2}$, the "width" of the distribution of $D_1(t)$, and that $[\ell_1 - (\mu_0 - \mu_1)t]$ in (7.8a and b) will be of order $[(\Delta_0 + \Delta_1)t]^{1/2}$. If (7.2b) is true, then the second and third terms of (7.8a) and the second term of (7.8b) are small compared with the first terms and we can expand (7.8) in powers of these second terms,

$$P\{Q_1(t) > \ell_1 | D_0(t) = x_0\} \approx \Phi\left(\frac{x_0 - \ell_1 - y_1 - \mu_1 t}{(\Delta_1 t)^{1/2}}\right)$$

$$+ \frac{1}{(2\pi\Delta_1 t)^{1/2}} \exp\left\{\frac{-(x_0 - \ell_1 - y_1 - \mu_1 t)^2}{2 \Delta_1 t}\right\} \frac{\exp(-|\alpha_1|(y_0 - y_1)}{|\alpha_1|} \tag{$($}$$

$$\cdot \left\{1 - \frac{[\ell_1 - (\mu_0 - \mu_1)t][1 + |\alpha_1|(y_0 - y_1)]}{(\mu_0 - \mu_1)t} - \frac{[x_0 - \ell_1 - y_1 - \mu_1 t]}{|\alpha_1| \Delta_1 t} + \cdots\right.$$

If we compare (7.9) with the power series expansion of a displaced $\Phi$-function

$$\Phi(z+\varepsilon) = \Phi(z) + (2\pi)^{-1/2} \exp(-z^2/2)\varepsilon[1 - \varepsilon z/2 + \cdots] , \tag{7.9a}$$

we see that the normal density in the second line of (7.9) has the same argument as the $\phi$-function in the first line. Thus (7.9) is, indeed, approximately a normal distribution in $\ell_1$; which confirms the above more intuitive arguments based upon the central limit theorem.

A displacement of the mean $E\{D_1(t)\}$ by some constant (relative to as in (7.6a) has a larger effect upon the distribution (7.9) than the constant displacement of the variances, in (7.6b,c). The displacement of the mean must, in effect, be compared with the width of the distribution, which is of order $t^{1/2}$. The displacements of the variances, however, are to be compared with undisplaced variances which are of order $t^1$. In (7.9), the displacement of the mean is determined by the leading term of the third line, which is of order $t^{-1/2}$, whereas the variances are determined by the second and third terms, which are of order $t^{-1}$.

From (7.9) one can easily verify that

$$E\{D_1(t)\} \simeq \mu_1 t + y_1 - |\alpha_1|^{-1} \exp[-|\alpha_1| (y_0 - y_1)] , \qquad (7.10a)$$

$$E\{Q_1(t)\} \simeq (\mu_0 - \mu_1)t + (y_0 - y_1) + |\alpha_1|^{-1} \exp[-|\alpha_1| (y_0 - y_1)] , \qquad (7.10b)$$

$$\text{cov}\{D_0(t), D_1(t)\} \simeq \frac{[1 + |\alpha_1| (y_0 - y_1)] 2\Delta_0}{|\alpha_1|^2 (\Delta_0 + \Delta_1)} \exp[- \alpha_1 (y_0 - y_1)] , \qquad (7.10c)$$

$$\text{Var}\{D_1(t)\} \simeq \Delta_1 t - \frac{\exp[-|\alpha_1| (y_0 - y_1)]}{|\alpha_1|^2} \left\{ \frac{[1 + |\alpha_1| (y_0 - y_1)] 4\Delta_1}{(\Delta_1 + \Delta_0)} \right.$$

$$\left. - 2 + \exp[-|\alpha_1| (y_0 - y_1)] \right\} , \qquad (7.10d)$$

$$\text{Var}\{Q_1(t)\} \simeq (\Delta_0 + \Delta_1)t - |\alpha_1|^2 \exp[-|\alpha_1| (y_0 - y_1)]\{[1 + 2|\alpha_1| (y_0 - y_1)]2$$

$$+ \exp[-|\alpha_1| (y_0 - y_1)]\}. \qquad (7.10e)$$

All correction terms due to the boundary contain the factor $\exp[-|\alpha_1| (y_0 - y_1)]$ , a decreasing function of the initial queue length $(y_0 - y_1)$. This factor can be interpreted as the probability that the queue will ever vanish, if it starts from the positive value $(y_0 - y_1)$ and has an increasing mean. All customer counts in the correction terms are also measured in units of $|\alpha_1|^{-1}$ , the only "natural" unit of length. Since the queue vanishing will interrupt the service at 1, the correction to (7.10a) is negative, whereas that in (7.10b) is positive.

The covariance (7.10c) is always positive because a negative fluctuation in $D_0(t)$ , proportional to $\Delta_0$ , increases the likelihood that the queue will vanish. This causes an interruption of server 1 and a negative

86

contribution to $D_1(t)$ . The correction to $\text{Var}\{D_1(t)\}$ is more complicate
and could be either positive or negative. If $\Delta_1$ were arbitrarily small
the first term of (2.10d) would vanish, i.e., $D_1(t)$ would have zero var
ance without the barrier. The barrier would give it a positive variance
(the second term in the correction). On the other hand, a positive fluctuation of $D_1(t)$ , proportional to $\Delta_1$ , is likely to cause the queue
vanish. These fluctuations are curtailed by the barrier causing a decreas
in $\text{Var}\{D_1(t)\}$ proportional to $\Delta_1$ (the first term in the correction).
The last correction term in (2.10d) is generated by $E^2\{D_1(t)\}$.

Equation (7.10e) is deduced from (7.10c) and (7.10d), and $\text{Var}\{D_0(t)\}$
$= \Delta_0 t$ . The queue evolution depends upon $\Delta_0$ and $\Delta_1$ only in the combination $\Delta_0 + \Delta_1$ . The barrier curtails negative queue fluctuations and
gives a negative correction in (7.10e).

8. <u>Discussion.</u> The above analysis of a single server (plus an input server)
has been directed toward two goals, firstly as an end in itself, and secondly as a possible prelude to an analysis of two or more server systems.

As an end in itself, one would probably be most interested in the
effect of a finite storage $c_1$ on the longtime mean service rate $\mu$ , (3.
as discussed in section 3. A second measure of system performance is the
longtime variance of the output $\Delta t$ , (5.3), discussed in section 5. Tha
one can evaluate the evolution of the marginal queue distribution $G^*(\ell_1,t)$
may also be of some interest. We did not actually write out the complete
time-dependent solution of (2.1), (2.3), although it was noted above (2.7)
that $G^*(\ell_1,t) - G^*(\ell_1)$ vanishes at both $\ell_1 = 0$ and $\ell_1 = c_1$ . The
complete solution of this deviation from the equilibrium distribution can
be written either as an infinite Fourier series, the first term of which
has the form (2.7), or as an infinite series of images generated by

successive reflections over both boundaries $\ell_1 = 0$ and $\ell_1 = c_1$ , generalizing (2.4). The derivation of this is quite straightforward, but the details of the solution do not seem to be of much practical value.

The tedious analysis of the joint distribution of $D_0(t)$, $D_1(t)$ was, of course, motivated by the fact that the output $D_1(t)$ might become the input process to a server 2 (for $c_2 = \infty$ , for example). The evolution of the queue $Q_2(t)$ at the second server will depend upon properties of the process $D_1(t)$ , which, in turn, is described by the transition probabilities of the Markov process $D_0(t)$, $D_1(t)$ .

It is not clear, at this moment, what properties of $D_0(t)$, $D_1(t)$ are relevant to the analysis of a system with two or more servers. Lacking such direction, we have analysed those properties which led to understandable formulas, with particular emphasis on the short-time and longtime properties but avoiding the complicated time-dependent behavior in the intermediate time range when the distribution is bouncing off both boundaries (full and empty storages) simultaneously.

It is possible to obtain formal "exact" solutions of (1.1) and (1.2) or, equivalently (1.3) and (1.4), by means of Fourier and Laplace transforms. It is possible to express certain moments directly in terms of these transforms, or one can express f or g themselves in terms of integral representations induced by the inversion formulas for the transforms.

We can take the Laplace transform of (1.3) with respect to t and the Fourier transform with respect to $x_0$ and let

$$\overline{g}(k_0,\ell_1;s) = \int_0^\infty dt\, e^{-st} \int_{-\infty}^{+\infty} dx_0\, \exp(ik_0 x_0)\, g(x_0,\ell_1;t) . \qquad (8.1)$$

An integration by parts with respect to t on the term involving $\partial g/\partial t$

generates an "initial value term" at $t = 0$, but an integration by parts with respect to $x_0$ of the terms containing $\partial/\partial x_0$ does not produce any boundary terms, since $g$ vanishes rapidly enough for $x_0 \to \pm \infty$. We obtain for $\bar{g}$ an equation

$$- \int_{-\infty}^{+\infty} dx_0 \, \exp(ik_0 x_0) \, g(x_0, \ell_1; 0) \; =$$

$$(-s + ik_0 \mu_0 - \frac{k_0^2 \Delta_0}{2}) \, \bar{g} \; + \; (-\mu_0 + \mu_1 - ik_0 \Delta_0) \, \frac{d\bar{g}}{d\ell_1} \; + \; \frac{(\Delta_0 + \Delta_1)}{2} \, \frac{d^2 \bar{g}}{d\ell_1^2}$$

(8.

for all values of $k_0, s$. The boundary conditions (1.4) give

$$\left[ -\mu_0 + \mu_1 - ik_0 \frac{(\Delta_0 - \Delta_1)}{2} \right] \bar{g} \; + \; \frac{(\Delta_0 + \Delta_1)}{2} \, \frac{d\bar{g}}{d\ell_1} \; = \; 0 \; \text{at} \; \ell_1 = c_1, \quad (8.$$

$$\left[ -\mu_0 + \mu_1 - ik\Delta_0 \; \bar{g} \right] + \; \frac{(\Delta_0 + \Delta_1)}{2} \, \frac{d\bar{g}}{d\ell_1} \; = \; 0 \quad \text{at} \; \ell_1 = 0 \;. \quad (8.$$

The left-hand side of (8.2) is determined by the initial distribution. In particular, if at $t = 0$, $D_0(t) = y_0$, $D_1(t) = y_1$, this term is

$$- \exp(ik_0 y_0) \, \delta(\ell_1 - (y_0 - y_1)) \tag{8.4}$$

in which $\delta(\cdot)$ is the Dirac $\delta$-function. The exact solution of (8.2), (8.3a,b) is quite straightforward. It involves nothing worse than trigonometric or exponential functions in $\ell_1$ with a discontinuity in the formula at $\ell_1 = y_1 - y_0$. Although this can be done explicitly, the formula is quite clumsy and a rather unpleasant function of the $k_0$ and $s$. We will not even show it.

From the behavior of $\bar{g}(k_0, \ell_1; s)$ as $s \to 0$ one can determine the longtime average behavior of the Fourier transform of $g(x_0, \ell_1; t)$ with respect to $x_0$. One can evaluate the moments of $D_0(t)$ given $Q_1(t)$ from derivatives of $\bar{g}(k_0, \ell_1; s)$ at $k_0 = 0$, and in particular, determine the $\mu$ and $\Delta$. This can, no doubt, be done from the transforms more quickly than by the methods described in sections 3 and 5. To evaluate anything else from $\bar{g}$, however, is, generally, rather clumsy. Furthermore, the generalization of these transform techniques to the analysis of problems with two or more servers does not appear to give any very useful results. Certainly transforms of the solutions do not give a very good "intuitive picture" of what is happening.

## III. Equilibrium Queue Distributions, Two Servers, $\mu_0 = \mu_1 = \mu_2$, Theory

1. **Introduction.** We saw in chapter II that the analysis of a system consisti
of an input server, a finite storage, and one other server was tractable;
one could evaluate essentially anything one wishes, and most things that ar
of any practical significance can be evaluated without much difficulty. A
one adds additional servers and storages to the system, however, a complet
analysis immediately becomes prohibitively difficult. One may devise
schemes for evaluating special cases analytically (usually involving some
infinite storages, some regular servers, i.e., $\Delta_j = 0$ , or identical servers), or one can numerically evaluate, possibly by simulation, the performance of any specific system. To understand in detail, how the behavior
of the system depends upon the $\Delta_j$'s , $\mu_j$'s , and $c_j$'s , however, is
hopeless. Even if one could find an exact solution of the diffusion equation, the number of parameters in the solution would be so large that it
would be impossible to comprehend the effects of each.

As a practical matter, however, one can make some crude evaluations
of performance of quite complex systems using a combination of common sense
along with a few relatively simple formulas. The most important property
of a tandem queueing system is its longtime service rate $\mu$ . It seems
intuitively obvious that $\mu$ should be a monotone non-decreasing function
of all the $\mu_j$'s (making some server faster should not make the overall
performance worse), a non-decreasing function of all the $c_j$'s, and a non-
increasing function of all the $\Delta_j$'s (the smaller the $c_j$'s and the larger
the $\Delta_j$'s, the more likely that servers will be blocked). From these properties one can evaluate various bounds on the $\mu$ (usually upper bounds),
which, in many practical applications, should be quite close.

If one were to replace all the $\Delta_j$'s by zero, the system would behave as described in section I2, and $\mu$ would be the service rate of the bottleneck. Since an increase of the $\Delta_j$'s would cause a smaller $\mu$, we conclude that

$$\mu \leq \min_j \mu_j \quad . \tag{1.1}$$

To improve on this bound, we might next imagine that we made all the $\mu_m$'s infinite except two, for example, $\mu_j$ and $\mu_k$ with $j < k$. Clearly such a system must behave like a system consisting of simply an input server with service rate $\mu_j$ and variance rate $\Delta_j$, feeding a storage of capacity $c_{j+1} + c_{j+2} + \cdots + c_k$, followed by a server of service rate $\mu_k$ and variance rate $\Delta_k$. The behavior of this sytem would be as described in chapter II with $\mu_0$, $\Delta_0$ replaced by $\mu_j, \Delta_j$; $c_1$ replaced by $c_{j+1} + \cdots + c_k$; and $\mu_1, \Delta_1$ replaced by $\mu_k, \Delta_k$. In particular the service rate of the system is given by II(3.2), (2.5). The $\mu$ for the actual system must again be less than (or equal to) the service rate of the single storage system, for all choices of $j$ and $k$. Consequently $\mu$ is bounded by the minimum with respect to $j$ and $k$ of the appropriate $\mu$'s from II(3.2). If we were to replace $\Delta_j$ and $\Delta_k$ by zero or make the $c_m$'s infinite, the bound II(3.2) would reduce to $\min(\mu_j, \mu_k)$. Increasing the $c_m$'s or decreasing the $\Delta$'s, however, increases the service rate. The new bound with $\Delta_j, \Delta_k > 0$ is therefore less than (1.1).

To compute the bound on $\mu$ from II(3.2) for a system of $n + 1$ servers (including the input server $\mu_0$), one must compare the service rates for $n(n + 1)/2$ single storage systems, i.e., for all choices of $j$ and $k$, $0 \leq j, k \leq n$ with $j < k$. Actually one can usually identify quite quickly the likely candidates for the minimum service rate since the service rate will be low if $\mu_j$ or $\mu_k$ is low, the storage is small, and/or the $\Delta_j$, $\Delta_k$ are large.

If we could determine the service rate of three-server systems with two storages, we could generalize the above procedure and evaluate still better bounds on the service rate of systems with three or more servers. The general solution of the system with two finite storages is already too difficult, but, because of the monotone properties of the $\mu$ with respect to the $\mu_j$, $\Delta_j$ and $c_j$, solutions of any special cases would also provide bounds on the $\mu$ for systems with larger or smaller values of the parameters.

In this chapter we present a detailed analysis of the equilibrium queue distributions for a system with an input server followed by two other servers each with a finite storage, but for the special case of equal service rates for the individual servers, i.e., $\mu_0 = \mu_1 = \mu_2$. From this we will be able to determine $\mu$ as a function of the remaining parameters $\mu_0$, $\Delta_0$, $\Delta_1$, $\Delta_2$, $c_1$ and $c_2$.

The choice $\mu_0 = \mu_1 = \mu_2$ is actually made because it yields a very significant simplication in the analysis, but one can expect this to be an important special case because it will illustrate how the blocking by both queues combine to reduce the $\mu$ relative to its value for $c_1 = \infty$ or $c_2 = \infty$. Since, for only one finite storage, the blocking effects are largest for the special case $\mu_0 = \mu_1$, one might expect the same to be true with two storages and $\mu_0 = \mu_1 = \mu_2$. By analysing the complete equilibrium queue distributions, we will additionally acquire some understanding of how the other two queues interact, and gain some intuitive feeling as to how more complex systems will behave (even if we cannot evaluate their properties exactly).

2. <u>Formulation.</u> The equations to be considered here are (I 5.6) and (I 5.7) for the special case $n = 2$ . We consider only the equilibrium queue distribution

$$g^*(\ell_1, \ell_2; t) = g^*(\ell_1, \ell_2) \tag{2.1}$$

for which the time derivative term $\partial g^*/\partial t$ of (I 5.6) vanishes. If we further specialize to the case $\mu_0 = \mu_1 = \mu_2$ , the first derivative terms $\partial g^*/\partial \ell_j$ of (I 5.6) also disappear, as do the terms proportional to $g^*$ in the boundary conditions (I 5.7).

The equilibrium queue distribution, for $\mu_0 = \mu_1 = \mu_2$ , satisfies the system of equations

$$\frac{(\Delta_0 + \Delta_1)}{2} \frac{\partial^2 g^*}{\partial \ell_1^2} + \frac{(\Delta_1 + \Delta_2)}{2} \frac{\partial^2 g^*}{\partial \ell_2^2} - \Delta_1 \frac{\partial^2 g^*}{\partial \ell_1 \partial \ell_2} = 0 \,, \tag{2.2}$$

subject to the boundary conditions,

$$\frac{(\Delta_0 - \Delta_1)}{2} \frac{\partial g^*}{\partial \ell_2} + \frac{(\Delta_0 + \Delta_1)}{2} \frac{\partial g^*}{\partial \ell_1} = 0 \qquad \text{for } \ell_1 = 0 \,, \tag{2.3a}$$

$$\frac{(\Delta_1 + \Delta_2)}{2} \frac{\partial g^*}{\partial \ell_2} - \Delta_1 \frac{\partial g^*}{\partial \ell_1} = 0 \qquad \text{for } \ell_2 = 0 \,, \tag{2.3b}$$

$$\frac{(\Delta_0 + \Delta_1)}{2} \frac{\partial g^*}{\partial \ell_1} - \Delta_1 \frac{\partial g^*}{\partial \ell_2} = 0 \qquad \text{for } \ell_1 = c_1 \,, \tag{2.3c}$$

$$-\frac{(\Delta_1 - \Delta_2)}{2} \frac{\partial g^*}{\partial \ell_1} + \frac{(\Delta_1 + \Delta_2)}{2} \frac{\partial g^*}{\partial \ell_2} = 0 \qquad \text{for } \ell_2 = c_2 \,, \tag{2.3d}$$

94

and

$$g^*(0,c_2) \quad = \quad 0 \ . \tag{2.3e}$$

In addition, we shall see that it is necessary to impose, explicitly, the condition (I 7.8), which is equivalent to

$$(\Delta_0{+}\Delta_1)g_1^*(c_1) \;=\; (\Delta_0{+}\Delta_1)g_1^*(0) + (\Delta_1{+}\Delta_2)g_2^*(c_2) \;=\; (\Delta_1{+}\Delta_2)g_2^*(0) \ , \tag{2.3f}$$

in which $g_1^*(\ell_1)$ and $g_2^*(\ell_2)$ are the marginal probability densities of $Q_1$ and $Q_2$ , respectively,

$$g_1^*(\ell_1) \;=\; \int_0^{c_2} d\ell_2 \ g^*(\ell_1,\ell_2) \ , \qquad g_2^*(\ell_2) \;=\; \int_0^{c_1} d\ell_1 \ g^*(\ell_1,\ell_2) \ . \tag{2.4}$$

This system is represented schematically in Fig. III-1a. We wish to solve (2.2) in the rectangle of sides $c_1$, $c_2$ in the $\ell_1,\ell_2$-plane. Each of the boundary conditions (2.3a) to (2.3d) can be interpreted to mean that a directional derivative of $g^*$ vanishes at the boundary. Thus, for example, (2.3a) means that the derivative of $g^*$ vanishes in the direction of the vector $(\Delta_0 + \Delta_1, \Delta_0 - \Delta_1)$ in the $(\ell_1,\ell_2)$-plane. Equivalently, this is the direction of the contour lines, $g^*(\ell_1, \ell_2)$ = const at $\ell_1 = 0$ .

Depending upon the values of $\Delta_0$, $\Delta_1$, $\Delta_2$, the contour lines can have any slope between -1 and +1 at $\ell_1 = 0$ (with a slope of 0 if $\Delta_0 = \Delta_1$). For $\ell_2 = c_2$ , the reciprocal slope must be between -1 and +1 (a vertical slope if $\Delta_1 = \Delta_2$). At $\ell_2 = 0$ or $\ell_1 = c_1$ , the slope of the contour lines must be negative (equal to -1 if $\Delta_0 = \Delta_1 = \Delta_2$).

The marks along the boundaries in figure 1a represent the direction of the contour lines. In Fig. III-1a, the $\Delta_0$, $\Delta_1$, $\Delta_2$ have been arbitrarily

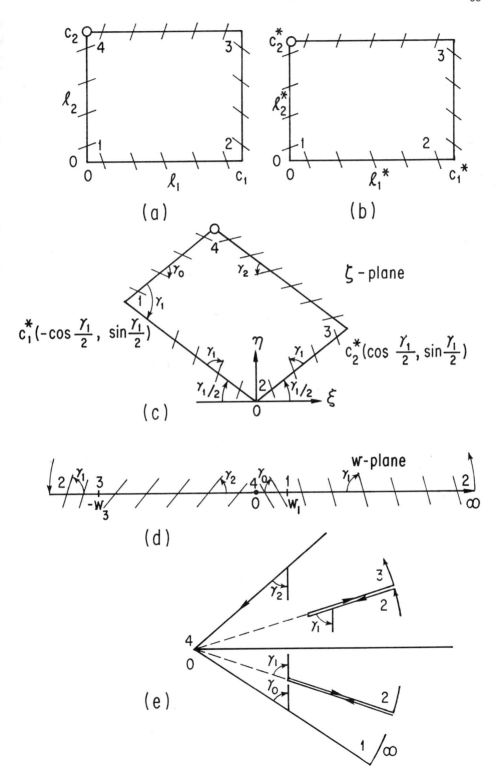

95

Fig. III-1.  A sequence of mappings.

chosen in the ratio 2:1:3, and $c_1$, $c_2$ have been chosen in the ratio 5:4
The boundary condition (2.3e) is identified in the figure by a circle arou
the point $(0, c_2)$ where $g*$ must vanish. Our problem is to determine
$g*(\ell_1, \ell_2)$ or, equivalently, the contour lines of $g*$ which satisfy (2.
and have the correct directions at the boundaries.

Since the direction of the contour lines differ along different bound
aries, $g*(\ell_1, \ell_2)$ must either have a stationary value at a corner or a
singularity. We shall see that, generally, $g*(\ell_1, \ell_2)$ is nonanalytic a
every corner.

The above equations will be solved through a sequence of mappings sho
by Figs. III-1b, c, d, and e. We first rescale the lengths $\ell_1$, $\ell_2$ to
convert (2.2) into a more symmetrical form, thus mapping the rectangle of
Fig. III-1a into another rectangle in Fig. III-1b. We next make a non-
orthogonal linear transformation to convert (2.2) into Laplace's equation.
This maps Fig. III-1b into the parallelogram of Fig. III-1c. The next tran
formation is a conformal mapping which maps the interior of the parallelogr
of Fig. III-1c into the upper half w-plane of Fig. III-1d. Finally, Fig.
III-1d is mapped into a G-plane such that the contour lines are vertical al
all boundaries. In this space of Fig. III-1e the contour lines of $g*$ wil
be vertical everywhere, i.e., the solution is known. The solution is then
mapped back to the original space of Fig. III-1a. In essence, the determin
tion of the solution of (2.2), (2.3) is converted into a problem of determining the appropriate mappings.

As the first step in the above sequence, it seems advantageous to rescale the lengths $\ell_1$ and $\ell_2$ so that the first two terms of (2.2) have
the same coefficient, thus making (2.2) symmetric with respect to interchange of the two coordinates. We, therefore, choose new coordinates

$$\ell_1^* = \ell_1 \left[ \frac{\Delta^*}{\Delta_1 + \Delta_0} \right]^{1/2} \quad , \quad \ell_2^* = \ell_2 \left[ \frac{\Delta^*}{\Delta_1 + \Delta_2} \right]^{1/2} \tag{2.5}$$

for some positive constant $\Delta^*$. It will be convenient, for reasons which are not yet obvious, to choose $\Delta^*$ as

$$\Delta^* \equiv (\Delta_0 \Delta_1 + \Delta_1 \Delta_2 + \Delta_0 \Delta_2)^{1/2} . \tag{2.5a}$$

We define $c_1^*$ and $c_2^*$ as the values of $\ell_1^*$, $\ell_2^*$ corresponding to $\ell_1 = c_1$, $\ell_2 = c_2$.

If we interpret the symbol $g^*$ to mean the mathematical function $g^*(\ell_1, \ell_2)$, then a transformation of coordinates would ordinarily be interpreted to mean that $g^*$ maps into a new function, say $g^{**}(\ell_1^*, \ell_2^*)$ such that $g^*(\ell_1, \ell_2) = g^{**}(\ell_1^*, \ell_2^*)$, when $\ell_1, \ell_2$ and $\ell_1^*, \ell_2^*$ are related through (2.5), i.e., the numerical value of $g^{**}$ is the same as the numerical value of $g^*$ at corresponding points of the two spaces. Because of this equality of the numerical values, some people might use just one symbol $g^*$, to represent the numerical value of the density rather than the function, or considered as a function of $\ell_1^*, \ell_2^*$, it is the function $g^*(\ell_1(\ell_1^*), \ell_2(\ell_2^*))$.

In the present problem, $g^*$ is a probability density of $Q_1, Q_2$, and we have still another possible interpretation of the mapping (2.5). We can rescale the queue lengths by introducing new random variables

$$Q_1^* \equiv Q_1 \left[ \frac{\Delta^*}{\Delta_1 + \Delta_0} \right]^{1/2} \quad , \quad Q_2^* = Q_2 \left[ \frac{\Delta^*}{\Delta_1 + \Delta_2} \right]^{1/2} \tag{2.5b}$$

and define $g^{**}(\ell_1^*, \ell_2^*)$ as the probability density of $Q_1^*, Q_2^*$ at $Q_1^* = \ell_1^*$,

$$Q_2^* = \ell_2^* \; .$$

Regardless of how one interprets the mappings (2.5), one will be led to the same type of transformed differential equation, but if we interpret it as a transformation of the random variables (2.5b), then the $g^{**}(\ell_1^*, \ell_2^*)$ would be normalized so that

$$\int_0^{c_1^*} d\ell_1^* \int_0^{c_2^*} d\ell_2^* \; g^{**}(\ell_1^*, \ell_2^*) \;\; = \;\; 1 \qquad (2.6)$$

and the $g^*$, $g^{**}$ would be related by

$$g^{**}(\ell_1^*, \ell_2^*) \;\; = \;\; g^*(\ell_1, \ell_2) \; (\Delta_1 + \Delta_0)^{\frac{1}{2}} (\Delta_1 + \Delta_2)^{\frac{1}{2}}/\Delta^* \qquad (2.7)$$

when $\ell_1, \ell_2$, $\ell_1^*, \ell_2^*$ are related by (2.5).

Since the equations (2.2), (2.3) are linear homogeneous, any multiple of a solution is also a solution. The specific solution of interest is that one scaled so as to give total probability 1. The rescaling in (2.7) merely changes the amplitude of the solution so that the probability density is normalized to 1 in the new coordinates.

The above transformations map (2.2), (2.3) into the form

$$\frac{\partial^2 g^{**}}{\partial \ell_1^{*2}} + \frac{\partial^2 g^{**}}{\partial \ell_2^{*2}} - 2 \cos \gamma_1 \frac{\partial^2 g^{**}}{\partial \ell_1^* \partial \ell_2^*} \;\; = \;\; 0 \qquad (2.8)$$

with

$$0 \le \cos \gamma_1 \equiv (1 + \Delta_0/\Delta_1)^{-1/2}(1 + \Delta_2/\Delta_1)^{-1/2} \le 1 \qquad (2.9)$$

subject to the boundary conditions

$$\frac{\partial g^{**}}{\partial \ell_1^*} - (1 - \frac{\Delta_0}{\Delta_1}) \cos \gamma_1 \frac{\partial g^{**}}{\partial \ell_2^*} = 0 \qquad \text{for } \ell_1^* = 0, \qquad (2.10a)$$

$$\frac{\partial g^{**}}{\partial \ell_2^*} - 2 \cos \gamma_1 \frac{\partial g^{**}}{\partial \ell_1^*} = 0 \qquad \text{for } \ell_2^* = 0, \qquad (2.10b)$$

$$\frac{\partial g^{**}}{\partial \ell_1^*} - 2 \cos \gamma_1 \frac{\partial g^{**}}{\partial \ell_2^*} = 0 \qquad \text{for } \ell_1^* = c_1^*, \qquad (2.10c)$$

$$\frac{\partial g^{**}}{\partial \ell_2^*} - (1 - \frac{\Delta_2}{\Delta_1}) \cos \gamma_1 \frac{\partial g^{**}}{\partial \ell_1^*} = 0 \qquad \text{for } \ell_2^* = c_2^*, \qquad (2.10d)$$

and

$$g^{**}(0, c_2^*) = 0 . \qquad (2.10e)$$

If we define

$$g_1^{**}(\ell_1^*) = \int_0^{c_2^*} d\ell_2^* \, g^{**}(\ell_1^*, \ell_2^*) , \qquad g_2^{**}(\ell_2^*) = \int_0^{c_1^*} d\ell_1^* \, g^{**}(\ell_1^*, \ell_2^*) \qquad (2.11)$$

as the marginal probability densities of $Q_1^*$, $Q_2^*$, analogous to (2.4), then (2.3f) maps into

$$(\Delta_0 + \Delta_1)^{\frac{1}{2}} g_1^{**}(c_1^*) = (\Delta_0 + \Delta_1)^{\frac{1}{2}} g_1^{**}(0) + (\Delta_1 + \Delta_2)^{\frac{1}{2}} g_2^{**}(c_2^*) = (\Delta_1 + \Delta_2)^{\frac{1}{2}} g_2^{**}(0) . \qquad (2.10f)$$

The figure, Fig. III-1b, associated with (2.8), (2.10) is basically the same as Fig. III-1a. In the special case $\Delta_0 - \Delta_2$ ($\Delta_1$ arbitrary), the scaling (2.5) is the same for $\ell_1$ and $\ell_2$ so that the picture does not change at all (except possibly in size). What we have gained by this rescaling, for $\Delta_0 \neq \Delta_2$ , is that (2.8) is symmetric with respect to interchange of $\ell_1^*$ and $\ell_2^*$ . Also the slopes of the contour lines along $\ell_2^* = 0$ and along $\ell_1^* = c_1^*$ are reciprocals, i.e., the boundary conditions (2.10b) and (2.10c) are symmetric with respect to the interchange of $\ell_1^*$ , $\ell_2^*$ relative to the corner $(c_1^*, 0)$ .

The second mapping is a nonorthogonal linear transformation of co-ordinates from Fig. III-1b to III-1c defined by

$$
\begin{pmatrix} \xi \\ \eta \end{pmatrix} = \begin{pmatrix} \cos(\gamma_1/2) & \cos(\gamma_1/2) \\ -\sin(\gamma_1/2) & \sin(\gamma_1/2) \end{pmatrix} \begin{pmatrix} \ell_1^* - c_1^* \\ \ell_2^* \end{pmatrix} . \tag{2.12}
$$

The primary purpose of this transformation is to map (2.8) into Laplace's equation.

$$
\frac{\partial^2 g^{**}}{\partial \xi^2} + \frac{\partial^2 g^{**}}{\partial \eta^2} = 0 \quad , \quad g^{**} = g^{**}(\ell_1^*(\xi, \eta), \ell_2^*(\xi, \eta)) . \tag{2.13}
$$

Since Laplace's equation is invariant to rotations, reflections, change of scale, and translations, there is considerable freedom in the choice of mappings which will yield (2.13). Because of the above symmetry relative to the corner $(c_1^*, 0)$ of the $(\ell_1^*, \ell_2^*)$-plane, we have chosen the arbitrary translation so as to map this point into the origin $\xi = \eta = 0$ . We have chosen the arbitrary rotation so as to map the symmetry axis of slope -1 at $(c_1^*, 0)$ of Fig. III-1b into the vertical direction $\xi = 0$ in Fig. III-1c.

The boundary 2-3 $(\ell_1^* = c_1^*)$ of Fig. III-1b maps into the line 2-3 of Fig. III-1c making an angle $\gamma_1/2$ with the horizontal. Correspondingly, the boundary 1-2 $(\ell_2^* = 0)$ of Fig. III-1b maps into a line making an angle $-\gamma_1/2$

with the horizontal.  Since, by symmetry again, the scale of length along 2-3

must be the same as along 1-2, it is convenient to choose the scale of units

for  $(\xi , \eta)$  so that the Euclidean length of 2-3 is the same in Figs. III-1b

and III-1c, namely  $c_2^*$ .  This will then, at the same time, make the Euclidean

length of 1-2 equal to  $c_1^*$  in the  $(\xi , \eta)$-plane, as in the   $(\ell_1^*, \ell_2^*)$-plane.

Of course, the linear transformation maps parallel lines into parallel lines,

so that the rectangle of Fig. III-1b maps into a parallelogram in Fig. III-1c.

The transformation (2.12) has merely changed the angles at the corners.

The directions of the contour lines at the boundaries of Fig. III-1b map

into new directions in Fig. III-1c (also new angles relative to the bound-

aries).  Thus, for example, the condition (2.10c) that the contour line has

the direction  $(1, -2\cos \gamma_1)$  in the  $(\ell_1 , \ell_2)$  space along the boundary 2-3

maps into a condition that the contour line has the direction

$$\left( (1 - 2\cos \gamma_1) \cos(\gamma_1/2), -(1 + 2\cos \gamma_1) \sin(\gamma_1/2) \right)$$

$$= \left( -\cos(3\gamma_1/2), -\sin(3\gamma_1/2) \right)$$

along 2-3 in the  $(\xi , \eta)$  plane.  Equivalently, the contour lines make an

angle  $\gamma_1$  with the boundary line 2-3 (which makes an angle  $\gamma_1/2$  with the

horizontal).  By symmetry, the contour lines along the boundary 1-2 also

make an angle  $\gamma_1$  (in the opposite direction) with the line 1-2, as shown

in Fig. III-1c.

One can similarly determine (as a function of the  $\Delta_k$'s) the direction

of the contour lines along the  boundaries 1-4 and 3-4 of Fig. III-1c, and,

correspondingly, the angles which they make with these boundaries.  These

angles are designated by  $\gamma_0$  and  $\gamma_2$ , respectively, as shown in Fig. III-1c.

After some algebraic manipulations, one can show that the angles $\gamma_j$ are determined by the equations

$$\text{ctn } \gamma_j = \Delta_j / \Delta^* , \qquad j = 0, 1, 2 . \qquad (2.14)$$

Since the $\Delta_k$'s are all non-negative, it follows that $0 \leq \gamma_j \leq \pi/2$. The extreme values $\gamma_j = \pi/2$ can arise if $\Delta_j = 0$ (regular service for the jth server), but the value $\gamma_j = 0$ can occur only if $\Delta_j > 0$ and the other two $\Delta_k$'2, $k \neq j$, both vanish. The latter cases are excluded from the present analysis, however, because the rescaling in (2.5) is not defined. If any two of the $\Delta_k$'s are zero, the diffusion equation degenerates to a one-dimensional equation. The methods described here do not apply because the diffusion equation cannot be mapped into Laplace's equation. Such cases are relatively easy to handle by other methods, although they can be analysed as limiting cases with some of the $\Delta_k$'s $\to 0$.

From (2.14), one can also show that

$$\gamma_0 + \gamma_1 + \gamma_2 = \pi . \qquad (2.15)$$

Thus the angles $\gamma_0, \gamma_1, \gamma_2$ can be interpreted as the interior angles of a triangle. From (2.15), one can show that the sides of the triangle opposite the angle $\gamma_j$ are proportional to $(\Delta_k + \Delta_\ell)^{1/2}$ with $(j,k,\ell)$ any permutation of $(1,2,3)$. Equivalently, the angles $\gamma_j$ satisfy the law of sines (as in Fig. III-2).

$$\frac{\sin \gamma_0}{(\Delta_1 + \Delta_2)^{1/2}} = \frac{\sin \gamma_1}{(\Delta_0 + \Delta_2)^{1/2}} = \frac{\sin \gamma_2}{(\Delta_0 + \Delta_1)^{1/2}} = \left[ \frac{\sin\gamma_0 \sin\gamma_1 \sin\gamma_2}{\Delta^*} \right]^{\frac{1}{2}} .$$

$$(2.16)$$

103

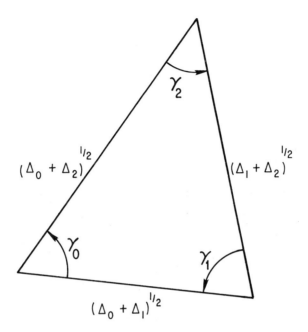

Fig. III-2. Relation between the angles $\gamma_j$ and the variance rates $\Delta_j$.

Our problem has now been mapped into the determination of a solution $g^{**}$ of Laplace's equation for which the contour lines have the directions specified in Fig. III-1c along the boundaries of a parallelogram.

Since the real (or imaginary) part of an analytic function of a complex variable is a solution of Laplace's equation, and conversely, it is convenient to introduce the complex variable representation of the $(\xi,\eta)$-plane. Let

$$\zeta = \xi + i\eta \;, \qquad\qquad i = \sqrt{-1} \;. \qquad (2.17)$$

We wish to determine a function $G(\zeta)$ which is analytic in the region of Fig. III-1c (except possibly at the corners) and for which

$$g^{**}(\ell_1(\zeta), \ell_2(\zeta)) = \operatorname{Re} G(\zeta) \qquad (2.18)$$

satisfies the boundary conditions shown in Fig. III-1b. Also $\operatorname{Re} G(\zeta)$ must vanish at point 4 and satisfy (2.10f).

Any analytic function $w(\zeta)$ can be interpreted as a mapping of the $\zeta$-plane into a w-plane or conversely. If $G(\zeta)$ is an analytic function of $\zeta$, then

$$G(\zeta(w)) \equiv H(w) \qquad (2.19)$$

is an analytic function of w . Thus, for any mapping $w(\zeta)$ , the problem of determining a particular analytic function $G(\zeta)$ of $\zeta$ can be mapped into a problem of determining a corresponding analytic function $H(w)$ of w .

Of course, the (unknown) function $G(\zeta)$ can itself be interpreted as a mapping of the $\zeta$-plane into a G-plane, which maps the contour lines $\operatorname{Re} G(\zeta)$ = constant in the $\zeta$-plane into vertical contours $\operatorname{Re} G$ = constant in the G-plane. Thus the problem of determining $G(\zeta)$ can also be interprete as a problem of finding a mapping $G(\zeta)$ for which the vertical contour

lines, Re $G$ = constant, satisfy the appropriate boundary conditions in

the $G$-plane as specified by the mapping of the boundary conditions from

the $\zeta$-plane into the $G$-plane.

To determine $G(\zeta)$ we first seek a mapping $w(\zeta)$ which maps the

parallelogram of Fig. III-1c into the upper-half $w$-plane as shown in Fig. III-1d.

We also determine the appropriate boundary conditions for $H(w)$ along the

image boundary, the real axis in the $w$-plane.

We finally seek a second mapping $H(w)$ into the $G$-plane of Fig. III-1e

such that the contour lines along the real $w$-axis map into vertical con-

tour lines in the $G$-plane. In this space (as implied by the notation)

the analytic function for which the real part satisfies the required bound-

ary conditions is the linear function $G$ itself.

Thus, in terms of the mappings $H(w)$ and $w(\zeta)$ , the solution of

(2.9), (2.10) is

$$g^{**}(\ell_1^*(\zeta), \ell_2^*(\zeta)) = \text{Re } G(\zeta) = \text{Re } H(w(\zeta)) . \tag{2.20}$$

If we could determine the functions $H(w)$ and $w(\zeta)$ explicitly, we could

also write (2.20) as

$$g^{**}(\ell_1^*, \ell_2^*) = \text{Re } H(w(\zeta(\ell_1^*, \ell_2^*)))$$

since the $\zeta(\ell_1^*, \ell_2^*)$ is known explicitly from (2.12) and (2.17). Actually,

we will not obtain the solution in quite this form. We will determine the

inverse mapping $\zeta(w)$ rather than $w(\zeta)$ and give the solution in the

"parametric form"

$$g^{**}(\ell_1^*(\zeta(w)), \ell_2^*(\zeta(w))) = \text{Re } H(w) . \tag{2.21}$$

For each point $w$ in the upper half $w$-plane, we can determine the value Re $H(w)$ of $g^{**}$ and the point $(\ell_1^*, \ell_2^*)$ where $g^{**}$ has this value.

3. <u>Conformal Mappings</u>. The mapping $w(\zeta)$ of Fig. III-1c into III-1d, or actually the inverse $\zeta(w)$, is required to be analytic everywhere in the upper half $w$-plane, having singularities only at points on the boundary which are the images of the corners 1, 2, 3, 4 of Fig. III-1c with coordinates $\zeta_1$, $\zeta_2 = 0$, $\zeta_3$ and $\zeta_4$. The scale and the origin of the $w$-plane are arbitrary. We have chosen to map $\zeta_4$ into the origin $w = 0$, $\zeta_2 = 0$ into $w = \infty$, and $\zeta_1$, $\zeta_3$ into (as yet unspecified) points $w_1$ and $-w_3$ along the real $(w_1 > 0$, $w_3 > 0)$.

Mappings of this type, known as Schwarz-Christoffel transformations [1,2], are determined by the angles at the corners 1, 2, 3, 4 of Fig. III-1. The function $\zeta(w)$ must satisfy an equation of the form

$$\frac{d\zeta}{dw} = e^{-i\gamma_1/2} \, Aw^{-\gamma_1/\pi} \, (w - w_1)^{-1+\gamma_1/\pi} \, (w + w_3)^{-1+\gamma_1/\pi} \, , \qquad (3.1)$$

for some real constant A. This equation has singularities at $w = 0$, $w_1$, $-w_3$, and $\infty$ of such a type as to guarantee that, as $w$ passes through each singularity along the real line $(dw = \text{real})$, the direction of $d\zeta$ changes so as to produce the appropriate corners of Fig. III-1c. The factor $\exp(-i\gamma_1/2)$ represents the direction of the line 1-2 of Fig. III-1c for $w > w_1$.

If we integrate (3.1) from an arbitrary point $\zeta$ (and its image $w$) to $\zeta_2 = 0$ in the $\zeta$-plane (and its image $\infty$ in the $w$-plane), we obtain

$$\zeta(w) = e^{i(\pi-\gamma_1/2)} \, A \int_w^\infty dz \, z^{-\gamma_1/\pi} \, (z - w_1)^{-1+\gamma_1/\pi} \, (z + w_3)^{-1+\gamma_1/\pi} \, . \qquad (3.2)$$

This equation contains three parameters $A$ , $w_1$ , and $w_3$ . Since the scale of the w-plane is arbitrary, we will specify the scale by choosing $A = 1$ . The two remaining parameters, $w_1$ and $w_3$ , must now be selected so that (3.2) produces the specified values of

$$c_1^* = |\zeta(w_1)| = |\zeta(-w_3) - \zeta(0)| \tag{3.3a}$$

$$c_2^* = |\zeta(-w_3)| = |\zeta(w_1) - \zeta(0)| \quad . \tag{3.3b}$$

Specifically, (for $A = 1$)

$$c_1^* = \int_{v_1}^{\infty} dz\ z^{-\gamma_1/\pi}\ (z - w_1)^{-1+\gamma_1/\pi}\ (z + w_3)^{-1+\gamma_1/\pi} \tag{3.4a}$$

$$= \int_0^{w_3} dz\ z^{-\gamma_1/\pi}\ (z + w_1)^{-1+\gamma_1/\pi}\ (w_3 - z)^{-1+\gamma_1/\pi} \tag{3.4b}$$

$$c_2^* = \int_{w_3}^{\infty} dz\ z^{-\gamma_1/\pi}\ (z + w_1)^{-1+\gamma_1/\pi}\ (z - w_3)^{-1+\gamma_1/\pi} \tag{3.4c}$$

$$= \int_0^{w_1} dz\ z^{-\gamma_1/\pi}\ (w_1 - z)^{-1+\gamma_1/\pi}\ (z + w_3)^{-1+\gamma_1/\pi} \quad . \tag{3.4d}$$

The above integrals can be expressed in terms of hypergeometric functions [3], but, basically, the method for evaluating $w_1$ and $w_3$ is first to rescale $z$ by $w_3$ in (3.4b) and by $w_1$ in (3.4d)

$$c_1^* = w_1^{-1+\gamma_1/\pi} \int_0^1 dx\ x^{-\gamma_1/\pi}\ (1 - x)^{-1+\gamma_1/\pi}\ (1 + xw_3/w_1)^{-1+\gamma_1/\pi} \tag{3.5a}$$

$$c_2^* = w_3^{-1+\gamma_1/\pi} \int_0^1 dx\ x^{-\gamma_1/\pi}\ (1 - x)^{-1+\gamma_1/\pi}\ (1 + xw_1/w_3)^{-1+\gamma_1/\pi} . \tag{3.5b}$$

If we divide these two equations

$$\frac{c_1^*}{c_2^*} = \left(\frac{w_1}{w_3}\right)^{-1+\gamma_1/\pi} \frac{\int_0^1 dx \; x^{-\gamma_1/\pi}(1-x)^{-1+\gamma_1/\pi}(1+xw_3/w_1)^{-1+\gamma_1/\pi}}{\int_0^1 dx \; x^{-\gamma_1/\pi}(1-x)^{-1+\gamma_1/\pi}(1+xw_1/w_3)^{-1+\gamma_1/\pi}} \;, \quad (3$$

we see that $c_1^*/c_2^*$ is (for given values of $\gamma_1$) a function of $w_1/w_3$ onl
From a graph of the right-hand side of (3.6) as a function of $w_1/w_3$, on
can determine $w_1/w_3$ as a function of $c_1^*/c_2^*$. For given values of $c_1^*$,
$c_2^*$, one would first determine $w_1/w_3$, then use (3.5a) or (3.5b) to
evaluate $w_1$ and $w_3$ separately.

The transformation (3.2) maps the contour lines $g^{**}$ = constant in
Fig. III-1c into image contour lines in Fig. III-1d. Since an analytic function defines a conformal mapping, i.e., it preserves angles, the angles
which the contour lines make with the boundary in Fig. III-1d are the same
as in Fig. III-1c. Thus in Fig. III-1d, the contour lines make angles $\gamma_0$,
$\gamma_1$, $\gamma_2$ with the real axis as shown. These angles are constant along each
segment of the real line between the singularities, but are different on
different segments.

Finally, we wish to determine a mapping $H(w)$ which satisifes the
conditions: (1) it is analytic everywhere in the upper-half w-plane except
possibly at $w = 0$, $w_1$, $-w_3$, and $\infty$; (2) it maps the boundary $w$ = real
so that the contour lines become vertical at all points along the image
boundary; and (3) it maps $w = 0$ so that $\text{Re } H(0) = \text{Re } G(\zeta_4) = 0$.
The imaginary part of $H(0)$ can be chosen arbitrarily since the addition
of any pure imaginary number to $H(w)$ will have no effect upon $g^{**}$. In
particular, we may specify that $H(0) = G(\zeta_4) = 0$, in place of condition 3.

Condition (1) implies that angles are preserved. This along with (2) means that the image in the G-plane of the boundary segment 4-1 in the w-plane must (everywhere) make an angle $\gamma_0$ with the vertical. Thus the image of the segment $0 < w < w_1$ must also be a straight line in the G-plane. From the last condition above, we further specify that it must start from the origin in the G-plane.

Similarly, the image in the G-plane of the boundary segment 4-3 in the w-plane must be a straight line segment from the origin in the G-plane making an angle $\gamma_2$ with the vertical. The images of the lines 1-2 and 3-2 in the w-plane must also be straight lines. They each make an angle $\gamma_1$ with the vertical, but in opposite directions.

Since the equations for $g^{**}$ are all linear, any multiple of a solution is also a solution of (2.8), (2.10); but, clearly, we want $g^{**} \geq 0$ everywhere (since $g^*$ is a probability density). This means that we want the image of the upper-half w-plane to map into the right-half G-plane. This establishes the direction of the lines 0-1 and 0-4 in the G-plane. The scale of the G-plane remains arbitrary (it will eventually be fixed by the condition that the total probability be normalized to 1).

Since the image of the real w-axis in the G-plane must form a polygon with sides making specified angles $\gamma_0$, $\gamma_1$, $\gamma_2$ with the vertical, the mapping $H(w)$ must belong also to the family of Schwarz-Christoffel transformations. It would seem that the transformation should be uniquely defined (except for scale) by the specification of the singular points of $H(w)$, (namely $0, w_1, -w_3$, and $\infty$) and the angles, but is not.

Although $H(w)$ is required to be analytic along the segment $0 < w < w_1$, and map this segment into a line segment in the G-plane at angle $\gamma_0$ with the vertical, it is not required that the mapping be one-to-one. It is not necessary that $H^{-1}(G)$ be analytic everywhere on the line segment. If, for example, $g^{**}(0,\ell_2^*)$ has an interior maximum along the boundary betwe points 1 and 4 of Fig. III-1b the image boundary in the G-plane would fol- low the line at angle $\gamma_0$ out to the maximum value of Re $G = g^{**}$, a then reverse directions, coming back along the same line again. This, in deed, may happen not just along the side 1-4 of Fig. III-1b but along any of the sides.

To uniquely determine the mapping $H(w)$ and the function $G(\zeta)$, it is necessary also to impose the condition (2.10f). To do this we must express the marginal probability densities $g_1^{**}(\ell_1^*)$ and $g_2^{**}(\ell_2^*)$ in ter of the $G(\zeta)$ and see what condition (2.10f) implies about the properties of $G(\zeta)$.

4. <u>Marginal Distributions.</u> Although the joint distribution $g^*(\ell_1^*, \ell_2^*)$ has interesting analytic properties, its detailed aspects are not particularly relevant to any design considerations. For most purposes, it suffices to know the marginal distributions of the queue length (2.11). In particular the equilibrium service rate of the system can be expressed in terms of the marginal distributions through (I 7.8).

$$\mu = \mu_0 - \frac{1}{2} (\Delta_0 + \Delta_1) \, g_1^*(c_1)$$

$$= \mu_1 - \frac{1}{2} (\Delta_0 + \Delta_1) \, g_1^*(0) - \frac{1}{2} (\Delta_1 + \Delta_2) \, g_2^*(c_2) \tag{4.1}$$

$$= \mu_2 - \frac{1}{2} (\Delta_1 + \Delta_2) \, g_2^*(0) \,,$$

or, in terms of the transformed coordinates

$$\mu = \mu_0 - \frac{1}{2}\Delta^{*1/2}(\Delta_0 + \Delta_1)^{1/2} g_1^{**}(c_1^*)$$

$$= \mu_1 - \frac{1}{2}\Delta^{*1/2}[(\Delta_0 + \Delta_1)^{1/2} g_1^{**}(0) + (\Delta_1 + \Delta_2)^{1/2} g_2^{**}(c_2^*)] \qquad (4.1a)$$

$$= \mu_2 - \frac{1}{2}\Delta^{*1/2}(\Delta_1 + \Delta_2)^{1/2} g_2^{**}(0) \quad .$$

Each of the integrals (2.11) can be represented as a line integral in the complex plane. In the $\ell_1^*$, $\ell_2^*$ space

$$g_1^{**}(\ell_1^*) = \int_0^{c_2^*} d\ell_2^* \ \text{Re}\ [G(\zeta(\ell_1^*,\ell_2^*))]; \ g_2^{**}(\ell_2^*) = \int_0^{c_1^*} d\ell_1^* \ \text{Re}\ [G(\zeta(\ell_1^*,\ell_2^*))]$$

are integrals along vertical and horizontal lines, respectively in Fig. III-1b. However, we can convert these into integrals in the $\zeta$-space. The first integral maps into a line integral parallel to the 1-4 or 2-3 directions of Fig. III-1c; the second integral maps into a line integral parallel to the 1-2 or 4-3 directions. Since the lengths of the sides of the parallelograms are the same in Figs. III-1b and III-1c

$$g_1^{**}(\ell_1^*) = \int_{\zeta(\ell_1^*,0)}^{\zeta(\ell_1^*,c_2^*)} d\zeta \ e^{-i\gamma_1/2} \ \text{Re}\ [G(\zeta)] = \text{Re}\int_{\zeta(\ell_1^*,0)}^{\zeta(\ell_1^*,c_2^*)} d\zeta \ G(\zeta) \ e^{-i\gamma_1/2}$$

$$(4.2)$$

and

$$g_2^{**}(\ell_2^*) = \text{Re}\int_{\zeta(0,\ell_2^*)}^{\zeta(c_1^*,\ell_2^*)} d\zeta \ G(\zeta) \ e^{+i\gamma_1/2} \quad . \qquad (4.2a)$$

Equation (4.2) is certainly valid if the path of integration is a straight line, $d\zeta \exp(-i\gamma_1/2)$ = real, but the last integral in (4.2) (and the integral in (4.2a)) is the integral of an analytic function $G(\zeta)$ between two points in the complex $\zeta$-plane. These integrals are independent of the path, as long as the path remains within the boundaries of the parallelogram of Fig. III-1c. The end points of these integrals are on the boundary; we can, therefore, choose the path of integration along (or just inside) the boundary going in either the clockwise or counterclockwise directions.

From (4.2) and (4.2a) we obtain

$$g_1^{**}(c_1^*) = \text{Re} \int_{\zeta_2=0}^{\zeta_3} d\zeta\, G(\zeta)\, e^{-i\gamma_1/2} \quad , \tag{4.3a}$$

$$g_1^{**}(0) = \text{Re} \int_{\zeta_1}^{\zeta_4} d\zeta\, G(\zeta)\, e^{-i\gamma_1/2} \quad , \tag{4.3b}$$

$$g_2^{**}(c_2^*) = \text{Re} \int_{\zeta_4}^{\zeta_3} d\zeta\, G(\zeta)\, e^{+i\gamma_1/2} \quad , \tag{4.3c}$$

and

$$g_2^{**}(0) = \text{Re} \int_{\zeta_1}^{\zeta_2=0} d\zeta\, G(\zeta)\, e^{+i\gamma_1/2} \quad . \tag{4.3d}$$

Suppose that in (4.3c) we choose the path of integration via the boundary $\zeta_4$ to $\zeta_1$ to $\zeta_2$ to $\zeta_3$. If we subtract (4.3d) from (4.3c), we obtain

$$g_2^{**}(c_2^*) - g_2^{**}(0) = \text{Re} \left\{ \int_{\zeta_4}^{\zeta_1} d\zeta\, G(\zeta)\, e^{+i\gamma_1/2} + \int_{\zeta_2}^{\zeta_3} d\zeta\, G(\zeta)\, e^{+i\gamma_1/2} \right\}.$$

But, from (2.10f) or (4.1a) we know that

$$(\Delta_1 + \Delta_2)^{1/2} [g_2^{**}(c_2) - g_2^{**}(0)] + (\Delta_0 + \Delta_1)^{1/2} g_1^*(0) = 0$$

or

$$(\Delta_1 + \Delta_2)^{1/2}\, \text{Re} \int_{\zeta_2}^{\zeta_3} d\zeta\, G(\zeta)\, e^{+i\gamma_1/2} = \text{Re}\,(\Delta_1+\Delta_2)^{1/2} \int_{\zeta_1}^{\zeta_4} d\zeta\, G(\zeta) e^{+i\gamma_1/2}$$

$$- \text{Re}\,(\Delta_0 + \Delta_1)^{1/2} \int_{\zeta_1}^{\zeta_4} d\zeta\, G(\zeta)\, e^{-i\gamma_1/2}. \tag{4.4}$$

From the results of the last section we know that the image of the boundary 4-1 in the G-plane is a line from the origin making an angle $\gamma_0$ with the vertical. Consequently, along 1-4, $d\zeta\, G(\zeta)\exp(-i\gamma_1/2)$ has the phase $(-\pi/2 + \gamma_0)$ and $d\zeta\, G(\zeta)\exp(+i\gamma_1/2)$ has the phase

$$- \pi/2 + \gamma_0 + \gamma_1 = \pi/2 - \gamma_2.$$

In (4.4) we have

$$\text{Re}\,(\Delta_1+\Delta_2)^{1/2} \int_{\zeta_1}^{\zeta_4} d\zeta\, G(\zeta)\, e^{+i\gamma_1/2} = (\Delta_1+\Delta_2)^{1/2} \sin \gamma_2 \left| \int_{\zeta_1}^{\zeta_4} d\zeta\, G(\zeta) \right|$$

and

$$\text{Re}\,(\Delta_0+\Delta_1)^{1/2} \int_{\zeta_1}^{\zeta_4} d\zeta\, G(\zeta)\, e^{-i\gamma_1/2} = (\Delta_0+\Delta_1)^{1/2} \sin \gamma_0 \left| \int_{\zeta_1}^{\zeta_4} d\zeta\, G(\zeta) \right|.$$

But from (2.16) we know that

$$(\Delta_1 + \Delta_2)^{1/2} \sin \gamma_2 = (\Delta_0 + \Delta_1)^{1/2} \sin \gamma_0 \; ,$$

consequently, the terms on the right-hand side of (4.4) cancel, leaving us with the condition

$$\text{Re} \int_{\zeta_2}^{\zeta_3} d\zeta \; G(\zeta) \; e^{+i\gamma_1/2} = 0 \; . \qquad (4.4\text{a})$$

In the last section we also showed that the image of the boundary 2-in the G-plane must be a straight line making an angle $-\gamma_1$ with the vertical, thus $G(\zeta)\exp(+i\gamma_1)$ is on a vertical line. We did not know, however, the location of the vertical line, i.e., the constant value of Re $G(\zeta) \exp(+i\gamma_1)$ . Along the line 2-3 in the $\zeta$-plane, $d\zeta$ has the phase $\exp(i\gamma_1/2)$ and consequently the real part of the integrand of (4.
is a constant, and (4.4a) forces this constant to be zero. From this we conclude that the image of the boundary 2-3 in the G-plane must be on the line <u>passing through the origin</u> at an angle $\pi/2 - \gamma_1$ .

If from (4.3) we had followed a similar procedure, sending the path of integration in (4.3b) from 1 to 2 to 3 to 4 instead of the path of (4.3c) from 4 to 1 to 2 to 3, and subsequently interchanging the roles of the $\ell_1^*$ and $\ell_2^*$ variables, we would be led to a companion conclusion tha the image of the boundary 1-2 in the G-plane must be on the straight line passing through the origin at an angle $-\pi/2 + \gamma_1$ .

Since we already knew that the images of 4-1 and 4-3 were lines throu the origin of the G-plane, we now conclude that the phase of $G(\zeta) = H(w)$ is constant along each of the four boundary line segments of Fig. III-1c or I

We are finally ready to determine the as yet unknown function $H(w)$ . A function which satisfies all the required conditions is the relatively simple one

$$H(w) = B e^{-i\pi/2} e^{i\gamma_0} w^{\gamma_1/\pi} (w_1 - w)^{(\gamma_0-\gamma_1)/\pi} (w + w_3)^{(\gamma_2-\gamma_1)/\pi} \qquad (4.5)$$

in which $B$ is some real positive constant. Since the boundary in the G-plane is known to form a polygon, we had previously argued that the mapping $H(w)$ would belong to the class of Schwarz-Christoffel transformations for which $H(w)$ would, in general, be represented as an integral in the $\zeta$-plane analogous to, but potentially more complicated than, the mapping (3.2) for $\zeta(w)$ . We might have obtained the form $H(w)$ by considering the appropriate class of Schwarz-Christoffel transformations and imposing various restrictions until we had narrowed the class down to the only acceptable ones. The form (4.5) was actually obtained, however, simply from a construction of the simplest possible function with branch point singularities of the proper type at each of the points $w = 0$, $w_1$, $-w_3$, and $\infty$ and a hope that all the other required conditions would also be met.

Fig. III-1e illustrates one of several possible types of mappings induced by (4.5). As $w$ traverses the real line from 0 to $w_1$ , $H(w)$ moves along the line with phase $-\pi/2 + \gamma_0$ making the required angle $\gamma_0$ with the vertical. This $H(w)$ also satisfies the condition that $H(0) = 0 = G(\zeta_4)$, since $\gamma_1 > 0$ .

As $w$ passes through $w_1$ (or actually around $w_1$ via a path in the upper-half w-plane), $H(w)$ must have a branch-point singularity which not only changes the phase of $dH(w)/dw$ to either $-\pi/2 + \gamma_1$ or $+\pi/2 + \gamma_1$

but also forces  H(w)  itself to have these phases, i.e.,  H(w)  must ju'

from one line through the origin to another.  The only places where we c.

permit this are at  G = 0  or  ∞ .  We must also do this in such a way

that the upper-half w-plane which is on the left-hand side of the path

to  $w_1$  in the w-plane maps into the interior of a polygon of the G-plane

to the left side of the image path.  These conditions force  H(w)  to be

proportional to the  $(\gamma_0 - \gamma_1)/\pi$  power of  $(w_1 - w)$  as given in (4.5).

As  $w \to w_1$,  H(w)  becomes infinite if  $\gamma_1 > \gamma_0$,  0 if  $\gamma_1 < \gamma_0$,  c

has a finite limit if  $\gamma_1 = \gamma_0$ .  Note that the case  $\gamma_1 = \gamma_0$ ,  which is

the diffusion approximation analogue of the exponentially distributed ser

vice times, is, indeed, quite special.  Fig. III-1d illustrates the case

$\gamma_1 > \gamma_0$ .  For  $\gamma_1 < \gamma_0$ ,  $|H(w)|$  must have a maximum value for some  w

$0 < w < w_1$ .  The image of the line  $0 < w < w_1$  starts at the origin  G

goes out along the line at angle  $-\pi/2 + \gamma_0$ ,  reverses direction and com

back to the origin.

For  $|w| \to \infty$ ,  (4.5) gives

$$H(w) \simeq B\, e^{-i\pi/2}\, e^{i\gamma_1}\, w^{(\gamma_0 + \gamma_2 - \gamma_1)/\pi} . \qquad (4.6)$$

But from (2.15), it follows that

$$(\gamma_0 + \gamma_2 - \gamma_1)/\pi = 1 - 2\,\gamma_1/\pi .$$

As  w  traverses an infinite semi-circle in the upper-half w-plane back to

the negative real axis, we have not only a condition that  dH(w)/dw  must

change phase but that  H(w)  itself must change phase to  $\pi/2 - \gamma_1$ .  The

function (4.6) satisfies this condition.

In the special case  $\gamma_1 = \pi/2$  which corresponds to regular service at 1, $\Delta_1 = 0$ , there is no singularity at $w = \infty$ . The $g^{**}$ at point 2

is finite, and the images of $w_1 < w < \infty$ and $-\infty < w < -w_3$ are both

along the real line of the G-plane. For $\Delta_1 > 0$ , however, $\gamma_1 < \pi/2$

and $G(\zeta_2) = H(\infty) = \infty$ . The probability density never vanishes at point 2.

As $w$ goes from $w_1$ to $+\infty$, $H(w)$ moves along a line at phase

$-\pi/2 + \gamma_1$ . For $\gamma_1 < \gamma_0$ it moves from the origin to $\infty$ if $\Delta_1 > 0$ or

to a finite value if $\Delta_1 = 0$ . For $\gamma_1 = \gamma_0$ it moves from some finite

value to $\infty$ ($\gamma_1 = \gamma_0 = \pi/2$ is excluded). For $\gamma_1 > \gamma_0$ it moves from $\infty$

to some finite point, reverses direction and goes back to $\infty$ again if

$\Delta_1 > 0$ (as shown in Fig. III-1d), or remains at a finite value if $\Delta_1 = 0$ .

As w continues to trace the boundary with $w$ going from $-\infty$ to $w_3$

to 0, $H(w)$ behaves in a manner analogous to that for the positive w-line.

Fig. III-1e illustrates the case $\gamma_2 < \gamma_1$ , for which $H(w)$ goes from $\infty$

to a finite value and back to $\infty$ as $w$ goes from $-\infty$ to $-w_3$ . Then

as w goes from $-w_3$ to 0 , $H(w)$ moves from $\infty$ back to the origin.

From the above description of the required properties of $H(w)$ , it

is clear that (4.5) is the unique solution, except for the unspecified

constant B . The value of B , however, will be determined by the normali-

zation (2.6).

This now completes the formal solution. The function $g^{**}$ is deter-

mined by (2.20), in which $\ell_1^*(\zeta), \ell_2^*(\zeta)$ is given by (2.12) and (2.17);

$\zeta(w)$ is given by (3.2) with $A = 1$ , and $H(w)$ is given by (4.5). The

parameters $w_1, w_3$ and B are determined from given values of $c_1^*, c_2^*$

through (3.5) and (2.6). These can be converted back to the original units

through (2.5) and (2.7).

Although the actual numerical evaluation of $g^{**}$ from the above for-

mulas is straightforward, it is, needless to say, quite tedious, mostly

118

because (3.2) is awkward to handle.

So far we have used the formulas for the marginal distribution only as a means to establish the solution $H(w)$. These marginal distribution however, are of considerable interest in themselves. Returning to (4.2) and (4.2a), we notice that in (4.2) we could integrate from $\zeta(\ell_1^*,0)$ to $\zeta(\ell_1^*,c_2^*)$ along the boundary either via points 1 and 4 or via 2 and 3. Along the line 1,2 , $d\zeta$ has the phase $-\gamma_1/2$ and G has the phase $-\pi/2 + \gamma_1$. The integral along this segment is pure imaginary and contri utes nothing to $g_1^{**}(\ell_1^*)$. The lower limit of integration in (4.2) can, therefore, be replaced by either $\zeta_1$ or $\zeta_2$. Similarly in (4.2a), the integral along 2,3 contributes nothing. The upper limit in (4.2a) can, therefore, be replaced by either $\zeta_2$ or $\zeta_3$.

Since our formulas actually describe $H(w)$ rather than $G(\zeta)$, it is advantageous to transform these integrals into the w-plane

$$g_1^{**}(\ell_1^*) = \text{Re} \int_{w_1}^{w(\zeta(\ell_1^*,c_2^*))} dw \ (d\zeta/dw) \ H(w) \ e^{-i\gamma_1/2} .$$

Substitution of (3.1) and (4.5) for $d\zeta/dw$ and $H(w)$ respectively, gives

$$g_1^{**}(\ell_1) = \text{Re} \ e^{i\pi/2} \ e^{i\gamma_0} \ B \int_{w_1}^{w(\zeta(\ell_1^*,c_2^*))} dw \ (w_1 - w)^{-1+\gamma_0/\pi} (w + w_3)^{-1+\gamma}$$

The image point $w(\zeta(\ell_1^*,c_2^*))$ of $(\ell_1^*, c_2^*)$ lies on the real line between $-w_3$ and 0 . If we integrate along the real line, the integrand is real and positive. Substitution of

$$x = (w_1 - w)/(w_1 + w_3)$$

reduces $g_1^{**}(\ell_1^*)$ to the form

$$g_1^{**}(\ell_1^*) = \frac{B \sin \gamma_0}{(w_1 + w_3)^{\gamma_1/\pi}} \int_0^{\frac{w_1 - w(\zeta(\ell_1^*, c_2^*))}{w_1 + w_3}} dx \; x^{-1+\gamma_0/\pi} (1-x)^{-1+\gamma_2/\pi} . \quad (4.7)$$

The final integration can, of course, be written as an incomplete Beta function.

Since (3.2) actually gives $\zeta$ as a function of $w$ rather than the inverse, it is again more convenient to express (4.7) in the parametric form

$$g_1^{**}(\ell_1^*(\zeta(w))) = \frac{B \sin \gamma_0}{(w_1 + w_3)^{\gamma_1/\pi}} \int_0^{\frac{(w_1-w)}{(w_1+w_3)}} dx \; x^{-1+\gamma_0/\pi} (1-x)^{-1+\gamma_2/\pi}, \quad \text{for } -w_3 < w < 0,$$

$$(4.8)$$

in which, from (3.2)

$$\ell_1^*(\zeta(w)) = \int_0^{-w} dz \; z^{-\gamma_1/\pi} (z + w_1)^{-1+\gamma_1/\pi} (w_3 - z)^{-1+\gamma_1/\pi} . \quad (4.9)$$

For any $w$, $-w_3 < w < 0$, (4.8) gives the probability density $g_1^{**}$, and (4.9) gives the value of $\ell_1^*$.

A similar procedure applied to $g_2^{**}(\ell_2^*)$ leads to

$$g_2^{**}(\ell_2^*(\zeta(w))) = \frac{B \sin \gamma_2}{(w_1 + w_3)^{\gamma_1/\pi}} \int_0^{\frac{(w+w_3)}{(w_1+w_3)}} dx \; x^{-1+\gamma_2/\pi} (1-x)^{-1+\gamma_0/\pi} \quad (4.8a)$$

in which

$$\ell_2^*(\zeta(w)) = \int_w^{w_1} dz \; z^{-\gamma_1/\pi} (w_1 - z)^{-1+\gamma_1/\pi} (z + w_3)^{-1+\gamma_1/\pi} \qquad (4.9a)$$

$$\text{for} \quad 0 < w < w_1 \; .$$

From (4.8) and (4.8a) one can evaluate $g_1^{**}(c_1^*)$, $g_1^{**}(0)$, $g_2^{**}(c_2^*)$ and $g_2^{**}(0)$ and reconfirm the consistency of (2.10f) or (4.1a). Furthermore, one can evaluate the $\mu$ from (4.1a),

$$\mu = \mu_0 - \frac{B\Delta^*[\sin\gamma_0 \sin\gamma_1 \sin\gamma_2]^{1/2} \Gamma(\gamma_0/\pi)\Gamma(\gamma_1/\pi)\Gamma(\gamma_2/\pi)}{(2\pi) (w_1 + w_3)^{\gamma_1/\pi}} \; . \qquad (4.10)$$

The normalization constant $B$ can either be determined from (2.6), as previously described, or from the marginal distributions (4.8), (4.8a), through either of the normalization conditions

$$\int_0^{c_1^*} d\ell_1^* \; g_1^{**}(\ell_1) = \int_0^{c_2^*} d\ell_2^* \; g_2^*(\ell_2^*) = 1 \; . \qquad (4.11)$$

Unfortunately, we have not succeeded in evaluating these integrals "explicitly." The determination of $\mu$ has come down to the calculation of the normalization constant $B$ but this must be done by numerical or analytic approximations. This will be discussed in more detail in chapter IV after we have analysed some of the properties of the $g^{**}(\ell_1^*, \ell_2^*)$ and $g_1^*(\ell_1^*)$, $g_2^*(\ell_2^*)$ .

. **Symmetry.** Although the problem as posed in section 2 involved six parameters $\mu_0$ $(= \mu_1 = \mu_2)$, $\Delta_0$, $\Delta_1$, $\Delta_2$, $c_1$ and $c_2$, all solutions can, in fact, be simply expressed in terms of a three parameter family of "basic solutions" depending upon only $\Delta_0/\Delta_1$, $\Delta_2/\Delta_1$, and $c_2/c_1$. Furthermore, any solution with $c_2/c_1 \geq 1$ can be related to one with $c_2/c_1 < 1$.

The parameter $\mu_0$ actually never appears in the equations (2.2) and (2.3); it dropped out when $\mu_0$, $\mu_1$, $\mu_2$ were made equal. Furthermore, with the $\mu_j$'s eliminated, (2.2) and (2.3) are homogeneous linear in the $\Delta_j$'s. We can divide all equations by $\Delta_1$, for example, so that the equations involve just $\Delta_0/\Delta_1$ and $\Delta_2/\Delta_1$ (but not also $\Delta_1$). Indeed the equations (2.8), (2.9), and (2.10) do involve the $\Delta_0/\Delta_1$ and $\Delta_2/\Delta_1$.

But also with the elimination of the terms depending on the $\mu_j$'s, (2.2) becomes homogeneous in the $\ell_1$, $\ell_2$ as do the equations 2.3a, b, ---. There is no "natural unit of length." If in (2.5) we replaced the $\Delta^*$ by any other constant, the subsequent equations would remain unchanged. (The $\Delta^*$ was chosen in (2.5) simply because it was a convenient parameter symmetric in the $\Delta_j$ and non-zero). In particular we could choose to measure $\ell_1^*$ and $\ell_2^*$ in units of $c_1^*$, i.e., let $\ell_1' = \ell_1^*/c_1^*$, $\ell_2' = \ell_2^*/c_1^*$. In this case the boundaries for $\ell_1'$, $\ell_2'$ would be $\ell_1' = 0$ and $1$, $\ell_2' = 0$ and $c_2^*/c_1^*$. In effect, $c_1^*$ becomes 1.

This change in units will affect the normalization (2.6), so that actually the symmetry implies

$$c_1^{*2} g^{**}(\ell_1^*, \ell_2^*; c_1^*, c_2^*) = g^{**}(\ell_1^*/c_1^*, \ell_2^*/c_1^*; 1, c_2^*/c_1^*) \tag{5.1}$$

or if we choose $c_2^*$ as the unit of length

$$c_2^{*2} g^{**}(\ell_1^*, \ell_2^*; c_1^*, c_2^*) = g^{**}(\ell_1^*/c_2^*, \ell_2^*/c_2^*; c_1^*/c_2^*, 1) . \tag{5.2}$$

Thus the solution for any $c_1^*$, $c_2^*$ is simply related to a solution with either $c_1^* = 1$ or $c_2^* = 1$ .

We could have introduced this symmetry earlier and eliminated one of the $c_j^*$'s from the equations of section 2. It does not really simplify the form of the equations, however, to replace $c_1^*$ or $c_2^*$ by 1. In fact, the equations look better with the more symmetrical notation. The symmetry is important only in the classification of actual numerical solutions or special cases.

Since the methods used here do not apply in the limiting cases $c_1^*$ or $c_2^* \to 0$ , but do apply for $c_1^*$ or $c_2^* \to \infty$ , it is convenient in applying (5.1) or (5.2) to choose the unit of length as the smaller of $c_1^*$ and $c_2^*$ i.e., use (5.1) if $c_2^*/c_1^* \ge 1$ and (5.2) if $c_1^*/c_2^* \ge 1$ .

Finally, there is one other symmetry property of $g^{**}$ which follows from the discussion of section I3. Customers passing from the source through servers 1 and 2 into the sink can also be interpreted as holes moving from the sink through servers 2 and 1 into the source. But if we thought of the holes as if they were "customers," they would also see the system as a tandem queueing system with a source having parameters $\mu_2$, $\Delta_2$ feeding a storage $c_2$, etc. This latter system would satisfy corresponding diffusion equations. An equilibrium queue distribution for customers impli an equilibrium distribution for the holes which in turn describes an equili rium queue distribution for another companion system in which the holes are reinterpreted as customers.

In general, for a system with parameters $\Delta_j$, $\mu_j$, $c_j$, the equilibrium queue distributions $g^*$ have, for $n = 2$ , the symmetry

$$g^*(\ell_1, \ell_2; \Delta_0, \mu_0, c_1, \Delta_1, \mu_1, c_2, \Delta_2, \mu_2) = g^*(c_2 - \ell_2, c_1 - \ell_1; \Delta_2, \mu_2, c_2, \Delta_1, \mu_1, c_1, \Delta_0, \mu_0)$$

$$(5.)$$

In particular, for a system with $\mu_0 = \mu_1 = \mu_2$

$$g^*(\ell_1,\ell_2;\Delta_0/\Delta_1,\Delta_2/\Delta_1,c_1,c_2) = g^*(c_2-\ell_2,c_1-\ell_1;\Delta_2/\Delta_1,\Delta_0/\Delta_1,c_2,c_1) \ . \qquad (5.4)$$

The same equation remains valid also if the $\ell_1$, $\ell_2$, $c_1$, $c_2$ are replaced by the $\ell_1^*$, $\ell_2^*$, $c_1^*$, $c_2^*$ . Thus, as applied to (5.1),

$$g^{**}(\frac{\ell_1^*}{c_1^*}, \frac{\ell_2^*}{c_1^*} ; \frac{\Delta_0}{\Delta_1}, \frac{\Delta_2}{\Delta_1}, 1, \frac{c_2^*}{c_1^*}) = g^{**}(\frac{c_2^*}{c_1^*} - \frac{\ell_2^*}{c_1^*}, 1-\frac{\ell_1^*}{c_1^*}; \frac{\Delta_2}{\Delta_1}, \frac{\Delta_0}{\Delta_1}, \frac{c_2^*}{c_1^*}, 1) \ . \qquad (5.5)$$

Equations (5.1), (5.2) and (5.5) together imply that the $g^*$ for any choice of parameters is simply related to the $g^*$ for some system with $c_1^* = 1$ , $c_2^* > 1$ (or with $c_2^* = 1$ and $c_1^* > 1$). This is particularly useful for systems with the additional symmetry $\Delta_2 = \Delta_0$ .

One can readily check that the solutions of section 3,4 do show the above symmetries. This has, in fact, been exploited already in the previous sections to avoid repetition of certain similar calculations.

In the previous sections, the notation has switched between $\Delta$'s and $c$'s, and $\gamma$'s and $w$'s. In the latter notation, the three parameter family of solutions is expressed through $\gamma_0$, $\gamma_1$, $\gamma_2$ (with $\gamma_0 + \gamma_1 + \gamma_2 = \pi$) and $w_1/w_3$ .

Even for $\mu_0 = \mu_1 = \mu_2$ , with the resulting reduction to a three parameter family of solutions, the investigation and interpretation of all solutions is indeed a formidable task, particularly since the equations for any single choice of parameters is quite complex. For any fixed choice of parameters one could have obtained approximate distributions by simulation or other numerical methods. The value of an analytic approach, particularly an approximate one, lies in its potential for investigation of the qualitative shapes of the distribution and their dependence upon the para

eters. If one has a computer and seeks an accurate numerical solution,

the evaluation of the solution from explicit formulas is not always the

fastest way.

Our goal here is not to provide formulas which are to be evaluated

by a computer or to compete with other computer methods for accuracy. It

is to demonstrate features of the solutions which numerical solutions

would not show in a convenient form, or to identify special features which

are worth investigation in more detail numerically. Of course, the most

useful benefit of the analytic approach is this (approximate) reduction

of the number of necessary parameters from six to three.

## 6. Saddle Points and Singularities.

If it were not for the fact that the queue from server 2 can back-up

and overrun the first server (which is the origin of the boundary condi-

tion $g^{**}(0, c_2^*) = 0$ at point 4 of Fig. III-1b), one might have guessed that

$g^{**}$ would be uniform, i.e., $g^{**}(\ell_1^*, \ell_2^*) =$ constant. A constant is indeed

a solution of (2.8) and the boundary conditions (2.10a-d). This condition

$g^{**}(0, c_2^*) = 0$ pushes the probability mass away from this corner into the

other corners. It also causes the service rate $\mu$ to be less than it

would be if the queues behaved independently (a uniform distribution).

There are, of course, other peculiar conditions at all corners.

Although the numerical evaluation of $g^{**}(\ell_1^*, \ell_2^*)$ is, in most cases,

quite tedious, the qualitative properties of $g^{**}(\ell_1^*, \ell_2^*)$ can be inferred

from its behavior near the corners and near saddle points. Since $g^{**}(\ell_1^*, \ell_2^*)$

has singularities at each of the corners, any efficient scheme of numerical

calculation would probably also involve some expansions of the functions

from the corners into the interior. We will consider here only the nature of these singularities, i.e., the first terms in the expansions, since the complete numerical evaluation of $g^{**}(\ell_1^*, \ell_2^*)$ is not of much practical value in itself. Most derived quantities, particularly the marginal distributions and the service rate $\mu$, can be deduced without numerical evaluation of the complete joint distributions.

We have already seen from (4.5) that $g^{**}(\ell_1^*, \ell_2^*)$ always vanishes at point 4 and (except for $\gamma_1 = \pi/2$) is infinite at point 2. Except for the special cases $\gamma_0 = \gamma_1$ or $\gamma_2 = \gamma_1$, it is also either 0 or $\infty$ at points 1 and 3. Consequently $g^{**}$ either vanishes at two or more points or is $\infty$ at two or more points, but, generally, we expect $g^{**}(\ell_1^*, \ell_2^*)$ to have at least two saddle points on the boundary, because it must have a maximum between two zeros and a minimum between two infinite points.

One can locate these saddle points quite easily. A necessary condition for a saddle point is that

$$0 = \frac{dG}{d\zeta} = \frac{dH}{dw}\frac{dw}{d\zeta} \ .$$

But since $dw/d\zeta \neq 0$ (see equation (3.1)), we must have

$$0 = \frac{dH}{dw} = \frac{H(w)}{\pi}\left[\frac{\gamma_1}{w} - \frac{(\gamma_0 - \gamma_1)}{(w_1 - w)} + \frac{(\gamma_2 - \gamma_1)}{(w + w_3)}\right] . \qquad (6.1)$$

Except possibly at the corners, corresponding to $w = 0$, $w_1$ or $-w_3$, we know that $H(w)[w(w_1 - w)(w + w_3)]^{-1} \neq 0$, consequently the only other possible saddle points satisfy

$$\gamma_1(w+w_3)(w_1-w) - (\gamma_0-\gamma_1)w(w+w_3) + (\gamma_2-\gamma_1)w(w_1-w) = 0 ,$$

or

$$w^2(\pi - 2\gamma_1) + w(\gamma_0 w_3 - \gamma_2 w_1) - \gamma_1 w_1 w_3 = 0 \quad . \tag{6.2}$$

This quadratic equation has two roots. Since $\pi - 2\gamma_1 \geq 0$ and $\gamma_1 w_1 w_3 \geq 0$, both roots are on the real line in the w-plane, which means that they map onto the boundary of Fig. III-1b or III-1c. For any particular values of the $\gamma$'s and w's, one can compute these points simply by solving the quadratic equation (6.2) for the w and substituting in (3.2) to obtain the $\zeta$.

For special values of the $\gamma$'s, the roots of (6.2) may occur at the corner points (and consequently are not necessarily roots of (6.1)). One can see directly from (6.1) that, if $\gamma_0 = \gamma_1$ or $\gamma_2 = \gamma_1$ ($\gamma_1 = 0$ is not allowed), there is only one non-corner root. Equivalently, one of the two roots of (6.2) will be at $w_1$ or $-w_3$, respectively. Also from (6.2) we see that if $\gamma_1 = \pi/2$ there is only one saddle-point. If $\gamma_0 = \gamma_1 = \gamma_2 = \pi/3$ there are no saddle points except possibly at corners. It is not possible here for $\gamma_1 = \pi/2 = \gamma_2$ or $\gamma_0$ because this corresponds to two of the $\Delta_j$'s vanishing.

The above special cases are precisely those described in section 4 for which $H(w)$ is not 0 or $\infty$ at some corner. Clearly, the only non-corner saddle-points of $g^{**}(\ell_1^*, \ell_2^*)$ lie on the boundary between neighboring corners at which $g^{**}$ has the same value (0 or $\infty$). Knowledge of the minimum points ($g^{**} = 0$), the maximum points ($g^{**} = \infty$), and the saddle-points is all one needs in order to sketch the qualitative shape of the contour lines of $g^{**}$. Note that this topology of the contour lines depends upon the $\gamma_j$'s but not the $w_1$, $w_3$ (i.e., the $c_1$, $c_2$).

Fig. III-3 shows four possible topologies of the contour lines over the triangular region of the $\ell_1^*$, $\ell_2^*$ plane on one side of the diagonal

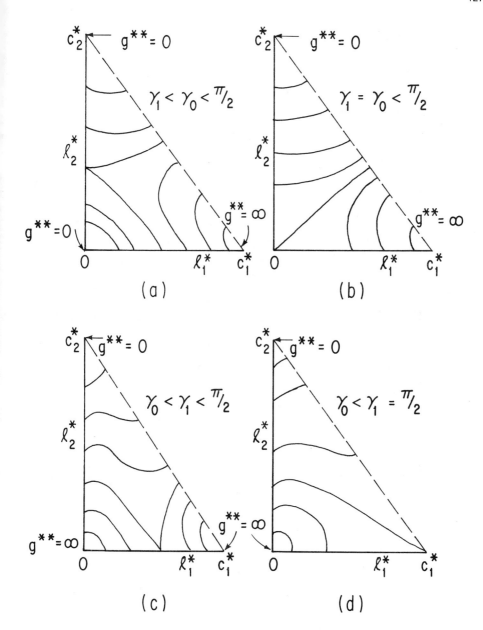

Fig. III-3. Possible topologies for contour lines.

of Fig. III-1b. Figs. III-3a,b,c show the cases $\gamma_1 < \pi/2$ for which g** is zero at point 4, $\infty$ at point 2, and 0 , finite, or $\infty$ at point 1 accordingly as $\gamma_0 > \gamma_1$ , $\gamma_0 = \gamma_1$ or $\gamma_0 < \gamma_1$ . Fig. III-3d shows the only other admissible case $\gamma_1 - \pi/2$ and $\gamma_0 < \gamma_1 = \pi/2$ .

The topologies on the opposite side of the diagonal have, by symmetry, a similar classification according to the values of $\gamma_2$ instead of $\gamma_1$ . Each of Figs. III-3a,b, or c can be matched with any of the three corresponding cases on the opposite side of the diagonal, giving a total of 9 combinations. Fig. III-1d, however, with $\gamma_1 = \pi/2$ , $\gamma_0 < \gamma_1$ can be matched only with its counterpart $\gamma_2 < \gamma_1 = \pi/2$ . Altogether there are 10 cases.

The contours of Fig. III-3 are not drawn to scale; nor are values of g** labeled, except for the values 0 and $\infty$ . The detailed shapes of the contours depend upon the $\gamma_j$'s and the $w_j$'s (i.e., $c_1^*$ , $c_2^*$) . For any values of these parameters, however, one can easily locate the saddle points and determine (except possibly for the numerical factor B) the values of g** at the saddle points. If we were to determine the analytic form of $g^{**}(\ell_1^*, \ell$ near each corner and near each saddle point, we could make at least a crude graphical interpolation and obtain qualitative estimates of the function $g^{**}(\ell_1^* , \ell_2^*)$ everywhere. This is probably as much as one would care to know about $g^{**}(\ell_1^* , \ell_2^*)$ anyway.

Consider first the behavior near point 4 $(\ell_1^* = 0 , \ell_2^* = c_2^*)$ . If $c_1^*$ and $c_2^*$ are both finite, then $w_1$ and $w_3$ are nonzero. For $|w| \ll W_1$ and $w_3$ , we can make an expansion of (3.2) in powers of $w$ ;

$$\zeta_4 - \zeta(w) = e^{i\gamma_1/2} \int_0^w dz \, z^{-\gamma_1/\pi} (w_1 - z)^{-1+\gamma_1/\pi} (z + w_3)^{-1+\gamma_1/\pi}$$

(6.3)

$$\simeq e^{i\gamma_1/2} (1 - \gamma_1/\pi)^{-1} (w/w_1 w_3)^{1-\gamma_1/\pi} .$$

Actually (6.3) is multiplied by a factor $1 + 0(w/w_1) + 0(w/w_3)$ or, more precisely, an analytic function of $w$ with value 1 at $w = 0$. To keep the formulas as compact as possible, however, we shall not indicate explicitly the magnitudes of terms other than the dominant ones. This can correspondingly be inverted to give $w$ as a function of $\zeta$

$$w(\zeta) \simeq w_1 w_3 [(1 - \gamma_1/\pi) \, e^{-i\gamma_1/2} \, (\zeta_4 - \zeta)]^{1/(1-\gamma_1/\pi)} . \tag{6.3a}$$

Now from (4.5) we see for $|w| \ll w_1$, $w_3$, that

$$H(w) \simeq B \, e^{-i\pi/2} \, e^{i\gamma_0} \, w_1^{\gamma_1/\pi} \, w_1^{(\gamma_0-\gamma_1)/\pi} \, w_3^{(\gamma_2-\gamma_1)/\pi}$$

and, therefore,

$$G(\zeta) = H(w(\zeta)) \simeq B e^{-i\pi/2} \, e^{i\gamma_0} \, w_1^{\gamma_0/\pi} \, w_3^{\gamma_2/\pi} \, [(1-\gamma_1/\pi)e^{-i\gamma_1/2} \, (\zeta_4-\zeta)]^{1/(-1+\pi/\gamma_1)} . \tag{6.4}$$

Since $g^{**}(\ell_1^*(\zeta), \ell_2^*(\zeta))$ is equal to Re $G(\zeta)$, and $\ell_1^*$, $\ell_2^*$ are related to $\zeta$ through the simple non-orthogonal linear transformation (2.12); (6.4), in essence, gives $g^{**}(\ell_1^*, \ell_2^*)$ explicitly in terms of $\ell_1^*$, $\ell_2^*$. The most important qualitative feature of this is the power of $(\zeta_4 - \zeta)$. As $\zeta \to \zeta_4$ along any radial from $\zeta_4$ in Fig. III-1c, or as $(\ell_1^*, \ell_2^*) \to (0, c_1^*)$ along any radial from point 4 of Fig. III-1b, $g^{**} \to 0$ like $|\zeta_4 - \zeta|$ to the power $(-1 + \pi/\gamma_1)^{-1}$. Since $0 < \gamma_1 \leq \pi/2$

$$0 < (-1 + \pi/\gamma_1)^{-1} \leq 1 . \tag{6.5}$$

Thus $g^{**}$ vanishes as some fractional power of the distance from point 4. This power depends only upon $\gamma_1$, but is independent of $\gamma_0, \gamma_2, w_1$ and $w_3$.

The actual numerical value of $g^{**}$ at any point $\ell_1^*, \ell_2^*$ depends upon all the parameters; the normalization $B$, in particular, depends upon the parameters in a rather complicated way. The contour lines $g^{**}$ = const., however, have a local shape which depends only upon the $\gamma_j$'s. If we write $\zeta_4 - \zeta$ in the form

$$\zeta_4 - \zeta = |\zeta_4 - \zeta| \exp(i \, \pi/2 + \phi_4)$$

so that $\phi_4$ represents the angle which the vector $\zeta_4 - \zeta$ makes with the vertical in Fig. III-1c, then Re $G(\zeta)$ = const implies that

$$\text{Re } |\zeta_4 - \zeta|^{1/(-1+\pi/\gamma_1)} \exp\left[i \, \frac{(\gamma_0-\gamma_2)}{2} + \frac{\phi_4}{-1 + \pi/\gamma_1}\right] = \text{const}$$

or

$$|\zeta_4 - \zeta| = (\text{const}) \left\{\cos\left[\frac{(\gamma_0-\gamma_2)}{2} + \frac{\phi_4}{-1 + \pi/\gamma_1}\right]\right\}^{-(-1+\pi/\gamma_1)} . \tag{6.6}$$

The constant in (6.6) depends upon the value of $g^{**}$, but contours for various values of $g^{**}$ differ only in a scale of length for the distance $|\zeta_4 - \zeta|$; except for the scale, all contours have the same shape relative to the corner at point 4 of Fig. III-1c (at least in the neighborhood of this corner). Furthermore, except for a rotation of coordinates around point 4, i.e., a change of the origin of the angle $\phi_4$, the contour lines of Fig. III-1c actually depend only upon $\gamma_1$.

The contour lines in Fig.III-1c can be drawn quite easily from (6.6). The analytic form of the contours of Fig.III-1b are more cumbersome, but it is quite straightforward to map the contours from Fig. III-1c back to Fig. III-1a via the linear mappings. The contours do have a variety of shapes which must adjust so as to meet the boundaries in the proper directions as shown in Figs. III-1a, III-1b, or III-1c. Some examples will be given later.

To obtain the behavior of $g^{**}(\ell_1^*, \ell_2^*)$ near point 2 of Fig. III-1, we can expand (3.2) in powers of $w^{-1}$ for $|w| \gg w_1$ and $w_3$;

$$\zeta(w) \simeq e^{i(\pi-\gamma_1/2)} w^{-1+\gamma_1/\pi} (1 - \gamma_1/\pi)^{-1} \qquad (6.7)$$

or

$$w(\zeta) = e^{i\pi/2} \left[ (1 - \gamma_1/\pi) e^{-i\pi/2} \zeta \right]^{-1/(1-\gamma_1/\pi)} .$$

From (4.5) we have, for $|w| \gg w_1, w_3$

$$G(\zeta) \simeq B \left[ (1 - \gamma_1/\pi) e^{-i\pi/2} \zeta \right]^{-(1-2\gamma_1/\pi)/(1-\gamma_1/\pi)} . \qquad (6.8)$$

Again, the most important feature of this is the power of $\zeta$ which, for $0 < \gamma_1 \le \pi/2$ is

$$-1 < -(1 - 2\gamma_1/\pi)/(1 - \gamma_1/\pi) \le 0 . \qquad (6.9)$$

Except for $\gamma_1 = \pi/2$, $G(\zeta)$ becomes infinite as some negative fractional power of $\zeta$ for $\zeta \to 0$; the power depends only upon the parameter $\gamma_1$. Although $g^{**}(\ell_1^*, \ell_2^*)$ becomes infinite at point 2, the singularity is "weak enough" (power greater than -1) so as to give a finite probability to any area including point 2. The contour lines of $g^{**}$ in the vicinity of point 2 have a shape, analogous to (6.6), which depends upon only $\gamma_1$ (independent of $\ell_0, \ell_2, w_1$ and $w_3$).

To obtain the behavior of $g^{**}$ near points 1 or 3 of Fig. III-1, we expand (3.2) in powers of $(w - w_1)$ or $(w + w_3)$, respectively:

$$\zeta(w) - \zeta_1 \simeq e^{-i\gamma_1/2} \; w^{-\gamma_1/\pi} \; (w_1 + w_3)^{-1 + \gamma_1/\pi} \; (\pi/\gamma_1)(w - w_1)^{\gamma_1/\pi},$$

$$(6.10)$$

$$\zeta_3 - \zeta(w) \simeq e^{-i\gamma_1/2} \; w_3^{-\gamma_1/\pi} \; (w_1 + w_3)^{-1 + \gamma_1/\pi} \; (\pi/\gamma_1)(w + w_3)^{\gamma_1/\pi}.$$

Correspondingly we find, for $\zeta$ close to $\zeta_1$ or $\zeta_3$

$$G(\zeta) \simeq B \, e^{-i\gamma_2/2} \; w_1^{\gamma_0/\pi} \; (w_1 + w_3)^{(\gamma_2 - \gamma_0)/\pi} \left[ (w_1 + w_3)(\gamma_1/\pi)(\zeta - \zeta_1) \right]^{-1 + \gamma_0/\gamma_1},$$

$$G(\zeta) \simeq B \, e^{+i\gamma_0/2} \; w_3^{\gamma_2/\pi} \; (w_1 + w_3)^{(\gamma_0 - \gamma_2)/\pi} \left[ (w_1 + w_3)(\gamma_1/\pi)(\zeta_3 - \zeta) \right]^{-1 + \gamma_2/\gamma_1}.$$

$$(6.11)$$

Again $G(\zeta)$ behaves as some power of the distance from the corner. The powers $-1 + \gamma_0/\gamma_1$ or $-1 + \gamma_2/\gamma_1$ are greater than $-1$ (the probability density is integrable) but, for small $\gamma_1$, could be very large and positive (there is a small probability that the queue lengths will be near these corners). The contour lines of $g^{**}$ again depend only upon the $\gamma_j$'s, not $w_1$ or $w_3$.

Finally, in the neighborhood of any non-corner saddle point along the boundary of Fig. III-1c, $G(\zeta)$ is analytic and can be approximated by

$$G(\zeta) = G(\zeta_0) + \frac{d^2 G(\zeta_0)}{2 \, d\zeta_0^2} (\zeta - \zeta_0)^2 + \cdots,$$

$$(6.11)$$

if $\zeta_0$ represents the position of a saddle point where $dG(\zeta_0)/d\zeta_0 = 0$. The value of $d^2 G(\zeta_0)/d\zeta_0^2$ can be evaluated easily from (3.1) and (4.5). At the saddle point $dH/dw = 0$ and so

$$\frac{d^2 G(\zeta)}{d\zeta^2} = \frac{d^2 H}{dw^2} \left(\frac{dw}{d\zeta}\right)^2 = \frac{d^2 H}{dw^2} \left(\frac{d\zeta}{dw}\right)^{-2} . \tag{6.12}$$

The shape of the contours, however, depends only upon the complex phase of (6.12), which can be read directly from Figs. III-1c and 1e. For example, on the line 1-2 $d\zeta$ has the phase $-\gamma_1/2$ and $dH$ has the phase $\pm\pi/2 + \gamma_1$, therefore (6.12) has the phase $\pm\pi/2 + 2\gamma_1$. The contours $Re\ G(\zeta) = const.$ have the form

$$Re\ (\zeta - \zeta_0)^2 \exp(\pm\frac{\pi}{2}i + 2\gamma_1 i) = const = |\zeta - \zeta_0|^2 (\pm)\sin(2\phi_0 + \gamma_1), \tag{6.13}$$

in which $\phi_0$ is the angle $\zeta - \zeta_0$ makes with the boundary line 1-2 at angle $-\gamma_1/2$ .

The contours (6.13) are (locally) the usual hyperbolas associated with analytic saddle points, having asymptotes at $\phi_0 = -\gamma_1/2$ and $\phi_0 = -\gamma_1/2 + \pi/2$ . Equation (6.13) could also be written in the more common form

$$\xi'^2 - \eta'^2 = \pm const \tag{6.14}$$

in which $\xi'$, $\eta'$ represent a rotation of $\xi, \eta$ through an angle $-\gamma_1 + \pi/4$. Geometrically, the asymptotes of the hyperbolas bisect the angles $\gamma_1$ and $\pi - \gamma_1$ which the contour lines of Fig. III-1c make with the boundary 1-2. Similarly if the saddle point is on any other boundary of Fig. III-1c, the contours of $g^{**}$ near the saddle point are hyperbolas having asymptotes which bisect the angles the contour lines make with the boundary.

If one maps the contours $g^{**} = const.$ from Fig. III-1c back to Figs. III-1b or 1a, the contours near the saddle point are still hyperbolas in figures 1b or 1a; but the two asymptotes no longer make an angle of $\pi/2$, since the non-orthogonal linear transformations from Figs. III-1a to 1b to 1c do not preserve angles.

It is straightforward, but somewhat tedious, to extend the above expansions one or more terms beyond those described. The functions are sufficiently smooth between the corners and saddles, however, that one can easily interpolate between expansions and sketch the complete contour plot, for any given values of the $\gamma_j$'s and $w_1$, $w_3$ or $c_1^*$, $c_2^*$. Although the shapes of the contours near corners or saddle-points are independent of $w_1$, $w_3$, the locations of the saddle points do depend upon $w_1$ and $w_3$; so do the $g^{**}$ values along the contours and correction terms to the formulas described above.

The simple formulas given here will be useful in describing the qualitative way in which the queue distributions depend upon the variance rates $\Delta_j$ and the storage capacities $c_j$.

'. <u>One Large Storage.</u> The formulas of the last section apply for any finite values of $c_1^*$, $c_2^*$, but they do not describe very well the behavior of $g^{**}$ for $c_2^*/c_1^* \gg 1$ or $c_1^*/c_2^* \gg 1$.

Since, according to section 5, we can use either $c_1^*$ or $c_2^*$ as a unit of length, the form of $g^{**}$ does not change if we let $c_1^* \to \infty$, $c_2^* \to \infty$ with $c_1^*/c_2^*$ fixed. The probability density simply becomes spread over a larger range of $\ell_1^*$, $\ell_2^*$; consequently $g^{**}$ decreases as $c_1^{*-2}$, and all expected queue lengths increase proportional to $c_1^*$.

If, however, we hold $c_1^*$ fixed and let $c_2^* \to \infty$, the second storage will hardly ever become full, so there will be no blockage of server 1. Server 1 should operate independently of the queue length in $c_2^*$ and have a service rate as described in II, namely, $\mu_0[1 - (\Delta_0 + \Delta_1)/2\mu_0 c_1] < \mu_0 = \mu_1 =$ Server 2 thus sees a traffic intensity less than 1, but the stochastic properties of the arrival process to server 2 (the output from 1) is rather complicated (as was discussed in chapter II). We would expect, however, that there should be a limit probability density associated with $c_2^* \to \infty$ with all queue lengths measured in units of $c_1^*$ .

If, on the other hand, we let $c_2^*$ be fixed and $c_1^* \to \infty$ , servers 1 and 2 will interact through the finite storage $c_2^*$ causing a service rate less than $\mu_0$ . If $c_1^*/c_2^* \gg 1$ but finite, the first storage will become nearly full, i.e., hardly every empty. It is more convenient, therefore, to describe this system in terms of holes rather than customers. Indeed, according to the symmetry conditions (5.4) or (5.5), we can convert the system with $c_1^* \to \infty$ into a corresponding system with $c_2^* \to \infty$. If there exists an equilibrium distribution of customers in the latter system, there must be an equilibrium distribution of holes for the former. Because of this symmetry, it suffices to consider only the cases $c_2^*/c_1^* \gg 1$ .

The formulas of sections 2, 3, and 4 remain valid in the limit $c_2^*/c_1^* \to \infty$. From Fig. III-1 it is clear that if $c_2^*/c_1^* \to \infty$, points 3 and 4 go to $\infty$ in Figs. III-1a,b and c. Since $\infty$ in the $\zeta$-plane maps into the origin of the w-plane and the G-plane, it follows that point 3 must coalesce with point 4, i.e., $w_3 \to 0$ . Indeed one can verify this also from (3.6).

The formulas of section 3 simplify considerably for $w_3 \to 0$ (although the mappings are still not expressible in terms of elementary functions). Equation (3.2) becomes

$$
\zeta(w) = e^{i(\pi-\gamma_1/2)} \int_w^\infty dz \, z^{-1}(z-w_1)^{-1+\gamma_1/\pi} = e^{i(\pi-\gamma_1/2)} w_1^{-1+\gamma_1/\pi} \int_{w/w_1}^\infty dz \, z^{-1}(z-1)^{-1+\gamma_1/\pi}
$$

$$
\tag{7.1}
$$

$$
= e^{i(\pi-\gamma_1/2)} c_1^* + w_1^{-1+\gamma_1/\pi} e^{i\gamma_1/2} \int_{w/w_1}^1 dz \, z^{-1} (1-z)^{-1+\gamma_1/\pi} .
$$

This integral can be expressed as an incomplete Beta function or a hyper-geometric function, but this would not be of much help here. Equation (3.4a), however, gives, for $w_3 \to 0$

$$c_1^* = w_1^{-1+\gamma_1/\pi} \int_1^\infty dz \, z^{-1} (z-1)^{-1+\gamma_1/\pi} = w_1^{-1+\gamma_1/\pi} \pi/\sin \gamma_1 \quad , \quad (7.2)$$

so we do have a simple relation between $c_1^*$ and $w_1$.

Equation (4.5) simplifies to

$$H(w) = B \, e^{-i\pi/2} \, e^{i\gamma_0} \, w^{\gamma_2/\pi} \, (w_1 - w)^{(\gamma_0 - \gamma_1)/\pi} \, . \qquad (7.3)$$

The nature of the singularities of $g^*$ near points 1 and 2 of Fig. I is not really affected by the limit $c_2^* \to \infty$, $w_3 \to 0$, except in so far as $c_2^*$ influences the scale of $g^{**}$ (particularly through the B). Our main concern here is with the behavior of $g^*$ near points 3 and 4 (i.e., for $\ell_2^* \to \infty$).

For $w \to 0$, $\zeta(w)$ has a logarithmic singularity. From (7.1) and (7.2) we obtain

$$\zeta(w) = e^{i(\pi-\gamma_1/2)} c_1^* + e^{i\gamma_1/2} (c_1^*/\pi) \sin \gamma_1 [-\ell n(w/w_1)$$

$$- \psi(\gamma_1/\pi) + \psi(1) + O(w)] \qquad (7.4)$$

in which $\psi(\cdot)$ is the digamma function [reference 4, page 259]. Inversion of (7.4) gives

$$w(\zeta) \approx w_1 \exp \left\{ - \frac{\left[ \zeta - c_1 e^{i(\pi-\gamma_1/2)} \right] e^{-i\gamma_1/2}}{c_1^* \sin \gamma_1} \pi + \psi(1) - \psi(\gamma_1/\pi) \right\} \qquad (7.5)$$

and substitution into (7.3) produces

$$
G(\zeta) = H(w(\zeta)) \simeq B \, w_1^{1-2\gamma_1/\pi} \exp \left\{ - \frac{\left[ \zeta - c_1 e^{i(\pi-\gamma_1/2)} \right] e^{-i\gamma_1/2}}{c_1^* \sin \gamma_1} \gamma_2 \right.
$$

$$
\left. - \frac{i\pi}{2} + i\gamma_0 + \frac{\gamma_2}{\pi} \psi(1) - \frac{\gamma_2}{\pi} \psi(\frac{\gamma_1}{\pi}) \right\}. \tag{7.6}
$$

This can be expressed directly in terms of $\ell_1^*$, $\ell_2^*$ through the substitution

$$
\left[ \zeta - c_1^* e^{i(\pi-\gamma_1/2)} \right] e^{-i\gamma_1/2} = (\ell_2^* + \ell_1^* \cos \gamma_1) - i \, \ell_1 \sin \gamma_1 \ .
$$

The real part of $G(\zeta)$, the probability density $g^{**}(\ell_1^*, \ell_2^*)$ therefore behaves, for $\ell_2^*/c_1^* \gg 1$, like

$$
g^{**}(\ell_1^*, \ell_2^*) \simeq B' \exp \left\{ \frac{-\gamma_2 (\ell_2^* + \ell_1^* \cos \gamma_1)}{c_1^* \sin \gamma_1} \right\} \sin \left( \gamma_0 + \frac{\gamma_2 \ell_1^*}{c_1^*} \right) , \tag{7.7}
$$

with $B'$ independent of $\ell_1^*$, $\ell_2^*$.

Since (7.7) can be written as a product of a function of $\ell_1^*$ and a function of $\ell_2^*$, this suggests that the queue lengths $Q_1^*$ and $Q_2^*$, for $c_2^* = \infty$, are nearly statistically independent. The formulas, however, only apply for $\ell_2^*/c_1^* \gg 1$. The behavior of $g_1^{**}(\ell_1^*, \ell_2^*)$ for $\ell_2^*/c_1^* \ll 1$ clearly disproves independence. Furthermore, for $c_2^* \to \infty$, the second queue cannot block the first server. The marginal distribution of $Q_1^*$ must, therefore, be the same as for a single server queueing system, a uniform distribution (for $\mu_0 = \mu_1$). The two factors of (7.7) are certa

not the marginal distributions of $Q_1^*$, $Q_2^*$ .

The shape of the dependence of $g^{**}(\ell_1^*, \ell_2^*)$ on $\ell_1^*$ depends upon th

parameters $\gamma_j$ , since the slopes of the contour lines along the bounda

1-4 and 2-3 of Fig. III-1b also vary with the $\gamma_j$ . Although, from (2.10c

the slope of the contour along 2-3 is always negative, the slope along 1-

may be either positive or negative. The form of the $\ell_1^*$-dependence is

typical of a "damped oscillation"; $g^{**}(\ell_1^*, \ell_2^*)$ is definitely decreasing

with $\ell_1^*$ , as $\ell_1^* \to c_1^*$ , but for $\ell_1^* = 0$ it will either increase or

decrease accordingly as $\Delta_1 < \Delta_0$ or $\Delta_1 > \Delta_0$ .

The $\ell_2^*$ dependence of $g^{**}$ is exponential (for $\ell_2^*/c_1^* \gg 1$), wit

a parameter which is a fairly complex function of the $\Delta_j$'s. The $\ell_2^*$ is

measured in terms of $c_1^*$, the only "length parameter" that remains after

let $c_2^* \to \infty$ .

For $c_2^* \to \infty$ ($w_3 \to 0$), the marginal distributions $g_1^{**}(\ell_1^*)$ and $g_2^{**}($

(4.8) and (4.8a), simplify considerably. From (4.8) we see that, for

$-w_3 < w < 0$ and $w_3 \to 0$ , $g_1^{**}(\ell_1^*)$ has a limit which is independent of

(the expected uniform marginal distribution for $Q_1$). Specifically we ob

tain from (4.8)

$$g_1^{**}(\ell_1^*) = \frac{B \sin \gamma_0 \sin \gamma_1 \, \Gamma(\gamma_0/\pi) \, \Gamma(\gamma_1/\pi) \, \Gamma(\gamma_2/\pi)}{\pi \, w_1^{\gamma_1/\pi}} . \qquad (7.8)$$

So far we have not explicitly determined the value of $B$ . Generall

it can be found only by a numerical integration of (4.11). In the presen

case, $c_2^* \to \infty$, however, the fact that $g_1^{**}(\ell_1^*)$ is a constant allows us

to determine $B$ from the obvious condition

$$g_1^{**}(\ell_1^*) \;\;=\;\; 1/c_1^* \; . \tag{7.9}$$

Having determined the  B  from (7.8), (7.9),  it can be used also in the formulas for  $g^{**}(\ell_1^*,\ell_2^*)$  and  $g_2^*(\ell_2^*)$.

With  $w_3 \to 0$ ,  the above value of  B ,  and (7.2), the formulas (4.8a) and (4.9a) for  $g_2^{**}(\ell_2^*)$  now simplify to

$$g_2^*(\ell_2^*(\zeta(w))) \;\;=\;\; \frac{\pi\,\sin\gamma_2}{c_1^*\sin\gamma_0\sin\gamma_1\Gamma(\gamma_0/\pi)\Gamma(\gamma_1/\pi)\Gamma(\gamma_2/\pi)}\int_0^{\frac{w}{w_1}}dx\;x^{-1+\gamma_2/\pi}\,(1-x)^{-1+\gamma_0/} \tag{7.10}$$

$$\ell_2^*(\zeta(w)) \;\;=\;\; \frac{c_1^*\sin\gamma_1}{\pi}\int_{w/w_1}^1 dz\; z^{-1}\,(1-z)^{-1+\gamma_1/\pi} \; . \tag{7.11}$$

This marginal distribution of  $Q_2^*$  generated by a source having a finite storage  $c_1^*$  is a result of particular interest.  Unfortunately, this is still in a parametric form which cannot obviously be simplified further since both (7.10) and (7.11) involve incomplete Beta functions.  We can, however, obtain expansions for  $\ell_2^*/c_1^* \ll 1$  and  $\ell_2^*/c_1^* \gg 1$,  for general values of the  $\gamma_j$'s.  For intermediate values of  $\ell_2^*/c_1^*$ ,  it is not too difficult to evaluate  $g^{**}$  numerically for any particular choice of the  $\gamma_j$'s.

8.  Expansions of the Marginal Distributions.  Most of the discussion, here-after, will deal with the properties of  $g_1^{**}(\ell_1^*)$  and  $g_2^{**}(\ell_2^*)$, because most of  the usual measures of performance can be evaluated directly from these marginal probability densities.

From the parametric representation of  $g_1^{**}$  in (4.8) and (4.9), we see that  $g_1^{**}$  is a monotone decreasing function of  w ,  as is  $\ell_1^*$ .

140

Therefore, $g_1^{**}(\ell_1^*)$ is a monotone increasing function of $\ell_1^*$; i.e., th

distribution of $Q_1^*$ is weighted in favor of a full storage. Correspondi

from (4.8a) and (4.9a), $g_2^{**}(\ell_2^*)$ is a monotone decreasing function of $\ell$

the distribution of $Q_2^*$ is weighted in favor of an empty storage for ser

As compared with $c_2^* = \infty$, it is this increasing behavior of $g_1^{**}(\ell_1^*)$

which causes $g_1^{**}(c_1^*)$ to be larger than $1/c_1^*$ which, in turn, describes

the lower service rate $\mu$ for $c_2^* < \infty$ than for $c_2^* = \infty$.

Because of the symmetry between the formulas for $g_1^{**}(\ell_1^*)$ and $g_2^{**}($

we will derive formulas only for the latter and use the symmetry to obtain

corresponding formulas for $g_1^{**}(\ell_1^*)$.

To describe the behavior of $g_2^{**}(\ell_2^*)$ near $\ell_2^* = 0$, we note that

$\ell_2^* = 0$ corresponds to $w = w_1$. We can write (4.8a) in the form

$$\frac{g_2^{**}(\ell_2^*(\zeta(w)))}{g_2^{**}(0)} = \frac{\pi}{\sin\gamma_1 \Gamma(\gamma_0/\pi)\Gamma(\gamma_1/\pi)\Gamma(\gamma_2/\pi)} \int_0^{\frac{w+w_3}{w_1+w_3}} dx \, x^{-1+\gamma_2/\pi} (1-x)^{-1+\gamma_0/\pi}$$

(8.1a)

$$= 1 - \frac{\pi}{\sin\gamma_1 \Gamma(\gamma_0/\pi)\Gamma(\gamma_1/\pi)\Gamma(\gamma_2/\pi)} \int_0^{\frac{w_1-w}{w_1+w_3}} dx \, x^{-1+\gamma_0/\pi} (1-x)^{-1+\gamma_2/\pi}$$

(8.1b)

and, for $(w_1 - w)/(w_1 + w_3) \ll 1$, expand (8.1b) in powers of this param-

eter,

$$\frac{g_2^{**}(\ell_2^*(\zeta(w)))}{g_2^{**}(0)} = 1 - \frac{\pi^2 \, [(w_1 - w)/(w_1 + w_3)]^{\gamma_0/\pi}}{\gamma_0 \sin \gamma_1 \, \Gamma(\gamma_0/\pi) \, \Gamma(\gamma_1/\pi) \, \Gamma(\gamma_2/\pi)}$$

(8.1c)

$$\cdot \left[ 1 + \frac{(1 - \gamma_2/\pi)}{(1 + \pi/\gamma_0)} \frac{(w_1 - w)}{(w_1 + w_3)} + \cdots \right].$$

Similarly (4.9a) can be written in the form

$$
\ell_2^*(\zeta(w)) = (w_1+w_3)^{-1+2\gamma_1/\pi}\, w_1^{-\gamma_1/\pi} \int_0^{\frac{w_1-w}{w_1+w_3}} dx\; x^{-1+\gamma_1/\pi}\,(1-x)^{-1+\gamma_1/\pi}
$$

$$
\cdot\,[1-(w_1+w_3)\,x/w_1]^{-\gamma_1/\pi} \tag{8.2}
$$

and expanded

$$
\ell_2^*(\zeta(w)) = (w_1+w_3)^{-1+2\gamma_1/\pi}\, w_1^{-\gamma_1/\pi}\,(\pi/\gamma_1)[(w_1-w)/(w_1+w_3)]^{\gamma_1/\pi} \tag{8.2a}
$$

$$
\cdot\left\{1+\frac{[1+(w_3/w_1)(\gamma_1/\pi)](\gamma_1/\pi)}{(1+\gamma_1/\pi)}\frac{(w_1-w)}{(w_1+w_3)}+\cdots\right\}.
$$

The inversion of (8.2a) gives

$$
\frac{w_1-w}{w_1+w_3}=\frac{w_1(\gamma_1\ell_2^*/\pi)^{\pi/\gamma_1}}{(w_1+w_3)^{2-\pi/\gamma_1}}\left\{1-\frac{[1+(w_3/w_1)(\gamma_1/\pi)]\,w_1(\gamma_1\ell_2^*/\pi)^{\pi/\gamma_1}}{(1+\gamma_1/\pi)(w_1+w_3)^{2-\pi/\gamma_1}}+\cdots\right\}
$$

in powers of $\ell_2^{*\,\pi/\gamma_1}$, and substitution into (8.1c) gives

$$
\frac{g_2^{**}(\ell_2^*)}{g_2^{**}(0)}=1-\frac{\pi^2 w_1^{\gamma_0/\pi}(w_1+w_3)^{-2\gamma_0/\pi+\gamma_0/\gamma_1}(\gamma_1\ell_2^*/\pi)^{\gamma_0/\gamma_1}}{\gamma_0\sin\gamma_1\,\Gamma(\gamma_0/\pi)\,\Gamma(\gamma_1/\pi)\,\Gamma(\gamma_2/\pi)} \tag{8.3}
$$

$$
\cdot\left\{1+\frac{\gamma_0}{\pi}\left[\frac{(1-\gamma_2/\pi)}{(1+\gamma_0/\pi)}-\frac{1+(w_3/w_1)(\gamma_1/\pi)}{1+\gamma_1/\pi}\right]\frac{w_1(\gamma_1\ell_2^*/\pi)^{\pi/\gamma_1}}{(w_1+w_3)^{2-\pi/\gamma_1}}+\cdots\right\}.
$$

142

The dependence of this on the $w_1$, $w_3$, and $\gamma_j$ is rather complicated but we are mostly concerned here with the dependence on $\ell_2^*$. The $g_2^{**}(\ell$ decreases from $g_2^{**}(0)$ as the $(\gamma_0/\gamma_1)$th power of $\ell_2^*$, multiplied by a power series in $\ell_2^{*\pi/\gamma_1}$. The power $\gamma_0/\gamma_1$ can have any positive value from near zero if $\Delta_1$ and $\Delta_2$ are small (nearly regular service at 1 and 2) to a very large value if $\Delta_0$ and $\Delta_2$ are small. In the former case $g_2^{**}(\ell_2^*)$ will decrease very rapidly, in the latter case $g_2^{**}(\ell_2^*$ will be nearly uniform. For $c_1^*/c_2^* \to \infty$, $w_1 \to 0$ and $g_2^{**}(\ell_2^*)$ becomes the uniform distribution as one would expect, as the counterpart of the uniform distribution of $Q_1^*$ for $c_2^* \to \infty$ given in (7.9).

To describe the behavior of $g_2^{**}(\ell_2^*)$ near $\ell_2^* = c_2^*$, we can first expand (8.1a) in powers of $w/(w_1 + w_3)$,

$$\frac{g_2^{**}(\ell_2^*(\zeta(w)))}{g_2^{**}(0)} = \frac{g_2^{**}(c_2^*)}{g_2^{**}(0)} + \frac{\pi}{\sin\gamma_1 \Gamma(\gamma_0/\pi)\Gamma(\gamma_1/\pi)\Gamma(\gamma_2/\pi)}$$

$$\cdot \left(\frac{w_3}{w_1+w_3}\right)^{-1+\gamma_2/\pi}\left(\frac{w_1}{w_1+w_3}\right)^{-1+\gamma_0/\pi}\left(\frac{w}{w_1+w_3}\right)\left\{1 + \left[\frac{(-1+\gamma_2/\pi)}{w_3} + \frac{(-1+\gamma_0/\pi)}{w_1}\right]\frac{w}{2}\right.$$

This describes $g_2^{**}(\ell_2^*(\zeta(w)))$ as an analytic function of $w$ near $w = 0$. It may be necessary, however, to evaluate the first term of (8.4) numerical from (8.1a). There is a further complication that this expansion converges only for $w/w_1 < 1$ and $w/w_3 < 1$ because of the non-analytic behavior of (8.1a) at $w = w_1$ or $w_3$. The expansion will, therefore, not be very useful for small values of $w_1$ or $w_3$, i.e., large $c_1^*$ or $c_2^*$. These cases, however, can be handled separately.

For $\ell_2^*$ close to $c_2^*$, we write (4.9a) in the form

$$c_2^* - \ell_2^*(\zeta(w)) = w_1^{-1+\gamma_1/\pi} \int_0^{w/w_3} dz\, z^{-\gamma_1/\pi} (1+z)^{-1+\gamma_1/\pi} (1 - w_3 z/w_1)^{-1+\gamma_1/\pi} \quad (8.5)$$

and expand this in powers of $w/w_3$

$$c_2^* - \ell_2^*(\zeta(w)) = \frac{1}{(1-\gamma_1/\pi)}\left(\frac{w}{w_1 w_3}\right)^{1-\gamma_1/\pi}\left[1 - \frac{(1-\gamma_1/\pi)^2}{(2-\gamma_1/\pi)}(1-w_3/w_1)\left(\frac{w}{w_3}\right) + \cdots\right]. \quad (8.5a)$$

Thus by inversion

$$\frac{w}{w_1 w_3} \simeq \left[(1-\gamma_1/\pi)(c_2^*-\ell_2^*)\right]^{\pi/(\pi-\gamma_1)}\left\{1 + \frac{(1-\gamma_1/\pi)}{(2-\gamma_1/\pi)}(1-\frac{w_3}{w_1})w_1\left[(1-\gamma_1/\pi)(c_2^*-\ell_2^*)\right]^{\frac{\pi}{(\pi-\gamma_1)}}+ \cdots\right\}.$$

Substitution in (8.4) then gives

$$\frac{g_2^{**}(\ell_2^*) - g_2^{**}(c_2^*)}{g_2^{**}(0)} = \frac{\pi w_3^{\gamma_2/\pi} w_1^{\gamma_0/\pi} (w_1+w_3)^{\gamma_1/\pi}}{\sin\gamma_1 \Gamma(\gamma_0/\pi)\Gamma(\gamma_1/\pi)\Gamma(\gamma_2/\pi)}\left[(1-\frac{\gamma_1}{\pi})(c_2^* - \ell_2^*)\right]^{\pi/(\pi-\gamma_1)}$$

$$\cdot \left\{1 + \left[(1 - \gamma_1/\pi)(c_2^* - \ell_2^*)\right]^{\pi/(\pi-\gamma_1)}\right.$$

$$\left[\frac{(1 - \gamma_1/\pi)}{(2 - \gamma_1/\pi)}(w_1-w_3) - \frac{w_1}{2}(1 - \frac{\gamma_2}{\pi}) - \frac{w_3}{2}(1 - \frac{\gamma_0}{\pi})\right]+ \cdots\right\}.$$

$$(8.6)$$

Thus as $\ell_2^* \to c_2^*$ , $g_2^{**}(\ell_2^*)$ approaches its limit $g_2^{**}(c_2^*)$ like $(c_2^* - \ell_2^*)^{\pi/(\pi-\gamma_1)}$ , and also has a series expansion in integer powers of $(c_2^* - \ell_2^*)^{\pi/(\pi-\gamma_1)}$ . Since $0 < \gamma_1 \le \pi/2$ , this power satisfies $1 < \pi/(\pi - \gamma_1) \le 2$ . The derivative of $g_2^{**}(\ell_2^*)$ vanishes at $\ell_2^* = c_2^*$ like

144

$$(c_2^* - \ell_2^*)^{\gamma_1/(\pi-\gamma_1)} \quad .$$

If neither $w_3/w_1$ nor $w_1/w_3$ is small compared with 1, the expansion (8.6) will, generally, join quite smoothly with the expansion (8.3). The $g_2^{**}(\ell_2^*)$ first decreases from $g_2^{**}(0)$ like $\ell_2^{*\gamma_0/\gamma_1}$ and then flattens out approaching $g_2^{**}(c_2^*)$ with zero slope as $\ell_2^* \to c_2^*$. This is also true for $w_1/w_3 \ll 1$ but, in this case, one can make some other simplifications.

For $w_1/w_3 \ll 1$, the expansion (8.1c) converges very rapidly for all values of $w$, $0 < w < w_1$, but (8.2a) converges rapidly only for $w/w_1 \ll 1$. If we neglect all but the leading term of (8.1c), then

$$1 - \frac{g_2^{**}(\ell_2^*(\zeta(w)))}{g_2^{**}(0)} \simeq \frac{\pi^2[(1 - w/w_1)(w_1/w_3)]^{\gamma_0/\pi}}{\gamma_0 \sin\gamma_1 \, \Gamma(\gamma_0/\pi)\Gamma(\gamma_1/\pi)\Gamma(\gamma_2/\pi)} \quad , \tag{8.7}$$

which is proportional to $(1 - w/w_1)^{\gamma_0/\pi}$. In place of (8.2), we can write

$$\ell_2^*(\zeta(w)) = (w_1 + w_3)^{-1+\gamma_1/\pi} \int_0^{1-w/w_1} dx \, x^{-1+\gamma_1/\pi} (1-x)^{-\gamma_1/\pi} \left(1 - \frac{w_1}{w_1 + w_3} x\right)^{-1+\gamma_1/\pi} \tag{8.}$$

which, for $w_1/w_3 \ll 1$, can be approximated by

$$\ell_2^*(\zeta(w)) \simeq w_3^{-1+\gamma_1/\pi} \int_0^{1-w/w_1} dx \, x^{-1+\gamma_1/\pi} (1-x)^{-\gamma_1/\pi} \quad , \tag{8.9}$$

an incomplete Beta function.

Although, in general, (8.9) cannot be expressed in terms of elementary functions, its inverse does describe $(1 - w/w_1)$ as a function of only $\ell_2^* w_3^{-1-\gamma_1/\pi}$ and $\gamma_1$. Thus (8.7) describes $1 - g_2^{**}(\ell_2^*)/g_2^{**}(0)$ as a function which depends upon the $w_1$ and $w_3$ (i.e., the storages $c_1^*$ and $c_2^*$) only through a choice of scale for the quantity (8.7) and a choice of scale for $\ell_2^*$. Except for the choice of scale, the function (8.7) depends upon $\gamma_0$ and $\gamma_1$ only; in fact, it is the $\gamma_0/\pi$ power of a function whose shape depends upon only $\gamma_1$. From a graph of the incomplete Beta-function (8.9), one can easily graph (8.7) for each value of $\gamma_1$.

For $w_3/w_1 \ll 1$, the evaluation of $g_2^{**}(\ell_2^*)$ is a bit more complicated. For $\ell_2^*/c_1^* \ll 1$, $(w_1 - w)/w_3 \ll 1$, the expansions (8.1c) to (8.3) are still the appropriate ones to use. Also (8.4) to (8.6) are valid for $\ell_2^*$ sufficiently close to $c_2^*$ that $(w/w_3) \ll 1$ but neither converges (very well, if at all) in the range $w_3 \lesssim w \lesssim w_1 - w_3$, particularly for $w \sim w_3$.

If $(w + w_3)/(w_1 + w_3) \ll 1$, the best approximation to (8.1a) is the series

$$\frac{g_2^{**}(\ell_2^*(\zeta(w)))}{g_2^{**}(0)} = \frac{\pi^2 [(w + w_3)/(w_1 + w_3)]^{\gamma_2/\pi}}{\gamma_2 \sin \gamma_1 \ \Gamma(\gamma_0/\pi)\Gamma(\gamma_1/\pi)\Gamma(\gamma_2/\pi)} \tag{8.10}$$

$$\cdot \left[ 1 + \frac{(1 - \gamma_0/\pi)}{(1 + \pi/\gamma_2)} \frac{(w + w_3)}{(w_1 + w_3)} + \cdots \right] .$$

For the mapping $\ell_2^*(\zeta(w))$, (8.8), however, the singularities of the integrand at $x = 1$ and $x = 1 + w_3/w_1$ coalesce for $w_3 \to 0$ causing $\ell_2^*(\zeta(w))$ to vary rapidly if $w_3/w_1 \ll 1$ and $w$ is comparable with $w_3$ ($\ell_2^*$ near $c_2^*$).

For $w_3$ actually equal to zero, we saw in section 7 that one could evaluate the normalization $B$ explicitly thereby determining

$$g_2^{**}(0) = \frac{\sin \gamma_2}{c_1^* \sin \gamma_0} \cdot \qquad (8.11)$$

Equation (8.10) then simplifies to

$$g_2^*(\ell_2(\zeta(w))) = \frac{\pi^2 \sin \gamma_2 \, (w/w_1)^{\gamma_2/\pi}}{\gamma_2 c_1^* \sin \gamma_0 \sin \gamma_1 \, \Gamma(\gamma_0/\pi)\Gamma(\gamma_1/\pi)\Gamma(\gamma_2/\pi)}$$

$$(8.10)$$

$$\cdot \left[ 1 + \frac{(1 - \gamma_0/\pi)}{(1 + \pi/\gamma_2)} \left(\frac{w}{w_1}\right) + \cdots \right] \cdot$$

The evaluation of $\ell_2(\zeta(w))$ for $w/w_1 \ll 1$ from (7.11) is similar to the evaluation of (7.4) from (7.1) and gives

$$\ell_2^*(\zeta(w)) = \frac{c_1 \sin \gamma_1}{\pi} \left[ -\ln(w/w_1) - \psi(\gamma_1/\pi) + \psi(1) - (1 - \gamma_1/\pi)(w/w_1) + \cdots \right.$$

which inverts to

$$\frac{w}{w_1} \simeq \exp\left[-\psi(\gamma_1/\pi) + \psi(1)\right] \exp\left(-\frac{\pi \ell_2^*}{c_1^* \sin \gamma_1}\right)$$

$$(8.12)$$

$$\left[ 1 - (1 - \gamma_1/\pi) \exp\left[-\psi(\gamma_1/\pi) + \psi(1)\right] \exp\left(-\frac{\pi \ell_2^*}{c_1^* \sin \gamma_1}\right) + \cdots \right] \cdot$$

Thus $w/w_1$ is represented as a power series in an exponential of $\ell_2^*$, a

$$g_2^{**}(\ell_2^*) = \frac{\pi^2 \sin \gamma_2 \, \exp[-(\gamma_2/\pi)\psi(\gamma_1/\pi) + (\gamma_2/\pi)\psi(1)]\exp[-\gamma_2\ell_2^*/c_1^* \sin \gamma_1]}{\gamma_2 \, c_1^* \sin \gamma_0 \, \sin \gamma_1 \, \Gamma(\gamma_0/\pi)\Gamma(\gamma_1/\pi)\Gamma(\gamma_2/\pi)}$$

$$\cdot \left\{ 1 - \frac{(\gamma_2/\pi)[1 - (2\gamma_1/\pi) - (\gamma_1\gamma_2/\pi^2)]}{(1 + \gamma_2/\pi)} \right.$$

$$\left. \cdot \, \exp[-\psi(\gamma_1/\pi) + \psi(1)] \, \exp\left(- \frac{\pi \, \ell_2^*}{c_1^* \sin \gamma_1}\right) + \cdots \right\} \, .$$

The $g_2^{**}(\ell_2^*)$ decreases like $\exp[-\gamma_2\ell_2^*/c_1^*\sin \gamma_1]$ for large $\ell_2^*$ .

References - Chapter III

1. H. J. Jeffreys and B. S. Jeffreys, <u>Methods of Mathematical Physics</u>, Cambridge, 1956.

2. L. A. Pipes, <u>Applied Mathematics for Engineers and Physicists</u>, McGraw-Hill, 1958.

3. A. Erdílyi, <u>Higher Transcendental Functions</u>, Vol. 1, McGraw-Hill, 19

4. M. Abramowitz and L. A. Stegun, <u>Handbook of Mathematical Functions</u>, U.S. Government Printing Office, Washington, 1964.

IV. Equilibrium Queue Distributions,
Two Servers $\mu_0 = \mu_1 = \mu_2$,
Numerical Results

Introduction. Chapter III has presented a formal representation of the joint equilibrium queue distribution $g^*(\ell_1, \ell_2)$ of the $Q_1$ and $Q_2$ , or, in rescaled units, the joint distribution $g^{**}(\ell_1^*, \ell_2^*)$ of $Q_1^*, Q_2^*$ . It also gave formulas for the marginal distributions $g_1^{**}(\ell_1^*), g_2^{**}(\ell_2^*)$ of $Q_1^*$ and $Q_2^*$ , the service rate $\mu$ , and numerous expansions around singular points, saddle points, etc., i.e., most of the analytic properties. Unfortunately, it is still quite difficult to present an interpretation or tabulation of these solutions because, even after a non-dimensionalization of the problem, there is a three parameter family of such joint distributions, i.e., a three parameter family of functions $g^{**}(\ell_1^*, \ell_2^*)$ in a two-dimensional space.

Since the purpose of obtaining an analytic solution of the queue distribution is to investigate qualitative properties, the analysis would not be complete without some description of how the solutions actually behave. In particular, we would like some actual numerical evaluations of $\mu$ as a function of the storages $c_1$ and $c_2$ (and the $\Delta_j$'s).

To determine the $\mu$ one must, in general, first evaluate one or both of the marginal distributions, because $\mu$ contains the normalization constant, for which we have not found any simple formulas. As a preliminary step, however, we will analyse the distribution $g_2^{**}(\ell_2^*)$ for $c_2^* = \infty$ (or equivalently $g_1^*(\ell_1^*)$ for $c_1^* = \infty$). This is of considerable interest in itself because server 2 with $c_2^* = \infty$ sees an input process like that described in chapter II. One basic problem which has eluded previous investigators is how to evaluate the queue distribution (or even the mean queue length) for a service facility fed by another server (the output from which is not a

Poisson process).

After we have analysed the dependence of $g_2^{**}(\ell_2^*)$ on the parameters $\gamma_0$, $\gamma_1$ (i.e., the $\Delta_j$'s) for $c_2^* = \infty$ , we will add another dimension and investigate the dependence of $g_2^{**}(\ell_2^*)$ upon the $c_2^*/c_1^*$ . This will lead us into an evaluation of how the service rate $\mu$ depends upon the parameters $c_2^*/c_1^*$, $\gamma_0$, and $\gamma_1$ .

This will be followed by a few illustrations of some joint distributions $g^{**}(\ell_1^*, \ell_2^*)$ , or at least some examples of contour plots near corn[...]

2. <u>Marginal Distributions for $c_2 = \infty$</u>. For $c_2^* = \infty$, the marginal distributi[...] of $Q_1^*$ is uniform, (III 7.9), over $0 \leq Q_1^* \leq c_1^*$ . We will be concerned only with the evaluation of $g_2^{**}(\ell_2^*)$ given by (III 7.10, 7.11) and its various expansions described in section III 8.

To illustrate the accuracy of the expansions, we consider first the special case of identical servers $\gamma_0 = \gamma_1 = \gamma_2 = \pi/3$ $(\Delta_0 = \Delta_1 = \Delta_2)$. F[...] $w_3 = 0$ , $w_1$ given by (III 7.2), and $g_2^{**}(0) = 1/c_1^*$ from (III 8.11), th[...] expansion (III 8.3) for small $\ell_2^*$ becomes

$$c_1^* g_2^{**}(\ell_2^*) = 1 - \frac{4\pi^2}{3\Gamma^3(1/3)} \left(\frac{\ell_2^*}{c_1^*}\right) \left[ 1 - \frac{1}{12} \left(\frac{2\pi}{3\sqrt{3}} \frac{\ell_2^*}{c_1^*}\right)^3 + \cdots \right]$$

(2.1)

$$\simeq 1 - (0.686)(\ell_2^*/c_1^*) \left[ 1 - (1/12)(1.21 \, \ell_2^*/c_1^*)^3 + \cdots \right] .$$

This function decreases linearly in $\ell_2^*$ for small $\ell_2^*$ , but subsequent terms in the expansion contain only powers 1, 4, 7, $\cdots$ of $\ell_2^*$ . The leng[...] $\ell_2^*$ is measured in units of the storage $c_1^*$ , the only natural unit of "length." For large $\ell_2^*$, (III 8.13) becomes

$$c_1^* g_2^{**} (\ell_2^*) \simeq \frac{2\sqrt{3}\ \pi}{\Gamma^3(1/3)}\ \exp\left[-\frac{1}{3}\ \psi(1/3) + \frac{1}{3}\ \psi(1)\right]\ \exp\left[-\frac{2\pi}{3\sqrt{3}}\ \frac{\ell_2^*}{c_1^*}\right]$$

$$\cdot \left\{1 - \frac{1}{18}\ \exp\left[-\psi(1/3) + \psi(1)\right]\ \exp\left[-\frac{2\pi}{\sqrt{3}}\ \frac{\ell_2^*}{c_1^*}\right] + \cdots \right\} \qquad (2.2)$$

$$\simeq (1.333)\exp(-1.21\ \ell_2^*/c_1^*)\ [1 - (0.72)\exp(-3.63\ \ell_2^*/c_1^*) + \cdots]\ ,$$

which decreases exponentially in $\ell_2^*$ with subsequent terms which decay more rapidly.

In Fig. IV-1, the solid line represents the value of $c_1^* g_2^{**} (\ell_2^*)$ as determined from a numerical evaluation of the exact formulas (III 7.10, 7.11). The dashed line shows just the first two terms of (2.1), the linear approximation. This is nearly indistinguishable from the exact curve for $\ell_2^*/c_1^*$ ≲ 0.5. The three term approximation of (2.1), not shown in Fig. IV-1, has a comparable accuracy out to $\ell_2^*/c_1^* \simeq 0.8$.

The upper dashed curve of Fig. IV-1 represents just the first term of (2.2). It is indistinguishable from the exact curve for $\ell_2^*/c_1^* \gtrsim 1$ . The two term expression (2.2) is nearly exact for $\ell_2^*/c_1^* \gtrsim 0.5$. For $0.5 ≲ \ell_2^*/c_1^* ≲ 0.8$, (2.1) and (2.2) give virtually the same values (to within about 1%).

This queue distribution for $c_2^* = \infty$ does not depend upon the service rate $\mu_0$ or the variance coefficient $\Delta_0$; it is uniquely determined if the queue length $Q_2^*$ is measured in units of the storage $c_1^*$ (and $g_2^{**}(\ell_2^*)$ is measured in corresponding units).

152

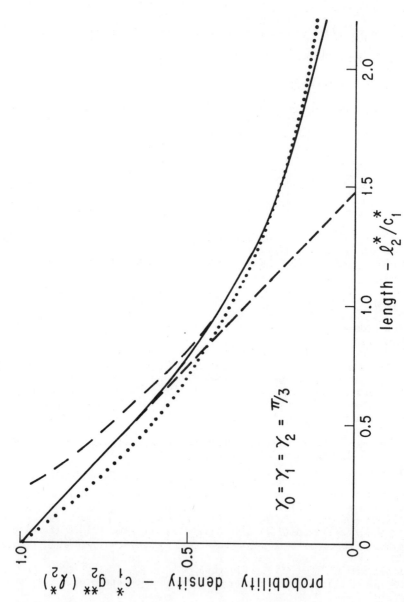

probability density — $c_1^* g_2^{**}(\ell_2^*)$

length — $\ell_2^*/c_1^*$

$\gamma_0 = \gamma_1 = \gamma_2 = \pi/3$

Fig. IV-1. Marginal queue distribution for identical servers $c_1 < \infty$, $c_2 = \infty$. The solid line is the exact distribution; the broken lines are small and large argument approximations; the dotted line is an exponential distribution.

The storage capacity $c_1$ determines the traffic intensity at server 2, namely $1 - \Delta_0/\mu_0 c_1$. It is natural that we should compare the distribution $g_2^*(\ell_2)$ with that for a single server serving a traffic stream with the same traffic intensity and the same $\Delta_0$ and $\mu_0$. In the diffusion approximation, the latter distribution is exponential, $g(\ell) = c_1^{-1}\exp(-\ell/c_1)$. This exponential distribution is also shown in Fig. IV-1 by the dotted curve.

The distribution $g_2^{**}(\ell_2^*)$ has similar qualitative shape to the exponential. It differs in that it remains nearly linear over a rather wide range of $\ell_2$. Also the tail of $g_2^{**}(\ell_2^*)$ is proportional to $\exp(-1.21\ell_2^*/c_1^*)$ instead of $\exp(-\ell_2^*/c_1^*)$. As a consequence of both of these, the mean queue $E\{Q_2^*\}$ is less than for the exponential. A numerical integration gives $E\{Q_2^*\} = 0.87\ c_1^*$, whereas the exponential distribution would give a mean of $c_1^*$. Of course, the mean of the first queue, $E\{Q_1^*\}$, is $c_1^*/2$ for the uniform distribution.

The formulas for $g_2^{**}(\ell_2^*)$ are so complicated because the function is unusually smooth. One does not ordinarily expect large and small argument expansions of a function to join so smoothly with just two or three terms in each. We shall enjoy such good fortune in many of the subsequent evaluations also.

Fig. IV-2 shows some queue distributions for several choices of the $\gamma$'s including the curve of Fig. IV-2 for $\gamma_1 = \gamma_2 = \gamma_3 = \pi/3$. For purposes of comparison, it is convenient, however, to return to the original coordinates of section III 1, $\ell_2$, $c_1$ instead of $\ell_2^*$, $c_1^*$,

$$\ell_2^*/c_1^* = (\ell_2/c_1)(\sin \gamma_2/\sin \gamma_0) \tag{2.3}$$

and to plot the probability density of $Q_2$, $g_2^*(\ell_2)$ in units of $c_1^{-1}$ rather than $g_2^{**}(\ell_2^*)$ in units of $c_1^{*-1}$,

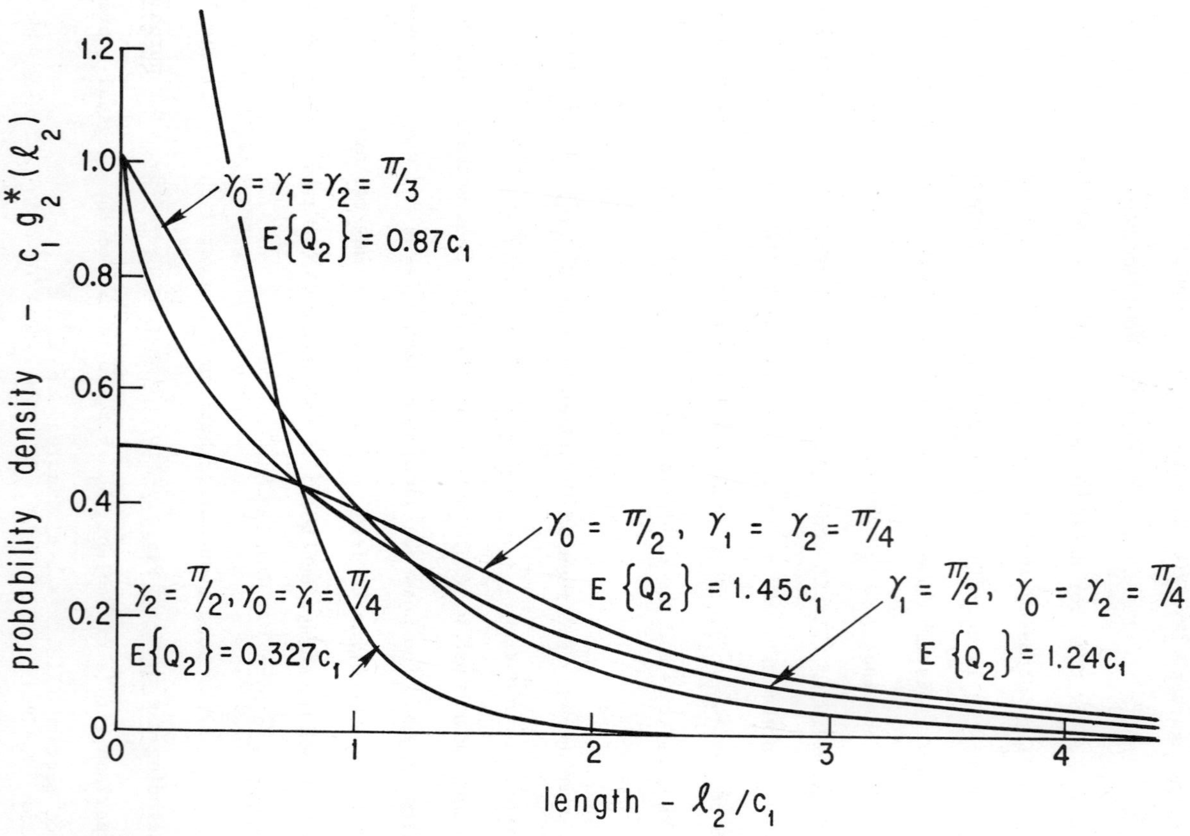
1.2
1.0
0.8
0.6
0.4
0.2
0
probability density - $c_1 g_2^*(\ell_2)$
0
1
2
3
4
length - $\ell_2/c_1$
$\gamma_0 = \gamma_1 = \gamma_2 = \pi/3$
$E\{Q_2\} = 0.87c_1$
$\gamma_0 = \pi/2,\ \gamma_1 = \gamma_2 = \pi/4$
$E\{Q_2\} = 1.45c_1$
$\gamma_2 = \pi/2, \gamma_0 = \gamma_1 = \pi/4$
$E\{Q_2\} = 0.327c_1$
$\gamma_1 = \pi/2,\ \gamma_0 = \gamma_2 = \pi/4$
$E\{Q_2\} = 1.24c_1$

Fig. IV-2. Some examples of marginal queue distributions for $c_1 < \infty$, $c_2 = \infty$, for various combinations of $\gamma_0$, $\gamma_1$, $\gamma_2$ $(\Delta_0, \Delta_1, \Delta_2)$.

$$c_1 \overset{*}{g_2}(\ell_2) = \overset{*}{c_1} \overset{**}{g_2}(\overset{*}{\ell_2})(\sin \gamma_2/\sin \gamma_0) \ . \tag{2.4}$$

Regular service for the jth server, $\Delta_j = 0$ , corresponds to $\gamma_j = \pi/2$.
Fig. IV-2 shows three cases $\gamma_0 = \pi/2$, $\gamma_1 = \gamma_2 = \pi/4$; $\gamma_1 = \pi/2$, $\gamma_0 = \gamma_2 = \pi/4$;
and $\gamma_2 = \pi/2$ , $\gamma_0 = \gamma_1 = \pi/4$ . In each case, the curves drawn from the
small and large argument expansions (III 8.3) and (III 8.13) join very
smoothly over some intermediate range of $\ell_2$ so that these formulas were
sufficiently accurate to construct the curves of $\overset{*}{g_2}(\ell_2)$ and to compute the
mean queue lengths.

For small $\ell_2$ , we see from (III 8.3) that the $\ell_2$ dependence is
dominated by the term proportional to $\ell_2^{\gamma_0/\gamma_1}$ . For $\gamma_0 = \pi/2$, $\gamma_1 = \gamma_2$
$= \pi/4$ , this term is proportional to $\ell_2^2$; for $\gamma_1 = \pi/2$, $\gamma_0 = \gamma_2 = \pi/4$ it
is proportional to $\ell_2^{1/2}$; and for $\gamma_2 = \pi/2$, $\gamma_0 = \gamma_1 = \pi/4$ it is proportional to $\ell_2$ . The $\overset{*}{g_2}(\ell_2)$ and its singularities were derived from the
joint distributions which have various singularities in the corners. There
is no obvious simple explanation why these curves should behave so differently near $\ell_2 = 0$ .

For large $\overset{*}{\ell_2}$ , the behavior of $\overset{*}{g_2}(\ell_2)$ is dominated by the exponential factor of (III 8.13) with exponent

$$- \frac{\gamma_2}{\sin \gamma_1}\left(\frac{\overset{*}{\ell_2}}{\overset{*}{c_1}}\right) = - \frac{\gamma_2 \sin \gamma_2}{\sin \gamma_0 \sin \gamma_1}\left(\frac{\ell_2}{c_1}\right) \ . \tag{2.5}$$

The factor $\gamma_2\sin \gamma_2/\sin \gamma_0 \sin \gamma_1$ has the values $\pi/4$, $\pi/4$, and $\pi$ respectively for the three cases $\gamma_0$, $\gamma_1$, and $\gamma_2$ equal to $\pi/2$. The corresponding mean queue lengths, $E\{Q_2\}$ are approximately $1.45c_1$, $1.24c_1$, and
$0.327c_1$ .

It is interesting to compare these three cases because one might ima
a hypothetical situation in which one had three servers that could be arr
in any order.  In particular, one might have a server of relatively small
variance,  $\Delta_j = 0$ ,  and two others which are nearly identical.  One coul
then ask which order is "best"; where should we place the regular server

It would appear from Fig. IV-2 that the best arrangement is to choose
$\Delta_2 = 0$   $(\gamma_2 = \pi/2)$ since this gives the smallest  $E\{Q_2\}$,  but one must al
consider the overall service rate  $\mu$ .  From (III 4.1) we see that the
service rate for  $\Delta_2 = 0$ ,  $\Delta_0 = \Delta_1$  is

$$\mu = \mu_0 - \frac{1}{2} (\Delta_0 + \Delta_1)/c_1 = \mu_0 - \Delta_0/c_1 \qquad (2.6)$$

whereas, for  $\Delta_0 = 0$  or  $\Delta_1 = 0$ ,  the service rate is  $\mu_0 - (1/2)\Delta_2/c_1$ .
Part of the reason that  $E\{Q_2\}$  is smallest for  $\Delta_2 = 0$  is that the service
rate from server 1 is smallest.  Since the overall service rate is the mos
important measure of performance,  $\Delta_2 = 0$  is actually the poorest arrangeme

The other two cases  $\Delta_0 = 0$  and  $\Delta_1 = 0$  do give the same service
rate  $\mu$ ,  but  $\Delta_1 = 0$  gives the shorter average queue length.

The probability density at zero queue length is only half as large
for  $\Delta_0 = 0$  as for  $\Delta_1 = 0$.  This is a direct consequence of (III 4.1)

$$\frac{1}{2} (\Delta_1 + \Delta_2) \, g_2^*(0) = \frac{1}{2} (\Delta_0 + \Delta_1)/c_1 \quad ; \qquad (2.7)$$

$g_2^*(0)$  must be twice as large for  $\Delta_1 = 0$  in order to give the same servi
rate at server 2.  More generally, if, for any values of the  $\Delta_j$'s, we fix
$\Delta_2$  and interchange  $\Delta_0$  and  $\Delta_1$,  $g_2^*(0)$  will be smaller if  $\Delta_1 > \Delta_0$ .
The density in Fig. IV-2 varies as  $\ell_2^2$  for  $\Delta_0 = 0$  and  $\ell_2^{1/2}$  for
$\Delta_1 = 0$  near  $\ell_2 = 0$ .  Generally, since the density varies as  $\ell_2^{\gamma_0/\gamma_1}$

near $\ell_2 = 0$ , an interchange of $\Delta_0$ and $\Delta_1$ will invert the power of $\ell_2$ (interchange $\gamma_0$ and $\gamma_1$). This suggests that it may, generally, be advantageous to have $\Delta_1 < \Delta_0$ rather than $\Delta_0 < \Delta_1$ .

For large $\ell_2$ , both $\Delta_0 = 0$ and $\Delta_1 = 0$ have the same exponential factor (2.5), but not the same amplitude. An exponential distribution with this same exponent would have a mean queue length of $(4/\pi)c_1 \simeq 1.27c_1$ only slightly larger than that for $\Delta_1 = 0$ . More generally, the exponential coefficient (2.5) is invariant to the interchange of $\Delta_0$ and $\Delta_1$ ($\gamma_0$ and $\gamma_1$), a result which is undoubtedly related to the fact that both the mean and longtime variance ($\mu$ and $\Delta$) of the output from server 1 depend upon ($\Delta_0 + \Delta_1$), see chapter II.

There are three other limiting cases that are worth examination. Although the formulas derived in chapter III do not apply for any $\gamma_j = 0$ (two of the $\Delta_k$'s equal to zero), they do apply for $\gamma_j \ll 1$. We shall now look at the behaviors of $\gamma_2 \ll 1$ , $\gamma_0 \ll 1$ , and $\gamma_1 \ll 1$ .

For $\gamma_2 \ll 1$ we must have $\Delta_0/\Delta_2$ and $\Delta_1/\Delta_2 \ll 1$ . Consequently the traffic intensity to server 2 will be very close to 1

$$1 - \mu/\mu_0 = \tfrac{1}{2} (\Delta_0 + \Delta_1)/c_1\mu_0 \qquad\qquad (2.8)$$

and the arrival process to server 2 will have a small variance. The behavior of the queue at server 2 must, therefore, be determined primarily by the fluctuations at server 2 competing against its small excess capacity. We would expect the queue at server 2 to behave essentially as for a D/G/1 system with arrival rate $\mu$ and variance rate $\Delta_2$ .

For $\gamma_2 \to 0$ , we see from figure III 2 that $\gamma_0$ and $\gamma_1$ must both go to $\pi/2$ . In (III 8.13), the second exponential term not only has a very short range compared with the first term, but the coefficient also vanishes for $\gamma_2 \to 0$ . For $\gamma_2 \ll 1$ , the exponential distribution gives a very accurate representation of $g_2^{**}(\ell_2^*)$ for all $\ell_2^*$ . One can also check th even the small argument expansion (III 8.3) behaves like an exponential.

$$g_2^{**}(\ell_2^*) \simeq \frac{\gamma_2}{c_1^* \sin \gamma_1} \exp\left[\frac{-\gamma_2 \ell_2^*}{c_1^* \sin \gamma_1}\right] \quad , \tag{2.9}$$

$$g_2^*(\ell_2) \simeq \frac{\gamma_2 \sin \gamma_2}{c_1 \sin \gamma_0 \sin \gamma_1} \exp\left[\frac{-\gamma_2 \sin \gamma_2 \ell_2}{c_1 \sin \gamma_0 \sin \gamma_1}\right] , \tag{2.9a}$$

with

$$E\{Q_2\} \simeq \frac{c_1 \sin \gamma_0 \sin \gamma_1}{\gamma_2 \sin \gamma_2} \quad . \tag{2.10}$$

The mean of $Q_2$ is still measured in units of $c_1$ but, for $\gamma_2 \to 0$ it is approximately $c_1/\gamma_2^2 \gg c_1$ with $\gamma_2^2 \simeq (\Delta_0 + \Delta_1)/\Delta_2$ . One can show that the error in (2.10) is fractionally of order $\gamma_2^4$ , consequently we can expand (2.10) in powers of $\Delta_0/\Delta_2$ and $\Delta_1/\Delta_2$ out to this order and obtain

$$E\{Q_2\} = c_1 \left[\frac{\Delta_2 + (\Delta_0 + \Delta_1)/3}{\Delta_0 + \Delta_1}\right] \left[1 + 0\left(\frac{\Delta_0 + \Delta_1}{\Delta_2}\right)^2\right] . \tag{2.10a}$$

We would have expected, for a D/G/1 system of traffic intensity (2.8) and a variance rate $\Delta_2$ , that

$$E\{Q_2\} \simeq \frac{(\Delta_2/\mu_0)}{2[1 - \mu/\mu_0]} \simeq c_1 \frac{\Delta_2}{\Delta_0 + \Delta_1} \quad ,$$

which agrees with the leading term of (2.10a). But more generally, for a G/G/1 system, we would expect the average queue to be proportional to the sum of variance rates of the server and the arrivals. In section II 5 we saw, (II 5.3c), that the longtime variance rate of the output from server 1 is $(\Delta_0 + \Delta_1)/3$. Thus (2.10a) confirms that, to the next order in $\Delta_0/\Delta_2$, $\Delta_1/\Delta_2$, the variance rate of the arrivals is simply added to the variance rate $\Delta_2$ in the formulas for $E\{Q_2\}$.

It is helpful to understand why one can simply add these two variance rates, because this argument can be generalized also to certain situations with $\mu_0 \neq \mu_1 \neq \mu_2$. In chapter II, the natural unit of time was (II 2.8), which for $\mu_1 = \mu_2$ is $2c_1^2/\pi^2(\Delta_0 + \Delta_1)$. This is the time scale over which the variance of the output can be considered to grow like $(\Delta_0 + \Delta_1)t/3$. For server 2, the natural unit of time, the time it takes the queue distribution to reach an equilibrium once it has been disturbed, is of order

$$\frac{\Delta_2}{(\mu_0 - \mu_1)^2} = \frac{4\,\Delta_0\,c_1^2}{(\Delta_0 + \Delta_1)^2} . \qquad (2.11)$$

This latter time constant is larger by a factor of about $2\pi^2\Delta_2/(\Delta_0+\Delta_1) \gg 1$.

On the time scale (2.11) and for a scale of queue lengths (2.10a), $Q_2$ does not see the detailed irregularities in the arrival process from server 1 generated by $Q_1$ hitting the boundaries 0 or $c_1$; it only sees a process that looks like a diffusion process of variance rate $\Delta$.

One cannot take seriously the values of numerical coefficients in the above estimates of time scales, but neither should one disregard the presence of the factor $2\pi^2 \sim 20$ in the above ratio of time scales. The formula (2.10) is surprisingly accurate, possibly because the time scales are quite different even if $\gamma_2$ is not very small. For example, with $\Delta_0 = \Delta_1 = \Delta_2$ ($\gamma_1 = \gamma_2 = \gamma_3 = \pi/3$), (2.10) gives $E\{Q_2\} \approx (5/6)c_1 = 0.833c_1$, whereas the correct value is $0.87c_1$; with $\Delta_0 = 0$, $\Delta_1 = \Delta_2$ ($\gamma_0 = \pi/2$, $\gamma_1 = \gamma_2$ = $\pi/4$) or $\Delta_1 = 0$, $\Delta_0 = \Delta_2$ ($\gamma_1 = \pi/2$, $\gamma_0 = \gamma_2 = \pi/4$), (2.10) gives $E\{Q_2\}$ = $(4/3)c_1 = 1.33c_1$, whereas the correct values are $1.45c_1$ and $1.24c_1$ respectively. All of these examples are, of course, well outside the ran. of "small" $\Delta_0/\Delta_2$, $\Delta_1/\Delta_2$.

For $\gamma_0 \ll 1$, we must have $\Delta_1/\Delta_0$ and $\Delta_2/\Delta_0 \ll 1$. In contrast wi the case $\gamma_2 \ll 1$ which gave large queues (because of the high traffic intensity), $\gamma_0 \ll 1$ gives very short queues. Although the output from server 1 has a longtime variance rate of $(\Delta_0 + \Delta_1)/3 \approx \Delta_0/3$, the fluct tions are "one-sided." For a regular server at 1, the interdeparture time cannot exceed $1/\mu_0$ but they can be less than $1/\mu_0$ when $Q_1$ vanishes (this is what causes the variance of the output). A regular server of service rate $\mu_0$ also at 2 can always match the maximum arrival rate from server 1. Consequently for $\Delta_1 = \Delta_2 \to 0$, $Q_2 \to 0$ with probability 1 for any $\Delta_0 > 0$.

In the diffusion approximation, we deal with probability densities by imagining that the average queue length is comparable or large compared wi 1 and customer "counts" can be treated as if they were continuous (non-integer) random variables. The formulas derived in chapter III will apply (even for $\gamma_0 \ll 1$) if the traffic intensity at server 2 is sufficiently close to 1 (because $c_1$ is large, for example) and $\Delta_1/\Delta_0$, $\Delta_2/\Delta_0$ are sufficiently large as to create (most of the time) a non-zero $Q_2$, while at the same time, we have $\Delta_1/\Delta_0$ and $\Delta_2/\Delta_0 \ll 1$. We are obviously look-ing for a queue distribution heavily concentrated at short queues but not short compared with 1; actually we want most of the probability in the range of $Q_2$ , $1 \leq Q_2 \ll c_1$ .

For $\gamma_0 \to 0$ ($\gamma_1$ and $\gamma_2 \to \pi/2$), (III 8.13) has a limit

$$c_1^* \, g_2^{**}(\ell_2^*) \to \frac{4}{\pi} \exp\left(-\frac{\pi \ell_2^*}{2c_1^*}\right) \left[ 1 + \frac{1}{3} \exp\left(-\frac{\pi \ell_2^*}{c_1^*}\right) + \cdots \right] \tag{2.12}$$

$$\text{for } \pi \ell_2^*/c_1 \gg 1.$$

This immediately suggests that the random variable $Q_2^*/c_1^*$ has a limit distribution for $\gamma_2 \to 0$ . Thus, $Q_2^*/c_1^*$ is $0(1)$ relative to $\gamma_0$ ,

$$\frac{Q_2}{c_1} = \frac{Q_2^*}{c_1^*} \frac{\sin \gamma_0}{\sin \gamma_2} \simeq \gamma_0 \frac{Q_2^*}{c_1^*} \tag{2.13}$$

is of order $\gamma_0 \simeq [(\Delta_1 + \Delta_2)/\Delta_0]^{1/2}$ , and $Q_2$ is of order $\gamma_0 c_1 \ll c_1$ (for the diffusion approximation to be meaningful we want $\gamma_0 c_1 \gtrsim 1$).

For $\pi \ell_2^*/c_1 \ll 1$, the behavior of $g_2^{**}(\ell_2^*)$ is more complicated, with $\gamma_0 \ll 1$. From (III 8.11) we see that $c_1^* g_2^{**}(0) = \sin \gamma_2 / \sin \gamma_0 \simeq \gamma_0^{-1}$ becomes infinite for $\gamma_0 \to 0$ . In order to estimate $c_1^* g_2^{**}(\ell_2^*)$ to order 1 relative to $\gamma_0$ from (III 8.3), it is necessary to retain at least two terms in the expansion of (III 8.3) in powers of $\gamma_0$ . In particular, one must expand the $\Gamma$-functions to terms linear in $\gamma_0$ using a relation

$$\frac{\Gamma(\frac{1}{2} + \frac{\gamma_1}{\pi} - \frac{1}{2}) \, \Gamma(\frac{1}{2} + \frac{\gamma_2}{\pi} - \frac{1}{2})}{\Gamma(1 - \gamma_0/\pi)} \simeq \pi(1 - \frac{2\gamma_0}{\pi} \ell n \, 2) \simeq \pi 2^{-2\gamma_0/\pi} ,$$

for $\gamma_0 + \gamma_1 + \gamma_2 = \pi$. With this, (III 8.3) can be approximated by

$$
c_1^* g_2^{**}(\ell_2^*) \simeq \frac{1}{\gamma_0} \left\{ 1 - \left[\frac{\pi\ell_2^*}{4c_1^*}\right]^{2\gamma_0/\pi} \left[ 1 - \frac{\gamma_0}{6\pi}\left(\frac{\pi\ell_2^*}{2c_1^*}\right)^2 + \cdots \right] \right\} \quad , \qquad (2.14)
$$

$$
\text{for} \quad \pi\ell_2^*/c_1^* \ll 1
$$

For sufficiently small $\ell_2^*$, $g_2^{**}(\ell_2^*)$ decreases with $\ell_2^*$ in proportion to $\ell_2^{*2\gamma_0/\pi}$, a small fractional power. The derivative of $g_2^{**}(\ell_2^*)$ becomes infinite at $\ell_2^* = 0$ like $\ell_2^{*(-1+2\gamma_0/\pi)}$, almost like $\ell_2^{*-1}$. If, however, we write

$$
\left(\frac{\pi\ell_2^*}{4c_1^*}\right)^{2\gamma_0/\pi} = \exp\left[\frac{2\gamma_0}{\pi}\ell n\left(\frac{\pi\ell_2^*}{4c_1^*}\right)\right] \quad ,
$$

we see that, for $\gamma_0 \ll 1$, and

$$
e^{-\pi/2\gamma_0} \ll \frac{\pi\ell_2^*}{4c_1^*} \ll 1 \quad , \qquad (2.15)
$$

the exponential can be expanded to give

$$
c_1^* g_2^{**}(\ell_2^*) \simeq \frac{2}{\pi}\left|\ell n\left(\frac{\pi\ell_2^*}{4c_1^*}\right)\right| + \frac{1}{6\pi}\left(\frac{\pi\ell_2^*}{2c_1^*}\right)^2 + \cdots \quad . \qquad (2.14a)
$$

Thus, for $\gamma_0 \ll 1$, $c_1^* g_2^{**}(\ell_2^*)$ has a "near" logarithmic singularity for $\ell_2^* \to 0$. As $\ell_2^*$ decreases toward zero $c_1^* g_2^*(\ell_2^*)$ increases like $|\ell n\,\ell_2^*|$ until it becomes of order $\gamma_0^{-1}$. Then the deviations from (2.14a) cause $c_1^* g_2^*(\ell_2^*)$ to approach a finite (but large) limit as $\ell_2^* \to 0$ instead of $\infty$ , in accordance with (2.14).

Significant deviations from (2.14a) occur over such a narrow range of $\ell_2^*$ , $\ell_2^*/c_1^* = 0(e^{-\pi/2\gamma_0})$ , that, for most purposes (except the evaluation of the service rate from $g_2^*(0)$), one can approximate $c_1^* g_2^{**}(\ell_2^*)$ by (2.14a) for all $\pi \ell_2^*/c_1^* \ll 1$ . Although (2.14a) becomes infinite for $\ell_2^* \to 0$ , this singularity is too weak to have much influence on properties such as $E\{Q_2\}$ .

The limit distribution of $Q_2^*/c_1^*$ for $\gamma_0 \to 0$ can be evaluated explicitly from (III 7.10, 7.11);

$$g_2^{**}(\ell_2^*(\zeta(w))) \to \frac{1}{c_1^* \pi} \int_0^{w/w_1} dx \ x^{-1/2} (1 - x)^{-1} = \frac{1}{c_1^* \pi} \ln \left[ \frac{1 + (w/w_1)^{1/2}}{1 - (w/w_1)^{1/2}} \right]$$

$$\ell_2^*(\zeta(w)) \to \frac{c_1^*}{\pi} \int_0^{1-w/w_1} dx \ x^{1/2} (1 - x)^{-1} = \frac{c_1^*}{\pi} \ln \left[ \frac{1 + (1 - w/w_1)^{1/2}}{1 - (1 - w/w_1)^{1/2}} \right] .$$

By eliminating $w/w_1$ between these two equations, one can show that $g_2^{**}$ and $\ell_2^*$ are related through the simple equation

$$\sinh \left( \frac{c_1^* \pi g_2^*}{2} \right) \sinh \left( \frac{\pi \ell_2^*}{2c_1^*} \right) = 1 . \tag{2.16}$$

One can readily check that the solution of (2.16) for $g_2^*$ as a function of $\ell_2^*$ does have expansions consistent with (2.12) and (2.14a), but (2.16) shows a symmetric relation between the variables $c_1^* \pi g_2^*/2$ and $\pi \ell_2^*/2c_1^*$ . This limit distribution is shown in Fig. IV-3 by the curve $\gamma_0 = 0$, $\gamma_1 = \gamma_2 = \pi/2$.

164

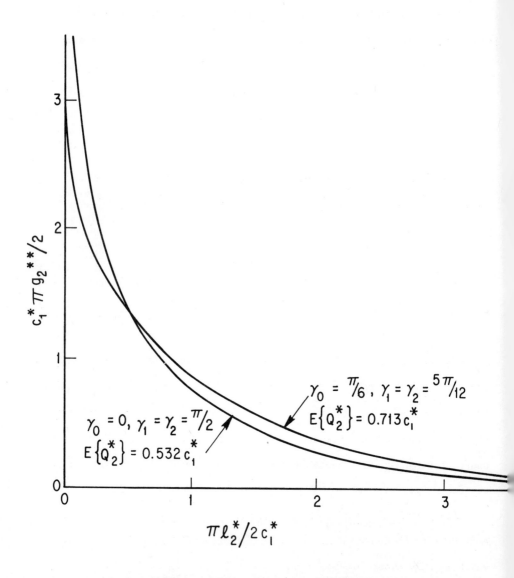

Fig. IV-3.  The limiting queue distribution for $\Delta_1 = \Delta_2 \to 0$ is shown by the curve $\gamma_0 = 0$ . A queue distribution for small $\gamma_0$ is shown by the curve for $\gamma_0 = \pi/6$ .

This limit distribution has a mean of approximately $(0.532)c_1^*$, which means that, for $\gamma_0 \ll 1$

$$E\{Q_2\} \simeq (0.532) \frac{\sin \gamma_0}{\sin \gamma_2} c_1 \simeq (0.532) \left[\frac{\Delta_1 + \Delta_2}{\Delta_0}\right]^{1/2} c_1 , \qquad (2.17)$$

for $(\Delta_1 + \Delta_2)/\Delta_0 \ll 1$ .

The limit properties described above for $\gamma_0 \to 0$ seem to bear little relation to any of the well-known queueing formulas. If one imagined that server 2 were fed by an input characterized only by the variance rate $(\Delta_0 + \Delta_1)/3 \simeq \Delta_0/3$ , and used (2.10a), one would have guessed that $E\{Q_2\} \simeq (1/3)c_1$ . Our preliminary discussion for $\gamma_0 \ll 1$ suggested that the correct result would be considerably less than this; the correct result is, in fact, of order $[(\Delta_1 + \Delta_2)/\Delta_0]^{1/2}$ smaller. On the other hand, if we imagined that server 2 were fed by an input having a variance rate equal to that of server 1, $\Delta_1$ , but an arrival rate $\mu$ , we would have guessed that $E\{Q_2\} \simeq (\Delta_1 + \Delta_2)c_1/\Delta_0$ which is too small by the same order of magnitude. Server 1 actually has an output variance rate of $\Delta_1$ while busy but an overall variance rate of $(\Delta_0 + \Delta_1)/3$ . It is not intuitively obvious why $E\{Q_2\}$ should be proportional to $(\Delta_1 + \Delta_2)^{1/2}$ .

The formula (2.10) based upon an exponential distribution with the correct rate of decay would have given $E\{Q_2\} \simeq (2/\pi)\gamma_0 c_1 \simeq (0.637) \gamma_0 c_1$ which is only about 20% too high.

To illustrate the rate of convergence to the limit distribution as $\gamma_0 \to 0$ , Fig. IV-3 also shows the queue distribution for $\gamma_0 = \pi/6$, $\gamma_1 = \gamma_2 = 5\pi/12$. This curve of $g_2^{**}(\ell_2^*)$ varies near $\ell_2^* = 0$ like $\ell_2^{*-2/5}$ , but stays quite close to the limit distribution despite the fact that $\gamma_0 = \pi/6$ is not particularly small. The angles $\gamma_j$ vary as the

166

square root of the $\Delta_k$'s as illustrated in figure III 2; the angles chang
much slower than the $\Delta_k$'s. The $\gamma_0 = \pi/6$ corresponds to $\Delta_0/\Delta_1 = \Delta_0/\Delta_2$
$\simeq 6.5$.

Finally, we consider the case $\gamma_1 \ll 1$ ($\gamma_0$ and $\gamma_2 \simeq \pi/2$), which corre
ponds to $\Delta_0/\Delta_1$ and $\Delta_2/\Delta_1 \ll 1$.

In the limit $\Delta_0 = \Delta_2 \to 0$, regular servers at both 0 and 2, all sto
astic effects are generated by server 1. If server 1 should temporarily
serve at a faster (slower) than average rate, it will cause the queue $Q_1$
to decrease (increase) but $Q_2$ to increase (decrease) by exactly the sam
amount, i.e., $Q_1 + Q_2$ remains fixed, provided servers 0 and 2 are kept
busy. If $Q_1 + Q_2 > c_1$ (with $0 \leq Q_1 \leq c_1$), then $Q_2 > 0$ and server 2
must remain busy. Server 0 may be blocked part of the time when $Q_1 = c_1$
however. As long as $Q_1 + Q_2$ remains greater than $c_1$, it can decreas
but cannot increase. Such a state is transient; once the system has lef
it, there is no way to return. Consequently, for the equilibrium distrib
tion, $Q_1 + Q_2 \leq c_1$, with probability 1, and, in particular $Q_2 \leq c_1$
with probability 1.

On the other hand, if $Q_1 + Q_2 < c_1$, then $Q_1 < c_1$ and, therefore,
server 0 must remain busy. Server 2 may at times be interrupted when
$Q_2 = 0$. As long as $Q_1 + Q_2$ remains less than $c_1$, it can only increase
The states $Q_1 + Q_2 < c_1$ are therefore also transient. We conclude that
the equilibrium joint distribution of $Q_1$, $Q_2$ must be concentrated on the
line $Q_1 + Q_2 = c_1$, for $\gamma_1 \to 0$.

Since $Q_1$ is known to have a uniform marginal distribution over
$(0, c_1)$ for $c_2 = \infty$, it follows that the joint distribution of $Q_1$, $Q_2$
must be uniform over the line $\ell_1 + \ell_2 = c_1$ of figure III 1a. The margin
distribution of $Q_2$ is, therefore, also uniform over the interval $(0, c_1)$.

This behavior for $\gamma_1 \to 0$ must emerge from the limit behavior of the joint distribution $g^*(\ell_1, \ell_2)$ as described in chapter III, but this is not immediately apparent from the rather complex formal solution as presented in chapter III.

Although the above arguments were made under the hypothesis that $c_2 = \infty$ (and $\gamma_1 = 0$), it is clear that, if $Q_1$ never exceeds the value $c_1$, one does not need more than $c_1$ of the storage $c_2$. The equilibrium queue distributions must be independent of $c_2$ for any $c_2 > c_1$. If storage costs money, there is no reason to provide any more storage at 2 than $c_1$. By virtue of the symmetry between holes and customers, as described in section III 5, the queue distributions for $\gamma_1 \to 0$, generally, depend only upon $\min(c_1, c_2)$.

For $0 < \gamma_1 \ll 1$, we expect that the distribution $g_2^*(\ell_2)$ will be close to the uniform distribution for $\gamma_1 = 0$. Since, for $\gamma_2$, $\gamma_0 \simeq \pi/2$, $\ell_2^*/c_1^* \simeq \ell_2/c_1$; the distribution $c_1^* g_2^{**}(\ell_2^*)$ should also be nearly uniform on $(0, c_1^*)$.

From (III 8.3) we obtain, for $\gamma_1 \ll 1$,

$$c_1^* g_2^{**}(\ell_2^*) \simeq 1 - \frac{2}{\pi}\left(\frac{\ell_2^*}{c_1^*}\right)^{\pi/2\gamma_1}\left[1 - \frac{1}{3}\left(\frac{\ell_2^*}{c_1^*}\right)^{\pi/\gamma_1} + \cdots\right]$$

which does show that $c_1^* g_2^{**}(\ell_2^*)$ is close to 1 for $\ell_2^*/c_1^* < 1$. If we write

$$\left(\frac{\ell_2^*}{c_1^*}\right)^{\pi/2\gamma_1} = \left[1 - \left(1 - \frac{\ell_2^*}{c_1^*}\right)\right]^{\pi/2\gamma_1} \simeq \exp\left[-\frac{\pi}{2\gamma_1}\left(1 - \frac{\ell_2^*}{c_1^*}\right)\right],$$

this also shows that the probability density decays rapidly when $\ell_2^*/c_1^* = 1 - 0(\gamma_1)$. Equation (III 8.13), in turn, shows that $c_2^* g_2^{**}(\ell_2^*)$ is nearly 0 for $\ell_2^*/c_1^* > 1$ with a similar "transition range" $|1 - \ell_2^*/c_1^*|$ $= 0(\gamma_1)$ . Neither of these equations, however, is particularly well sui⌐ for showing the shape of $c_1^* g_2^{**}(\ell_2^*)$ through the transition. This can be evaluated more easily from (III 7.10, 7.11).

For $\gamma_0, \gamma_2 \to \pi/2$ , (III 7.10) gives

$$c_1^* g_2^{**}(\ell_2^*(\zeta(w))) \to \frac{1}{\pi} \int_0^{w/w_1} dx \; x^{-1/2} \; (1 - x)^{-1/2} \; = \; \frac{2}{\pi} \sin^{-1}(w/w_1)^{1/2} \; , \qquad (2.1$$

a well-behaved function of the parameter $w/w_1$ . The singular behavior c $c_1^* g_2^{**}(\ell_2^*)$ for $\gamma_1 \to 0$ arises entirely from the limit behavior of (III 7.1

$$\ell_2^*(\zeta(w)) \;\simeq\; \frac{c_1^* \gamma_1}{\pi} \int_0^{1-w/w_1} dz \; z^{-1+\gamma_1/\pi} \; (1 - z)^{-1}$$

$$= \; \frac{c_1^* \gamma_1}{\pi} \int_0^{1-w/w_1} dz \left[ z^{-1+\gamma_1/\pi} \; + \; (1 - z)^{-1} \; - \; \frac{(1 - z^{\gamma_1/\pi})}{(1 - z)} \right] \; .$$

For $\gamma_1/\pi \ll 1$ in the last term

$$1 - z^{\gamma_1/\pi} \;=\; 1 - \exp[(\gamma_1/\pi)\ln z] \;\simeq\; -(\gamma_1/\pi)\ln z \; .$$

This integral is finite and contributes a quantity of order $\gamma_1^2$ . The mai⌐ contribution comes from the first two terms,

$$\ell_2^*(\zeta(w)) \;\simeq\; c_1^* [(1 - w/w_1)^{\gamma_1/\pi} \; - \; (\gamma_1/\pi)\ln(w/w_1) + 0(\gamma_1^2)]$$

$$\simeq\; c_1^* \left[ 1 + (\gamma_1/\pi)\ln\left(\frac{w_1}{w} - 1\right) \; + \; 0(\gamma_1^2) \right] \; ,$$

from which we deduce that

$$\frac{w_1}{w} - 1 \;\simeq\; \exp[-(1 - \ell_2^*/c_1^*)\pi/\gamma_1] \; .$$

Substitution of this into (2.18) leads to the approximation

$$c_1^* g_2^{**} (\ell_2^*) \;\simeq\; \frac{2}{\pi} \, \tan^{-1} \left\{ \exp\left[ \left( 1 - \frac{\ell_2^*}{c_1^*} \right) \frac{\pi}{2\gamma_1} \right] \right\} . \qquad (2.19)$$

For $\gamma_1 \ll 1$ , (2.19) describes the probability density near the "cut-off" of the approximately rectangular distribution by measuring $\ell_2^*/c_1^*$ relative to $\ell_2^*/c_1^* = 1$ and in "units" of $2\gamma_1/\pi$ . For $\ell_2^*/c_1^* < 1$ , the exponential in (2.19) becomes very large, the inverse tangent goes to $\pi/2$ and $c_1^* g_2^{**} (\ell_2^*)$ goes to 1. For $\ell_2^*/c_1^* > 1$ , the exponential becomes very small and $c_1^* g_2^{**} (\ell_2^*)$ goes to 0. The shape of $c_1^* g_2^{**} (\ell_2^*)$ is symmetric with respect to reflections through the point $\ell_2^*/c_1^* = 1$, $c_1^* g_2^{**} (\ell_2^*) = \frac{1}{2}$ . The curve labeled "limit distribution" in Fig. IV-4 is the function (2.19) drawn relative to the coordinates $(\ell_2^*/c_1^* - 1)\pi/2\gamma_1$ . This is a "magnified view" of the curve $c_1^* g_2^{**} (\ell_2^*)$ at the cut-off.

To illustrate the convergence of $c_1^* g_2^{**} (\ell_2^*)$ to (2.19) for $\gamma_1 \to 0$ , Fig. IV-4 also shows the correct distribution $c_1^* g_2^{**} (\ell_2^*)$ for $\gamma_1 = \pi/6$ , $\gamma_0 = \gamma_2 = 5\pi/12$ (the companion distribution to that shown in Fig. IV-3 with servers 0 and 1 interchanged). For $\gamma_1 = \pi/6$ , $1 - c_1^* g_2^* (\ell_2^*)$ behaves near $\ell_2^* = 0$ like $\ell_2^{*5/2}$ . Despite the fact that $\gamma_1$ is not small enough to make this power very large, the distribution for $\gamma_1 = \pi/6$ already has a shape very similar to the limit distribution for $\gamma_1 \to 0$ .

The few illustrations described above demonstrate most of the qualitative features of $g_2^*(\ell_2)$ . First, in all the numerical evaluations of Figs. IV-1-4, except the limit distributions, the graphs could be drawn accurately from (III 8.3) and (III 8.13). In every case, the large and small argument expansions joined very smoothly such as illustrated in Fig. IV-1.

170

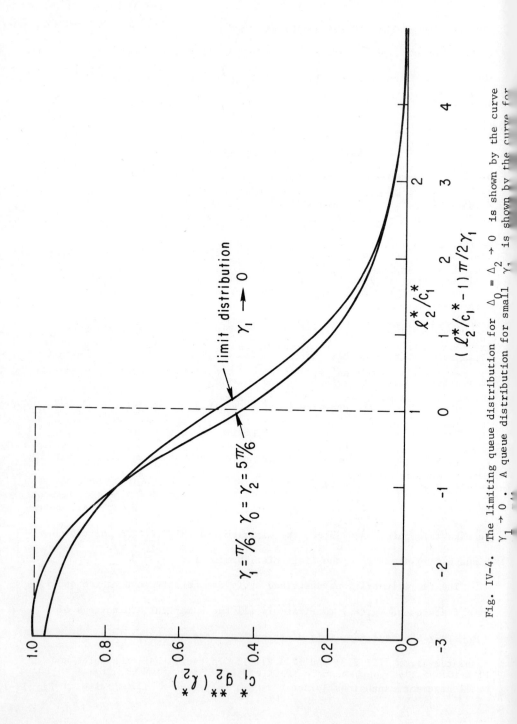

Fig. IV-4. The limiting queue distribution for $\Delta_0 = \Delta_2 \to 0$ is shown by the curve $\gamma_1 \to 0$. A queue distribution for small $\gamma_1$ is shown by the curve for

The same should be true for any other values of the $\gamma$'s. Although we have a rather complex two parameter family of distributions, the shapes are quite obvious from inspection of (III 8.3) and (III 8.13). The curves for $c_1^* g_2^{**} (\ell_2^*)$ decrease from the value 1 at $\ell_2^* = 0$ like $\ell_2^{*\gamma_0/\gamma_1}$ but then decay exponentially.

Relation between $c_1^*$, $c_2^*$ and $w_1$, $w_3$ . Most of the formulas of chapter III describing the properties of the marginal and joint distributions were expressed in terms of the parameters $w_1$ and $w_3$ of the conformal mapping, section III 3, rather than the original storage capacities $c_1$, $c_2$ , or the rescaled storages $c_1^*$, $c_2^*$ .

The relation between the $c_1^*$, $c_2^*$ and the $w_1$, $w_3$ was given by (III 3.5, 3.6). Although these are rather cumbersome formulas, they contain only one extra parameter $\gamma_1$ . It is possible, therefore, to construct some graphs for various values of $\gamma_1$ from which one can evaluate numerical values of the $w_1$, $w_3$ from $c_1$, $c_2$ or $c_1^*$, $c_2^*$ .

The integrals (III 3.5a,b) are of the form which defines the hypergeometric function. For numerical evaluation, however, it is more convenient to express them in the form

$$c_1^* = (w_1 + w_3)^{-1+\gamma_1/\pi} \int_0^1 dx\; x^{-1+\gamma_1/\pi} (1-x)^{-\gamma_1/\pi} \left(1 - \frac{x\, w_3}{w_1 + w_3}\right)^{-1+\gamma_1/\pi} , \qquad (3.1a)$$

$$c_2^* = (w_1 + w_3)^{-1+\gamma_1/\pi} \int_0^1 dx\; x^{-1+\gamma_1/\pi} (1-x)^{-\gamma_1/\pi} \left(1 - \frac{x\, w_1}{w_1 + w_3}\right)^{-1+\gamma_1/\pi} . \qquad (3.1b)$$

In terms of the hypergeometric function (ref III 3, page 59), these are

$$c_1^* = \frac{\pi (w_1 + w_3)^{-1+\gamma_1/\pi}}{\sin \gamma_1} \; F(1 - \gamma_1/\pi, \; \gamma_1/\pi; \; 1; \; \frac{w_3}{w_1 + w_3}) \quad , \tag{3.2a}$$

$$c_2^* = \frac{\pi (w_1 + w_3)^{-1+\gamma_1/\pi}}{\sin \gamma_1} \; F(1 - \gamma_1/\pi, \; \gamma_1/\pi; \; 1; \; \frac{w_1}{w_1 + w_3}) \; . \tag{3.2b}$$

$$\frac{c_1^*}{c_2^*} = \frac{F(1 - \gamma_1/\pi, \; \gamma_1/\pi; \; 1; \; w_3/(w_1 + w_3))}{F(1 - \gamma_1/\pi, \; \gamma_1/\pi; \; 1; \; 1 - w_3/(w_1 + w_3))} \; . \tag{3.2c}$$

If we had graphs of $F(1 - \gamma_1/\pi, \; \gamma_1/\pi; \; 1; \; z)$ as a function of $z$ for $0 < z < 1$ and all values of $\gamma_1/\pi$, $0 < \gamma_1/\pi \le 1/2$, the evaluation of $c_1^*, c_2^*$ would reduce to simple algebra. We can, in fact, not only constr these graphs, but also obtain various limit values, expansions, etc.

The function $F(1 - \gamma_1/\pi, \gamma_1/\pi; \; 1; \; z)$ has the value 1 at $z = 0$ and is infinite for $z = 1$. Therefore

$$c_1^* = \frac{\pi w_1^{-1+\gamma_1/\pi}}{\sin \gamma_1} \quad , \qquad c_2^* = \infty \qquad \text{for} \; w_3 = 0 \tag{3.3}$$

a result which we have already derived in (III 7.2) and used in section 2. For $w_3 = w_1$, the integrals in (III 3.5, 3.6) can be expressed as (compl Beta functions giving

$$c_1^* = c_2^* = w_1^{-1+\gamma_1/\pi} \; \frac{\Gamma\left(\dfrac{1 - \gamma_1/\pi}{2}\right) \Gamma(\gamma_1/\pi)}{2 \; \Gamma\left(\dfrac{1 + \gamma_1/\pi}{2}\right)} \qquad \text{for} \; w_3 = w_1 \; . \tag{3.4}$$

For small values of $z$, the hypergeometric function is most easily
evaluated from the power series

$$F(1 - \gamma_1/\pi, \gamma_1/\pi; 1; z) = \sum_{n=0}^{\infty} (1 - \gamma_1/\pi)_n \, (\gamma_1/\pi)_n \, z^n/(n!)^2 \qquad (3.5)$$

$$(a)_n \equiv a(a + 1), \cdots, (a + n - 1)$$

$$F(1 - \gamma_1/\pi, \gamma_1/\pi; 1; z) = 1 + \frac{\gamma_1}{\pi} \left\{ (1 - \gamma_1/\pi)z + \left[1 - \left(\frac{\gamma_1}{\pi}\right)^2\right]\left[1 - \left(\frac{\gamma_1}{2\pi}\right)\right]\frac{z^2}{2} \right.$$

$$\left. + \left[1 - \left(\frac{\gamma_1}{\pi}\right)^2\right]\left[1 - \left(\frac{\gamma_1}{2\pi}\right)^2\right]\left[1 - \left(\frac{\gamma_1}{3\pi}\right)\right]\frac{z^3}{3} + \cdots \right\}. \qquad (3.5a)$$

This actually converges for $0 \leq z < 1$ but, for $z$ close to $1/2$, it is
more convenient to exploit the quadratic transformation (ref. III 3, page 65)

$$F(1 - \frac{\gamma_1}{\pi}, \gamma_1/\pi, 1; z) = \frac{\Gamma(\frac{1}{2})F(\frac{1}{2} - \frac{\gamma_1}{2\pi}, \gamma_1/2\pi; 1/2; (2z - 1)^2)}{\Gamma(1 - \gamma_1/2\pi)\Gamma(1/2 + \gamma_1/2\pi)} \qquad (3.6)$$

$$+ \frac{2(2z - 1)\Gamma(\frac{1}{2})F(1 - \frac{\gamma_1}{2\pi}, \frac{1}{2} + \frac{\gamma_1}{2\pi}; \frac{3}{2}; (2z - 1)^2)}{\Gamma(\frac{1}{2} - \gamma_1/2\pi)\Gamma(\gamma_1/2\pi)}$$

$$= \frac{\Gamma(\frac{1}{2})}{\Gamma(1 - \gamma_1/2\pi)\Gamma(\frac{1}{2} + \gamma_1/2\pi)}\left[1 + 2(1 - \frac{\gamma_1}{\pi})(\frac{\gamma_1}{\pi})(z - \frac{1}{2})^2 + \cdots\right] \qquad (3.6a)$$

$$+ \frac{4(z - 1/2)\Gamma(1/2)}{\Gamma(\frac{1}{2} - \frac{\gamma_1}{2\pi})\Gamma(\gamma_1/2\pi)}\left[1 + \frac{4(1 - \frac{\gamma_1}{2\pi})(1 + \frac{\gamma_1}{\pi})}{3}(z - \frac{1}{2})^2 + \cdots\right].$$

For $z$ close to 1, the hypergeometric function can be evaluated from the

174

expansion (ref. III 3, page 74)

$$F(1 - \gamma_1/\pi, \gamma_1/\pi; 1; z) = \frac{\sin \gamma_1}{\pi} \cdot \sum_{n=0}^{\infty} \frac{(1 - \gamma_1/\pi)_n (\gamma_1/\pi)_n}{(n!)^2}$$

(3.7)

$$\cdot \left[ 2\psi(n + 1) - \psi(1 + n - \gamma_1/\pi) - \psi(n + \gamma_1/\pi) - \ln(1 - z) \right] (1 - z)^n .$$

Curves of $F(1 - \gamma_1/\pi, \gamma_1/\pi; 1; z)$ vs $z$ can be drawn very easily for any $\gamma_1$ if one uses only two or three terms of the expansion (3.5) fⲟ $0 < z < 1/4$, (3.6) for $1/4 \lesssim z \lesssim 3/4$, and (3.7) for $3/4 \lesssim z < 1$. Some examples are illustrated in Fig. IV-5 From this one can then draw curves of $c_2^*/c_1^*$, (3.2c), as a function of $w_3/(w_1 + w_3)$, as shown in Fig. IV-6. Fig.IV-6 is drawn only for $0 \leq w_3/(w_1 + w_3) \leq 1/2$, because aꞥ interchange of $w_1$ and $w_3$ maps $w_3/(w_1 + w_3)$ into $w_1/(w_1 + w_3) = 1 - w_3/(w_1 + w_3)$ and $c_2^*/c_1^*$ into $c_1^*/c_2^*$. This same graph will therefore describe $c_1^*/c_2^*$ as a function of $w_1/(w_1 + w_3)$ for $1/2 < w_3/(w_1 + w_3) < 1$.

Each curve of Fig. IV-5 monotone increasing in $x$ and has a logarithmic singularity at $x = 1$. For each $x$, the curves are monotone increasing with $\gamma_1$ and approach the constant $F = 1$ for $\gamma_1 \to 0$ (except for $x = 1$). In Fig. IV-6 $c_2^*/c_1^*$ has a logarithmic singularity at $w_3 = 0$ and decreases to 1 as $w_3/(w_1 + w_3) \to 1/2$. These curves are also monotone in $\gamma_1$.

For given values of $c_1^*$, $c_2^*$, and $c_2^*/c_1^*$, one will first use Fig. IV- or equations (3.2c), (3.5, 6 or 7) to determine $w_3/(w_1 + w_3)$. The corres₋ ponding values of the $F$ can then be found from Fig. IV-5 and used in (3.2₋ or (3.2b) to determine $(w_1 + w_3)$, and, therefore, also $w_3$ and $w_1$.

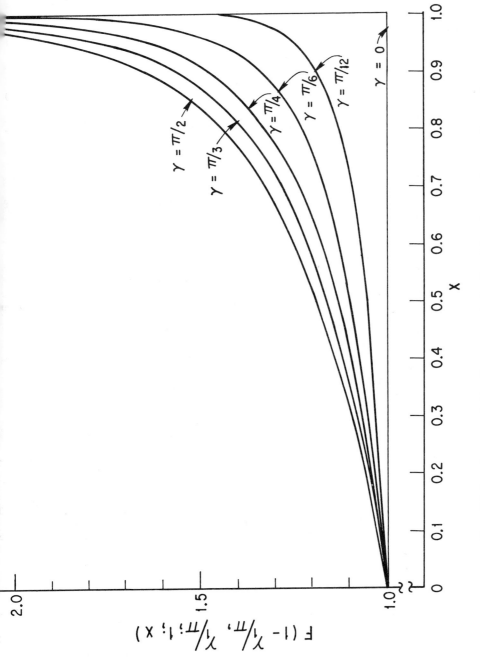

Fig. IV-5. Curves of the Hypergeometric function for various values of $\gamma_1$.

176

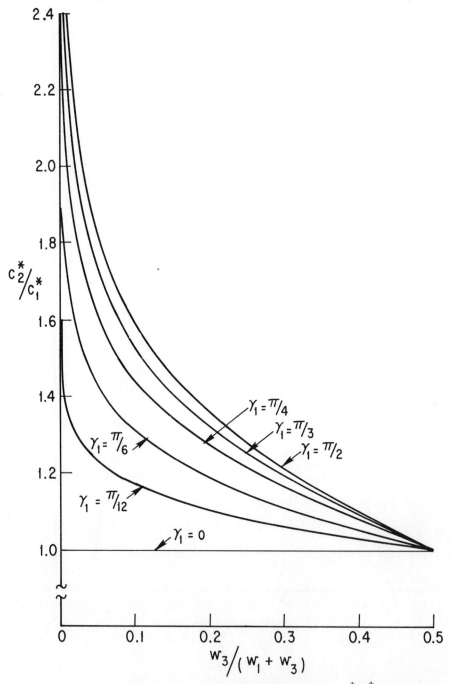

Fig. IV-6. Relation between the storage ratios $c_2^*/c_1^*$ and the parameter $w_3/(w_1 + w_3)$, for various values of $\gamma_1$.

The extreme case $\gamma_1 = \pi/2$ is somewhat easier, because all formulas can be expressed in terms of complete elliptic integrals and related functions, all of which are well tabulated. In particular, for $\gamma_1 = \pi/2$

$$c_1^* = (w_1 + w_3)^{-1/2} \int_0^1 dx \; x^{-1/2}(1 - x)^{-1/2}\left(1 - \frac{x\,w_3}{w_1 + w_3}\right) = (w_1 + w_3)^{-\frac{1}{2}} 2K\left(\frac{w_3}{w_1 + w_3}\right)$$
(3.8)

$$c_2^* = (w_1 + w_3)^{-1/2} 2K\left(\frac{w_1}{w_1 + w_3}\right) = (w_1 + w_3)^{-1/2} 2K'\left(\frac{w_3}{w_1 + w_3}\right)$$

in which $K$ and $K'$ are complete elliptic integrals of the first kind (ref III 4, page 590)

$$c_1^*/c_2^* = \frac{K(w_3/(w_1 + w_3))}{K'(w_3/(w_1 + w_3))} = -\frac{1}{\pi} \ln q\left(\frac{w_1}{w_1 + w_3}\right)$$
(3.9)

in which $q$ is the Nome.

For $\gamma_1 = \pi/2$ one will determine $w_1/(w_1 + w_3)$ from (3.9) and tables of $q$, then evaluate $(w_1 + w_3)$ from (3.8) and tables of $K$.

For numerical evaluations, it is worthy of note that, from the inverse relations implied by Fig. IV-6, the value of $w_3/(w_1 + w_3)$ is quite sensitive to the value of $c_2^*/c_1^*$. An increase in $c_2^*/c_1^*$ from 1.0 to 1.2 causes $w_3/(w_1 + w_3)$ to drop from 0.5 to about 0.2 or 0.3 for $\gamma_1$ in the range of $\pi/6$ to $\pi/2$.

For $w_3/(w_1 + w_3)$ close to 0, one can approximate the curves fairly well by

$$\frac{c_2^*}{c_1^*} \simeq \frac{\sin \gamma_1}{\pi}\left[2\psi(1) - \psi(1 - \frac{\gamma_1}{\pi}) - \psi(\frac{\gamma_1}{\pi}) - \ln(w_3/(w_1 + w_3))\right]$$
(3.10)

obtained from just the first terms of (3.5) and (3.7) . Inversion of this gives

$$\frac{w_3}{w_1 + w_3} \simeq \exp\left[-\left(\frac{\pi}{\sin \gamma_1}\right)\frac{c_2^*}{c_1^*}\right] \exp[2\psi(1) - \psi(1 - \gamma_1/\pi) - \psi(\gamma_1/\pi)] . \quad (3$$

The sensitivity of $w_3/(w_1 + w_3)$ to $c_2^*/c_1^*$ is reflected here in the sizeable exponential coefficient $\pi/\sin \gamma_1 > 3$ .

For $w_3/(w_1 + w_3)$ close to $1/2$, one can use the first two terms of (3.6a) to give the linear approximation

$$\frac{c_2^*}{c_1^*} - 1 \simeq \left[\frac{4}{\pi^2} \sin \gamma_1 \ \Gamma^2 \ (1 - \frac{\gamma_1}{2\pi})\Gamma^2(\frac{1}{2} + \frac{\gamma_1}{2\pi})\right]\left[\frac{1}{2} - \left(\frac{w_3}{w_1 + w_3}\right)\right] + \cdots . \quad (3$$

4. <u>Marginal Distributions $c_1^*, c_2^* < \infty$.</u> A finite value of $c_2^*$ will not only the distribution of $Q_2$, $g_2^*(\ell_2)$, to deviate from that described in secti but it will also cause $g_1^*(\ell_1)$ to deviate from the uniform distribution associated with $c_2^* = \infty$ . The finite storage $c_2^*$ causes server 1 to be blocked occasionally when $Q_2^* = c_2^*$, which, in turn, causes $Q_1^*$ to incre equivalently it increases $g_1^*(\ell_1)$ for larger values of $\ell_1$ .

In analysing the behavior of both $g_1^*(\ell_1)$ and $g_2^*(\ell_2)$, we have the option of exploiting the symmetry between holes and customers to restrict the discussion to $c_2^*/c_1^* > 1$ , as we have been doing, or we could consid the complete range of $c_2^*/c_1^*$ from 0 to $\infty$ , but confine the discussio to the properties of $g_2^*(\ell_2)$ only; $g_1^*(\ell_1)$ for $c_2^*/c_1^* > 1$ can be relat to an appropriate $g_2^*(\ell_2)$ for $c_2^*/c_1^* < 1$ . Formally, it is perhaps easi to use the latter, but in applications one would wish to look at both $g_1^*$ and $g_2^*$ simultaneously for the same system. Furthermore, it will be advantageous to exploit again the fact that the normalization $B$ in (III 4.8) is the same as the $B$ in (III 4.8a), a fact which is not easily deduced directly; by evaluation of $B$ from (III 4.8) and (III 4.9), and comparing it with the value deduced from (III 4.8a) and (III 4.9a). For $c_2^* = \infty$ we previously exploited this in (III 7.9) to evaluate $B$ from (III 4.8) and use it in (III 4.8a).

Various expansions of $g_1^*(\ell_1)$ and $g_2^*(\ell_2)$ have already been described in section III 8. To see how these behave, we can follow the evolution of these distributions as $c_2^*$ decreases from $c_2^* = \infty$ .

The most obvious consequence of $c_2^* < \infty$ is that the distribution of $Q_2^*$ must be cut off at $\ell_2^* = c_2^*$ . If one chooses a $c_2^*$ sufficiently large, however, that $\ell_2^* = c_2^*$ is already well into the tail of the distribution $g_2^{**}(\ell_2^* | c_2^* = \infty)$, as evaluated in section 2, then the consequences of having $c_2^*$ finite should be quite "small." It should be unnecessary to provide a storage in excess of what one typically would use if one had an infinite storage; and one would not expect the distribution $g_2^{**}(\ell_2^*)$ to be affected very much by a finite $c_2^*$ except for $\ell_2^*$ close to (or in excess of) $c_2^*$ .

These intuitively obvious properties are confirmed by the equations. In (III 8.1a) or (III 8.10), we see that the distribution $g_2^{**}(\ell_2^*)/g_2^{**}(0)$ , considered as a function of $w$ , actually is a function of $(w+w_3)/(w_1+w_3)$. The effect of making $w_3 > 0$ $(c_2^* < \infty)$ involves nothing more than a slight translation (by $w_3$) and rescaling (by $1 + w_3/w_1$) of the w-coordinate, and a possible rescaling of $g^{**}$ by a new $g^{**}(0)$. The $\ell_2^*$ in (III 8.2) is, for any $w$ , also a continuous function of $w_3$ at $w_3 = 0$, except for $w = - w_3$. For $w = w_3$ and $w_3 \to 0$ , $\ell_2^*$ becomes infinite.

Fig. IV-7 illustrates the way in which $g_2^{**}(\ell_2^*)$ varies with $c_2^*$ in special case $\gamma_0 = \gamma_2 = \pi/4$ , $\gamma_1 = \pi/2$ . This particular choice of the $\gamma_j$'s was selected because it is somewhat easier to calculate than the ot choices. The graph was evaluated directly from the parametric form (III 8.2).

From (III 8.2), (III 8.1), and (3.8), one can show that (for this cl of the $\gamma$'s)

$$\frac{\ell_2^* (\zeta(w))}{c_1^*} = \frac{F(\cos^{-1}(w/w_1)^{1/2}, w_1/(w_1 + w_3))}{K (w_3/(w_1 + w_3))} \quad , \tag{4.1}$$

and

$$\frac{g_2^{**}(\ell_2^*)}{g_2^{**}(0)} = \frac{1}{B_1(1/4, 1/4)} \; B_{\frac{w+w_3}{w_1+w_3}} (1/4, 1/4) \quad , \tag{4.2}$$

in which $F(\cdot,\cdot)$ is the incomplete elliptic integral of the first kind, $K(\cdot)$ is the complete elliptic integral, $B_z(\cdot,\cdot)$ is an incomplete Beta-function, and $B_1(\cdot,\cdot)$ is the complete Beta-function. The elliptic inte grals are well tabulated, so that one can easily evaluate (4.1) as a func tion of $w$ for any choice of $w_1/w_3$. In (4.2), one need only draw one graph of $B_z(1/4, 1/4)$ as a function of $z$ to determine $g_2^{**}(\ell_2^*)/g_2^*(0)$ as a function of $w/w_3$ for any choice of $w_1/w_3$ . Thus (4.1) and (4.2) can be used to evaluate the graphs in parametric form (parameter $w$) for series of values of $w_3/w_1$ .

The curve $c_2^* = \infty$ is equivalent to the curve of Fig. IV-2 for $\gamma_0 = $ $= \pi/4, \gamma_1 = \pi/2$ . The values of $c_2^*$ for the other curves of Fig. IV-7 ca be identified by the cut-off. Thus the curve for $c_2^*/c_1^* \simeq 2.43$ terminates

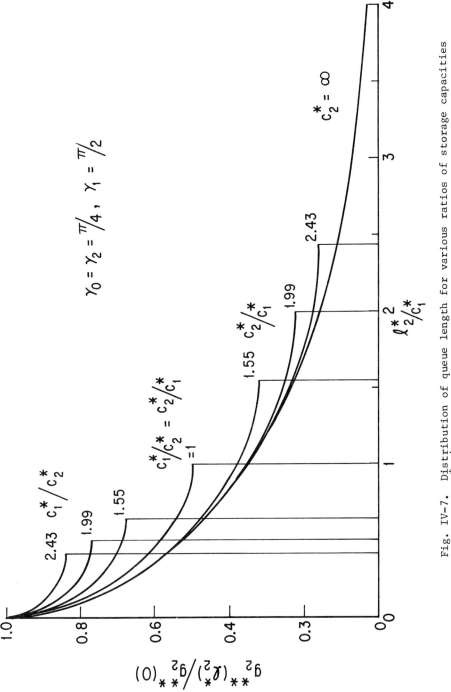

Fig. IV-7. Distribution of queue length for various ratios of storage capacities $c_1^*/c_2^*$, for $\gamma_0 = \gamma_2$.

at $\ell_2^*/c_1^* = c_2^*/c_1^* \simeq 2.43$. These curves were drawn for conveniently sele

choices of $w_3/(w_1 + w_3)$ or actually $\sin^{-1}((w_3/w_1 + w_3)^{1/2})$, rather th

$c_2^*/c_1^*$, to simplify the evaluation of the $F(\cdot,\cdot)$ from tables. The c

= 2.43 corresponds to a quite small value of $w_3$, $w_3/(w_1 + w_3) \simeq 0.007$

The curve $c_2^*/c_1^* \simeq 2.43$ follows that for $c_2^* = \infty$ very closely unt:

$\ell_2^*/c_1^* \simeq 2$; it then flattens, in order to achieve a horizontal slope as

$\ell_2^* \to c_2^*$, as required by (III 8.6). For comparisons we have drawn

$g_2^{**}(\ell_2^*)/g_2^{**}(0)$ rather than the properly normalized $g_2^{**}(\ell_2^*)$. To obtai

$g_2^{**}(\ell_2^*)$ one must divide by the area under the curve. In comparing the a

for $c_2^* = \infty$ and $c_2^*/c_1^* \simeq 2.43$, one can see that the difference in areas

out to $\ell_2^* = c_2^*$ is quite small compared with the area under the curve fc

$c_2^* = \infty$ beyond $\ell_2^* = c_2^*$. Thus one can obtain a good approximation to

$g_2^{**}(\ell_2^*)$ for $c_2^* < \infty$ by cutting off the tail of the distribution for $c_2^*$

at $\ell_2^* = c_2^*$ and renormalizing (provided the cut-off is well out in the

tail of the distribution for $c_2^* = \infty$).

As $c_2^*/c_1^*$ continues to decrease toward 1, the shape of the distribu

tion remains approximately the same, but the magnitude of the deviation,

for $\ell_2^* < c_2^*$, of the distribution from that for $c_2^* = \infty$ increases, and

of course, the distribution is cut-off at smaller values of $\ell_2^*$. This

pattern persists even for $c_2^*/c_1^* < 1$, but, for $c_2^*/c_1^* < 1$, the distr

tion deviates considerably from the curve for $c_2^* = \infty$, even for small

values of $\ell_2^*/c_1^*$. For $c_2 \to 0$, i.e., $c_1^*/c_2^* \to \infty$, the distribution

becomes nearly uniform over $0 < \ell_2^* < c_2^*$.

Fig. IV-7 can also be used to describe the properties of $g_1^{**}(\ell_1^*)$.

From (III 5.1) and (III 5.4), we conclude that for $\gamma_0 = \gamma_2$ $(\Delta_0 = \Delta_2)$

$$g_1^{**}(\ell_1^*; c_1^*, c_2^*) = g_2^{**}(c_1^* - \ell_1^*; c_2^*, c_1^*) , \qquad (4.3)$$

and

$$\frac{g_1^{**}(\ell_1^{*}; c_1^{*}, c_2^{*})}{g_1^{**}(c_1^{*}; c_1^{*}, c_2^{*})} = \frac{g_2^{**}(c_1^{*} - \ell_1^{*}; c_2^{*}, c_1^{*})}{g_2^{**}(0; c_2^{*}, c_1^{*})} \quad . \tag{4.3a}$$

Thus, for example, the graph of $g_1^{**}$ corresponding to the value $c_2^{*}/c_1^{*}$ = 2.43 is the same as the graph of $g_2^{**}$ but for $c_1^{*}/c_2^{*}$ = 2.43; except for a change of both the vertical and horizontal scales, and a reflection $\ell_1^{*} \leftrightarrow c_1^{*} - \ell_1^{*}$ .

This can be exploited not only to describe the form of the $g_1^{**}$ which corresponds to any curve $g_2^{**}$ , but also, possibly, to simplify the numerical evaluation of the normalization for $g_2^{**}$ . It follows from (4.3a) and (III 4.1a) that the area under the curve for any value of $c_2^{*}/c_1^{*}$ in Fig. IV-7 is just $c_2^{*}/c_1^{*}$ times the area under curve for the corresponding value of $c_1^{*}/c_2^{*}$ , i.e., the area under the curve $c_2^{*}/c_1^{*}$ = 2.43 is just 2.43 times the area under the curve $c_1^{*}/c_2^{*}$ = 2.43. It is obviously easier to evaluate numerically the area under the curve $c_1^{*}/c_2^{*}$ = 2.43 by comparing it with a uniform distribution than to evaluate the area under the curve for $c_2^{*}/c_1^{*}$ = 2.43. It is also easier to obtain analytic approximations to $g_2^{**}$ for small values of $c_2^{*}/c_1^{*}$ ($g_1^{**}$ for large values of $c_2^{*}/c_1^{*}$) than for large values of $c_2^{*}/c_1^{*}$ .

For $w_1/w_3 \ll 1$ and $\gamma_1 = \pi/2$, (III 8.9) can be integrated to give

$$\ell_2^{*} \simeq w_3^{-1/2} 2 \sin^{-1}(1 - w/w_1)^{1/2}$$

or

$$1 - w/w_1 \simeq \sin^2(\ell_2^{*}\pi/2c_2^{*}) \quad .$$

From (III 8.7) we then obtain

$$\frac{g_2^{**}(\ell_2^*)}{g_2^{**}(0)} \simeq 1 - \frac{\pi^{3/2}(w_1/w_3)^{\gamma_0/\pi} \sin^{2\gamma_0/\pi}(\ell_2^*\pi/2c_2^*)}{\gamma_0 \, \Gamma(\gamma_0/\pi) \, \Gamma(\frac{1}{2} - \gamma_0/\pi)} .$$

For $w_1/w_3 \ll 1$, one can also deduce from (3.9) or (3.10) that

$$w_1/w_3 \simeq 16 \exp(-\pi c_1^*/c_2^*) ,$$

so

$$\frac{g_2^{**}(\ell_2^*)}{g_2^{**}(0)} \simeq 1 - \frac{\pi^{3/2} \, 2^{4\gamma_0/\pi} \exp(-\gamma_0 c_1^*/c_2^*) \sin^{2\gamma_0/\pi}(\ell_2^*\pi/2c_2^*)}{\gamma_0 \, \Gamma(\gamma_0/\pi) \, \Gamma(\frac{1}{2} - \gamma_0/\pi)} . \qquad (4.4)$$

In particular, if $\gamma_0 = \pi/4$

$$\frac{g_2^{**}(\ell_2^*)}{g_2^{**}(0)} \simeq 1 - \frac{8 \, \pi^{1/2} \exp(-\pi c_1^*/4c_2^*) \sin^{1/2}(\ell_2^*\pi/2c_2^*)}{\Gamma^2(1/4)} . \qquad (4.4a)$$

The fractional error in the second term of (4.4) is of order $w_1/w_3$, but actually (4.4a) is correct to within a few percent even for $w_1 = w_3$ $(c_1^* = c_2^*)$ .

Equation (4.4a) shows that, for $c_1^* > c_2^*$, the deviation of $g_2^{**}(\ell_2^*)$ from a uniform distribution is proportional to $\exp(-\pi c_1^*/4c_2^*)$ . Equivalen for $c_2^* > c_1^*$, the deviation of $g_1^{**}(\ell_1^*)$ from a uniform distribution is proportional to $\exp(-\pi c_2^*/4c_1^*)$ .

The normalization of the approximate distribution (4.4) can be evalua explicitly,

$$\frac{\int_0^{c_2^*} d\ell_2^* \, g_2^{**}(\ell_2^*)}{g_2^{**}(0)} = \frac{1}{g_2^{**}(0)} \simeq c_2^* \left[ 1 - \frac{2^{4\gamma_0/\pi} \exp(-\gamma_0 c_1^*/c_2^*) \Gamma(\tfrac{1}{2} + \gamma_0/\pi)}{\Gamma^2(1 + \gamma_0/\pi) \Gamma(1/2 - \gamma_0/\pi)} \right].$$

$$(4.5)$$

Although the above analysis has dealt mostly with the special case $\gamma_0 = \gamma_2 = \pi/4$, $\gamma_1 = \pi/2$, for which $\ell_2^*(\zeta(w))$ could be expressed in terms of the tabulated elliptic integral, it is not much more difficult to construct graphs like Fig. IV-7 for any other choices of the $\gamma$'s. The construction of graphs for $\gamma_1 = \pi/2$ and any other $\gamma_2 = \pi/2 - \gamma_0$ is, in fact, no more difficult than for $\gamma_0 = \pi/4$ because (4.1) is true for $\gamma_1 = \pi/2$ and any choice of $\gamma_0$; only (4.2) generalizes to

$$\frac{g_2^{**}(\ell_2^*)}{g_2^{**}(0)} = \frac{1}{B_1(\gamma_0/\pi, \tfrac{1}{2} - \gamma_0/\pi)} \, B_{\frac{w+w_3}{w_1+w_3}}(\tfrac{1}{2} - \gamma_0/\pi, \, \gamma_0/\pi) \, . \qquad (4.6)$$

For any other choice of $\gamma_0$, one need only draw a single graph of $B_z(\tfrac{1}{2} - \gamma_0/\pi, \, \gamma_0/\pi)$ and proceed as for $\gamma_0 = \pi/4$ . Figures IV-8 and IV-9 distributions for $\gamma_0 = \pi/6$, $\gamma_2 = \pi/3$ and $\gamma_0 = \pi/3$, $\gamma_0 = \pi/6$ (the $\Delta_0$, $\Delta_1$, $\Delta_2$ in the ratios 1:0:3 or 3:0:1, respectively.)

For any choice of $\gamma_1$ (including $\pi/2$), the graphs of $g_2^{**}$ or $g_1^{**}$ can be drawn quite accurately from the expansions of section III 8. For any values of $\gamma_0$, $\gamma_1$, $\gamma_2$ and $c_1^*$, $c_2^*$, one will first evaluate $w_1$ and $w_3$ from the graphs of section 2. For small $\ell_2^*$, one will then use the expansion (III 8.3). This shows that $g_2^{**}(\ell_2^*)$ decreases proportional to $\ell_2^{*\gamma_0/\gamma_1}$ for any $w_1$ and $w_3$ ($c_1^*$ and $c_2^*$). In particular for $\gamma_0 = \pi/4$,

186

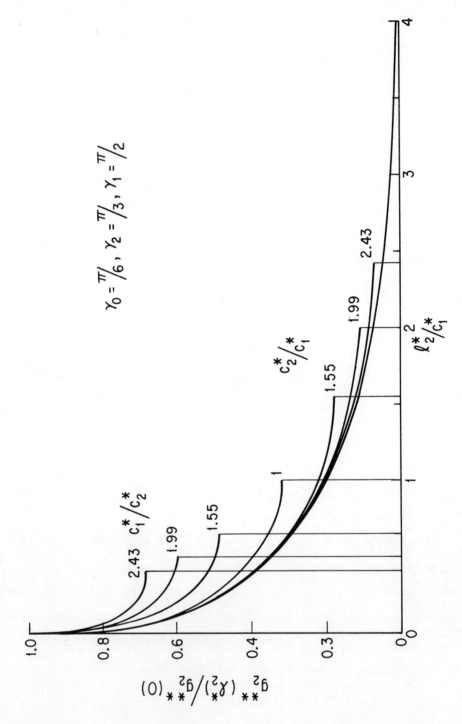

Fig. IV-8. Distribution of queue length for various ratios of storage capacities $c_1^*/c_2^*$ for $\gamma = \pi/6$, $\gamma = \pi/3$

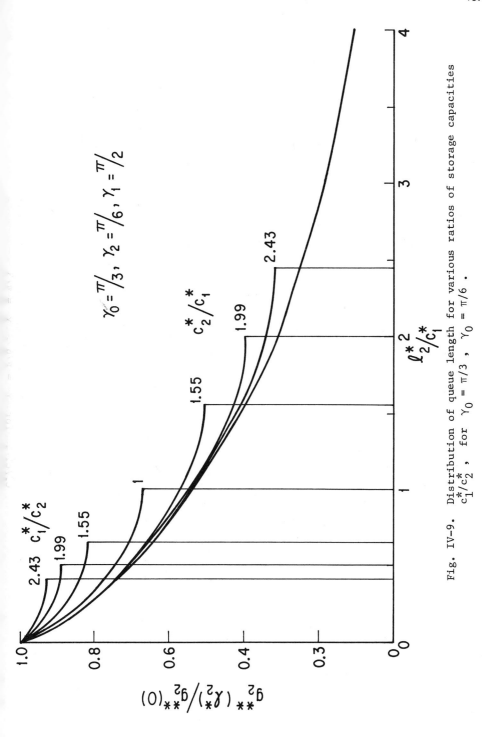

Fig. IV-9. Distribution of queue length for various ratios of storage capacities $c_1^*/c_2^*$, for $\gamma_0 = \pi/3$, $\gamma_0 = \pi/6$.

$\gamma_1 = \pi/2$ , $g_2^{**}$ decreases proportional to $\ell_2^{*1/2}$ for all curves of Fig

but the coefficient of the $\ell_2^{*1/2}$ depends upon $c_2^*/c_1^*$; the larger $c_2^*/$

the more rapid the decrease. For $c_2^* \to 0$ , the coefficient vanishes an

$g_2^{**}$ becomes uniform. Similarly in Fig. IV-8, $g_2^{**}$ decreases like $\ell_2^{*1/}$

and in Fig. IV-9 like $\ell_2^{*2/3}$ , for all values of $c_2^*/c_1^*$ .

For sufficiently small values of $c_2^*$ $(w_1/w_3 \ll 1)$, one can also dr.

a graph of the Beta-function in (III 8.9) for given values of $\gamma_1$, thus

from its inverse obtain $1 - w/w_1$ in terms of $\ell_2^*$ . Substitution of th.

in (III 8.7) then gives the curve for $g_2^{**}$. This would provide the gene:

ization of the formula (4.4) which for $\gamma_1 = \pi/2$ involves only trigono-

metric functions instead of inverse Beta-functions. Except for a rescal:

of the coordinates for $1 - g_2^{**}(\ell_2^*)/g_2^{**}(0)$ and $\ell_2^*$ , the curves for var

values of (small) $w_1/w_3$ (i.e., $c_2^*/c_1^*$) are all identical, as is demon-

strated in Figs. IV-7, 8 and 9 for $\gamma_1 = \pi/2$ .

For any values of $w_1/w_3$ (particularly for $w_1/w_3$ comparable with

one can evaluate $g_2^{**}(c_2^*)/g_2^{**}(0)$ from (III 8.1a) or (III 8.1b) with

$w = 0$ . From a single graph of $B_z(\gamma_0, \gamma_2)$ as a function of $z$ , for gi

values of $\gamma_0, \gamma_2$ , one will obtain $g_2^{**}(c_2^*)/g_2^{**}(0)$ for all values of

$w_1/w_3$ (in Figs IV-7, 8, and 9, the values of the curves at $\ell_2^* = c_2^*$ were

in fact, obtained in this way). From (III 8.6), one can now obtain the

curves for $\ell_2^*$ near $c_2^*$ . For $\gamma_1 = \pi/2$ as in Figs. IV-7, 8, and 9, the

curves all vary like $(c_2^* - \ell_2^*)^2$ , but, more generally, they vary like

$(c_2^* - \ell_2^*)^{\pi/(\pi-\gamma_1)}$ .

For $w_1/w_3 \lesssim 1$ , the expansions from $\ell_2^* = 0$ and from $\ell_2^* = c_2^*$ wi

join quite smoothly in some intermediate range. For $w_1/w_3 \gtrsim 1$ , howeve

$g_2^{**}(\ell_2^*)/g_2^{**}(0)$ will behave, for small to moderate values of $\ell_2^*$ , like :

does for $c_2^* = \infty$. The small argument expansion will join smoothly to the expansion (III 8.13), which, in turn, can be used until $\ell_2^*$ comes suffi-

ciently close to $c_2^*$ that the curve joins with the expansion near $c_2^*$.

One can see from the shapes of Figs. IV-7, 8, and 9 that such a procedure

will give a fairly accurate approximation to the curves, particularly if

one uses at least two terms in each expansion. One can draw these curves

fairly easily for any particular values of $\gamma_0, \gamma_1, \gamma_2$, although it obvi-

ously becomes quite tedious to repeat for many choice of the $\gamma$'s.

Again one can exploit the symmetry to describe the distribution $g_1^*$.

For any choice of $c_2^*/c_1^*$ and curve $g_2^{**}(\ell_2^*)$ from Fig. IV-8, the corres-

ponding curve for $g_1^{**}(\ell_1^*)$ is obtained by interchanging $\gamma_0$ with $\gamma_2$,

$c_2^*$ with $c_1^*$, and $\ell_2^*$ with $c_1^* - \ell_1^*$; thus it is described by the curve

of Fig. IV-9 with the corresponding values of $c_1^*/c_2^*$. Figs. IV-8 and 9

therefore, also determine $g_1^{**}(\ell_1)$ for the same choice of the $\gamma_0, \gamma_2$,

$\gamma_1 = \pi/2$. In Figs. IV-7 with $\gamma_0 = \gamma_2$, $g_2^{**}$ and $g_1^{**}$ were described by

the same family of curves.

The symmetry can also be used to simplify the normalization. It suf-

fices to normalize either the $g_2^{**}$ or the $g_1^{**}$, whichever is the easier

to approximate, and use it to determine the normalization of the other.

5.  The Service Rate.  The formulas of sections 2 and 4 have given some indica-

tion of how the $g^{**}$'s vary with the $\gamma_j$ and $c_j$. For one thing, $g_1^{**}(\ell_1^*)$

is monotone increasing in $\ell_1^*$ and $g_2^{**}(\ell_2^*)$ is monotone decreasing in $\ell_2^*$.

Therefore

$$ g_1^{**}(0) \leq 1/c_1^* \leq g_1^{**}(c_1^*) \; ; \qquad g_2^{**}(0) \geq 1/c_2^* \geq g_2^{**}(c_2^*) \; , $$

and, from (III 4.1a), we can obtain simple upper and lower bounds on the

loss in service, $\mu_0 - \mu$, due to blockage

$$\frac{1}{2} \Delta^{*1/2} \max\left\{\frac{(\Delta_0 + \Delta_1)^{1/2}}{c_1^*}, \frac{(\Delta_1 + \Delta_2)^{1/2}}{c_2^*}\right\} \leq \mu_0 - \mu$$

(5.1a)

$$\leq \frac{1}{2} \Delta^{*1/2} \left\{\frac{(\Delta_0 + \Delta_1)^{1/2}}{c_1^*} + \frac{(\Delta_1 + \Delta_2)^{1/2}}{c_2^*}\right\}.$$

Equivalently,

$$\max\left\{\frac{\sin\gamma_2}{c_1^*}, \frac{\sin\gamma_0}{c_2^*}\right\} \leq \frac{2(\mu_0-\mu_1)(\sin\gamma_0 \sin\gamma_1 \sin\gamma_2)^{\frac{1}{2}}}{\Delta^*} \leq \frac{\sin\gamma_2}{c_2^*} + \frac{\sin\gamma_0}{c_2^*}$$

(5.1b)

or, in the original units of (III 4.1)

$$\frac{1}{2} \max\left\{\frac{\Delta_0 + \Delta_1}{c_1}, \frac{\Delta_1 + \Delta_2}{c_2}\right\} \leq \mu_0 - \mu \leq \frac{1}{2}\left\{\frac{(\Delta_0 + \Delta_1)}{c_1} + \frac{(\Delta_1 + \Delta_2)}{c_2}\right\}.$$

(5.1c)

Thus, the overall service rate $\mu$ is always less (for finite storage $c_1$ and $c_2$) than it would be for either servers 0 and 1 alone, or server and 2 alone with intermediate storages $c_1$ and $c_2$, respectively. But the loss in service due to blockage can be no worse than the sum of the losses of these two two-server systems by themselves. It follows also that the right-hand side of the inequalities (5.1a,b,c) can be no more than twice the left-hand side; $\mu_0 - \mu$ is determined to within a factor of 2 at worst.

The above lower bounds are special cases of those described (but not proved) in section III 1. There is still another bound predicted in section III 1; $\mu$ should be less than that which would result if one set

$\mu_1 = \infty$ and produced, in effect, a two-server system with intermediate storage $c_1 + c_2$. This leads to the bound

$$\frac{1}{2}\left(\frac{\Delta_0 + \Delta_2}{c_1 + c_2}\right) \leq \mu_0 - \mu .$$

This lower bound, however, is never larger than the lower bound (5.1c). The bound is correct, but gives no improvement over (5.1c).

It is difficult to show graphically the dependence of $\mu_0 - \mu$ on all the relevant parameters, $\gamma_0$, $\gamma_1$, $\gamma_2$, $c_1$, and $c_2$, but, in many potential applications, the service facilities are given and one is primarily interested in the dependence of $\mu$ on the storages $c_1$ and $c_2$. We will, therefore, concentrate our attention mostly on the dependence of $\mu_0 - \mu$ on $c_1$ and $c_2$ treating the $\gamma_j$ (or the $\Delta_j$) as given parameters.

From (III 4.1) we see that

$$1 = \frac{(\Delta_0 + \Delta_1)g_1^*(c_1)}{2(\mu_0 - \mu)} = \frac{(\Delta_1 + \Delta_2)g_2^*(0)}{2(\mu_0 - \mu)}$$

$$= \frac{(\Delta_0 + \Delta_1)g_1^*(0)}{2(\mu_0 - \mu)} + \frac{(\Delta_1 + \Delta_2)g_2^*(c_2)}{2(\mu_0 - \mu)} .$$

(5.2)

But $c_1 g_1^*(c_1)$ or $c_2 g_2^*(0)$ can be considered as "dimensionless" densities which depend upon $c_1$ and $c_2$ only through the dimensionless ratio $c_1/c_2$, as described in section III 5. If we consider $\mu_0 - \mu$ as a function in a $c_1$, $c_2$-space (for fixed $\gamma_j$), the contours $\mu_0 - \mu = $ const. will all have the same shape, differing only in a change of scale for $c_1$, $c_2$.

We can express this relation in terms of a single graph by considering (5.2) as the equation of a curve in a space of coordinates $(\mu_0 - \mu)c_1$
$(\mu_0 - \mu)c_2$ . Note that, since $c_1 g_1^*(c_1)$ is a function of $c_1/c_2$ , it
can also be considered as a function of $(\mu_0 - \mu)c_1/(\mu_0 - \mu)c_2 = c_1/c_2$ .
From such a graph, we can evaluate $\mu_0 - \mu$ for any values of $c_1$, $c_2$ by
first drawing a line of slope $c_2/c_1$ through the origin in the $(\mu_0 - \mu)c_1$
$(\mu_0 - \mu)c_2$ space. The coordinates of intersection of this line with the
graph of (5.2) determine $(\mu_0 - \mu)c_1$ and $(\mu_0 - \mu)c_2$ , from which one
obtains $\mu_0 - \mu$ . The following analysis will deal primarily with properties of the graphs of (5.2) in the space $(\mu_0 - \mu)c_1$, $(\mu_0 - \mu)c_2$ for vari
ous values of the $\gamma_j$'s (equivalently the $\Delta_j$, or actually the ratios $\Delta_0/\Delta_1$
$\Delta_2/\Delta_1$).

For some purposes, it may be most convenient to draw the graph of (5.
in the space $(\mu_0 - \mu)c_1$, $(\mu_0 - \mu)c_2$; for other purposes it may be conven
ient to draw it in the space $[(\mu_0 - \mu)c_1]^{-1}$ , $[(\mu_0 - \mu)c_2]^{-1}$ . In the
latter space, the curves (5.2) must, according to (5.1c), lie within the
region bounded by straight lines

$$\frac{(\Delta_0 + \Delta_1)}{2} [(\mu_0 - \mu)c_1]^{-1} + \frac{(\Delta_1 + \Delta_2)}{2}[(\mu_0 - \mu)c_2]^{-1} \geq 1 \qquad (5.3a)$$

$$\frac{(\Delta_0 + \Delta_1)}{2}[(\mu_0 - \mu)c_1]^{-1} \leq 1 \quad , \qquad \frac{(\Delta_1 + \Delta_2)}{2}[(\mu_0 - \mu)c_2]^{-1} \leq 1 \qquad (5.3b)$$

as shown in Fig. IV-10a by the broken lines. In the space $(\mu_0 - \mu)c_1$ ,
$(\mu_0 - \mu)c_2$ , (5.3b) still represents a region bounded by vertical and hor
zontal lines, but (5.3a) maps into the hyperbola

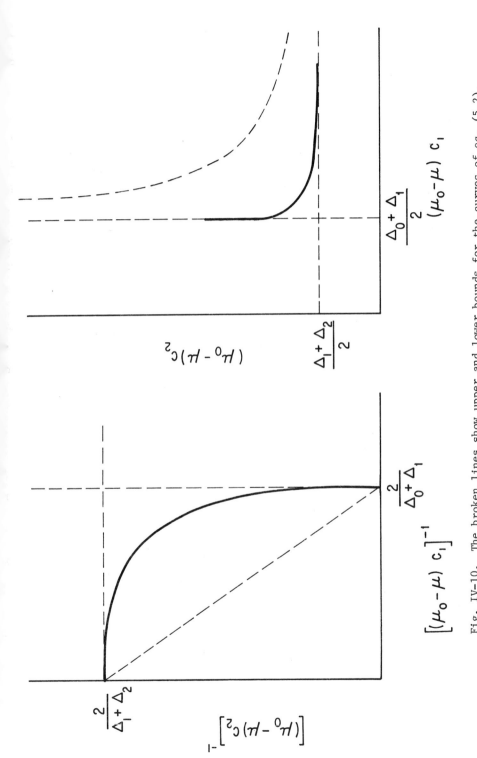

Fig. IV-10. The broken lines show upper and lower bounds for the curves of eq. (5.2).

$$\left[ (\mu_0 - \mu)c_1 - \left( \frac{\Delta_0 + \Delta_1}{2} \right) \right] \left[ (\mu_0 - \mu)c_2 - \frac{(\Delta_1 + \Delta_2)}{2} \right] = \frac{(\Delta_0 + \Delta_1)(\Delta_1 + \Delta_2)}{4} .$$

$$(5.3c)$$

as shown in Fig. IV-10b. The solid lines of Figs. IV-10a and b represent a possible (as yet undetermined) curve of (5.2).

Although Fig. IV-10a is clearly a more elegant representation of the bounds (5.1c), Fig. IV-10b will be the more natural space in which to analyse the important question: for a fixed total storage $c_1 + c_2$, what is the value of $c_1/c_2$ which maximizes $\mu$? From the correct curve of Fig. IV-10b this ratio can be found from the point of tangency with a line $c_1 + c_2 = $ const. of slope $-1$.

For fixed $c_1 + c_2$, the lower bounds on $\mu_0 - \mu$ give a minimum at the intersection of the two lines of Fig. IV-10b, i.e., for

$$\frac{c_1}{c_2} = \frac{\Delta_0 + \Delta_1}{\Delta_1 + \Delta_2} , \qquad (5.4a)$$

but the upper bounds on $\mu_0 - \mu$ give a minimum at

$$\frac{c_1}{c_2} = \left( \frac{\Delta_0 + \Delta_1}{\Delta_1 + \Delta_2} \right)^{1/2} . \qquad (5.4b)$$

There is no reason why either (5.4a) or (5.4b) should give a good approximation to the optimal $c_1/c_2$ for (5.2), but one might expect the correct ratio to lie between the values (5.4a) and (5.4b).

We can use (5.4a,b) to put bounds on the maximum service rate $\mu_{max}$, for fixed $c_1 + c_2$. These are

$$\frac{(\Delta_0 + \Delta_1) + (\Delta_1 + \Delta_2)}{2(c_1 + c_2)} \leq \mu_0 - \mu_{max} \leq \frac{[(\Delta_0 + \Delta_1)^{1/2} + (\Delta_1 + \Delta_2)^{1/2}]^2}{2(c_1 + c_2)}.$$

$$(5.5)$$

If $(\Delta_0 + \Delta_1) \ll (\Delta_1 + \Delta_2)$, i.e., $\Delta_0, \Delta_1 \ll \Delta_2$, or if $(\Delta_0 + \Delta_1) \gg (\Delta_1 + \Delta_2)$, i.e., $\Delta_2, \Delta_1 \ll \Delta_0$; these bounds are quite close. In the former case, either (5.4a) or (5.4b) imply that one should use most of the available storage in $c_2$ with only a small storage between the more regular servers 0 and 1. Having done so, the maximum service rate is essentially that of the two server system, servers 1 and 2, with most of the available storage $c_1 + c_2$ between them. Correspondingly, in the latter case, one will use only a small storage between servers 1 and 2. If $\Delta_0 + \Delta_1 \simeq \Delta_1 + \Delta_2$, i.e., $\Delta_0 \simeq \Delta_2$ one expects the optimal split of the storage to be $c_1 \simeq c_2$, but the upper and lower bounds on $\mu_0 - \mu_{max}$ now differ by a factor of 2.

To obtain more accurate estimates of $\mu$, it is necessary to evaluate the normalizations of the $g^*$'s, and, from them, the values of the $g_1^*(c_1)$ or $g_2^*(0)$ in (5.2). It suffices to consider only the evaluation of $g_2^*(0)$. If we also wish the value of $g_1^*(c_1)$, it can be determined from the formulas for $g_2^*(0)$ through the symmetry with respect to interchange of servers 0 and 2. From (III 8.1), we wish to evaluate

$$\frac{1}{c_2 g_2^*(0)} = \frac{1}{c_2^* g_2^{***}(0)} = \frac{1}{c_2^*} \int_0^{c_2^*} \frac{g_2^{**}(\ell_2^*)}{g_2^{**}(0)} d\ell_2^* \qquad (5.6)$$

as a function of $c_1/c_2$, $c_1^*/c_1^*$, or $w_1/w_3$.

Rather than trying to express $g_2^{**}(\ell_2^*)$ explicitly as a function of $\ell_2^*$ and integrating with respect to $\ell_2^*$, we will change integration variables to

$$z \;=\; 1 \;-\; w/w_1 \quad,$$

the natural choice in view of (III 8.8). As $\ell_2^*$ goes from 0 to $c_2^*$, $z$ goes from 0 to 1. We can now integrate (5.6) as

$$\frac{1}{c_2^* g_2^{**}(0)} \;=\; \frac{1}{c_2^*} \int_0^1 \frac{g_2^{**}(\ell_2^*)}{g_2^{**}(0)} \frac{d\ell_2^*}{dz}\, dz$$

$$= \; 1 \;-\; \frac{\pi(w_1 + w_3)^{-1+\gamma_1/\pi}}{c_2^* \sin\gamma_1 \, \Gamma(\frac{\gamma_0}{\pi})\Gamma(\frac{\gamma_1}{\pi})\Gamma(\frac{\gamma_2}{\pi})} \int_0^1 dz\; z^{-1+\gamma_1/\pi}\,(1-z)^{\frac{-\gamma_1}{\pi}}\left(1 - \frac{w_1\, z}{w_1+w_3}\right)^{-1+}$$

$$\cdot \int_0^{w_1 z/(w_1+w_3)} dx\; x^{-1+\gamma_0/\pi}\,(1 - x)^{-1+\gamma_2/\pi} \quad. \tag{5.7a}$$

Rather than have both the $c_2^*$ and the $w_1$ and $w_3$ in the same formula, we can use (IV 3.1b) to eliminate the $c_2^*$ in the second term of (5.7a);

$$\frac{1}{c_2^* g_2^{**}(0)} = 1 \;-\; \frac{\pi}{\sin\gamma_1 \,\Gamma(\frac{\gamma_0}{\pi})\Gamma(\frac{\gamma_1}{\pi})\Gamma(\frac{\gamma_2}{\pi})}\Biggl\{\int_0^1 du\; u^{-1+\gamma_1/\pi}\,(1-u)^{\frac{-\gamma_1}{\pi}}\left(1 - \frac{w_1\, u}{w_1+w_3}\right)^{-1+\gamma_1/\pi}\Biggr\}^-$$

$$\cdot \int_0^1 dz\; z^{-1+\gamma_1/\pi}\,(1-z)^{-\gamma_1/\pi}\left(1 - \frac{w_1\, z}{w_1+w_3}\right)^{-1+\gamma_1/\pi}\int_0^{w_1 z/(w_1+w_3)} dx\; x^{-1+\gamma_0/\pi}\,(1 - x)^{-1+\gamma_2/\pi} \quad .$$

$$\tag{5.7b}$$

The above integrals cannot be evaluated in any convenient form. We can either revert to a numerical integration for special choices of the $\gamma_j$, make approximations (for limiting values of the $\gamma_j$), or try to improve the bounds described by Fig. IV-10. The straight lines of Fig. IV-10B were obtained by setting $c_2 g_2^*(0) = 1$ (and $c_1 g_1^*(c_1) = 1$), which corresponds to the neglect of the second (negative) term of (5.7). Any (low) estimate of this second term would improve the former lower bounds.

To estimate the second term of (5.7b), we note that the last integral is an increasing function of $z$. The whole second term is, essentially, a weighted average of this integral. If we change the weight so as to decrease the weight on the larger $z$, we will underestimate this average. This will happen if we discard the factor $[1 - w_1 u/(w_1 + w_3)]^{-1+\gamma_1/\pi}$ and the corresponding factor in the $z$ integral. Thus

$$\frac{1}{c_2 g_2^{* **}(0)} \le 1 - \frac{1}{\Gamma(\frac{\gamma_0}{\pi})\Gamma(\frac{\gamma_1}{\pi})\Gamma(\frac{\gamma_0}{\pi})} \int_0^1 dz\, z^{-1+\gamma_1/\pi}(1-z)^{-\gamma_1/\pi}$$

$$\cdot \int_0^{w_1 z/(w_1+w_3)} dx\, x^{-1+\gamma_0/\pi}(1-x)^{-1+\gamma_2/\pi} . \tag{5.8a}$$

If we also discard the factor $(1-x)^{-1+\gamma_2/\pi}$, we will further increase the right-hand side, therefore

$$\frac{1}{c_2 g_2^{* **}(0)} \le 1 - \frac{[w_1/(w_1+w_3)]^{\gamma_0/\pi}\Gamma(1-\gamma_2/\pi)\Gamma(1-\gamma_1/\pi)}{\Gamma(\gamma_1/\pi)\Gamma(\gamma_2/\pi)\Gamma^2(1+\gamma_0/\pi)} . \tag{5.8b}$$

To obtain tighter bounds, we can expand the integrals in (5.7b) and obtai

$$\frac{1}{c_2 g_2^*(0)} = \frac{1}{c_2^* g_2^{**}(0)} \le 1 - \frac{[w_1/(w_1 + w_3)]^{\gamma_0/\pi} \Gamma(1 - \gamma_2/\pi)\Gamma(1 - \gamma_1/\pi)}{\Gamma(\gamma_1/\pi)\Gamma(\gamma_2/\pi)\Gamma^2(1 + \gamma_0/\pi)}$$

(5.8c)

$$\cdot \left\{ 1 + \left(\frac{w_1}{w_1 + w_3}\right)\left(\frac{\gamma_0}{\pi}\right)\left[\frac{\left(1 - \frac{\gamma_2}{\pi}\right)^2}{\left(1 + \frac{\gamma_0}{\pi}\right)^2} + \frac{\left(1 - \frac{\gamma_1}{\pi}\right)^2}{\left(1 + \frac{\gamma_0}{\pi}\right)} - \right] + \cdots \right\}$$

This formula, or its companion for $c_1^* g_1^{**}(c_1^*)$ , are the most accurate we have found short of piecing together several expansions over different ranges of the integration or evaluating the integrals numerically. We ca also obtain lower bounds for $[c_2^* g_2^{**}(0)]^{-1}$ but none that give a significar improvement over those in (5.1c).

Substitution of (5.8c) into (5.2) gives a lower bound for $\mu_0 - \mu$ o equivalently a new lower bound for the curve associated with Fig. IV-10b. From the formulas or graphs for $c_2^*/c_1^*$ vs $w_3/(w_1 + w_3)$ of section 2, Fig. IV-6, (5.8c) can be evaluated in terms of $c_1^*/c_2^*$ or $c_1/c_2$ , or one can evaluate (5.2) parametrically in terms of the parameter $w_1/(w_1 + w_3)$.

Fig. IV-11 shows some curves of (5.2), (5.8c) for some symmetric cases $\gamma_0 = \gamma_2$ and $\gamma_1 = \pi/2, \pi/3$, and $\pi/6$ . For these special cases $\gamma_0 = \gamma_2$ $\Delta_0 = \Delta_2$, it is convenient to plot the curves (5.2) in the space of coordinates $2(\mu_0 - \mu)c_1/(\Delta_0 + \Delta_1)$, $2(\mu_0 - \mu)c_2/(\Delta_1 + \Delta_2)$ because the curves for various $\gamma_1$ (i.e., for various values of $\Delta_0/\Delta_1 = \Delta_2/\Delta_1$) all have the same asymptotes and the same bounds (5.3). The vertical and horizonta broken lines correspond to the lower bounds (5.3b); the broken line curve corresponds to the upper bound (5.3c). The solid line curves with the horizontal asymptote are the curves obtained from (5.8c). The curves with the vertical asymptotes are derived from the companion relation to (5.8c) for $c_1 g_1^*(c_1)$ . They are (for $\gamma_0 = \gamma_2$) simply the reflection of the former curves over the $45°$ line. Both the curve from (5.8c) and its reflection are lower bounds for the correct curve, for each value of $\gamma_1$ .

The error in (5.8c) is an increasing function of $w_1/(w_1 + w_3)$ and, for $w_1/(w_1 + w_3) \leq 1/2$, $(c_1^* \geq c_2^*)$, is largest at $c_1^* = c_2^*$ , $c_1 = c_2$ , i.e., along the 45º line of Fig. IV-10  An accurate numerical evaluation of $g_2^*(0)$ is quite tedious and was done only in a few special cases. From an evaluation of the area under the curves of Fig. IV-7, one can determine $g_2^*(0)$ for $\gamma_0 = \gamma_2 = \pi/4$, $\gamma_1 = \pi/2$ and $c_2/c_1 = 1$, 1.55, 1.99 and 2.43. For $c_1/c_2 = 1.55$ or 1.99, the points on the graph of Fig. IV-11 determined from a numerical integration are indistinguishable from the curves of (5.8c). These points are labeled by an x along the curves $\gamma_0 = \gamma_2 = \pi/4$, $\gamma_1 = \pi/2$ . The correct point corresponding to $c_1/c_2 = 1$, however, does lie slightly off the curve at coordinates (1.60, 1.60), whereas the lower bounds (5.8c) give the coordinates (1.58₅, 1.58₅) at $c_1 = c_2$ . Thus, even at the point where the bounds (5.8c) are least accurate, they are in error by only 1%. Since the correct curve has a continuous derivative at $c_1 = c_2$ and is symmetric, it must have a slope $-1$ at $c_1 = c_2$ . If one simply made an interpolation between the two crossing curves of Fig.IV-11, smoothing out the discontinuity in slope, one would certainly come very close to the correct curve.

As a further check, the correct $g_2^*(0)$ was also evaluated numerically for $\gamma_0 = \gamma_1 = \gamma_2 = \pi/3$ and $c_1 = c_2$ . The corresponding point in Fig. IV-11. is shown at coordinates (1.42, 1.42);  the lower bound curves cross at

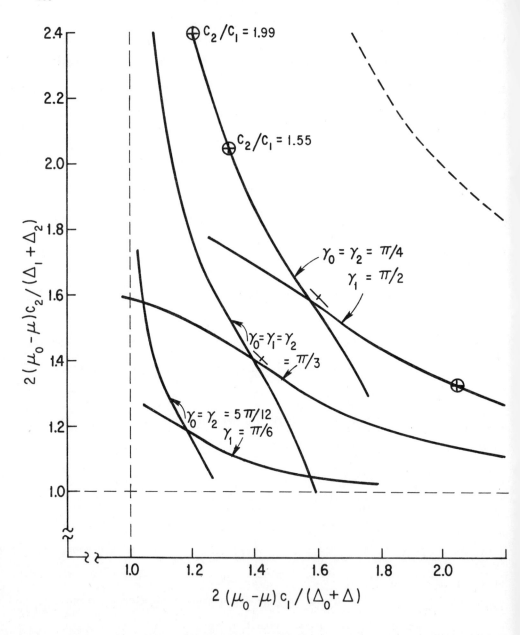

Fig. IV-11. The solid lines are lower bounds for the curves of eq. (5.2) in which the service rate μ can be evaluated as a function of $c_2/c_1$, for $\gamma_0 = \gamma_2$.

(1.40 , 1.40 ), again an error of only about 1%.

The curves of Fig. IV-11 illustrate clearly the consequences of the interaction between the two finite storages. For $c_2 = \infty$, figure IV-11 shows that $2(\mu_0 - \mu)c_1/(\Delta_0 + \Delta_1) = 1$, i.e.,

$$\mu = \mu_0 - \frac{(\Delta_0 + \Delta_1)}{2 c_1} \qquad \text{for } c_2 = \infty \qquad (5.9a)$$

as described previously for a single server system. But in the symmetric case $c_1 = c_2$, $\Delta_0 = \Delta_2$ and $\Delta_1 = 0$ $(\gamma_1 = \pi/2)$, Fig. IV-11 shows that

$$2(\mu_0 - \mu)c_1/(\Delta_0 + \Delta_1) \simeq 1.60$$

i.e.,

$$\mu \simeq \mu_0 - \frac{\Delta_0}{2c_1}(1.60) \qquad \text{for } c_1 = c_2, \ \Delta_1 = 0. \qquad (5.9b)$$

The second terms of (5.9a,b) represent the loss in service rate due to blocking by the finite storages. A comparison of the two cases shows that, if one had a finite storage $c_1$ between a server with variance rate $\Delta_0$ and a regular server, and one were then to add a server 2 with $\Delta_2 = \Delta_0$ and a storage $c_2 = c_1$, the reduction in service rate due to blocking, $\mu_0 - \mu$, would increase by 60%. If, on the other hand, one had two identical servers, identified as servers 0 and 2 $(\Delta_0 = \Delta_2)$, in series with a finite storage $c = c_1 + c_2$ between them, and one were to insert a regular server between servers 0 and 2 splitting the storage equally $(c_1 = c_2)$, the loss in service due to blocking would again increase by 60%, from

$$\mu = \mu_0 - \frac{\Delta_0}{c} \qquad \text{to } \mu \simeq \mu_0 - \frac{\Delta_0}{c}(1.60). \qquad (5.9c)$$

If one inserted the regular server so as to split the storage unequally, $c_1 \neq c_2$, the loss would be still higher.

The case of identical servers $\gamma_0 = \gamma_1 = \gamma_2$ is less extreme but perhaps more important. If we go from two servers in series $\Delta_0 = \Delta_1$, $c_2 = \infty$ to three servers in series $\Delta_0 = \Delta_1 = \Delta_2$, $c_1 = c_2$, the service rate drops from

$$\mu = \mu_0 - \frac{\Delta_0}{c_1} \quad \text{to} \quad \mu \simeq \mu_0 - \frac{\Delta_0}{c_1} (1.42) \quad , \tag{5.9d}$$

a 42% increase in the loss due to blockage. If, on the other hand, we had two in series with storage $c = c_1 + c_2$ and we inserted a server in the middle, the service rate would drop from

$$\mu = \mu_0 - \frac{\Delta_0}{c} \quad \text{to} \quad \mu \simeq \mu_0 - \frac{2\Delta_0}{c} (1.42) \quad ; \tag{5.9e}$$

the loss would increase by a factor of 2.84. This confirms one's expectations, that if one must insert a server (with $\mu_1 = \mu_0 = \mu_2$) between two identical servers, the least damage is done if the server is regular $\Delta_1 = $ (compare the factor 2.84 with the 1.60 of equation (5.9c)).

Since the effect of going from 2 identical servers in series to three in series with $c_1 = c_2$ increases the loss due to blockage by a factor of 1.42, one could ask the question: what will happen if we take infinitely many identical servers in series with $c_1 = c_2 = \cdots$ ? Unfortunately, we do not know the answer, but a reasonable conjecture is that the loss, compared with that of a single storage, would increase by approximately a factor of 2. The argument is that the marginal queue distributions for queues well in the interior of the sequence are likely to be nearly uniform. If so, these probability densities would be $1/c_1$ and each server would be interrupted equally often by an empty queue or a blocked storage.

The curves of Fig. IV-11 for $\gamma_0 = \gamma_2 = 5\pi/12$, $\gamma_1 = \pi/6$ illustrate the continued trend from the above cases $\gamma_1 = \pi/2$, $\gamma_1 = \pi/3$. A small value of $\gamma_1$ means that $\Delta_0$ and $\Delta_2$ are small compared with $\Delta_1$. We saw in Fig. II-4 that even for $c_2 = \infty$, the distribution $g_2^*(\ell_2)$ was nearly rectangular with an approximate cut-off at $\ell_2 = c_1$. The effect of having a finite storage $c_2$ with $c_2$ only slightly larger than $c_1$ was small. For $\gamma_1 \to 0$ we expect that the service rate will be determined by the smaller of $c_1$ and $c_2$. Fig. IV-11 indeed shows that as $\gamma_1$ becomes smaller, the curves approach the two horizontal and vertical asymptotes. If one has a regular server $\Delta_0 = 0$, a finite storage $c_1$, and a server 1 with $\Delta_1 > 0$; and one then adds another regular server $\Delta_2 = 0$ and a finite storage $c_2 \geq c_1$, there is no further reduction in the overall service rate $\mu$.

Fig. IV-11 shows only cases with $\gamma_0 = \gamma_2$. To analyse, in detail, the behavior of $\mu$ for $\gamma_0 \neq \gamma_2$ is quite tedious. Fig. IV-12. however, shows a number of representative graphs, from which one can infer some simple but crude approximations.

In Fig. IV-12, the horizontal and vertical coordinates have been scaled by $\sin \gamma_2$ and $\sin \gamma_0$, respectively, relative to those of Fig. IV-11. The horizontal and vertical asymptotes of the curves for various $\gamma_j$'s are no longer at the coordinate 1 as in Fig. IV-11, but cover a wide range of values less than 1. Fig. IV-12 shows again the three cases of Fig. IV-11 (rescaled), but the sequence of curves for $\gamma_1 = \pi/2$, $\pi/3$, and $\pi/6$, $\gamma_0 = \gamma_2$, no longer has the monotone trend of Fig. IV-11. For these cases, the horizontal and vertical axes are scaled by the same factor $\sin \gamma_0 = \sin \gamma_2$, but for $c_1 = c_2$ (along the $45^\circ$ line) the curve

204

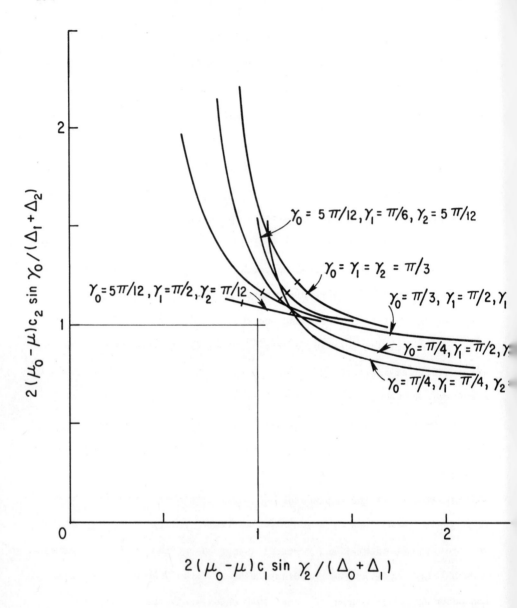

Fig. IV-12. The solid lines are lower bounds for the curves of eq. (5.2)
which the service rate of $\mu$ can be evaluated as a function
$c_2/c_1$, for $\gamma_0 = \gamma_2$. The crosses along the curves indica
the optimal ratio of $c_1/c_2$ with $c_1 + c_2$ fixed.

for $\gamma_1 = \pi/2$ is nearest the origin, $\gamma_1 = \pi/3$ is furthest, and $\gamma_1 = \pi/6$ is between them. For $\gamma_1 \to 0$, however, the curves will come in closer and pass through the point $(1,1)$. The asymptotes of this family with $\gamma_0 = \gamma_2$ do behave monotonically; most pairs of curves will cross each other.

For all curves with $\gamma_0 = \gamma_2$, the optimal split of a total storage $c = c_1 + c_2$ is an equal split $c_1 = c_2$. The point to be observed here, as compared with Fig. IV-11, is that for $c_1 \sim c_2$, most of these curves cross the $45^\circ$ line at coordinates in the range from about 1.1 to 1.2, despite a much wider range of variation in the coordinates of the asymptotes.

Fig. IV-12 also shows a sequence of three curves all with $\gamma_1 = \pi/2$ and with $\gamma_0 = \gamma_2 = \pi/4$ (also in the above sequence); $\gamma_0 = \pi/3$, $\gamma_2 = \pi/6$; and $\gamma_0 = 5\pi/12$, $\gamma_2 = \pi/12$. This sequence is for $\Delta_1 = 0$ and $\Delta_0/\Delta_2 = 1$, 1/3, and 1/14. For $\gamma_2 \to 0$ $(\Delta_0 \to 0)$, the curve of Fig. IV-12 would approach the horizontal line at height 1.

Whereas in Fig. IV-10, the split of $c_1 + c_2$ which maximizes $\mu$ is determined by the point on the curve where the slope is $-1$, in Fig. IV-12 it is a point where the slope is $-\sin \gamma_2 / \sin \gamma_0$. Such points are marked in Fig. IV-12 by the crossmark on each curve. Actually the graphs in Fig. IV-12 were drawn from an interpolation between bounds (5.8c) and may be in error by a fraction of a percent. A slight error in the slope can cause a much larger error in the point of tangency with a line of fixed slope, consequently the location of these crossmarks may be noticeably in error. But conversely, a small error in the split $c_1/c_2$ near the optimal will have little effect upon the value of $\mu$.

What one should notice in this sequence is that the optimal $c_1/c_2$ is not very far from the $45^\circ$ line of Fig. IV-12 sufficiently close, in fact, that to approximate the optimal split by a point on the $45^\circ$ line would have little effect upon the value of $\mu$ (less than about 1%). Although we have only two curves for $\gamma_0 \neq \gamma_2$ and $\gamma_1 = \pi/2$, it is clear from the smooth trend in the shape of these curves that the same conclusions would be true for other values of $\gamma_2$.

Fig. IV-12 shows also one other curve for $\gamma_0 = \pi/4$, $\gamma_1 = \pi/4$, $\gamma_2 = \pi$ $(\Delta_2 = 0)$, for which the optimal split is also rather close to the $45^\circ$ line. Not shown in Fig. IV-12 are the curves corresponding to an interchange of $\gamma_0$ and $\gamma_2$. For any curve with $\gamma_0 \neq \gamma_2$, we could have drawn a comparison curve with $\gamma_2$ and $\gamma_0$ interchanged, simply by interchanging the axes (reflect the curve over the $45^\circ$ line).

Although an accurate evaluation of $\mu$ can be quite complex, Fig. IV-demonstrates that the optimal split is for

$$\frac{c_1 \sin \gamma_2}{(\Delta_0 + \Delta_1)} \simeq \frac{c_2 \sin \gamma_0}{(\Delta_1 + \Delta_2)}$$

$$\frac{c_1}{c_2} \simeq \frac{\sin \gamma_2}{\sin \gamma_0} = \left(\frac{\Delta_0 + \Delta_1}{\Delta_1 + \Delta_2}\right)^{1/2} , \qquad (5.10)$$

the same as in (5.4b). In view of the results of section 2, particularly (2.17) that, for $(\Delta_1 + \Delta_2)/\Delta_0 \ll 1$, the equilibrium queue length for $c_2 = \infty$ would be of order $[(\Delta_1 + \Delta_2)/\Delta_0]^{1/2} c_1$, it is not surprising that the optimal $c_2$ would be such as to assign it a value comparable with the mean queue length for $c_2 = \infty$. The result (2.17), however, was the one for which there was no simple explanation in terms of conventional queueing theory logic.

Also from Fig. IV-12 we see that, for most values of the $\gamma$'s, the optimal $\mu$ is given by

$$2(\mu_0 - \mu) \, c_1 \sin \gamma_2 / (\Delta_0 + \Delta_1) \quad \approx \quad 1.1 \ \text{to} \ 1.2$$

for the $c_j$ chosen as in (5.10)

$$c_1 + c_2 \ = \ c \ = \ \frac{c_1}{(\Delta_0 + \Delta_1)^{1/2}} \ [(\Delta_1 + \Delta_2)^{\frac{1}{2}} + (\Delta_0 + \Delta_1)^{\frac{1}{2}}] \ .$$

Thus

$$\frac{\sin \gamma_2}{(\Delta_0 + \Delta_1)^{1/2}} \ \frac{2 \, (\mu_0 - \mu) \, c}{[(\Delta_1 + \Delta_2)^{1/2} + (\Delta_0 + \Delta_1)^{1/2}]} \ \approx \ 1.1 \ - \ 1.2 \ . \quad (5.11)$$

The factor $\sin \gamma_2 / (\Delta_0 + \Delta_1)^{1/2}$ is a symmetric function of the $\Delta_j$ or $\gamma_j$ . From (III 2.16)

$$\frac{\sin \gamma_2}{(\Delta_0 + \Delta_1)^{1/2}} \ = \ \left[ \frac{\sin \gamma_0 \sin \gamma_1 \sin \gamma_2}{\Delta^*} \right]^{\frac{1}{2}} \ = \ \left[ \frac{\Delta_2 \Delta_1 + \Delta_0 \Delta_2 + \Delta_0 \Delta_1}{(\Delta_0 + \Delta_1)(\Delta_2 + \Delta_1)(\Delta_2 + \Delta_0)} \right]^{\frac{1}{2}} \ .$$

$$(5.12)$$

The factor $[(\Delta_1 + \Delta_2)^{1/2} + (\Delta_0 + \Delta_1)^{1/2}]$ , however, is not symmetric to interchange of the $\Delta_j$'s. It is, of course, symmetric to the interchange of $\Delta_0$ and $\Delta_2$ by virtue of the symmetry of section III 5. Server 1 is exceptional in that this server can be interrupted either by an empty queue upstream or a full storage downstream. If it is possible to inter-change servers, one should put the server with the smallest $\Delta_j$ in the middle, $\Delta_1 < \Delta_0, \Delta_2$ .

208

6. **Joint Distributions.** Because of the large variety of special forms for the joint probability distribution of $Q_1$, $Q_2$ as described in section I and 4, it is not possible to give an exhaustive description of it here. We will merely give a few illustrations of relatively simple cases.

For $\gamma_0 = \gamma_1 = \gamma_2 = \pi/3$ , (III 4.5) simplifies to

$$H(w) = B e^{-i\pi/6} w^{1/3} .$$

If we further specialize to $c_1^* = c_2^*$ (i.e., $w_1 = w_3$), (III 3.2) gives

$$\zeta(w) = e^{i5\pi/6} w_1^{-2/3} \int_{w/w_1}^{\infty} dz\ z^{-1/3} (z^2 - 1)^{-2/3}$$

or

$$\frac{\zeta(w)}{c_1^*} = \frac{\Gamma(2/3)\ e^{i5\pi/6}}{\Gamma^2(1/3)} \int_0^{(w_1/w)^2} dv\ (1 - v)^{-2/3} v^{-2/3} . \tag{6.1}$$

From the numerical integration of the marginal distribution $g_2^{**}(\ell_2^*)$ which was needed to evaluate the point (1.42, 1.42) of Fig. IV-11, one can determine the constant B . One finds that

$$g^{**} = \text{Re } H(w) \simeq \frac{1.03}{c_1^{*2}} \left|\frac{w}{w_1}\right|^{\frac{1}{3}} \cos(\frac{\theta}{3} - \frac{\pi}{6}) \tag{6.2}$$

in which $\theta$ is the complex phase of $w$ .

For each value of $|(w/w_1)|$ and $\theta$ , one can evaluate $\zeta(w)$ from (6. and the corresponding value of $g^{**}$ at that point from (6.2). Fig. IV-1. shows a contour plot of $g^{**}$ in the $\zeta$-plane of Fig. III-1c and Fig. IV-13b

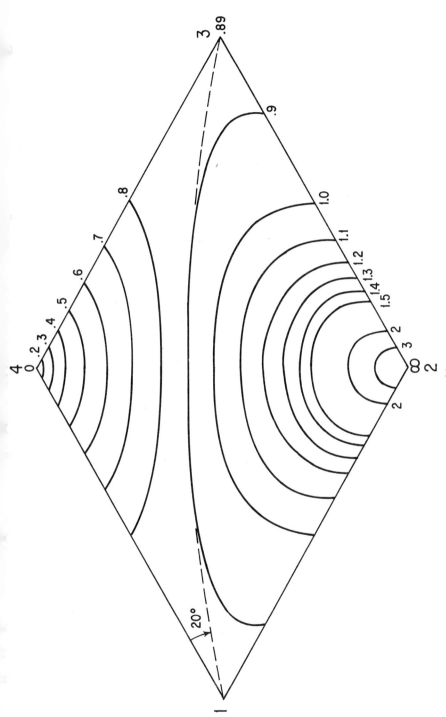

Fig. IV-13a. Contour plot of $g^{**}$ in the $\zeta$-plane for $\gamma_0 = \gamma_1 = \gamma_2$ , $c_1 = c_2$ .

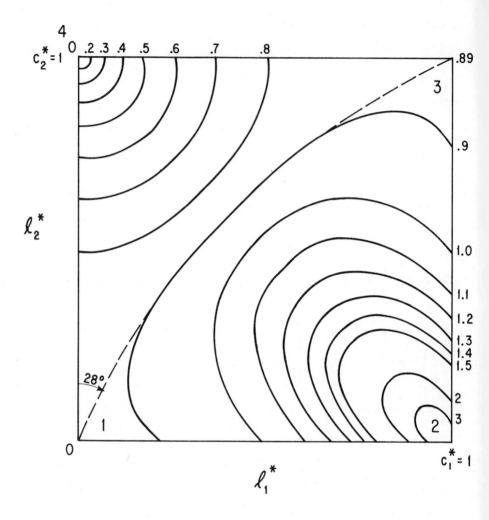

Fig. IV-13b. Contour plot of $g^{**}$ in the $\ell_1^*$, $\ell_2^*$ space $\gamma_0 = \gamma_1 = \gamma_2$ , $c_1 = c_2$ .

shows the mapping of this into the $\ell_1^*$, $\ell_2^*$ plane of Fig. III 1b. The numerical values of $g^{**}$ along the contours are nondimensional values corresponding to $c_1^* = c_2^* = 1$ (equivalently, the $g^{**}$ is measured in units of $c_1^{*-2}$).

Actually Fig. IV-13a and b were sketched from some rather crude interpolations, because it is a bit tedious to evaluate (6.1) for complex values of $(w_1/w)^2$. In the vicinity of point 4, $g^{**}$ vanishes as the 1/2 power of the distance from the corner, as described in (III 6.4), and the contours have a shape as described by (III 6.6). Locally the contours differ only in a scale of length from this corner. The angles which the contours make with the edges is specified by the boundary conditions (they meet the boundary at an angle of $\pi/3$). Similarly near point 2, the contours are described by (III 6.8); $g^{**}$ becomes infinite like $\zeta^{-1/2}$. The shape of the contours is easily evaluated from (III 6.8).

To determine the shape of the contours near points 1 or 3, one must carry the expansions one term beyond that given in (III 6.11). For $\gamma_1 = \gamma_2 = \gamma_3$, (III 6.11) merely predicts that $g^{**}$ has a non-zero finite value, specifically it is approximately 0.89. The next term in the expansion is proportional to $(\zeta - \zeta_1)^3$ which means that $g^{**}$ changes very slowly. Note that the contour for $g^{**} = 0.9$ is already quite a distance from the corner. The local contours near point 1 or 3 are asymptotic to a line making an angle of about $20^{\circ}$ with the boundaries 1-4 or 3-4 (shown by the broken line).

In addition to the expansions from the corners, it is also relatively easy to evaluate $g^{**}$ from (6.1), (6.2) along the boundaries and along the vertical line from 4 to 2. In each case (6.1) can be expressed in terms of the incomplete Beta function $B_x(1/3, 1/3)$ for real $x$. From a single graph of the Beta function one can evaluate $g^{**}$ along these line

One also knows the slope of the contours along the boundaries and the ver

tical axis (the vertical axis is an axis of symmetry).

From the sketch in Fig. IV-13a, the contours of Fig. IV-13b were draw

from the linear mapping. In Fig. IV-13b, the contours near point 4 meet

the boundary at right angles and appear like circles; actually the radiu

of a contour from point 4 varies by only a few percent locally. Near poi

4, the contours bulge slightly in the $45°$ direction, but as $g^{**}$ increas

the contours become flatter in the $45°$ direction (the latter can be seen

in the figure).

Despite the fact that $g^{**}$ vanishes at point 4 and is infinite at

point 2, it actually does not change very much over most of the area. Th

value of $g^{**}$ is between 0.7 and 1.3 over about 3/4 of the total area.

The distribution differs from a uniform distribution in that some probabi

ity mass has been removed from the corner at point 4 and added to region

near point 2.

As a second illustration we consider the case $\gamma_1 = \pi/2$, $\gamma_0 = \gamma_2 = \pi$

$c_2 = \infty$ (regular service at 1, infinite storage at 2). Actually the prop·

erties of all systems with $\gamma_1 = \pi/2$ can be evaluated in terms of tabula

elliptic functions. The main difficulty in most numerical evaluations

originates from the mapping (III 3.2) which, however, for $\gamma_1 = \pi/2$ , be-

comes an elliptic integral, specifically

$$e^{-i\pi/4}\left[\zeta(w) - \zeta_1\right] = \frac{2}{(w_3+w_1)^{1/2}}\int_0^{(1 - w/w_1)^{1/2}} dx\ (1 - x^2)^{-1/2}\left[1 - \frac{w_1\ x^2}{(w_1+w_3)}\right]^{-1/}$$

The inverse of this can be expressed as

$$\frac{w}{w_1} = cn^2 u \quad ,$$

$$u = \frac{(w_3 + w_1)^{1/2}}{2} e^{-i\pi/4} [\zeta - \zeta_1] \tag{6.3}$$

in which $cn$ is the elliptic function of parameter $w_1/(w_1 + w_3)$. With this, we can express $G(\zeta) = H(w(\zeta))$ explicitly in terms of $\zeta$ through (III 4.5).

$$G(\zeta) = B \, w_1^{\gamma_0/\pi} (w_3 + w_1)^{\frac{\gamma_2}{\pi} - \frac{1}{2}} e^{-i\pi/2} e^{i\gamma_0} cn \, u \left[ sn \, u \right]^{\frac{2\gamma_0}{\pi} - 1} \left[ dn \, u \right]^{\frac{2\gamma_2}{\pi} - 1}$$

$$\tag{6.4}$$

in which $sn$ and $dn$ are also elliptic functions of parameter $w_1/(w_1+w_3)$.

From (6.4) one can write an explicit (but complicated) formula for $g^{**}(\ell_1^*, \ell_2^*)$, except for the normalization factor $B$. Since $\zeta = \xi + i\eta$ is a simple function of $\ell_1^*, \ell_2^*$, (III 2.12), $u$ can be written in terms of $\ell_1^*, \ell_2^*$, or $\ell_1, \ell_2$. Their are formulas for the real and imaginary parts of each of the elliptic functions of a complex argument, and, of course, one can also write formulas for the real and imaginary parts of any power of a complex number or products of complex numbers. Consequently, one can evaluate $g^{**} = $ Real $G(\zeta)$ explicitly in terms of trigonometric and elliptic functions. It is still quite tedious, however, to construct the contour map of $g^{**}$.

If we further specialize to the case $c_2 = \infty$ ($w_3 = 0$), the parameter of the elliptic function becomes 1 and the elliptic functions are expressible

214

in terms of elementary functions. Equation (6.4) simplifies to

$$G(\zeta) = B\, e^{-i\pi/2}\, e^{i\gamma_0}\, [\sinh u]^{-2\gamma_2/\pi} \; . \tag{6.4a}$$

From (III 7.8), (III 7.9) one can determine the normalization $B$ ,

$$B = \frac{\pi^{1/2}}{c_1^{*2}} \frac{\Gamma(\tfrac{1}{2} + \gamma_2/\pi)}{\Gamma(\gamma_2/\pi)} \; ,$$

and, for $\gamma_1 = \pi/2$ , the mapping from the $\ell_1^*,\ \ell_2^*$ plane to the $\zeta$-plane (figure III 1) is simply a rotation which preserves the $90^\circ$ corner at point 1. Consequently, $G$ can be expressed directly in terms of $\ell_1^*,\ \ell_2^*$ and

$$g^{**}(\ell_1^*,\ \ell_2^*) = \frac{\pi^{\frac{1}{2}}\Gamma(\tfrac{1}{2} + \gamma_2/\pi)}{c_1^{*2}\,\Gamma(\gamma_2/\pi)} \; \mathrm{Re} \left\{ \sin\left[\frac{\pi(\ell_1^* + i\ell_2^*)}{2\,c_1^*}\right] \right\}^{\frac{-2\gamma_2}{\pi}} . \tag{6.4b}$$

Fig. IV-4 shows a contour plot of (6.4b) for $\gamma_0 = \gamma_2 = \pi/4$, $c_1^* = 1$ Since, in this case, $\ell_1/\ell_1^* = \ell_2/\ell_2^*$ , this can also be interpreted as a contour plot of $g^*(\ell_1,\ell_2)$ for $c_1 = 1$ . The contours meet the line $\ell_1^* = 0$ at $45^\circ$, but meet the lines $\ell_1^* = 1$ or $\ell_2^* = 0$ at right angles. The density becomes infinite at $\ell_1^* = \ell_2^* = 0$ like the $- 1/2$ power of the distance from the origin. There is a saddle point at $\ell_1^* = 1$ , $\ell_2^* = 0$ . The marginal distribution $g_1^{**}(\ell_1^*)$, the integral of $g^{**}(\ell_1^*,\ \ell_2^*)$ up a vertical line at $\ell_1^*$ is independent of $\ell_1^*$, whereas $g_2^{**}(\ell_2^*)$, the integral along a horizontal line, gives the distribution shown in Fig. IV-2.

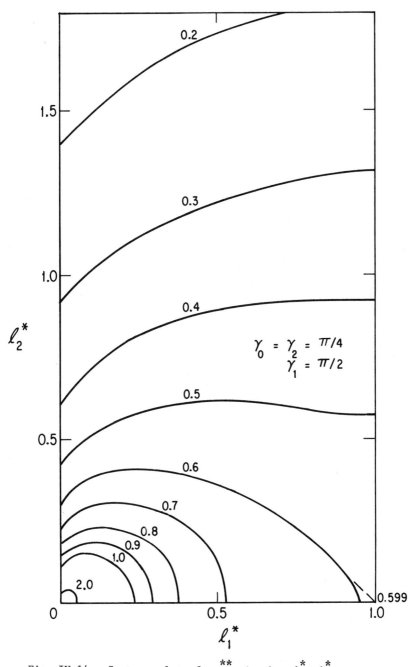

Fig. IV-14. Contour plot of $g^{**}$ in the $\ell_1^*$, $\ell_2^*$ space for $\gamma_0 = \gamma_2 = \pi/4$ .

Fig. IV-15 shows a contour plot of (6.4b) for $\gamma_2 = \pi/2$, $\gamma_0 \to 0$ ($\Delta_1$ $\Delta_2 \to 0$). This represents a limiting distribution because, from (2.13), we see that the queue length $Q_2/c_1$ is actually $\gamma_0 Q_2^*/c_1^*$ with $\gamma_0 \to 0$. Thus the vertical coordinate of Fig. IV-15 is proportional to $\ell_2/\gamma_0$. Th contours near $\ell_1^* = \ell_2^* = 0$ are circles tangent to the vertical axis at $\ell_1^* = 0$. The contours are supposed to meet the boundary $\ell_1^* = 0$ at zero angle, but the line $\ell_1^* = 0$ is highly singular, $g^{**}(\ell_1^*, \ell_2^*)$ vanishes along this line everywhere except at the origin. Despite this behavior a $\ell_1^* = 0$, the integral of $g^{**}(\ell_1^*, \ell_2^*)$ up any vertical line $\ell_1^* > 0$ is in dependent of $\ell_1^*$. The integral of $g^{**}(\ell_1^*, \ell_2^*)$ along a horizontal line gives the limit distribution shown in Fig. IV-3.

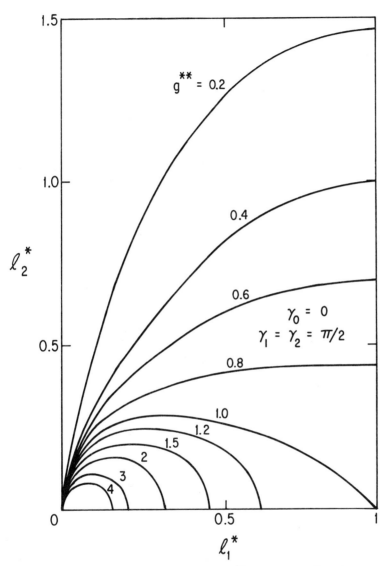

Fig. IV-15. Contour plot of $g^{**}$ in the $\ell_1^*$, $\ell_2^*$ space for $\gamma_0 = 0$, $c_2 = \infty$.

# V. Time-dependent Solutions, $\Delta_0 = \Delta_1 = \Delta_2$

1. **Introduction.** Most of the techniques used to analyse equilibrium or time-dependent solutions of the diffusion equation for $n = 1$, as described in Chapter II, do not have simple generalizations for $n \geq 2$. We saw, for example, in Chapters III and IV, that the derivation of the equilibrium queue distribution was already quite difficult even in the special case $\mu_0 = \mu_1 = \mu_2$. Furthermore, the methods used there do not have obvious generalization for $\mu_0 \neq \mu_1 \neq \mu_2$.

We are not even attempting here to present a systematic treatment of tandem queues, but are content to look for whatever can be had easily. Much of the existing literature on tandem queues deals with systems for which a Poisson input process gives a Poisson output process, or other related systems for which the equilibrium queue lengths $Q_1$, $Q_2$, --- are statistically independent. So far we have not taken advantage of any special features of the diffusion equation associated with the fact that certain problems have been solved exactly.

A server with exponential service time has a variance rate $\Delta_j$ equal to its service rate $\mu_j$, but in the diffusion equation we will not obtain significant queues unless the input rate is approximately equal to the service rate, which means that the service rates $\mu_j$ must be nearly equal. The diffusion analogue of the known soluble problems is not what one might at first suspect, namely that $\Delta_j = \mu_j$, but rather that the $\Delta_j$ are all equal to each other, $\Delta_j = \Delta_0$ for all $j$. The known soluble problems are also ones with infinite storage $c_j = \infty$, all $j$, since any finite storage obviously complicates the probability structure of the input or output process.

In this chapter we shall investigate what is special about the case $\Delta_0 = \Delta_1 = \Delta_2$, $c_1 = c_2 = \infty$, at least in the case $n = 2$. Most of the results described here for $n = 2$ will, however, have generalizations to $n > 2$.

Image Solution. We shall see later that the equilibrium queue distributions for $\Delta_j = \Delta_0$, $c_j = \infty$ are indeed trivial. We will attack the more difficult time-dependent problem, generalizing the solution of section II 6, from which the equilibrium distributions will follow.

The solution of the diffusion equation for $n = 1$ obtained in section II 6 by the method of images applied for any choice of $\Delta_1$, $\Delta_0$, $\mu_1$, $\mu_0$ but $c_1 = \infty$. The formulas for the special case $\Delta_0 = \Delta_1$ are not really much simpler than for $\Delta_0 \neq \Delta_1$. The main simplification is in eq. (II 6.2). The image transformation is, in this case, a permutation or reflection, i.e.,

$$x_0' = x_1, \qquad x_1' = x_0 .\qquad (2.1)$$

There is also a slight simplification in that the normal distributions are rotationally symmetric.

It follows from (II 6.1) by superposition of various solutions or, equivalently, by integration over any initial probability distribution of the coordinates $y_0$, $y_1$, that, if $f_0(x_0,x_1;t)$ is any solution of the diffusion equation (not necessarily satisfying the boundary conditions), then

$$f(x_0,x_1;t) = f_0(x_0,x_1;t) + \frac{\partial}{\partial x_1}\left\{\exp\left[\frac{(\mu_1-\mu_0)(x_1-x_0)}{\Delta_0}\right]\int_{x_0}^{\infty}dy\, f_0(x_1,y;t)\right\}$$

$$(2.2)$$

220

is also a solution of the diffusion equation (for $\Delta_0 = \Delta_1$). Furthermore (2.2) also satisfies the boundary condition (II 1.2b), namely,

$$(-\mu_0 + \mu_1)f \;+\; \Delta_0\, \partial f/\partial x_0 \;=\; 0 \qquad \text{at } x_0 = x_1. \qquad (2.3)$$

In other words, the linear operator on the function $f_0(\cdot,\cdot;\cdot)$ described by the right-hand side of (2.2) transforms $f_0$ into another function $f(\cdot,\cdot;\cdot)$ which satisfies the differential equation plus the boundary condition (2.3). This is the "image" transformation. In section II 6, this was specifically applied only to the "fundamental" solution generated by an initial state $(y_0,y_1)$ at time $t_0$ .

For $n = 2$ , $\Delta_0 = \Delta_1 = \Delta_2$ , $c_1 = c_2 = \infty$ , we wish to obtain a solution $f(x_0,x_1,x_2;t)$ of the diffusion equation

$$\frac{\partial f}{\partial t} \;=\; -\mu_0 \frac{\partial f}{\partial x_0} - \mu_1 \frac{\partial f}{\partial x_1} - \mu_2 \frac{\partial f}{\partial x_2} \;+\; \frac{\Delta_0}{2}\left[\frac{\partial^2 f}{\partial x_0^2} + \frac{\partial^2 f}{\partial x_1^2} + \frac{\partial^2 f}{\partial x_2^2}\right] \qquad (2.4)$$

in the region $x_0 \geq x_1 \geq x_2$ , subject to the boundary conditions

$$(-\mu_0 + \mu_1)f \;+\; \Delta_0\, \partial f/\partial x_0 \;=\; 0 \qquad \text{at } x_0 = x_1 \qquad (2.5a)$$

$$(-\mu_1 + \mu_2)f \;+\; \Delta_0\, \partial f/\partial x_1 \;=\; 0 \qquad \text{at } x_1 = x_2 . \qquad (2.5b)$$

In the space $(x_1,x_2,x_3)$, $f$ is defined only in the part of the space shown in Fig. V-1 bounded by the planes $x_0 = x_1$ and $x_1 = x_2$ .

It is clear from a comparison of the case $n = 2$ and $n = 1$ , that one can generate solutions of (2.4) which satisfy (2.5a) simply by applying the image transformation (2.2) to any solution of (2.4) (the fundamental solution, for example). One can also obtain solutions of

221

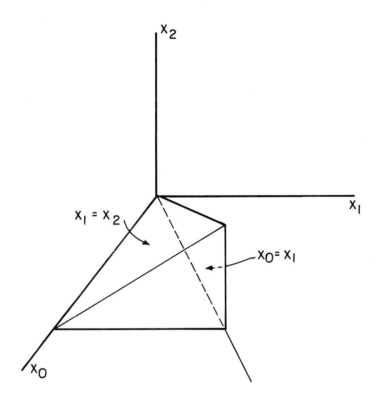

Fig. V-1. Boundaries of the region over which f is defined.

(2.4) which satisfy (2.5b) by applying the analogue of (2.2) but with $x_0, x_1$ replaced by $x_1, x_2$. Each of these image transformations could, individually, be generalized to the case $\Delta_0 \neq \Delta_1 \neq \Delta_2$ through use of the more general image transformation described by (II 6.1).

In principle, one could write a solution of (2.4) which simultaneously satisfies both (2.5a) and (2.5b), even for $\Delta_0 \neq \Delta_1 \neq \Delta_2$. One would first generate a solution of (2.4) satisfying (2.5a) by applying the transformation (II 6.1) to some solution of (2.4); i.e., one reflects $f_0$ over the plane $x_0 = x_1$. The second step is to take this solution of (2.4) as a new $f_0$ and reflect it over the other plane $x_1 = x_2$. This reflected solution, which now satisfies (2.5b), no longer satisfies (2.5a). We now take this as a new $f_0$ and reflect it over the plane $x_0 = x_1$. We continue to reflect solutions over the two boundaries until either the scheme, by accident, happens to terminate, or, hopefully, the infinite series of images converges to an f satisfying both boundary conditions.

A special feature of the case $\Delta_0 = \Delta_1 = \Delta_2$ is that the sequence of reflections terminates in finitely many steps. The reason for this is that the mapping (2.1) is simply a permutation, as is the corresponding reflection over the boundary $x_1 = x_2$. The succession of images terminates when one has exhausted all permutations of the numbers $(x_0, x_1, x_2)$. The solution of (2.4), (2.5a,b) defined only for $x_0 \geq x_1 \geq x$ is obtained from an $f_0$ defined for all values of $x_0, x_1, x_2$. Specifically, for any $f_0$ satisfying (2.4), the following function satisfies (2.4), (2.5a), and (2.5b).

$$f(x_0,x_1,x_2;t) \quad = \quad f_0(x_0,x_1,x_2;t)$$

$$+ \frac{\partial}{\partial x_1}\left\{\exp\left[\frac{(\mu_1-\mu_0)(x_1-x_0)}{\Delta_0}\right]\int_{x_0}^{\infty}dz_0\, f_0(x_1,z_0,x_2;t)\right\}$$

$$+ \frac{\partial}{\partial x_2}\left\{\exp\left[\frac{(\mu_2-\mu_1)(x_2-x_1)}{\Delta_0}\right]\cdot\int_{x_1}^{\infty}dz_1\, f_0(x_0,x_2,z_1;t)\right\}$$

$$+ \frac{\partial}{\partial x_1}\left\{\exp\left[\frac{(\mu_1-\mu_0)(x_1-x_0)}{\Delta_0}\right]\int_{x_0}^{\infty}dz_0\frac{\partial}{\partial x_2}\left\{\exp\left[\frac{(\mu_2-\mu_1)(x_2-z_0)}{\Delta_0}\right]\cdot\int_{z_0}^{\infty}dz_1\, f_0(x_1,x_2,z_1;t)\right\}\right\}$$

$$+ \frac{\partial}{\partial x_2}\left\{\exp\left[\frac{(\mu_2-\mu_1)(x_2-x_1)}{\Delta_0}\right]\int_{x_1}^{\infty}dz_1\frac{\partial}{\partial x_2}\left\{\exp\left[\frac{(\mu_1-\mu_0)(x_2-x_0)}{\Delta_0}\right]\cdot\int_{x_0}^{\infty}dz_0\, f_0(x_2,z_0,z_1;t)\right\}\right\}$$

$$+ \frac{\partial}{\partial x_2}\left\{\exp\left[\frac{(\mu_2-\mu_1)(x_2-x_1)}{\Delta_0}\right]\int_{x_1}^{\infty}dz_1\frac{\partial}{\partial x_2}\left\{\exp\left[\frac{(\mu_1-\mu_0)(x_2-x_0)}{\Delta_0}\right]\right.\right.$$

$$\left.\left.\cdot\int_{x_0}^{\infty}dz_0\frac{\partial}{\partial z_1}\left\{\exp\left[\frac{(\mu_2-\mu_1)(z_1-z_0)}{\Delta_0}\right]\int_{z_0}^{\infty}dz_2\, f_0(x_2,z_1,z_2;t)\right\}\right\}\right\}\quad.$$

(2.6)

This expression consists of six terms. The first is some arbitrary solution of (2.4) defined for all $x_0,x_1,x_2$, and $t$. The second term results from reflection of $f_0$ over the boundary $x_0 = x_1$, and the third term from reflection of $f_0$ over the boundary $x_1 = x_2$. The fourth term is the reflection of the third term over $x_0 = x_1$ and the fifth term is the reflection of the second term over $x_1 = x_2$. The sixth term, as written, results from a reflection of the fourth term over $x_1 = x_2$, but this last term can be simplified. The integrand of the $z_1$-integration appears as the derivative of some function with respect to $z_1$ ; consequently this integration can be performed, giving for the last term

$$- \frac{\partial}{\partial x_2} \left\{ \exp\left[ \frac{(\mu_2-\mu_1)(x_2-x_1)}{\Delta_0} \right] \frac{\partial}{\partial x_2} \left\{ \exp\left[ \frac{(\mu_1-\mu_0)(x_2-x_0)}{\Delta_0} \right] \right. \right.$$

$$\left. \left. \cdot \int_{x_0}^{\infty} dz_0 \, \exp\left[ \frac{(\mu_2-\mu_1)(x_1-z_0)}{\Delta_0} \right] \int_{z_0}^{\infty} dz_2 \, f_0(x_2,x_1,z_2;t) \right\} \right\} \quad .$$

But now one can also combine the first and third exponential factors simplifying this to

$$- \frac{\partial}{\partial x_2} \int_{x_0}^{\infty} dz_0 \, \exp\left[ \frac{(\mu_2-\mu_1)(x_2-z_0)}{\Delta_0} \right] \frac{\partial}{\partial x_2} \left\{ \exp\left[ \frac{(\mu_1-\mu_0)(x_2-x_0)}{\Delta_0} \right] \cdot \int_{z_0}^{\infty} dz_1 \, f_0(x_2,x_1,z_1;t) \right.$$

$$\tag{2.6a}$$

If one reflects the fifth term of (2.6) over the boundary $x_0 = x_1$ , one finds that this also gives a term which is equal to (2.6a), i.e., the sixth term of (2.6) obtains either from a reflection of the fourth term over the second boundary or the fifth term over the first boundary. It is this special feature of the case $\Delta_0 = \Delta_1 = \Delta_2$ which terminates the series of successive reflections. If one applies a reflection transformation to (2.6) over either boundary, one generates simply a multiple of the same f (actually 2f); therefore (2.6) must satisfy both boundary conditions.

As a further check on the validity of (2.6), one will recall that the boundary condition (2.5b) was originally derived from a requirement that, if $Q_2(t)$ should vanish, this would interrupt the service at server 2 but would have no effect on the evolution of $D_0(t)$ or $D_1(t)$. In the present case with $c_1 = c_2 = \infty$, this means that the marginal distribution of $D_0(t)$, $D_1(t)$ for $n = 2$ should be equal to the distribution of $D_0(t)$, $D_1(t)$ for a system with $n = 1$; the existence of a second server should not affect the behavior of servers 0 and 1.

If we integrate (2.6) with respect to $x_2$ from $-\infty$ to $x_1$, we should obtain

$$f(x_0,x_1;t) = \int_{-\infty}^{x_1} dx_2 \, f(x_0,x_1,x_2;t) \quad ,$$

in which the left-hand side satisfies (2.2) and the integrand on the right-hand side satisfies (2.6), provided that the $f_0$'s satisfy the same relation. One can indeed verify that this is true. The integrals of the first and third terms of (2.6) combine to give the first term of (2.2); the integrals of the second and fifth terms of (2.6) combine to give the second term of (2.2); and the integrals of the fourth and sixth terms of (2.6) cancel each other.

The boundary condition (2.5a) is supposed to guarantee that if $Q_1 = 0$ and server 1 is interrupted, this shall have no immediate effect upon the evolution of $D_0(t)$ and $D_2(t)$, as long as $Q_2(t)$ stays positive. In terms of the solution (2.6), this means that, if we choose the $f_0(x_0,x_1,x_2;t)$ so that it is certainly zero for $x_2 > x_0$ or $x_2 > x_1$ but not necessarily for $x_1 > x_0$, then the marginal distribution of $D_0(t)$, $D_2(t)$ should be equal to the corresponding marginal distribution of $f_0(x_0,x_1,x_2;t)$. This is verified also by (2.6). The condition that $f_0$ vanish for $x_2 > x_0$ or $x_1$ guarantees that all integrals of the $f_0$ in the third to sixth terms of (2.6) vanish. If one integrates the first and second terms of (2.6) with respect to $x_1$

up to $x_1 = x_0$ from a lower limit below which $f_0$ vanishes anyway

(actually from $x_2$ to $x_0$), the two terms combine to give the integral

of $f_0(x_0,x_1,x_2;t)$ with respect to $x_1$ from $-\infty$ to $+\infty$ .

It is possible to rearrange (2.6) in many ways but none seems to

achieve any significant simplification. One could not expect to have a

simple formula, however, because the formula must describe a wide variety

of different types of detailed behavior. If we take $f_0(x_0,x_1,x_2;t)$ to

be the fundamental solution of (2.4) starting from an arbitrary initial

state $(y_0,y_1,y_2)$ at time $t = t_0$ , $f_0$ describes a distribution whose

center is traveling with velocity $(\mu_0,\mu_1,\mu_2)$ in the $(x_0,x_1,x_2)$-space

and spreading with a standard deviation $(\Delta_0 t)^{1/2}$ in all directions.

The formula (2.6) describes the evolution of $f$ for arbitrary choices

of velocities or initial states $(y_0,y_1,y_2)$, with $y_0 > y_1 > y_2$ .

If $\mu_0 < \mu_1$ , the velocity has a positive component perpendicular

to the plane $x_0 = x_1$ and the unreflected distribution $f_0$ will even-

tually pass through this plane. If $\mu_0 > \mu_1$ , it will run away from

the plane $x_0 = x_1$ , although some of the distribution may penetrate

the plane and be reflected (interrupting server 1). Similarly if

$\mu_1 < \mu_2$ , the unreflected distribution will penetrate the plane $x_1 = x_2$.

Even in the limit of arbitrarily small $\Delta_0 t$ where we would use the de-

terministic approximations discussed in Chapter I, there is a variety

of transient behaviors of $D_0(t)$, $D_1(t)$, $D_2(t)$ in which a queue might

at first decrease to (nearly) zero and later reform, or start to grow

but later decrease. Such behaviors are described in (2.6) by the terms

corresponding to multiple reflections from the boundaries.

The case $\mu_0 < \mu_1, \mu_2$ is of special interest since we expect the

distribution of $Q_1(t)$, $Q_2(t)$ to approach an equilibrium. In (2.6) one

can easily show for $x_0 > x_1 > x_2$ and sufficiently large $t$ , that all terms except the fifth will decrease very rapidly with t (exponentially fast). Furthermore in the fifth term the integrals with respect to $z_0$ and $z_1$ are essentially over the entire range of the distribution $f_0$, so the lower limits of integration can be replaced by $-\infty$. Thus

$$f(x_0,x_1,x_2;t) \rightarrow \frac{\partial}{\partial x_2} \left\{ \exp\left[\frac{(\mu_2-\mu_1)(x_2-x_1)}{\Delta_0}\right] \frac{\partial}{\partial x_2} \left\{ \exp\left[\frac{(\mu_1-\mu_0)(x_2-x_0)}{\Delta_0}\right] \right.\right.$$

$$\left.\left. \cdot \int_{-\infty}^{+\infty} dz_0 \int_{-\infty}^{+\infty} dz_1 \, f_0(x_2,z_0,z_1;t) \right\} \right\} \,. \tag{2.7}$$

If we take for $f_0$ the solution with initial state $(y_0,y_1,y_2)$ at time 0, the integrals with respect to $z_0$ and $z_1$ give simply the marginal distribution of $D_0(t)$ evaluated, however, at $x_2$ rather than $x_0$. Instead of expanding the derivatives in (2.7), which will generate several terms, one can integrate to obtain a simple expression for the joint distribution function of $D_0(t)$, $Q_1(t)$, $Q_2(t)$,

$$P\{D_0(t) \le x_0, \, Q_1(t) > \ell_1, \, Q_2(t) > \ell_2\} \rightarrow$$

$$\tag{2.7a}$$

$$\exp\left[\frac{-(\mu_2-\mu_0)\ell_2}{\Delta_0}\right] \exp\left[\frac{-(\mu_1-\mu_0)\ell_1}{\Delta_0}\right] \Phi\left(\frac{x_0-\ell_1-\ell_2-y_0-\mu_0 t)}{(\Delta_0 t)^{1/2}}\right) \,.$$

The first two factors of (2.7a) are what we would have expected for the joint equilibrium queue distribution. Indeed, if we let $x_0 \rightarrow \infty$ so as to produce the marginal distribution of $Q_1(t)$, $Q_2(t)$, the third factor goes to 1 for all values of $\ell_1$ and $\ell_2$. Thus the marginal distribution of $Q_1(t)$, $Q_2(t)$ approaches an equilibrium with $Q_1$ and $Q_2$ statistically independent and exponentially distributed.

If we set $\ell_2 = 0$ , we obtain the joint marginal distribution of $D_0(t)$, $Q_1(t)$, which agrees with that analysed in section II 6. If we set $\ell_1 = 0$ , we obtain the joint marginal distribution of $D_0(t)$, $Q_2(t)$ which has exactly the same form, i.e., the marginal distribution of $D_0(t)$, $Q_2(t)$ is the same as if server 1 were not there.

From (2.7a) we can also obtain the conditional distribution of $Q_1(t)$ $Q_2(t)$ given $D_0(t) = x_0$ . As one might expect from the analysis of section II 6, the value of $\mu_0$ becomes irrelevant.

$$P\{Q_1(t) > \ell_1, \; Q_2(t) > \ell_2 | D_0(t) = x_0\} \quad \rightarrow$$

(2.8)

$$\exp\left[\frac{-(\mu_2 - (x_0 - y_0)/t)\ell_2}{\Delta_0}\right] \exp\left[\frac{-(\mu_1 - (x_0 - y_0)/t)\ell_1}{\Delta_0}\right] \exp\left[\frac{-(\ell_1 + \ell_2)^2}{2\,\Delta_0\,t}\right] \quad .$$

If, per chance, server zero were to serve $x_0 - y_0$ customers in time $t$ with $(x_0 - y_0)/t$ significantly different from the expected rate $\mu_0$ , servers 1 and 2 would react as if the arrival rate were $(x_0 - y_0)/t$ . For sufficiently large $t$ , the last factor of (2.8) approaches 1; $Q_1(t)$, $Q_2(t)$ become statistically independent and exponentially distributed with parameter as if the arrival rate were $(x_0 - y_0)/t$ .

Although the above results are asymptotic results for "sufficiently large t," we have retained some time dependent aspects. The terms which we have discarded are ones which decrease exponentially fast in time after the unreflected distribution has crossed the boundaries. Discarding these terms eliminates the dependence of the distribution on the initial queue lengths $y_0 - y_1$ and $y_1 - y_2$ . The time-dependence which we have retained is that caused by fluctuations in the total number of customers served by server 0. The effects of this decay much slower (like powers of $t^{-1}$ rather than exponentials in $t$). In (2.8), the last factor does approach 1 for $t \to \infty$ but the tails of the queue distribution are relatively slow to reach an equilibrium. Furthermore, this last factor shows some lingering statistical dependence between $Q_1(t)$ and $Q_2(t)$; if $Q_1$ is large, for example, this tends to retard the formation of large values of $Q_2$ .

Time-dependent Queue Distribution. In Chapter I we saw that the queue distribution $g^*(\ell_1,\ell_2;t)$ satisfies a diffusion equation of its own. The fact that we can evaluate the joint distribution of $D_0(t)$, $Q_1(t)$, $Q_2(t)$ for $\Delta_0 = \Delta_1 = \Delta_2$ , of course, implies that we can determine the corresponding marginal distribution of $Q_1(t)$, $Q_2(t)$, i.e., solutions of the time-dependent equation for $g^*(\ell_1,\ell_2;t)$ .

One might have thought that it would be easier to solve the diffusion equation for $g^*(\ell_1,\ell_2;t)$ directly than to solve the equations of higher dimension for $f(x_0,x_1,x_2;t)$ and obtain the $g^*$ by integrating over one of the variables. Anytime one can evaluate the $f$ , one can certainly evaluate the $g^*$ but not necessarily conversely. That there is an image method for finding $f$ means that there is also a corresponding image method for finding $g^*$ .

In Chapter III we did not see anything special about the equilibrium distribution for $\Delta_0 = \Delta_1 = \Delta_2$ and $c_1$, $c_2$ finite (actually the simple cases in Chapter III were those with one or more of the $\Delta_j$ equal to 0). In the diffusion equation, however, a cross-derivative term was eliminated by a linear mapping which changed the angles of the parallelogram (see Figure III-1) over which $g^*$ was defined. In the special case $\Delta_0 = \Delta_1 = \Delta_2$ the angles were changed from $\pi/2$ to $\pi/3$ or $2\pi/3$ ; also the angles which the contours made with the boundary were all $\pi/3$ . The

230

same mapping could also be applied to the time-dependent equation since these mappings do not change the term $\partial g^*/\partial t$ .

If we had tried to solve the diffusion equation for $g^*$ directly by a method of images, we would have had some hope of finding a solution by reflection over the two boundaries at angle $\pi/3$ . If it were to succeed, however, we would have eventually created images in each of the six sectors corresponding to the angles from $j\,\pi/3$ to $(j + 1)\pi/3$, $j = 0, 1, \cdots, 5,$ and we would have not had much hope of success unless the angles of the contour lines also were periodic as one rotated through the images. In other words, this special case $\Delta_0 = \Delta_1 = \Delta_2$ is one of very few (possibly the only) cases for which one would expect an image method to give a solution in finitely many steps. The fact that the image solution would have six terms means that the solution obtained directly from the equations for $g^*$ is not obviously any easier to derive than the solution for f . The equation for f has higher dimension but more obvious symmetry. Since we have the solution for f already, it is clearly easier at this stage to determine $g^*$ from f .

If one integrates (2.6) to obtain the joint marginal distribution of $Q_1$, $Q_2$, $P\{Q_1(t) < \ell_1, Q_2(t) < t_2\}$ starting from some initial queue lengths, it is possible to reduce all the multiple integrals from the various terms of (2.6) to two-dimensional integrals of some joint normal distribution over a wedged-shaped region. The various terms, however, do not combine easily and the result cannot be written in any compact form. We shall not even bother to write the formula because it seems too cumbersome to be very useful.

VI.  Laplace Transform Methods;
Equilibrium Queue Distributions
for $n = 2$, $\mu_0 < \mu_1 \neq \mu_2$ .

<u>Analysis of Transforms.</u>  The methods used in Chapter III for analysing

the behavior of the queue distributions for $\mu_0 = \mu_1 = \mu_2$ do not con-

veniently generalize to cases with $\mu_0 \neq \mu_1 \neq \mu_2$;  they depended heavily

upon the fact that the diffusion equation could be mapped into Laplace's

equation.  Some properties of the more general system with $\mu_0 \neq \mu_1 \neq \mu_2$,

however, can be deduced from the analysis of Laplace Transforms (moment

generating functions) of the probability distributions.

   If in (I 7.2) we let

$$Z(x_0, x_1, x_2) = \exp[-\lambda_0 x_0 - \lambda_1(x_0 - x_1) - \lambda_2(x_1 - x_2)] \quad ,$$

then

$$K(\lambda_0, \lambda_1, \lambda_2;t) \equiv E\{Z(D_0(t), D_1(t), D_2(t))\}$$

$$= \iiint dx_0\ dx_1\ dx_2\ f(x_0,x_1,x_2;t)\exp[-\lambda_0 x_0 - \lambda_1(x_0-x_1) - \lambda_2(x_1-x_2)]$$

$$= \iiint dx_0\ d\ell_1\ d\ell_2\ g(x_0,\ell_1,\ell_2;t)\exp[-\lambda_0 x_0 - \lambda_1\ell_1 - \lambda_2\ell_2]$$

$$\text{(1.1)}$$

defines the (triple) Laplace Transform of the distribution  f  or  g ;

equivalently, the moment generating function of  $D_0(t)$, $Q_1(t)$, $Q_2(t)$ .

Since  $D_0(t)$, $Q_1(t)$, $Q_2(t)$  are nonnegative random variables,  K  is a

real, positive, and a monotone decreasing function of  $\lambda_0$, $\lambda_1$, $\lambda_2$  for

$\lambda_0$, $\lambda_1$, $\lambda_2$  real and positive, with  $K(0, 0, 0;t) = 1$ .    For complex

values of  $\lambda_0$, $\lambda_1$, $\lambda_2$,  K  is analytic at least for  Re $\lambda_0$, $\lambda_1$, $\lambda_2 \geq 0$ .

Whereas (1.1) defines  K  in terms of  f  or  g ,  the function $K(\lambda_0,\lambda_1,\lambda_2;t)$

also uniquely determines  f  and  g .  Any equations which describe the evolution of  f  must also describe the evolution of  K ,  and vice versa

Substitution of (1.1) into (I 7.2) gives

$$\frac{d}{dt} K(\lambda_0, \lambda_1, \lambda_2; t) = E\left\{\left[-\mu_0^*(\lambda_0 + \lambda_1) + \mu_1^*(\lambda_1 - \lambda_2) + \mu_2^*\lambda_2 \right.\right.$$

$$\left.\left. + \frac{\Delta_0}{2}(\lambda_0 + \lambda_1)^2 + \frac{\Delta_1}{2}(\lambda_1 - \lambda_2)^2 + \frac{\Delta_2}{2}\lambda_2^2\right] Z(D_0(t), D_1(t), D_2(t))\right\} .$$

We can now substitute for $\mu_j^*$ from (I 6.3) to obtain

$$\frac{d}{dt} K(\lambda_0, \lambda_1, \lambda_2; t) = \left[-\mu_0(\lambda_0 + \lambda_1) + \mu_1(\lambda_1 - \lambda_2) + \mu_2\lambda_2\right.$$

$$\left. + \frac{\Delta_0}{2}(\lambda_0 + \lambda_1)^2 + \frac{\Delta_1}{2}(\lambda_1 - \lambda_2)^2 + \frac{\Delta_2}{2}\lambda_2^2\right] K(\lambda_0, \lambda_1, \lambda_2; t)$$

$$- \iiint dx_0 \, d\ell_1 \, d\ell_2 \left[\exp[-\lambda_0 x_0 - \lambda_1 \ell_1 - \lambda_2 \ell_2] g(x_0, \ell_1, \ell_2; t)\right.$$

$$\left. \cdot \left[\frac{-\mu_0(\lambda_0+\lambda_1)}{n_0} |\ell_1 - c_1|^+ + \frac{\mu_1(\lambda_1-\lambda_2)}{n_1}(|-\ell_1|^+ + |\ell_2-c_2|^+) + \frac{\mu_2\lambda_2}{n_2}|-\ell_2|^+\right]\right.$$

$$\text{(1.2)}$$

We have gone to the equations of sections I 6 and I 7 for the "soft boundaries" rather than use the differential equations plus boundary conditions as described in section I 4, because the nonanalytic behavior of  f  near corners causes some difficulties for the latter. We saw in sections I 6 and 7 that the device of approximating  f  for  $\ell_j < 0$  or $\ell_j > c_j$  by expressions like (I 6.8) and (I 6.9) with  $n_j \to 0$  guaranteed that  f  would satisfy the boundary conditions of section I 4, and also, apparently, any other necessary conditions.

If we let  $n_j \to 0$ ,  and use (I 6.8) and (I 6.9), the integrals in

(1.2) can be reduced. For example, the term containing $|-\ell_1|^+$ becomes

$$- \iiint dx_0 \, d\ell_1 \, d\ell_2 \, \exp[-\lambda_0 x_0 - \lambda_1 \ell_1 - \lambda_2 \ell_2] g(x_0, 0, \ell_2; t) \exp[-\eta_1 \ell_1^2] \left[\frac{\mu_1}{\eta_1}\right] (\lambda_1 - \lambda_2) |-\ell_1|^+ .$$

The integrand vanishes unless $\ell_1 < 0$ and is negligible except for small values of $|-\ell_1|$, of order $\eta_1^{-1/2}$. The factor $\exp(-\lambda_1 \ell_1)$ is approximately 1 over this range, and the integration of $\ell_1$ gives

$$- (\lambda_1 - \lambda_2) \frac{(\Delta_0 + \Delta_1)}{2} \iint dx_0 \, d\ell_2 \, \exp[-\lambda_0 x_0 - \lambda_2 \ell_2] \, g(x_0, 0, \ell_2; t) .$$

This is proportional to

$$K_1(\lambda_0, \lambda_2; t) \equiv \iint dx_0 \, d\ell_2 \, \exp[-\lambda_0 x_0 - \lambda_2 \ell_2] \, g(x_0, 0, \ell_2; t) , \qquad (1.3)$$

the Laplace transform with respect to $x_0$ and $\ell_2$ of the joint probability density evaluated at $Q_1 = 0$.

For $\lambda_0 \to 0$ and $\lambda_2 \to 0$, $K_1(0,0;t)$ gives the marginal probability density for $Q_1 = 0$. Since this contributes to the reduction in the service rate of server 1 as described in (I 7.4), the equations defining $K$ must guarantee that $K_1(0,0;t)$ is finite, which, in turn also guarantees that $K_1(\lambda_0, \lambda_2; t)$ is finite for $\mathrm{Re} \, \lambda_0, \lambda_2 \geq 0$.

If in (1.1) we let $\lambda_1 \to +\infty$, the integration with respect to $\ell_1$ is confined to an arbitrarily small range near $\ell_1 = 0$. We see that $K_1(\lambda_0, \lambda_2; t)$ can also be related to $K$ through

$$K_1(\lambda_0, \lambda_2; t) = \lim_{\lambda_1 \to +\infty} \lambda_1 K(\lambda_0, \lambda_1, \lambda_2; t) . \qquad (1.4)$$

Thus the term of (1.2) involving $\left|-\ell_1\right|^+$ becomes

$$- (\lambda_1 - \lambda_2) \frac{(\Delta_0 + \Delta_1)}{2} K_1(\lambda_0,\lambda_2;t) \qquad (1.5)$$

which is related to the (as yet unknown) $K(\lambda_0,\lambda_1,\lambda_2;t)$ .

By similar arguments, the last term of (1.2) can be expressed as

$$- \lambda_2 \frac{(\Delta_1 + \Delta_2)}{2} K_2(\lambda_0,\lambda_1;t) \qquad (1.6)$$

in which $K_2(\lambda_0,\lambda_1;t)$ is the analogous transform to (1.3) for $Q_2 = 0$ ,

$$K_2(\lambda_0,\lambda_1;t) = \iint dx_0 \, d\ell_1 \, \exp[-\lambda_0 x_0 - \lambda_1 \ell_1] \, g(x_0,\ell_1,0;t) \qquad (1.7)$$

and

$$K_2(\lambda_0,\lambda_1;t) = \lim_{\lambda_2 \to +\infty} \lambda_2 \, K(\lambda_0,\lambda_1,\lambda_2;t) \quad . \qquad (1.7a)$$

The solution must guarantee that $K_2(\lambda_0,\lambda_1;t)$ is finite for Re $\lambda_0$ , $\lambda_1 \geq 0$ .

If $c_1$ and $c_2$ are finite, the two terms of (1.2) involving $c_1$ and $c_2$ can be written as

$$e^{-\lambda_1 c_1} \frac{(\Delta_0 + \Delta_1)}{2} (\lambda_0 + \lambda_1) \, K_1^*(\lambda_0,\lambda_2;t) \qquad (1.8)$$

and

$$- e^{-\lambda_2 c_2} \frac{(\Delta_1 + \Delta_2)}{2} (\lambda_1 - \lambda_2) \, K_2^*(\lambda_0,\lambda_1;t) \qquad (1.8a)$$

in which

$$K_1^*(\lambda_0,\lambda_2;t) \equiv \iint dx_0 \, d\ell_2 \, \exp[-\lambda_0 x_0 - \lambda_2 \ell_2] \, g(x_0,c_1,\ell_2;t) \qquad (1.9)$$

and

$$K_2^*(\lambda_0,\lambda_1;t) \equiv \iint dx_0 \, d\ell_1 \exp[-\lambda_0 x_0 - \lambda_1 \ell_1] \, g(x_0,\ell_1,c_2;t) \qquad (1.9a)$$

describe the Laplace transforms of the probability density along $Q_1 = c_1$ and $Q_2 = c_2$, respectively. The $K_1^*$ and $K_2^*$ must be finite for Re $\lambda_0, \lambda_2 > 0$ and Re $\lambda_0, \lambda_1 > 0$, respectively.

The analogues of (1.4) and (1.7a) are:

$$K_1^*(\lambda_0,\lambda_2;t) = \lim_{\lambda_1 \to -\infty} e^{\lambda_1 c_1}(-\lambda_1)K(\lambda_0,\lambda_1,\lambda_2;t) \quad , \qquad (1.10)$$

$$K_2^*(\lambda_0,\lambda_1;t) = \lim_{\lambda_2 \to -\infty} e^{\lambda_2 c_2}(-\lambda_2)K(\lambda_0,\lambda_1,\lambda_2;t) \quad . \qquad (1.10a)$$

Equation (1.2) can now be written in the form

$$\frac{d}{dt} K(\lambda_0,\lambda_1,\lambda_2;t) = \left[ -\mu_0(\lambda_0+\lambda_1) + \mu_1(\lambda_1-\lambda_2) + \mu_2\lambda_2 + \frac{\Delta_0}{2}(\lambda_0+\lambda_1)^2 \right.$$

$$\left. + \frac{\Delta_1}{2}(\lambda_1-\lambda_2)^2 + \frac{\Delta_2}{2}\lambda_2^2 \right] K(\lambda_0,\lambda_1,\lambda_2;t) - (\lambda_1-\lambda_2)\frac{(\Delta_0+\Delta_1)}{2} K_1(\lambda_0,\lambda_2;t)$$

$$- \lambda_2 \frac{(\Delta_1+\Delta_2)}{2} K_2(\lambda_0,\lambda_1;t) + (\lambda_0+\lambda_1)\frac{(\Delta_0+\Delta_1)}{2} e^{-\lambda_1 c_1} K_1^*(\lambda_0,\lambda_2;t)$$

$$- (\lambda_1-\lambda_2)\frac{(\Delta_1+\Delta_2)}{2} e^{-\lambda_2 c_2} K_2^*(\lambda_0,\lambda_1;t)$$

$$(1.11)$$

in which the $K_1$, $K_2$, $K_1^*$, $K_2^*$ are related to the $K(\lambda_0,\lambda_1,\lambda_2;t)$ through (1.4), (1.7a), (1.9), and (1.9a). The boundary terms of (1.11) are such as to guarantee that for $\lambda_1 \to +\infty$, the terms of order $\lambda_1^2 K$ cancel;

the right-hand side of (1.11) has a finite limit for $\lambda_1 \to \infty$ . Similarly

it has a finite limit for $\lambda_1 \to -\infty$ or $\lambda_2 \to \pm \infty$ .

Although (1.11) appears to be a fairly straightforward linear dif-

ferential equation, there are certain subtle features of this which we

are not ready to attack yet in this general situation. Since the marginal

queue distribution $g^*(\ell_1, \ell_2)$ also satisfies a diffusion equation by

itself, we could have derived analogous equations for the Laplace trans-

forms of $g^*(\ell_1, \ell_2)$ . Alternatively, we can simply set $\lambda_0 = 0$ in (1.1

and define

$$K(\lambda_1,\lambda_2;t) \equiv K(0,\lambda_1,\lambda_2;t) = \iint d\ell_1 \, d\ell_2 \, g^*(\ell_1,\ell_2;t) \, \exp[-\lambda_1\ell_1 - \lambda_2\ell_2]$$

as the Laplace transform of $g^*$ . All equations relating to $K(\lambda_1,\lambda_2;t)$

can be obtained by setting $\lambda_0 = 0$ in the equations above. Thus, from

(1.11) we have

$$
\frac{d}{dt} K(\lambda_1,\lambda_2;t) = \left[ \lambda_1(\mu_1-\mu_0) + \lambda_2(\mu_2-\mu_1) + \frac{\Delta_0}{2}\lambda_1^2 + \frac{\Delta_1}{2}(\lambda_1-\lambda_2)^2 + \frac{\Delta_2}{2}\lambda_2^2 \right] K(\lambda.
$$

$$
- (\lambda_1 - \lambda_2)\frac{(\Delta_0 + \Delta_1)}{2} K_1(\lambda_2;t) - \lambda_2\frac{(\Delta_1 + \Delta_2)}{2} K_2(\lambda_1;t)
$$

$$
+ \lambda_1\frac{(\Delta_0+\Delta_1)}{2}e^{-\lambda_1 c_1}K_1^*(\lambda_2;t) - (\lambda_1-\lambda_2)\frac{(\Delta_1+\Delta_2)}{2}e^{-\lambda_2 c_2}K_2^*(\lambda_1;t)
$$

$$(1.12)$$

in which the $K_1$, $K_2$, etc., are the functions evaluated with $\lambda_0 = 0$ .

If $\mu_0$ is less than $\mu_1$ and $\mu_2$ we expect that an equilibrium

queue distribution will obtain for $t \to \infty$ . The equilibrium distribu-

tion must satisfy an equation with $dK/dt = 0$ , i.e.,

$$\left[\lambda_1(\mu_1 - \mu_0) + \lambda_2(\mu_2 - \mu_1) + \frac{\Delta_0}{2}\lambda_1^2 + \frac{\Delta_1}{2}(\lambda_1 - \lambda_2)^2 + \frac{\Delta_2}{2}\lambda_2^2\right] K(\lambda_1, \lambda_2)$$

$$= (\lambda_1 - \lambda_2)\frac{(\Delta_0 + \Delta_1)}{2} K_1(\lambda_2) + \lambda_2 \frac{(\Delta_1 + \Delta_2)}{2} K_2(\lambda_1)$$

$$- \lambda_1 \frac{(\Delta_0 + \Delta_1)}{2} e^{-\lambda_1 c_1} K_1^*(\lambda_2) + (\lambda_1 - \lambda_2)\frac{(\Delta_1 + \Delta_2)}{2} e^{-\lambda_2 c_2} K_2^*(\lambda_1)$$

$$\tag{1.13}$$

in which the K-functions refer, in all cases, to the corresponding functions in (1.12) evaluated for $t \to \infty$ .

We can use (1.13) to express $K(\lambda_1, \lambda_2)$ , a function of two variables $\lambda_1$, $\lambda_2$ , in terms of $K_1(\lambda_2)$, $K_2(\lambda_1)$, $K_1^*(\lambda_2)$, and $K_2^*(\lambda_1)$, four functions of one variable each. If we knew the probability density along the boundaries, $g^*(0, \ell_2)$, $g^*(\ell_1, 0)$, $g^*(c_1, \ell_2)$ , and $g^*(\ell_1, c_2)$, which would determine $K_1(\lambda_2)$, $K_2(\lambda_1)$, $K_1^*(\lambda_2)$, and $K_2^*(\lambda_1)$, we could obtain $K(\lambda_1, \lambda_2)$ from (1.13), which would determine $g^*(\ell_1, \ell_2)$ for all $\ell_1$, $\ell_2$ , $0 < \ell_1 < c_1$ , $0 < \ell_2 < c_2$ . But we do not know the boundary functions yet. Neither does (1.13) itself determine these functions directly. If we let $\lambda_1 \to \pm \infty$ or $\lambda_2 \to \pm \infty$ in (1.13) using (1.4), etc., to evaluate $K_1(\lambda_2)$ from $K(\lambda_1, \lambda_2)$, (1.13) merely confirms that the equations are consistent (in effect, we get an equation $0 = 0$).

To determine $K(\lambda_1, \lambda_2)$, $K_1(\lambda_2)$, etc., from (1.13), we must also exploit the fact that these functions must satisfy certain analytic properties in the complex $\lambda_1$ and $\lambda_2$ spaces. If $c_1$ and $c_2$ are finite, all of these functions must be entire functions (analytic for all finite values) of $\lambda_1$, $\lambda_2$ . If $c_1 = \infty$ , the boundary term containing $K_1^*(\lambda_2)$ disappears but all remaining functions must be analytic at least for Re $\lambda_1 \geq 0$ and $\lambda_2$ finite. If $c_2 = \infty$ , the boundary term containing

238

$K_2^*(\lambda_1)$ disappears but all remaining functions must be analytic at least for Re $\lambda_2 \geq 0$ and $\lambda_1$ finite. If both $c_1$ and $c_2$ are infinite, bot boundary terms with $K_1^*(\lambda_2)$ and $K_2^*(\lambda_1)$ disappear but the remaining functions must be analytic at least for Re $\lambda_1 \geq 0$ and Re $\lambda_2 \geq 0$ .

That $K(\lambda_1,\lambda_2)$ is analytic in both $\lambda_1$ and $\lambda_2$ implies that the left-hand side of (1.13) must vanish wherever $\lambda_1$ and $\lambda_2$ are related so that the coefficient of $K(\lambda_1,\lambda_2)$ vanishes. For all such combination of $\lambda_1$, $\lambda_2$ , one obtains an equation involving the functions $K_1$, $K_2$, $K_1^*$ and $K_2^*$ . In addition to this equation, we have the requirements that $K_1(\lambda_2)$ is not only analytic in the appropriate range of $\lambda_2$ , but it is real and positive for $\lambda_2$ real. Corresponding properties are true for $K_2(\lambda_1)$, $K_1^*(\lambda_2)$, and $K_2^*(\lambda_1)$ . Hopefully, all of these conditions, along with a normalization condition, $K(0,0) = 1$ , will uniquely determine the boundary functions and thus $K(\lambda_1,\lambda_2)$ . We will return to this question later as we try actually to determine these functions, at least in special cases.

If we can evaluate the boundary functions, we can also evaluate the Laplace transforms of the marginal distributions of $Q_1$ and $Q_2$ :

$$K(\lambda_1, 0) = \int d\ell_1 \, \exp(-\lambda_1 \ell_1) \, g_1^*(\ell_1) , \qquad (1.14)$$

$$K(0, \lambda_2) = \int d\ell_2 \, \exp(-\lambda_2 \ell_2) \, g_2^*(\ell_2) . \qquad (1.14a)$$

By setting $\lambda_2 = 0$ or $\lambda_1 = 0$ in (1.13), one can express $K(\lambda_1, 0)$ and $K(0, \lambda_2)$ directly in terms of $K_1$, $K_2$, etc. If we set $\lambda_2 = 0$ in (1.13) and divide both sides of $\lambda_1$ , we obtain

$$\left[ (\mu_1 - \mu_0) + \frac{(\Delta_0 + \Delta_1)}{2} \lambda_1 \right] K(\lambda_1, 0) = \frac{(\Delta_0 + \Delta_1)}{2} [K_1(0) - e^{-\lambda_1 c_1} K_1^*(0)] + \frac{(\Delta_1 + \Delta_2)}{2} K_2^*$$

$$(1.15)$$

If we set $\lambda_1 = 0$ in (1.13) and divide both sides by $\lambda_2$, we obtain

$$\left[(\mu_2 - \mu_1) + \frac{(\Delta_1 + \Delta_2)}{2}\lambda_2\right] K(0, \lambda_2) = \frac{(\Delta_1 + \Delta_2)}{2}[K_2(0) - e^{-\lambda_2 c_2}K_2^*(0)] - \frac{(\Delta_0 + \Delta_1)}{2} K_1(\lambda_2) .$$

$$(1.15a)$$

Since all functions are required to be analytic at $\lambda_1 = 0$ and $\lambda_2 = 0$, (1.15) must be true for $\lambda_1 \to 0$, despite the fact that we divided (1.13) by $\lambda_1$ to obtain (1.15). Similarly (1.15a) is true for $\lambda_2 \to 0$. If we set $\lambda_1 = 0$ in (1.15) and $\lambda_2 = 0$ in (1.15a), and take $K(0,0) = 1$, we do not obtain the same equations, even though both arise from (1.15) for $\lambda_1 \to 0$, $\lambda_2 \to 0$. Equation (1.15) gives

$$\mu_1 - \mu_0 = \frac{(\Delta_0 + \Delta_1)}{2}[K_1(0) - K_1^*(0)] + \frac{(\Delta_1 + \Delta_2)}{2} K_2^*(0) \qquad (1.16)$$

which is equivalent to

$$\mu_0 - \frac{(\Delta_0 + \Delta_1)}{2} g_1^*(c_1) = \mu_1 - \frac{(\Delta_0 + \Delta_1)}{2} g_1^*(0) - \frac{(\Delta_1 + \Delta_2)}{2} g_2^*(c_2) .$$

Equation (1.15a) gives

$$\mu_2 - \mu_1 = \frac{(\Delta_1 + \Delta_2)}{2} [K_2(0) - K_2^*(0)] - \frac{(\Delta_0 + \Delta_1)}{2} K_1(0) \qquad (1.16a)$$

which implies

$$\mu_2 - \frac{(\Delta_1 + \Delta_2)}{2} g_2^*(0) = \mu_1 - \frac{(\Delta_0 + \Delta_1)}{2} g_1^*(0) - \frac{(\Delta_1 + \Delta_2)}{2} g_2^*(c_2) .$$

These equations we recognize from (I 7.8). The analytic behavior of the various transforms thus guarantees that the equilibrium service rates of servers 0, 1, and 2 are all equal.

The above equations should also guarantee that, for $c_2 \rightarrow \infty$, the marginal distribution of server 1 be independent of the properties of server 2 (provided $\mu_1 > \mu_0$). This follows from (1.15) because, for $c_2 \rightarrow \infty$, $g_2^*(\ell_1, c_2) \rightarrow 0$ and, therefore, $K_2^*(\lambda_1) \rightarrow 0$ for all $\lambda_1$. Except for two as yet unknown numbers $K_1(0)$ and $K_1^*(0)$, $K(\lambda_1, 0)$ is a known function of $\lambda_1$. It contains two terms, one proportional to

$$[\alpha_1 + \lambda_1]^{-1} \quad \text{with} \quad \alpha_1 = 2(\mu_1 - \mu_0)/(\Delta_0 + \Delta_1)$$

and the other proportional to $[\alpha_1 + \lambda_1]^{-1} \exp(-\lambda_1 c_1)$.

The transform inversion of these two terms requires that $g_1^*(\ell_1)$ have the form

$$g_1^*(\ell_1) = \begin{cases} K_1(0) \, e^{-\alpha_1 \ell_1} & \text{for } \ell_1 < c_1 \\ \\ K_1(0) \, e^{-\alpha_1 \ell_1} - K_1^*(0) \, e^{-\alpha_1(\ell_1 - c_1)} & \text{for } \ell_1 > c_1 . \end{cases}$$

Although each of the two terms of $K(\lambda_1, 0)$ individually has a first order pole at $\lambda_1 = -\alpha_1$, $K(\lambda_1, 0)$ is required to be an entire function and $g_1^*(\ell_1)$ is required to be 0 for $\ell_1 > c_1$. These conditions force the right-hand side of (1.15) to vanish for $\lambda_1 = -\alpha_1$, thus $K_1(0) = \exp(+\alpha_1 c_1) K_1^*(0)$ and

$$g_1^*(\ell_1) = \begin{cases} K_1(0) \, e^{-\alpha_1 \ell_1} & \text{for } \ell_1 < c_1 \\ \\ 0 & \text{for } \ell_1 > c_1 . \end{cases} \tag{1.17}$$

The final unknown $K_1(0)$ is determined by the normalization $K(0,0) = 1$

241

which implies that

$$K_1(0) = \alpha_1 \left[ 1 - e^{-\alpha_1 c_1} \right]^{-1} .$$

This, of course, agrees with the results of section II 2.

That (1.15) and (1.15a) have somewhat similar forms is a consequence of the symmetry between customers and holes as discussed in section I 3.

Equilibrium Distributions, $c_1 = c_2 = \infty$ , $\Delta_0 = \Delta_2 = 0$ . In view of the complexity of the special solutions of Chapters III and IV, we do not really expect to obtain useable formulas for the general equilibrium queue distribution with arbitrary choices of the $\mu_j$ , $\Delta_j$ and $c_j$ . We continue to seek the solution for other relatively simple special cases. To illustrate how the imposition of analyticity conditions can determine a unique solution of (1.13), we consider here the special case of regular servers at 0 and 2, $\Delta_0 = \Delta_2 = 0$ , and infinite storages $c_1 = c_2 = \infty$ (and $\mu_0 < \mu_1, \mu_2$).

For $c_1 = \infty$ , $c_2 = \infty$ , we first set $K_1^*(\lambda_2) = 0$ and $K_2^*(\lambda_1) = 0$ because, for $\mu_0 < \mu_1, \mu_2$, we should have a proper limit distribution of $Q_1, Q_2$, thus zero probability density at $Q_1 = c_1$ , $Q_2 = c_2$ for $c_1, c_2 \to \infty$ . For $\Delta_0 = \Delta_2 = 0$ , (1.13) further simplifies to

$$[\alpha_1\lambda_1 + \alpha_2\lambda_2 + (\lambda_1 - \lambda_2)^2] K(\lambda_1,\lambda_2) = (\lambda_1 - \lambda_2)K_1(\lambda_2) + \lambda_2 K_2(\lambda_1)$$

$$(2.1)$$

with $\alpha_1 = 2(\mu_1 - \mu_0)/\Delta_1$ , $\alpha_2 = 2(\mu_2 - \mu_1)/\Delta_1$ .

It is convenient to rotate coordinates and express (2.1) in terms of the variables

$$z_1 = \lambda_1 + \lambda_2 , \qquad z_2 = \lambda_1 - \lambda_2$$

so that (2.1) becomes

$$\left[\frac{(\alpha_1 + \alpha_2)}{2} z_1 + \frac{(\alpha_1 - \alpha_2)}{2} z_2 + z_2^2\right] K\left(\frac{z_1 + z_2}{2}, \frac{z_1 - z_2}{2}\right)$$

(2.1a)

$$= z_2 K_1\left(\frac{z_1 - z_2}{2}\right) + \frac{(z_1 - z_2)}{2} K_2\left(\frac{z_1 + z_2}{2}\right) \quad .$$

Since $K(\lambda_1, \lambda_2)$ is required to be analytic at least for Re $\lambda_1$, $\lambda_2$ >
the left-hand side of (2.1a) must vanish whenever Re $\lambda_1$, $\lambda_2 > 0$ and also

$$z_1 = - z_2[(\alpha_1 - \alpha_2) + 2z_2]/(\alpha_1 + \alpha_2) \quad . \tag{2.2}$$

Thus for $z_1$ related to $z_2$ in this way, the right-hand side of (2.1a)
must also vanish, i.e.,

$$K_1\left(\frac{(\alpha_1/2)^2 - (z_2 + \alpha_1/2)^2}{(\alpha_1 + \alpha_2)}\right) = \frac{(\alpha_1 + z_2)}{(\alpha_1 + \alpha_2)} K_2\left(\frac{(\alpha_2/2)^2 - (z_2 - \alpha_2/2)^2}{(\alpha_1 + \alpha_2)}\right) \quad .$$

(2.3)

For an equilibrium queue distribution to exist, we must have $\mu_0 < \mu$
and $\mu_0 < \mu_2$ , i.e., $\alpha_1 > 0$ and $\alpha_1 + \alpha_2 > 0$ . In the $z_2$-space of
Fig.VI-1a, the argument of $K_1$ is real and nonnegative along the nega-
tive line segment $-\alpha_1 \leq z_2 \leq 0$ and along the vertical line Re $z_2 = -\alpha_1/2$
the dashed lines of Fig. VI-1a. Along these lines, $K_1$ is required to
be real and positive. In the neighborhood of $z_2 = -\alpha_1/2$ , $K_1$ must
be analytic and invariant to reflections, $(z_2 + \alpha_1/2) \rightarrow -(z_2 + \alpha_1/2)$ ,
of $z_2$ through the point $-\alpha_1/2$ . It also must be analytic in the region

$$\text{Re } (z_2 + \alpha_1/2)^2 \leq (\alpha_1/2)^2 \tag{2.4}$$

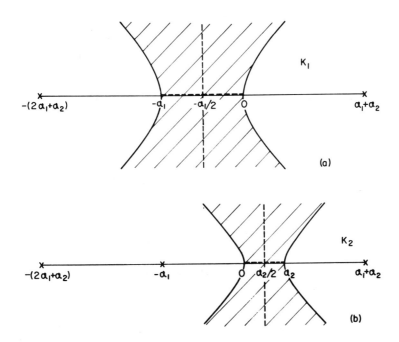

Fig. VI-1.  The shaded region of (a) is where $K_1$ is an
analytic function of $z_2$ . The shaded region
of (b) is where $K_2$ is analytic.

shown by the shaded region of Fig. VI-1a.

In the $z_2$-space of Fig. VI-1b, the argument of $K_2$ in (2.3) is real and nonnegative along the line segment between 0 and $\alpha_2$, and along the vertical line Re $z_2 = \alpha_2/2$. The value of $\alpha_2$ may be positive or negative but in any case the point $\alpha_2$ of Fig. VI-1b lies to the left of $-\alpha_1$ in Fig. VI-1a. The function $K_2$ must be invariant to reflections $(z_2 - \alpha_2/2) \rightarrow -(z_2 - \alpha_2/2)$ through the point $\alpha_2/2$ and analytic in the region

$$\text{Re } (z_2 - \alpha_2/2)^2 \leq (\alpha_2/2)^2 \qquad (2.4a)$$

shown by the shaded region of Fig. VI-1b.

Both $K_1$ and $K_2$ are required simultaneously to be analytic at least along the line Re $z_2 = 0$, and to satisfy (2.3). If $K_1$ and $K_2$ were known in some region where they were both analytic, they would each have a unique analytic continuation beyond the shaded regions of Fig. VI-1a, b and would continue to satisfy (2.3) in the region of continuation.

If we analytically continue $K_2$ into the shaded region of Fig. VI-1 where $K_1$ is analytic, (2.3) will require that $K_2$ also be analytic in this region except at the point $z_2 = -\alpha_1$ where the factor $(z_2 + \alpha_1)$ of (2.3) vanishes. At this point $K_1$ has the value $K_1(0)$ which must be positive. Since $K_1$ must be analytic in some neighborhood of $z_2 = -\alpha_1$ $K_2$ must have a simple pole at $z_2 = -\alpha_1$ with residue $(\alpha_1 + \alpha_2)K_1(0) > 0$

Since the analytic continuation of $K_2$ must still be invariant to reflections through $z_2 = \alpha_2/2$, the continuation to Re $z_2 < 0$ induces a continuation to Re $z_2 > \alpha_2$. $K_2$ will be analytic in the reflection of the region (2.4) except for a simple pole at $z_2 = \alpha_1 + \alpha_2$ (the refection of the pole at $z_2 = -\alpha_1$), also with residue $(\alpha_1 + \alpha_2)K_1(0)$.

If we now analytically continue $K_1$ into the shaded region of Fig. VI-1b and beyond, as far as $K_2$ has been defined so far, (2.3) will require $K_1$ to be analytic wherever $K_2$ is analytic. Since $K_2$ has a simple pole at $z_2 = \alpha_1 + \alpha_2$, (2.3) will require $K_1$ also to have a simple pole at $z_2 = \alpha_1 + \alpha_2$, with residue $K_1(0)(2\alpha_1 + \alpha_2)$. By symmetry of $K_1$ with respect to reflection through $z_2 = -\alpha_1/2$, $K_1$ must also have a simple pole at $z_2 = -(2\alpha_1 + \alpha_2)$. This, in turn, causes $K_2$ to have a simple pole also at $z_2 = -(2\alpha_1 + \alpha_2)$, and, by reflection, at $z_2 = 2(\alpha_1 + \alpha_2)$.

We can iterate the above scheme of reflecting $K_2$ through $\alpha_2/2$ and $K_1$ through $-\alpha_1/2$, thereby generating the continuation of $K_1$ and $K_2$ throughout the entire $z_2$-plane. The result of this is that $K_1$ and $K_2$ are both required to have simple poles at

$$z_2 = -[\alpha_1 + n(\alpha_1 + \alpha_2)] \quad \text{for } n = 1, 2, \text{--} \tag{2.5}$$

and at

$$z_2 = +n(\alpha_1 + \alpha_2) \quad \text{for } n = 1, 2, \text{--} . \tag{2.5a}$$

In addition $K_2$, but not $K_1$, has a pole at $z_2 = -\alpha_1$.

Since the gamma function $\Gamma(z)$ is analytic except for simple poles at $z = 0, -1, -2, \text{--}$, and has no zeros in the finite plane, we will write $K_1$ and $K_2$ in the form

$$K_1\left[\frac{(\alpha_1/2)^2 - (z_2 + \alpha_1/2)^2}{\alpha_1 + \alpha_2}\right] = C(z_2)\, \Gamma\left(\frac{z_2 + 2\alpha_1 + \alpha_2}{\alpha_1 + \alpha_2}\right) \Gamma\left(\frac{\alpha_1 + \alpha_2 - z_2}{\alpha_1 + \alpha_2}\right)$$

$$\tag{2.6}$$

$$K_2 \left[ \frac{(\alpha_2/2)^2 - (z_2 - \alpha_2/2)^2}{\alpha_1 + \alpha_2} \right] = \left[ \frac{\alpha_1 + z_2}{\alpha_1 + \alpha_2} \right]^{-1} C(z_2) \Gamma \left[ \frac{z_2 + 2\alpha_1 + \alpha_2}{\alpha_1 + \alpha_2} \right] \Gamma \left[ \frac{\alpha_1 + \alpha_2 - z_2}{\alpha_1 + \alpha_2} \right]$$

(2.6a)

$$= C(z_2) \Gamma \left[ \frac{z_2 + \alpha_1}{\alpha_1 + \alpha_2} \right] \Gamma \left[ \frac{\alpha_1 + \alpha_2 - z_2}{\alpha_1 + \alpha_2} \right]$$

with $C(z_2)$ some as yet unknown function. The $\Gamma$-functions describe all poles of $K_1$ and $K_2$ in the finite z-plane; consequently $C(z_2)$ is an entire function.

Since $K_1$ must be real along $\mathrm{Re}\ z_2 = -\alpha_1/2$ and the product of the $\Gamma$-functions in (2.6) is real there, $C(z_2)$ is required to be real for $\mathrm{Re}\ z_2 = -\alpha_1/2$. Similarly from (2.6a), $K_2$ must be real for $\mathrm{Re}\ z_2 = \alpha_2/2$, and, consequently, so must $C(z_2)$. $C(z_2)$ must also be real along the real axis $\mathrm{Im}\ z_2 = 0$.

In order for the imaginary part of $C(z_2)$ to vanish along the lines $\mathrm{Re}\ z_2 = -\alpha_1/2$, $\mathrm{Re}\ z_2 = +\alpha_2/2$, and $\mathrm{Im}\ z_2 = 0$, and $C(z_2)$ be an entire function, it must have a Taylor series expansion in powers of

$$\cos[2\pi(z_2 + \alpha_1/2)/(\alpha_1 + \alpha_2)] \qquad (2.7)$$

or an equivalent cosine series expansion in multiple angles. However, $K_1$ and $K_2$ are also required to be positive and monotone decreasing in $|\mathrm{Im}\ z_2|$ along the lines $\mathrm{Re}\ z_2 = -\alpha_1/2$ and $\mathrm{Re}\ z_2 = +\alpha_2/2$, respectively. The function (2.7) grows like $\exp[2\pi|\mathrm{Im}\ z_2|/(\alpha_1 + \alpha_2)]$ along these lines for large $|\mathrm{Im}\ z_2|$ which would overpower the decay of the $\Gamma$-functions in (2.6), (2.6a). We conclude from this that the only admissible term in the expansion is the constant term, i.e., $C(z_2) = C$, a constant. The value of $C$ will, of course, be determined by the normalization $K(0,0) = 1$ .

Equations (2.6), (2.6a) uniquely define the functions $K_1$ and $K_2$ . Although for many calculations it is easiest to work directly from (2.6), (2.6a), we can write the functions in terms of the original variables $\lambda_1, \lambda_2$ :

$$K_1(\lambda_2) = C \Gamma \left( 1 + \frac{\alpha_1}{2(\alpha_1 + \alpha_2)} + \left[ \left( \frac{\alpha_1}{2(\alpha_1 + \alpha_2)} \right)^2 - \frac{\lambda_2}{(\alpha_1 + \alpha_2)} \right]^{1/2} \right)$$

(2.8)

$$\cdot \Gamma \left( 1 + \frac{\alpha_1}{2(\alpha_1 + \alpha_2)} - \left[ \left( \frac{\alpha_1}{2(\alpha_1 + \alpha_2)} \right)^2 - \frac{\lambda_2}{(\alpha_1 + \alpha_2)} \right]^{1/2} \right)$$

$$K_2(\lambda_1) = C \Gamma \left( 1 - \frac{\alpha_2}{2(\alpha_1 + \alpha_2)} + \left[ \left( \frac{\alpha_2}{2(\alpha_1 + \alpha_2)} \right)^2 - \frac{\lambda_1}{(\alpha_1 + \alpha_2)} \right]^{1/2} \right)$$

(2.8a)

$$\cdot \Gamma \left( 1 - \frac{\alpha_2}{2(\alpha_1 + \alpha_2)} - \left[ \left( \frac{\alpha_2}{2(\alpha_1 + \alpha_2)} \right)^2 - \frac{\lambda_1}{(\alpha_1 + \alpha_2)} \right]^{1/2} \right) \ .$$

For $c_1 = c_2 = \infty$ , $\Delta_0 = \Delta_2 = 0$; (1.15), (1.15a) simplify to

$$(\alpha_1 + \lambda_1) K(\lambda_1, 0) = K_1(0) \ , \tag{2.9}$$

$$(\alpha_2 + \lambda_2) K(0, \lambda_2) = K_2(0) - K_1(\lambda_2) \ . \tag{2.9a}$$

Since $K(0,0) = 1$ , we conclude that

$$C = \frac{(\alpha_1 + \alpha_2)}{\Gamma\left(\dfrac{\alpha_1}{\alpha_1 + \alpha_2}\right)} \cdot \qquad (2.10)$$

Although the $\Gamma$-function is tabulated and its properties "well-known"
it is worth noting that $K_1$ and $K_2$ can be expressed in terms of trigonometric functions by exploiting the formulas

$$\Gamma(z)\ \Gamma(1 - z)\ =\ \pi/\sin \pi z\ , \qquad z\ \Gamma(z)\ =\ \Gamma(1 + z)$$

provided $\alpha_2/(\alpha_1 + \alpha_2)$ is integer-valued. Since $\alpha_2 > -\alpha_1$ , this is
true for $\alpha_2 = -\alpha_1 k/(k + 1)$ , $k = 0, 1, ---$ . In particular for $k = 0$
$\alpha_2 = 0$ , $\mu_2 = \mu_1$ ,

$$K_1(\lambda_2)\ =\ \frac{\pi\,\lambda_2}{\cos\left(\dfrac{\pi}{2}\left[1 - \dfrac{4\lambda_2}{\alpha_1}\right]^{1/2}\right)}\ , \qquad K_2(\lambda_1)\ =\ \frac{\alpha_1 \pi [\lambda_1/\alpha_1]^{1/2}}{\sinh(\pi[\lambda_1/\alpha_1]^{1/2})}\ \cdot \qquad (2.1$$

3. <u>Numerical Evaluations.</u> In the last section we obtained an explicit
formula for $K(\lambda_1,\lambda_2)$ with $\Delta_0 = \Delta_2 = 0$ , $c_1 = c_2 = \infty$ . It remains to
investigate how this solution behaves, and why.

The function $K(\lambda_1,\lambda_2)$ is particularly suited to the evaluation
of moments for $Q_1$ and $Q_2$ . Of special interest is

$$E\{Q_2\}\ =\ -\frac{d}{d\lambda_2}\ K(0,\lambda_2)\bigg|_{\lambda_2=0}\ ,$$

which, from (2.8), (2.8a), (2.9a), (2.10), has the value

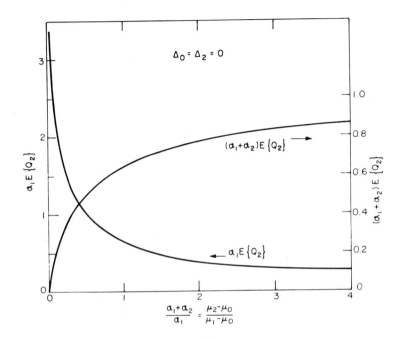

Fig. VI-2. Average queue length $E\{Q_2\}$ at server 2 if the input server 0 and server 2 are both regular ($\Delta_0 = \Delta_2 = 0$). The queue is measured on two scales as a function of the relative service rates $\mu_2 > \mu_0$, $\mu_1 > \mu_0$.

$$E\{Q_2\} = \alpha_2^{-1}\left[-\psi\left(1 + \frac{\alpha_1}{\alpha_1 + \alpha_2}\right) + \psi(1) + 1\right]. \qquad (3.1)$$

Since the digamma function $\psi(\cdot)$ is tabulated, we can easily evalu

ate $E\{Q_2\}$ as a function of the parameters $\alpha_1$ and $\alpha_2$ (for $\alpha_2 > -\alpha$

Fig. VI-2 shows graphs of $\alpha_1 E\{Q_2\}$ and $(\alpha_1 + \alpha_2)E\{Q_2\}$ vs $(\alpha_1 + \alpha_2)/\alpha_1$

$(\mu_2 - \mu_0)/(\mu_1 - \mu_0)$. Since $E\{Q_1\} = \alpha_1^{-1}$, $\alpha_1 E\{Q_2\} = E\{Q_2\}/E\{Q_1\}$ de-

scribes $E\{Q_2\}$ in units of $E\{Q_1\}$. The quantity $(\alpha_1 + \alpha_2)^{-1} = [2(\mu_2 - \mu_0)]$

can be interpreted as the average queue length for a hypothetical regular

server serving an arrival process with arrival rate $\mu_0$, variance rate

thus $(\alpha_1 + \alpha_2)E\{Q_2\}$ is the average queue measured in units of the mean

queue of this hypothetical system.

Suppose we were to keep server 1 fixed and vary the service rate $\mu_2$

of server 2. If we let $\mu_2$ decrease to $\mu_0$ (traffic intensity goes to

1), $\alpha_1 E\{Q_2\}$ becomes infinite, but not in the manner typical of a single

server system. For $\alpha_2 \rightarrow -\alpha_1$, the $\psi$-function has a logarithmic singu-

larity

$$\alpha_1 E\{Q_2\} \simeq \ln\left(\frac{\alpha_1}{\alpha_1 + \alpha_2}\right) - \psi(1) - 1 + --$$

$$(3.2)$$

$$E\{Q_2\} \simeq \frac{\Delta_1}{2(\mu_1 - \mu_0)}\left[\ln\left(\frac{\mu_1 - \mu_0}{\mu_2 - \mu_0}\right) - 0.423 + --\right]$$

for $\alpha_2 \rightarrow -\alpha_1$ or $\mu_2 \rightarrow \mu_0$.

If server 1 were not there (or if it were regular, $\Delta_1 = 0$, or

infinitely fast $\mu_1 = \infty$), we would have a regular input process (rate $\mu_0$

to a regular server (rate $\mu_2$) with $\mu_2 > \mu_0$. For any $\mu_2 > \mu_0$, $Q_2$

would be zero because the server could, at all times, serve customers as fast as they arrive. If, however, we now introduce a stochastic server at 1 with $\mu_1 > \mu_0$ , there is a nonzero probability that server 1 will actually serve at an apparently slow rate, less than $\mu_0$ , for any finite length of time and thereby build a sizable queue $Q_1$ . While doing so, it will feed server 2 at a slow rate (less than $\mu_2$) forcing $Q_2$ to decrease, probably to zero. Subsequently, server 1 will serve at an average rate $\mu_1 > \mu_2$ as long as $Q_1$ remains positive. This will cause $Q_2$ to grow at a rate of $\mu_1 - \mu_2$ . For $\mu_2$ sufficiently close to $\mu_0$ , one can generate arbitrarily large values of $Q_2$ in this way. This explains why $E\{Q_2\}$ becomes infinite for $\mu_2 \to \mu_0$ , although there is no simple explanation why it should be of order $-\ln(\mu_2 - \mu_0)$ .

If $\mu_1 - \mu_0$ were sufficiently small, the longtime average output rate from server 1 would be $\mu_0$ ; server 1 would serve at rate $\mu_1$ while busy but occasionally it would be idle (a fraction $1 - \mu_0/\mu_1$ of the time). The variance rate of the output would be $\Delta_1$ most of the time, reduced somewhat because server 1 is idle part of the time. The output from server 1 (the input to server 2) does, however, resemble that of a process with rate $\mu_0$ , variance rate $\Delta_1$ , particularly for small values of $1 - \mu_0/\mu_1$ . The curve for $(\alpha_1 + \alpha_2)E\{Q_2\}$ in Fig. VI-2 illustrates this. For $(\alpha_1 + \alpha_2)/\alpha_1 \to \infty$ , $(\alpha_1 + \alpha_2)E\{Q_2\} \to 1$ . As one might expect, $(\alpha_1 + \alpha_2)E\{Q_2\}$ is always less than 1, because the variance rate of the input to server 2 is actually somewhat less than $\Delta_1$ .

From Fig. VI-2, one can see that $\mu_1 - \mu_0$ "small" is to be interpreted as small compared with $\mu_2 - \mu_0$ . At the other extreme $(\mu_2 - \mu_0)/(\mu_1 - \mu_0) \to 0$ , $(\alpha_1 + \alpha_2)E\{Q_2\} \to 0$ because the hypothetical system with input rate $\mu_0$, variance rate $\Delta_1$ would cause a queue length of order $(\mu_2 - \mu_0)^{-1}$ instead of order $-\ln(\mu_2 - \mu_0)$ for $\mu_2 \to \mu_0$ .

Although the digamma function is tabulated, it is worth noting that for integer values of $\alpha_1/(\alpha_1 + \alpha_2)$ , namely

$$\alpha_1/(\alpha_1 + \alpha_2) \quad = \quad k + 1 , \qquad k = 1, 2, -- \qquad (3.3)$$

$$\psi\left(1 + \frac{\alpha_1}{\alpha_1 + \alpha_2}\right) = \psi(2+k) = \psi(1+k) + \frac{1}{k+1} = \psi(1) + 1 + \frac{1}{2} + \cdots + \frac{1}{k+}$$

Equation (3.1) now has the simple form

$$\alpha_1 E\{Q_2\} = \frac{(k+1)}{k} \left[\frac{1}{2} + \frac{1}{3} + \cdots + \frac{1}{k+1}\right] , \quad k = 1, 2, -- . \qquad (3.4)$$

In particular, for $k = 1$ , $\alpha_2 = -\alpha_1/2$ , $\mu_2 - \mu_0 = (\mu_1 - \mu_0)/2$

$$\alpha_1 E\{Q_2\} = 1 , \qquad E\{Q_2\} = E\{Q_1\} .$$

Equation (3.4) does not apply for $k = 0$ , which corresponds to $\alpha_2 = 0$
Although (3.1) contains a factor $\alpha_2^{-1}$ , $E\{Q_2\}$ is finite for $\alpha_2 \to 0$
(as shown in Fig. VI-2).

We could proceed now to evaluate covariances of $Q_1$ , $Q_2$ directly from $K(\lambda_1,\lambda_2)$ , and other higher moments, but the formulas become rather cumbersome and not very informative. It is more interesting to obtain some at least qualitative description of the shape of the marginal distribution $g_2^*(\ell_2)$ and perhaps also the joint distribution $g^*(\ell_1,\ell_2)$ . Evaluation of these, however, requires a Laplace transform inversion, which is difficult to evaluate exactly.

The inversion formula for $K(0,\lambda_2)$ is

$$g_2^*(\ell_2) = \frac{1}{2\pi i} \int_{-i\infty}^{+i\infty} d\lambda_2 \ e^{\lambda_2 \ell_2} K(0,\lambda_2) . \qquad (3.5)$$

To evaluate this, particularly for "large" $\ell_2$ , the simplest procedure is to close the path of integration up the imaginary axis with a semi-circle at infinity in the left-half $\lambda_2$-plane as in Fig. VI-3. One then moves the vertical path to the left, picking up the residues as the path is displaced past each pole of the integrand.

The right-hand side of (2.9a) vanishes at $\lambda_2 = -\alpha_2$ , so $K(0,\lambda_2)$ does not have a pole there. The poles of $K(0,\lambda_2)$ occur only at the poles of $K_1(\lambda_2)$ . Despite the fact that (2.8) contains some square roots, $K_1(\lambda_2)$ is an even function of the square root and has no branch point singularities, only poles at the values of $\lambda_2$ that cause the argument of the $\Gamma$-function to be 0, -1, -2, --.

The poles of $K_1(\lambda_2)$ occur at

$$\lambda_2 = -\lambda_{2n} \equiv -(n + 1)[\alpha_1 + (n + 1)(\alpha_1 + \alpha_2)] , \qquad n = 0, 1, 2, \text{ -- } .$$

$$(3.6)$$

By evaluating the residues at each pole one can show that

$$g_2^*(\ell_2) = \sum_{n=0}^{\infty} \frac{(-1)^n}{(n + 2)!} 2 \left[ n + 1 + \frac{\alpha_1}{2(\alpha_1 + \alpha_2)} \right] \left( \frac{\alpha_1}{\alpha_1 + \alpha_2} \right)_n \lambda_{2n} \exp(-\lambda_{2n}\ell_2) .$$

$$(3.7)$$

This infinite series converges for all $\ell_2 > 0$ . For

$$\alpha_1 \ell_2 \gtrsim 1 + \ln(\alpha_1/[\alpha_1 + \alpha_2]) \qquad (3.7a)$$

it can be approximated very well by the first few terms

$$g_2^*(\ell_2) \simeq \left[ 1 + \frac{\alpha_1}{2(\alpha_1 + \alpha_2)} \right] (2\alpha_1 + \alpha_2) \exp[-(2\alpha_1 + \alpha_2)\ell_2]$$

$$(3.7b)$$

$$- \frac{1}{3} \left[ 2 + \frac{\alpha_1}{2(\alpha_1 + \alpha_2)} \right] \left( \frac{\alpha_1}{\alpha_1 + \alpha_2} \right) 2(3\alpha_1 + 2\alpha_2) \exp[-2(3\alpha_1 + 2\alpha_2)\ell_2] + \text{ -- } .$$

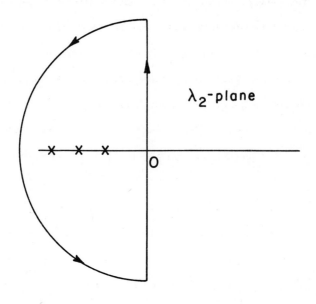

Fig. VI-3. Path of integration in the $\lambda_2$-space.

Since the $\lambda_n$ , the parameters in the exponentials, increase quadratically

in $n$ , the convergence of (3.7) is very rapid once the exponential fac-

tors overpower any possible growth in the coefficients (particularly for

$\alpha_1/(\alpha_1 + \alpha_2) \gg 1$).

Whenever (3.7) does not converge rapidly, one can estimate (3.5) more

easily by means of a saddle-point integration. Since both $K_1(\lambda_2)$ and

$K(0,\lambda_2)$ are transforms of nonnegative functions (probability densities),

they must be monotone decreasing in $\lambda_2$ for $\lambda_2$ real and $\lambda_2 > -\lambda_{2o} =$

$-(2\alpha_1 + \alpha_2)$. On the other hand, the factor $\exp(\lambda_2 \ell_2)$ , $\ell_2 > 0$ is

increasing in $\lambda_2$ .

The integrand of (3.5) is infinite at $\lambda_2 = -\lambda_{2o}$ and also for

$\lambda_2 \to + \infty$ (because $K(0,\lambda_2)$ decreases slower than an exponential in $\lambda_2$

for $\lambda_2 \to + \infty$). It must, therefore, have a minimum along the real line

$-\lambda_{2o} < \lambda_2 < \infty$ and, at least in any cases analysed here, it has only one

minimum. Since the integrand is analytic in $\lambda_2$ for Re $\lambda_2 > -\lambda_{2o}$ ,

the minimum point on the real line is a saddle-point in the complex plane.

If we displace the path of integration so as to pass vertically through

the saddle-point, the integrand will have a maximum at $\lambda_2$ real.

For sufficiently small $\ell_2$ , the factor $\exp(\lambda_2 \ell_2)$ will not overpower

the decay of $K(0,\lambda_2)$ until $\lambda_2$ is large, larger than $-\alpha_2$ at least

$(-\alpha_2 < \alpha_1)$ . To evaluate (3.5) for small $\ell_2$ , it is actually more con-

venient to treat the two terms from (2.9a) separately

$$g_2^*(\ell_2) \;=\; \frac{1}{2\pi i} \int_{a-i\infty}^{a+i\infty} d\lambda_2 \frac{e^{\lambda_2 \ell_2} K_2(0)}{\alpha_2 + \lambda_2} \;-\; \frac{1}{2\pi i} \int_{a-i\infty}^{a+i\infty} d\lambda_2 \frac{e^{\lambda_2 \ell_2} K_1(\lambda_2)}{\alpha_2 + \lambda_2} \;.$$

The   a   can be any real number   $a > -\lambda_{2o}$   but for small   $\ell_2$ ,   it will
be chosen to the right of   $-\alpha_2$ .

The first term can be evaluated by closing the contour in the left-
half plane and picking the residue at   $\lambda_2 = -\alpha_2$ .   The   $K_2(0)$   is known
from (2.8a) and (2.10), so

$$g_2^*(\ell_2) \;=\; (\alpha_1 + \alpha_2)e^{-\alpha_2\ell_2} \;-\; \frac{1}{2\pi i}\int_{a-i\infty}^{a+i\infty} d\lambda_2\; e^{\lambda_2\ell_2}\;\frac{K_1(\lambda_2)}{\alpha_2 + \lambda_2} \;. \tag{3.8}$$

In the second term   $K_1(\lambda_2)(\alpha_2 + \lambda_2)^{-1}$   is decreasing in   $\lambda_2$   for   $\lambda_2 > -\alpha_2$
and, for large   $\lambda_2$ ,   decreases much faster than   $K(0,\lambda_2)$ .   This inte-
gral can be evaluated quite accurately by a saddle-point integration.

For small   $\ell_2$ ,   the saddle-point will occur for large   $\lambda_2$   and the
integrand at the saddle-point will be very small.   Certainly for   $\ell_2 \to 0$,
the second terms of (3.8) goes to zero (very rapidly, as we will soon see),
and   $g_2^*(\ell_2) \to (\alpha_1 + \alpha_2)$ .   This value of   $g_2^*(0)$   is already known from
the requirement that the service rate of server 2 must be   $\mu_0$ .

The saddle-point of the integrand in (3.8) can be located by evaluation of that   $\lambda_2$   for which the logarithmic derivative of the integrand
vanishes, i.e.,

$$\ell_2 \;=\; -\frac{d}{d\lambda_2}\,\ell n\,K_1(\lambda_2) \;-\; \frac{1}{\alpha_2 + \lambda_2} \;. \tag{3.9}$$

For sufficiently large values of   $\lambda_2$ ,   one can use the asymptotic formulas for the $\Gamma$-functions in (2.7).   The leading terms in such an expan-
sion show that   $-\ell n\,K_1(\lambda_2)$   increases like   $\pi[\lambda_2/(\alpha_1 + \alpha_2)]^{1/2}$.   A first
approximation to the saddle-point would be

$$\ell_2 \simeq \frac{\pi}{2[(\alpha_1 + \alpha_2)\lambda_2]^{1/2}} \, , \qquad \lambda_2 = \left(\frac{\pi}{2\ell_2}\right)^2 \frac{1}{(\alpha_1 + \alpha_2)} \, .$$

By evaluating the integrand and its second derivative at the saddle-point one can show that the second term of (3.8) is approximately

$$\frac{2\sqrt{2} \, (\alpha_1 + \alpha_2)}{\Gamma\left(\frac{\alpha_1}{\alpha_1 + \alpha_2}\right)} \left[\frac{\pi}{2(\alpha_1 + \alpha_2)\ell_2}\right]^{\frac{1}{2} + \frac{\alpha_1}{\alpha_1 + \alpha_2}} \exp\left[-\frac{\pi^2}{4\ell_2(\alpha_1 + \alpha_2)}\right] \, , \qquad (3.10)$$

for sufficiently small $\ell_2$ .

Depending on the value of $(\alpha_1 + \alpha_2)$, (3.10) may be too crude an estimate to be very useful for numerical calculations in the range of $\ell_2$ where this term is significant. It is possible to solve (3.9) more accurately by use of several terms in the expansions of the $\Gamma$-functions, but this does not seem necessary. Equation (3.10) shows that the contribution to (3.8) from the second term goes to zero extremely fast as $\ell_2 \to 0$ .

Since the first term of (3.7b) and the first term of (3.8) are both upper bounds on $g_2^*(\ell_2)$ , the smaller of these is also an upper bound, which, in fact, gives a fair description of the shape of $g_2^*(\ell_2)$ . If one plots just the first term of (3.7b) on semi-log paper as a function of $\ell_2$ , one obtains a straight line of negative slope determined by the exponent $-(2\alpha_1 + \alpha_2)$ . Similarly the first term of (3.8) gives a straight line of slope determined by the exponent $-\alpha_2$ , which may be either positive or negative. The broken lines of Fig. VI-4 show the bounds defined by the first terms for several values of $\alpha_2$ , with

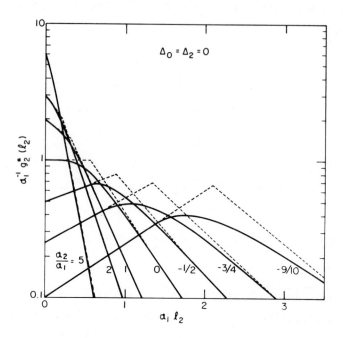

Fig. VI-4. Distributions of the queue length $Q_2$ for various service rates $\mu_0$, $\mu_1$, $\mu_2$; $\alpha_2/\alpha_1 = (\mu_2 - \mu_1)/(\mu_1 - \mu_0)$. The broken lines represent exponential approximations.

lengths measured in units of $\alpha_1^{-1}$ . The function $g_2^*(\ell_2)$ is shown by
the solid line curves.  It was calculated over most of the range of $\ell_2$
from (3.7).

From the discussion of Fig. VI-2, one would have guessed that for
large $\alpha_2$ or $(\alpha_2 + \alpha_1)/\alpha_1$ , $g_2^*(\ell_2)$ would be nearly exponential, because it should be similar to the queue distribution for a single server
system.  Fig. VI-4 shows that for large $\alpha_2$ (for example, $\alpha_2/\alpha_1 = 1$,
2, or 5) $g_2^*(\ell_2)$ starts at small $\ell_2$ to decrease like one exponential,
then makes a smooth transition to a more rapidly decreasing exponential.
For $\mu_2 = \mu_1$ , $\alpha_2 = 0$ , $g_2^*(\ell_2)$ is nearly constant for $\alpha_1\ell_2 \lesssim 1/2$ but
then decays nearly exponentially.  For $\mu_2 < \mu_1$ , $\alpha_2 < 0$ , however,
$g_2^*(\ell_2)$ increases exponentially for small $\ell_2$ , but decreases exponentially for large $\ell_2$ , and has a single maximum.  As $\mu_2$ approaches $\mu_0$,
$\alpha_2 \to -\alpha_1$ , the position of the maximum moves to large values of $\ell_2$ .
The "width" of the distribution appears to remain finite as the mean goes
to $\infty$ .  Certainly the shape is very narrow compared with the exponential
distribution associated with a single server system at traffic intensity
approaching 1.

It is also possible to evaluate the joint distribution of the two
queues by a double Laplace Transform inversion

$$g^*(\ell_1,\ell_2) = \frac{1}{(2\pi i)^2} \int_{-i\infty}^{+i\infty} d\lambda_1 \int_{-i\infty}^{+i\infty} d\lambda_2 \frac{(\lambda_1 - \lambda_2)K_1(\lambda_2) + \lambda_2 K_2(\lambda_1)}{\alpha_1\lambda_1 + \alpha_2\lambda_2 + (\lambda_1 - \lambda_2)^2} \exp(\lambda_1\ell_1+\lambda_2\ell_2).$$

$$(3.11)$$

The equations for $K_1(\lambda_2)$, $K_2(\lambda_1)$ guarantee that the integrand is analytic in $\lambda_1$, $\lambda_2$ where the denominator vanishes.  One can integrate
either $\lambda_2$ or $\lambda_1$ first by evaluating the residues at the poles.  The

poles of the integrand in the $\lambda_2$-space come from $K_1(\lambda_2)$ and are independ-

ent of $\lambda_1$; those in the $\lambda_1$-space come from $K_1(\lambda_2)$ and are independent

of $\lambda_2$. If we integrate $\lambda_2$ first we obtain

$$g^*(\ell_1,\ell_2) = \frac{1}{2\pi i} \int_{-i\infty}^{+i\infty} d\lambda_1 \; e^{\lambda_1\ell_1} \sum_{n=0}^{\infty} \left\{ \frac{(\lambda_1 + \lambda_{2n})(-\alpha_2 + \lambda_{2n})}{[\alpha_1\lambda_1 - \alpha_2\lambda_{2n} + (\lambda_1 + \lambda_{2n})^2]} \right.$$

$$\left. \cdot \frac{(-1)^n \, 2}{(n + 2)!} \left[ n + 1 + \frac{\alpha_1}{2(\alpha_1 + \alpha_2)} \right] \left( \frac{\alpha_1}{\alpha_1 + \alpha_2} \right)_n \lambda_{2n} \, \exp(-\lambda_{2n}\ell_2) \right\}$$

in which the $\lambda_{2n}$ are given by (3.6).

Each term of the sum is now a rational function of $\lambda_1$ having just

two poles in the $\lambda_1$-space. The $\lambda_1$ integration can be done also by

evaluation of the residues. It can be written in the form

$$g^*(\ell_1,\ell_2) = \alpha_1 \, e^{-\alpha_1\ell_1} \, (2\,\alpha_1 + \alpha_2) \, e^{-(2\alpha_1 + \alpha_2)\ell_2}$$

$$+ \sum_{n=0}^{\infty} \frac{(-1)^n \lambda_{1n+1} e^{-\lambda_{1n+1}\ell_1}}{(n + 2)!} \left( \frac{\alpha_1}{\alpha_1 + \alpha_2} \right)_{n+1} \left[ \lambda_{2n} e^{-\lambda_{2n}\ell_2} - \lambda_{2n+1} e^{-\lambda_{2n+1}\ell_2} \right]$$

$$\tag{3.12}$$

in which

$$\lambda_{1n} = -(n + 1)\,\alpha_2 + (n + 1)^2 \, (\alpha_1 + \alpha_2) \quad,$$

$$\tag{3.12a}$$

$$\lambda_{1n+1} = [(n + 2)/(n + 1)]\,\lambda_{2n} \quad.$$

The terms of (3.12) have been paired in such a way as to show

clearly that an integration of (3.12) with respect to $\ell_2$ from 0 to $\infty$

will cause each term in the sum to vanish; the integration of the terms in the square bracket cancel for every $n$. This immediately yields the known form for $g_1^*(\ell_1)$, namely, $\alpha_1 \exp(-\alpha_1 \ell_1)$. We could also regroup the terms so that an integration of (3.12) with respect to $\ell_1$ gives the form (3.7) for $g_2^*(\ell_2)$.

Since $\lambda_{1n}$ and $\lambda_{2n}$ both increase quadratically in $n$, the series (3.12) converges very rapidly, except possibly if $(\alpha_1 + \alpha_2)/\alpha_1 \ll 1$ or if both $\ell_1$ and $\ell_2$ are small. One can show directly from (3.11) that $g_1^*(\ell_1, \ell_2)$ goes to zero very rapidly for $\ell_1$ and $\ell_2 \to 0$ analogous to the behavior of (3.10). Any time the series (3.12) appears to converge slowly, the value of $g^*(\ell_1, \ell_2)$ is actually relatively small.

From (3.12) one can show that for values of $\alpha_1 \ell_1 \gtrsim 1$ and $\alpha_1 \ell_2 \gtrsim 1 + \ln(\alpha_1/(\alpha_1 + \alpha_2))$, the value of $g^*(\ell_1, \ell_2)$ is determined mostly by just the first term. The first term alone would describe $Q_1$ and $Q_2$ as being statistically independent, each with an exponential distribution, of mean $\alpha_1^{-1}$ and $(2\alpha_1 + \alpha_2)^{-1}$, respectively.

Successive terms in the series (3.12) involve more and more rapidly decreasing exponentials in $\ell_1$ and $\ell_2$, thus corrections to be made closer and closer to the origin $\ell_1 = \ell_2 = 0$. Most of the qualitative features of $g^*(\ell_1, \ell_2)$ can be seen from the behavior of just the first term of the series ($n = 0$). Since the "total probability mass" of each term vanishes, the positive and negative contributions can be interpreted as a shift of the probability from one place to another. For $n = 0$, the negative term has a factor $\exp(-\lambda_{2n+1} \ell_2)$, the positive term a factor $\exp(-\lambda_{2n} \ell_2)$ with $\lambda_{2o} = 2\alpha_1 + \alpha_2$. The probability which is shifted is mostly that with $\lambda_{1n+1} \ell_1 = (4\alpha_1 + 2\alpha_2)\ell_1 \lesssim 1$, i.e., relatively small $\ell_1$. It is taken away from the smaller $\ell_2$ values

262

and displaced to larger values (since $\lambda_{2n+1} > \lambda_{2n}$).

In essence, the complete series in (3.12) describes a displacement of the probability contained in the first term of (3.12) away from the small values of $\ell_1$, $\ell_2$ (where $g^*(\ell_1,\ell_2)$ actually vanishes) into the range of relatively small $\ell_2$ but large $\ell_1$. Thus $Q_1$ and $Q_2$ are negatively correlated, as would be expected from the discussion above explaining how a large value of $Q_2$ could be generated, particularly for $(\alpha_1 + \alpha_2)/\alpha_1 \ll 1$. A positive value of $Q_1$ at one time typically leads to a smaller $Q_1$ and a larger $Q_2$ at a later time. Thus the equilibrium distribution will show a tendency for small $Q_1$ to be associated with large $Q_2$.

One can calculate $g^*(\ell_1,\ell_2)$ from (3.12) very easily, but it is difficult to display graphically the manner in which this function varies with $\alpha_1$ and $\alpha_2$.

4. <u>Equilibrium Distributions, $c_1 = c_2 = \infty$</u>. Some of the techniques described in sections 2 and 3 for analysing the queue distributions in the special case $\Delta_0 = \Delta_2 = 0$, $c_1 = c_2 = \infty$, can be generalized to the case of arbitrary $\Delta_0$, $\Delta_1$, $\Delta_2$ but $c_1 = c_2 = \infty$. The results for the general case will not, however, be in quite as convenient a form.

We go back to (1.13), with $c_1 = c_2 = \infty$, and first make a substitution of coordinates expressing $\lambda_1$ and $\lambda_2$ in terms of two new variables $\theta_1$ and $\theta_2$ defined through the relations

$$\lambda_1 = \mu^\dagger \Delta^{*-3/2}(\Delta_1 + \Delta_2)^{1/2}[\cos\theta_1 - \cos(\theta^* - \gamma_1)] , \qquad (4.1)$$

$$\lambda_2 = \mu^\dagger \Delta^{*-3/2}(\Delta_0 + \Delta_1)^{1/2}[\cos\gamma_1 \cos\theta_1 + \sin\gamma_1 \sin\theta_2 - \cos\theta^*] \qquad (4.2)$$

in which $\gamma_0$, $\gamma_1$, $\gamma_2$ are the angles defined in Chapter III, equations
(III 2.9), (III 2.14), and (III 2.16), $\Delta^*$ is given by (III 2.5a), and
$\mu^\dagger$, $\theta^*$ are defined by

$$\mu^\dagger \equiv \Delta^{*-1/2}[\Delta_0(\mu_2 - \mu_1)^2 + \Delta_1(\mu_2 - \mu_0)^2 + \Delta_2(\mu_1 - \mu_0)^2]^{1/2} , \quad (4.3)$$

$$\tan \theta^* = (\mu_1 - \mu_0) \Delta^*/[\Delta_0(\mu_2 - \mu_1) + \Delta_1(\mu_2 - \mu_0)] , \quad (4.4)$$

$$\text{with} \quad 0 \le \theta^* \le \gamma_1 + \gamma_2 \le \pi . \quad (4.4a)$$

From these equations, one can also show that

$$\lambda_1 - \lambda_2 = \mu^\dagger \Delta^{*-3/2}(\Delta_0 + \Delta_2)^{1/2}[\cos \gamma_2 \cos \theta_1 - \sin \gamma_2 \sin \theta_2 + \cos(\gamma_0+\theta^*)].$$
$$(4.5)$$

This transformation can be deduced from (1.13) if one first seeks a
linear transformation of coordinates which reduces the quadratic coefficient of $K(\lambda_1,\lambda_2)$ ,

$$\lambda_1(\mu_1 - \mu_0) + \lambda_2(\mu_2 - \mu_1) + \tfrac{1}{2}[\Delta_0\lambda_1^2 + \Delta_1(\lambda_1 - \lambda_2)^2 + \Delta_2\lambda_2^2] \quad (4.6)$$

to a diagonal form with no linear terms. The new coordinates, however,
are identified as $\cos \theta_1$ and $\sin \theta_2$ . Thus (4.1) and (4.2) define $\lambda_1$
and $\lambda_2$ as linear functions of the new variables $\cos \theta_1$ and $\sin \theta_2$
with $\lambda_1$ independent of $\sin \theta_2$ . The coefficients in the linear transformation are determined so as to guarantee that (4.6) has the form

$$\tfrac{1}{2} \Delta^{*-3/2}\mu^\dagger[-1 + \cos^2\theta_1 + \sin^2\theta_2] = \tfrac{1}{2} \Delta^{*-3/2}\mu^\dagger[-\sin^2\theta_1 + \sin^2\theta_2] . \quad (4.6a)$$

The transformation (4.1), (4.2) is, in fact, uniquely determined by the specification that $\lambda_1$ be a linear function of $\cos \theta_1$ and $\lambda_2$ a linear function of $\cos \theta_1$ and $\sin \theta_2$ ; that the coefficients of $\cos \theta_1$, $\sin \theta_2$, and $\cos \theta_1 \sin \theta_2$ in (4.6) vanish; and that the coef ficients of $\cos^2 \theta_1$ and $\sin^2 \theta_2$ be equal to each other and to the con- stant term in (4.6a). One can, of course, confirm that (4.6a) is correc by substituting (4.1) and (4.2) into (4.6). It does take some manipula- tion to arrange the formulas in the specific form shown in (4.1) - (4.4)

The purpose in writing (4.6) in the form (4.6a) is to give a con- venient representation for the conditions under which this coefficient o $K(\lambda_1, \lambda_2)$ in (1.13) vanishes, namely for

$$\theta_1 = \pm \theta_2 \ . \tag{4.7}$$

Since $K(\lambda_1, \lambda_2)$ is analytic at least for Re $\lambda_1$, Re $\lambda_2 \geq 0$ , it follows that the right-hand side of (1.13) must vanish whenever Re $\lambda_1$ , Re $\lambda_2 \geq 0$ and also $\theta_1 = \pm \theta_2$ . Since $\lambda_1$ and $\lambda_2$ are functions of $\cos \theta_1$, an even function of $\theta_1$ , it is not necessary to consider sepa- rately both $\theta_1 = +\theta_2$ and $\theta_1 = -\theta_2$ . We will consider only $\theta_1 = +\theta_2$ For $c_1 = c_2 = \infty$ , the condition that the right-hand side of (1.13) vanishes for $\theta_1 = \theta_2$ implies that

$$-(\Delta_0 + \Delta_2)^{1/2} (\Delta_0 + \Delta_1)^{1/2} [\cos(\theta_1 + \gamma_2) + \cos(\gamma_0 + \theta^*)] K_1^\dagger(\theta_1)$$

$$\tag{4.8}$$

$$= (\Delta_1 + \Delta_2) [\cos(\theta_1 - \gamma_1) - \cos \theta^*] K_2^\dagger(\theta_1)$$

in which

$$K_2^\dagger(\theta_1) \equiv K_2(\lambda_1(\theta_1)) \tag{4.8a}$$

is the value of $K_2(\lambda_1)$ with $\lambda_1(\theta_1)$ evaluated from (4.1), and

$$K_1^\dagger(\theta_1) \equiv K_1(\lambda_2(\theta_1)|\theta_1 = \theta_2) \qquad (4.8b)$$

is the value of $K_1(\lambda_2)$ with $\lambda_2(\theta_1)$ evaluated from (4.2) with $\theta_1 = \theta_2$, namely,

$$\lambda_2 = \mu^\dagger \Delta^{*-3/2} (\Delta_0 + \Delta_1)^{1/2} [\cos(\theta_1 - \gamma_1) - \cos\theta^*] . \qquad (4.9)$$

Since $\gamma_0 + \gamma_1 + \gamma_2 = \pi$ , both sides of (4.8) vanish when

$$\theta_1 + \gamma_2 = \pi - \gamma_0 - \theta^* \quad \text{and} \quad \theta_1 - \gamma_1 = -\theta^*$$

i.e.,

$$\theta_1 = \gamma_1 - \theta^* . \qquad (4.10)$$

This is the value of $\theta_1$ at which both $\lambda_1(\theta_1)$ and $\lambda_2(\theta_1)$ vanish. It is a point at which (4.6) obviously vanishes and at which $K(\lambda_1,\lambda_2)$ is known to be analytic. Equation (4.8) is valid not only at the point (4.10) but also in some neighborhood of this point. By using the sum and difference formulas for trigonometric functions, one can factor and divide both sides of (4.7) by

$$\cos\left(\frac{\theta_1 + \theta^* + \pi - \gamma_1}{2}\right) = -\sin\left(\frac{\theta_1 + \theta^* - \gamma_1}{2}\right) ,$$

the factor which vanishes at (4.10), and reduce (4.7) to

$$-(\Delta_0 + \Delta_2)^{\frac{1}{2}}(\Delta_0 + \Delta_1)^{\frac{1}{2}} \cos\left(\frac{\theta_1 - \theta^* - \gamma_0 + \gamma_2}{2}\right) K_1^\dagger(\theta_1) = (\Delta_1 + \Delta_2)\sin\left(\frac{\theta_1 - \theta^* - \gamma_1}{2}\right) K_2^\dagger(\theta_1) .$$

$$(4.8c)$$

266

From (4.8c) and conditions of analyticity for $K_1(\lambda_2)$ and $K_2(\lambda_1)$, we wish to determine both $K_1(\lambda_2)$ and $K_2(\lambda_1)$ .

The coordinate transformation (4.1) maps each of the vertical strip $0 < \text{Re } \theta_1 \leq \pi$ and $-\pi < \text{Re } \theta_1 \leq 0$ in the complex $\theta_1$-space into the ent complex $\lambda_1$-space. The angle $\gamma_1 - \theta^*$ , (4.10), may be either positive negative (it is positive if $\mu_2 > \mu_1$ , negative for $\mu_2 < \mu_1$), but it 1 in one or the other of these two strips.

The condition that $K_2(\lambda_1)$ is analytic for $\text{Re } \lambda_1 \geq 0$ means, thro (4.1), (4.8a), that $K_2^+(\theta_1)$ is an analytic function of $\theta_1$ for

$$\text{Re cos } \theta_1 \geq \cos(\gamma_1 - \theta^*) , \qquad (4.11)$$

at least for $\theta_1$ contained in that strip of width $\pi$ which includes the point $\gamma_1 - \theta^*$ , defined as the primary image of $\lambda_1 = 0$ . Since the region (4.11) contains both the point $\gamma_1 - \theta^*$ and the origin $\theta_1 = 0$ , and $K_2(\lambda_1)$ is a function of $\cos \theta_1$ , the analytic continuation of $K_2^+(\theta_1)$ through the origin must satisfy the condition

$$K_2^+(\theta_1) = K_2^+(-\theta_1) \qquad (4.12)$$

at least in the symmetric region satisfying (4.11) and $-\pi < \text{Re } \theta_1 \leq +\pi$ . Furthermore, since $K_2(\lambda_1)$ must be real and positive for $\lambda_1$ real and positive, $K_2^+(\theta_1)$ is real and positive along the real line segment $-|\gamma_1 - \theta^*| \leq \theta_1 \leq |\gamma_1 - \theta^*|$, plus the imaginary axis $\text{Re } \theta_1 = 0$ .

For the corresponding conditions on $K_1^+(\theta_1)$ , we observe that (4.9) maps the strip $-\pi + \gamma_1 < \text{Re } \theta_1 \leq \gamma_1$ of the complex $\theta_1$-space into the entire $\lambda_2$-space; and this strip always contains the point $\gamma_1 - \theta^*$, the primary image of $\lambda_2 = 0$ . That $K_1(\lambda_2)$ is analytic for $\text{Re } \lambda_2 \geq 0$

means, through (4.8b) and (4.9), that $K_1^+(\theta_1)$ is an analytic function of $\theta_1$ in the region

$$\text{Re } \cos(\theta_1 - \gamma_1) \geq \cos \theta^* \qquad (4.13)$$

which contains both the point $\gamma_1 - \theta^*$ and $\theta_1 = \gamma_1$.

Since $K_1(\lambda_2)$ is a function of $\cos(\theta_1 - \gamma_1)$, the analytic continuation of $K_1^+(\theta_1)$ for $\text{Re } \theta_1 > \gamma_1$ must satisfy

$$K_1^+(\theta_1) = K_1^+(2\gamma_1 - \theta_1) \qquad (4.14)$$

at least in the region (4.13), which is symmetric to the reflection $\theta_1 \rightarrow 2\gamma_1 - \theta_1$. The function $K_1^+(\theta_1)$ must also be real and positive along the real line segment $\gamma_1 - \theta^* \leq \theta_1 \leq \gamma_1 + \theta^*$ and along the vertical line $\text{Re } \theta_1 = \gamma_1$.

Fig. VI-5 shows the regions (4.11) and (4.13) in which $K_2^+(\theta_1)$ and $K_1^+(\theta_1)$, respectively, are required to be analytic. Fig. VI-5a illustrates a case with $0 < \theta^* < \gamma_1 < \pi/2$, $0 < \gamma_1 - \theta^*$, which arises for $\mu_2 > \mu_1$. The two shaded regions representing (4.11) and (4.13) barely touch along the real axis but do overlap off the real line. Fig. VI-5b illustrates a case with $0 < \gamma_1 < \theta^* < \pi/2$, $\gamma_1 - \theta^* < 0$, in which the two regions also overlap along the real line. In the special case $\gamma_1 = \theta^*$ ($\mu_1 = \mu_2$), the region (4.11) touches the real axis at only one point $\theta_1 = 0$. In Fig. VI-5c, $0 < \gamma_1 < \pi/2 < \theta^*$, and $\cos \theta^* < 0$ in (4.13). This is similar to Fig. VI-5b except that the region (4.13) has a width greater than $\pi$ along the real line and bulges out. The lines along which $K_2^+(\theta_1)$ or $K_1^+(\theta_1)$ are known to be real and positive are shown by the heavy lines.

Equation (4.8c) is valid at least in the overlap of the regions

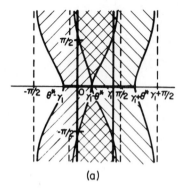

(a)

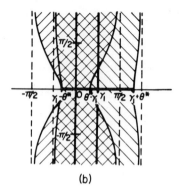

(b)

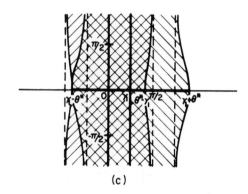

(c)

Fig. VI-5.  Regions of the complex $\theta_1$-plane in
which $K_1^+(\theta_1)$ and/or $K_2^+(\theta_1)$ are
analytic.

(4.11) and (4.13) which includes the point $\gamma_1 - \theta^*$ . If it is possible

to continue $K_1^\dagger(\theta_1)$ and $K_2^\dagger(\theta_1)$ analytically beyond the regions where

they are presently known to be analytic, they must also satisfy (4.8c)

in the region of continuation.

We can first continue $K_2^\dagger(\theta_1)$ into the region (4.13) where $K_1^\dagger(\theta_1)$

is analytic. The only possible singularity of $K_2^\dagger(\theta_1)$ in this region

is at the boundary point $\theta_1 = \gamma_1 + \theta^*$ where the coefficient of $K_2^\dagger(\theta_1)$

in (4.8a) vanishes. This continuation, however, also induces, through

(4.12), a continuation of $K_2^\dagger(\theta_1)$ into the reflection of region (4.13)

through the origin. We conclude that $K_2^\dagger(\theta_1)$ is analytic at least in

the strip $-(\gamma_1 + \theta^*) < \text{Re } \theta_1 < \gamma_1 + \theta^*$ , excluding the points $\theta_1 =$

$\pm (\gamma_1 + \theta^*)$ .

Applying similar arguments to $K_1^\dagger(\theta_1)$ , we can analytically con-

tinue $K_1^\dagger(\theta_1)$ into the region (4.11) and the reflection of (4.13), where

$K_2^\dagger(\theta_1)$ is known to be analytic. The only possible singularity of $K_1^\dagger(\theta_1)$

in this region occurs where the coefficient of $K_1^\dagger(\theta_1)$ in (4.8a) vanishes

at

$$\theta_1 - \theta^* - \gamma_0 + \gamma_2 = \pi$$

$$\theta_1 = \theta^* - \pi + \gamma_0 - \gamma_2 = \theta^* - \gamma_1 - 2\gamma_2 \leq -\gamma_2$$

which, for $\theta^* < \gamma_2$ , will actually be outside the region in question.

In any case, however, $K_1^\dagger(\theta_1)$ is analytic in the strip $0 \leq \text{Re } \theta_1 \leq \gamma_1$

and by virtue of (4.14) also in the larger strip $0 \leq \text{Re } \theta_1 \leq 2\gamma_1$ . Both

$K_1^\dagger(\theta_1)$ and $K_2^\dagger(\theta_1)$ are analytic in a region including the strip $0 \leq \text{Re } \theta_1$

$\leq \gamma_1$ , between the two heavy vertical lines of Fig. VI-5.

To continue $K_1^\dagger(\theta_1)$ and $K_2^\dagger(\theta_1)$ further, it is convenient to divide

(4.8c) by the same equation with $\theta_1$ replaced by $2\gamma_1 - \theta_1$. Then use (4.12) and (4.14) to obtain

$$
K_2^\dagger(\theta_1) = \frac{\cos\left(\dfrac{\theta_1 - \theta^* - \gamma_0 + \gamma_2}{2}\right) \sin\left(\dfrac{-\theta_1 - \theta^* + \gamma_1}{2}\right)}{\cos\left(\dfrac{-\theta_1 - \theta^* - \gamma_0 + \gamma_2 + 2\gamma_1}{2}\right) \sin\left(\dfrac{\theta_1 - \theta^* - \gamma_1}{2}\right)} \; K_2^\dagger(\theta_1 - 2\gamma_1) \; .
$$

(4.15)

If we divide (4.8c) by the same equation with $\theta_1$ replaced by $-\theta_1$ we similarly obtain

$$
K_1^\dagger(\theta_1) = \frac{\cos\left(\dfrac{-\theta_1 - \theta^* - \gamma_0 + \gamma_2}{2}\right) \sin\left(\dfrac{\theta_1 - \theta^* - \gamma_1}{2}\right)}{\cos\left(\dfrac{\theta_1 - \theta^* - \gamma_0 + \gamma_2}{2}\right) \sin\left(\dfrac{-\theta_1 - \theta^* - \gamma_1}{2}\right)} \; K_1^\dagger(\theta_1 + 2\gamma_1) \; .
$$

(4.15a)

Since $K_2^\dagger(\theta_1)$ is known to be analytic in the strip $-\gamma_1 \le \mathrm{Re}\,\theta_1 \le \gamma_1$ and $K_1^\dagger(\theta_1)$ in the strip $0 \le \mathrm{Re}\,\theta_1 \le 2\gamma_1$, the finite difference equations (4.15) and (4.15a) can be used to determine the singularities of $K_2^\dagger(\theta_1)$ and $K_1^\dagger(\theta_1)$ throughout the $\theta_1$-plane. One can show that $K_2^\dagger(\theta_1)$ and $K_1^\dagger(\theta_1)$ are also free of zeros in these same strips, so that (4.15) and (4.15a) also determine the zeros of $K_2^\dagger(\theta_1)$ and $K_1^\dagger(\theta_1)$ throughout the $\theta_1$-plane.

It follows from (4.15) and (4.15a) that all singularities of $K_2^\dagger(\theta_1)$ and $K_1^\dagger(\theta_1)$ in the finite $\theta_1$-plane are poles, and that all poles or zeros occur on the real $\theta_1$-axis. In general, however, the geometry of these is rather complex. As we analytically continue $K_1^\dagger(\theta_1)$, for example, in steps of $2\gamma_1$ in the negative direction using (4.15a), the first zero or pole of $K_1^\dagger(\theta_1)$ must be generated at the first point where the coefficient in (4.15a) vanishes or is infinite. Each zero or pole

generated in this way will, by iteration of (4.15a), create an infinite

sequence of zeros or poles at spacing $2\gamma_1$ . As $\theta_1$ proceeds down the

negative axis, it initiates a new sequence at each zero or pole of the

coefficient in (4.15a), two new zeros and two new poles in each interval

of width $2\pi$. For some values of the parameters, notably for $\gamma_1 = \gamma_0$ ,

the zeros and the poles may coalesce and annihilate each other, however.

Except in special cases, we shall not try to identify the functions

$K_2^\dagger(\theta_1)$ and $K_1^\dagger(\theta_1)$ through its zeros and poles as was done in section 2.

The behavior of $g^*(\ell_1,\ell_2)$ and $g_2^*(\ell_2)$ for large $\ell_1$ and $\ell_2$ , however,

depends primarily upon the location and nature of the singularities of

$K_2(\lambda_1)$ and $K_1(\lambda_2)$ which are nearest the origin.

For real values of $\lambda_1$ , $K_2(\lambda_1)$ must be a positive monotone de-

creasing function of $\lambda_1$ for all $\lambda_1$ to the right of the singularity

of $K_2(\lambda_1)$ which is nearest the origin; similarly for $K_1(\lambda_2)$ . The

$K_2^\dagger(\theta_1)$ must, therefore, be positive monotone increasing along the real

line $0 < \theta_1$ until $\theta_1$ reaches the first singularity of $K_2^\dagger(\theta_1)$ at

$\gamma_1 + \theta^*$ , provided $\gamma_1 + \theta^* < \pi$ . For $\gamma_1 + \theta^* < \pi$ , the pole singu-

larity of $K_2^\dagger(\theta_1)$ at $\gamma_1 + \theta^*$ induces a pole singularity of $K_2(\lambda_1)$ at

$$\lambda_1(\gamma_1 + \theta^*) = -\mu^\dagger \Delta^{*-3/2}(\Delta_1 + \Delta_2)^{1/2}2\sin\theta^* \sin\gamma_1$$

$$= -\frac{2(\mu_1 - \mu_0)}{(\Delta_0 + \Delta_1)} = -\alpha_1 \quad . \tag{4.16}$$

This result is not surprising in view of the fact that the marginal

distribution of $Q_1$ must be exponential and its transform $K(\lambda_1,0)$

proportional to $(\lambda_1 + \alpha_1)^{-1}$ , which also has a simple pole at $\lambda_1 = -\alpha_1$ .

272

If, however, $\gamma_1 + \theta^* > \pi$ (which is possible only if $\gamma_1 > \gamma_0$, i.e., $\Delta_1 < \Delta_0$), the first singularity of $K_2(\lambda_1)$ that one encounters, as $K_2(\lambda_1)$ is analytically continued along the negative real line from the origin, is a branch point singularity induced by the mapping (4.1) at $\theta_1 = \pi$. The branch point occurs at

$$\lambda_1(\pi) = -[\Delta_0(\mu_2 - \mu_1)^2 + \Delta_1(\mu_2 - \mu_0)^2 + \Delta_2(\mu_1 - \mu_0)^2]^{\frac{1}{2}} \Delta^{*-2}(\Delta_1 + \Delta_2)^{\frac{1}{2}}$$

$$- [\Delta_1(\mu_2 - \mu_0) + \Delta_2(\mu_1 - \mu_0)] \Delta^{*-2} . \qquad (4.16a)$$

(There is a simple pole in $K_2(\lambda_1)$ at the point (4.16), and it lies closer to the origin than (4.16a), but the pole singularity is on a different Reimann surface.)

Correspondingly, the function $K_1^\dagger(\theta_1)$ must be positive monotone decreasing for $\theta_1 < \gamma_1$ until, as $\theta_1$ decreases, $\theta_1$ reaches either the first singularity of $K_1^\dagger(\theta_1)$ or $-\pi + \gamma_1$ (where $K_1(\lambda_2(\theta_1))$ has a branch point). From (4.15a) we see that the first singularity of $K_1^\dagger(\theta_1)$ with $\theta_1 < \gamma_1$ occurs at

$$\theta_1 = \begin{cases} -\theta^* - \gamma_1 & \text{if } \theta^* \le \gamma_2 \\ \\ \theta^* - \gamma_1 - 2\gamma_2 & \text{if } \theta^* \ge \gamma_2 . \end{cases} \qquad (4.17)$$

If we keep $\mu_0$ and $\mu_1$ constant and let $\mu_2$ decrease from $\infty$ to $\mu_0$, (4.4) shows that $\theta^*$ increases continuously from $0$ to $\gamma_1 + \gamma_2$. The point $-\theta^* - \gamma_1$ in (4.17) decreases from $-\gamma_1$ to $-\gamma_2 - 2\gamma_1$, whereas $\theta^* - \gamma_1 - 2\gamma_2$ increases from $-\gamma_1 - 2\gamma_2$ to $-\gamma_2$. As $\theta^*$ passes through $\gamma_2$ these two points cross. For $\theta^* = \gamma_2$ both factors in the denominator of (4.15a) vanish simultaneously at $\theta_1 = -(\gamma_1 + \gamma_2) = -\pi + \gamma_0$ causing $K_1^+(\theta_1)$ to have a second order pole.

The pole singularities of $K_1^+(\theta_1)$ at (4.17) induce pole singularities in $K_1(\lambda_2)$ at

$$\lambda_2(-\theta^* - \gamma_1) = -2\mu^\dagger \Delta^{*-3/2}(\Delta_0 + \Delta_1)^{1/2}\sin\gamma_1\sin(\theta^* + \gamma_1)$$

(4.18a)

$$= \frac{-2[(\Delta_0 + \Delta_1)(\mu_2 - \mu_0) + (\Delta_1 - \Delta_0)(\mu_1 - \mu_0)]}{(\Delta_0 + \Delta_1)(\Delta_1 + \Delta_2)} \quad , \text{ if } \theta^* \leq \gamma_2$$

or

$$\lambda_2(\theta^* - \gamma_1 - 2\gamma_2) = -2\mu^\dagger \Delta^{*-3/2}(\Delta_0 + \Delta_1)^{1/2}\sin\gamma_0\sin(\theta^* + \gamma_0)$$

(4.18b)

$$= \frac{-2(\mu_2 - \mu_0)}{(\Delta_0 + \Delta_2)} \quad , \qquad \text{if } \theta^* \geq \gamma_2 \quad .$$

If, however, $\gamma_1 > \gamma_0$ $(\Delta_1 < \Delta_0)$, it is possible (as was true also for $K_2(\lambda_1)$) that the first singularity of $K_1(\lambda_2)$ along the negative axis is a branch point at the image of $\theta_1 = -\pi + \gamma_1$. For

$$\pi - 2\gamma_1 < \theta^* < \pi - 2\gamma_0$$

$$-(\gamma_1 - \gamma_0) < \theta^* - \gamma_2 < (\gamma_1 - \gamma_0) \quad , \qquad \gamma_1 > \gamma_0$$

the nearest singularity is at

$$\lambda_2(-\pi + \gamma_1) = -[\Delta_0(\mu_2 - \mu_1)^2 + \Delta_1(\mu_2 - \mu_0)^2 + \Delta_2(\mu_1 - \mu_0)^2]^{\frac{1}{2}}(\Delta_0 + \Delta_1)^{\frac{1}{2}}\Delta^{*-2}$$

$$- [\Delta_0(\mu_2 - \mu_1) + \Delta_1(\mu_2 - \mu_0)] \Delta^{*-2} \quad .$$

(4.18c)

One may eventually wish to use $K(\lambda_1,\lambda_2)$ and $K(0,\lambda_2)$ evaluated from (1.13) and (1.15a) to determine $g^*(\ell_1,\ell_2)$ and $g_2^*(\ell_2)$ . For sufficiently large values of $\ell_1$, $\ell_2$ , the Laplace transform inversion formulas will show that the behavior of $g^*(\ell_1,\ell_2)$ and $g_2^*(\ell_2)$ is determined primarily by the behavior of the functions $K_2(\lambda_1)$ and $K_1(\lambda_2)$ in the vicinity of the singular points (4.16) and (4.18) which are nearest the origin in the $\lambda_1$ or $\lambda_2$ space. If these singularities are both simple poles, $g_2^*(\ell_1,\ell_2)$ will behave asymptotically like the product of two exponentials, $\exp(\lambda_1\ell_1 + \lambda_2\ell_2)$ , with the (negative) $\lambda_1$ and $\lambda_2$ evaluated at the singular points. Similarly $g_2^*(\ell_2)$ will be proportional to $\exp(\lambda_2\ell_2)$ for large $\ell_2$ . If the singularity of $K_1(\lambda_2)$ is a second order pole (as for $\theta^* = \gamma_2$), then $g_2^*(\ell_2)$ will be proportional to $\ell_2\exp(\lambda_2\ell_2)$ for large $\ell_2$ . If the singularity is a branch point, the exponential dependence is replaced by $\ell_2^{-3/2}\exp(\lambda_2\ell_2)$ . If the branch point and the poles coalesce, one can obtain other powers of $\ell_2$ times exponentials, but for large $\ell_2$ the exponential will vary so rapidly compared with any power of $\ell_2$ that the qualitative behavior will be essentially dominated by the exponential factors.

With the above interpretation of the singularities, the meaning of (4.18b) is clear. For sufficiently small $\mu_2 - \mu_0$ (that $\theta^* > \gamma_2$), the second server should behave nearly as if there were no server 1. Server 1 merely delays somewhat the arrival of customers to a queue, $Q_2$ , that is usually quite large (compared with $Q_1$). Note that (4.18b) is the parameter of the exponential queue distribution that would exist without a server 1.

Since the special case $\Delta_0 = \Delta_1$ , $\gamma_0 = \gamma_1$ , is the diffusion analogue of exponential service times for servers 0 and 1, i.e., servers 0 and 1 represent an M/M/1 system which is known to give a Poisson output from server 1, we would expect this case to have special features. Actually the complete solution of this case is very simple as we shall see later, but its special properties manifest themselves here in that (4.18a) and (4.18b) give the same value for $\lambda_2$, and (4.18c) does not apply. For $\Delta_0 \neq \Delta_1$, however, the interpretation of (4.18a) or (4.18c) is not obvious.

The above analysis did not define the amplitude of the asymptotic exponential behavior of $g_2^*(\ell_2)$. The functions $K_1^\dagger(\theta_1)$ and $K_2^\dagger(\theta_1)$ have not been evaluated yet; we have not even established that they are uniquely defined. To prove that there are unique functions $K_1^\dagger(\theta_1)$ and $K_2^\dagger(\theta_1)$ which satisfy (4.8c) along with the various subsidiary conditions imposed by the fact they are Laplace transforms of probability densities, it is advantageous to consider the logarithms of both sides of (4.8c). Since $K_2^\dagger(\theta_1)$ is real and positive along the line $Re\ \theta_1 = 0$ and the real line segment $0 \leq \theta_1 \leq \gamma_1$, $\ell n\ K_2^\dagger(\theta_1)$ is also real along these lines, i.e., $Im\ \ell n\ K_1^\dagger(\theta_1) = 0$. Similarly $Im\ \ell n\ K_1^\dagger(\theta_1) = 0$ along the line $Re\ \theta_1 = \gamma_1$ and $0 \leq \theta_1 \leq \gamma_1$.

We know that $K_1^\dagger(\theta_1)$ and $K_2^\dagger(\theta_1)$ must be analytic in the strip $0 \leq Re\ \theta_1 \leq \gamma_1$ of Fig. VI-5. If they are also free of zeros, then $\ell n\ K_1^\dagger(\theta_1)$ and $\ell n\ K_2^\dagger(\theta_1)$ are also analytic in this strip. Consequently $Im\ \ell n\ K_1^\dagger(\theta_1)$ and $Im\ \ell n\ K_2^\dagger(\theta_1)$ must be solutions of Laplace's equation (so must the real parts).

From (4.8c) we have

$$\ell n\ K_1^\dagger(\theta_1) - \ell n\ K_2^\dagger(\theta_1) = \ell n\ \sin\left(\frac{-\theta_1 + \theta^* + \gamma_1}{2}\right) - \ell n\ \cos\left(\frac{\theta_1 - \theta^* - \gamma_0 + \gamma_2}{2}\right)$$

$$+ \ell n[(\Delta_1 + \Delta_2)(\Delta_0 + \Delta_2)^{-1/2}(\Delta_0 + \Delta_1)^{-1/2}] . \qquad (4.19)$$

Since

$$\text{Im } \ln K_2^\dagger(\theta_1) = 0 \qquad \text{for} \quad \text{Re } \theta_1 = 0 \quad \text{or} \quad 0 \le \theta_1 \le \gamma_1 \qquad (4.19a)$$

$$\text{Im } \ln K_1^\dagger(\theta_1) = 0 \qquad \text{for} \quad \text{Re } \theta_1 = \gamma_1 \quad \text{or} \quad 0 \le \theta_1 \le \gamma_1 \,, \qquad (4.19b)$$

it follows that

$$\text{Im } \ln K_1^\dagger(\theta_1) = \text{Im}\left[\ln \sin\left(\frac{-\theta_1 + \theta^* + \gamma_1}{2}\right) - \ln \cos\left(\frac{\theta_1 - \theta^* - \gamma_0 + \gamma_2}{2}\right)\right]$$

$$= \tan^{-1}\left[\tan\left(\frac{\theta^* + \gamma_1}{2}\right)\text{ctnh}\left(\frac{\text{Im }\theta_1}{2}\right)\right] - \tan^{-1}\left[\tan\left(\frac{\theta^* + \gamma_1 + 2\gamma_0}{2}\right)\text{ctnh}\left(\frac{\text{Im }\theta_1}{2}\right)\right] \,,$$

$$\text{for} \quad \text{Re } \theta_1 = 0 \,, \qquad (4.19c)$$

and

$$-\text{Im } \ln K_2^\dagger(\theta_1) = \text{Im}\left[\ln \sin\left(\frac{-\theta_1 + \theta^* + \gamma_1}{2}\right) - \ln \cos\left(\frac{\theta_1 - \theta^* - \gamma_0 + \gamma_2}{2}\right)\right]$$

$$= \tan^{-1}\left[\tan\left(\frac{\theta^*}{2}\right)\text{ctnh}\left(\frac{\text{Im }\theta_1}{2}\right)\right] - \tan^{-1}\left[\tan\left(\frac{\theta^* + 2\gamma_0}{2}\right)\text{ctnh}\left(\frac{\text{Im }\theta_1}{2}\right)\right] \,,$$

$$\text{for} \quad \text{Re } \theta_1 = \gamma_1 \,. \qquad (4.19d)$$

From (4.19c) one can see that as $\text{Im } \theta_1$ varies along the line $\text{Re } \theta_1 = 0$, $\text{ctnh}(\text{Im } \theta_1 / 2)$ varies from $\infty$ at $\text{Im } \theta_1 = 0$ to $\pm 1$ at $\text{Im } \theta_1 \to \pm \infty$. This causes $\text{Im } \ln K_1^\dagger(\theta_1)$ to be a monotone decreasing function of $\text{Im } \theta_1$, going from 0 at $\text{Im } \theta_1 = 0$ to $\mp \gamma_0$ at $\text{Im } \theta_1 =$ The shape of this variation with $\text{Im } \theta_1$ depends upon $\theta^*$ and $\gamma_1$ which

in turn, depends upon the $\Delta_j$'s and $\mu_j$'s , but the limit $-\gamma_0$ for
$\text{Im } \theta_1 \to \infty$ does not depend upon the $\mu_j$'s . Similarly from (4.19d) we
conclude that $\text{Im } \ln K_2^\dagger(\theta_1)$ is a monotone increasing function of $\text{Im } \theta_1$
along the line $\text{Re } \theta_1 = \gamma_1$ , going from 0 at $\text{Im } \theta_1 = 0$ to $\pm \gamma_0$ at
$\text{Im } \theta_1 = \pm \infty$ . Again, the limit for $\text{Im } \theta_1 \to \pm \infty$ is independent of the
service rate.

The above equations describe the values of the functions $\text{Im } \ln K_1^\dagger(\theta_1)$
and $\text{Im } \ln K_2^\dagger(\theta_1)$ on the boundaries of a rectangle $0 \le \text{Re } \theta_1 \le \gamma_1$ ,
$\text{Im } \theta_1 \ge 0$ , except for the values at $\text{Im } \theta_1 \to \infty$ , $0 \le \text{Re } \theta < \gamma_1$ . If
$K_1^\dagger(\theta_1)$ and $K_2^\dagger(\theta_1)$ are free of zeros in this rectangle, so that $\ln K_1^\dagger(\theta_1)$
and $\ln K_2^\dagger(\theta_1)$ are analytic, then the imaginary parts of the latter
would be solutions of Laplace's equation having known values on parallel
boundaries. The solution of Laplace's equation would be unique and could
be evaluated.

To show that $K_1^\dagger(\theta_1)$ and $K_2^\dagger(\theta_1)$ have no zeros in the rectangle,
we observe that, since $K_1^\dagger(\theta_1)$ and $K_2^\dagger(\theta_1)$ are analytic in the rectangle,
the number of zeros of $K_1^\dagger(\theta_1)$ , for example, is given by

$$\text{Re } \frac{1}{2\pi i} \int_C \frac{d}{d\theta_1} \ln K_1^\dagger(\theta_1) \, d\theta_1 \quad = \quad \frac{1}{2\pi} \int_C \frac{d}{d\theta_1} \text{Im } \ln K_1^\dagger(\theta_1) \, d\theta_1 \qquad (4.20)$$

integrated counterclockwise around the boundary $C$ of the rectangle.
The indefinite integral (4.20) is simply $(2\pi)^{-1} \text{Im } \ln K_1^\dagger(\theta_1)$ . The integral (4.20) around three sides of the rectangle, from $0 + i\infty$ to $0$ to
$\gamma_1$ to $\gamma_1 + i\infty$ , gives the value $\gamma_0/2\pi$ , with $0 \le \gamma_0/2\pi \le 1/4$ .
The integral along the last side, from $\gamma_1 + i\infty$ to $0 + i\infty$ , must therefore be $-\gamma_0/2\pi$ plus the number of zeros of $K_1^\dagger(\theta_1)$ inside the rectangle.

278

From (1.7a) we have

$$K_2(0) = \lim_{\lambda_2 \to +\infty} \lambda_2 K(0,\lambda_2) \quad,$$

and from (1.15a), with $c_2 = \infty$ , we conclude that $K_1(\lambda_2)$ must go to zero for $\lambda_2 \to +\infty$ . But since $K_1(\lambda_2)$ is a transform of a nonnegative function, it follows also that $|K_1(\lambda_2)| \leq K_1(\text{Re } \lambda_2)$ for $\text{Re } \lambda_2 \geq 0$ . Consequently, $K_1(\lambda_2) \to 0$ for $\lambda_2 \to \infty$ in the right-half $\lambda_2$-plane. Since the image of $\text{Im } \theta_1 \to \infty$ , $0 \leq \text{Re } \theta_1 \leq \gamma_1$ is $\lambda_2 \to \infty$ in the right-half plane, it follows also that $K_1^\dagger(\theta_1) \to 0$ for $\text{Im } \theta_1 \to \infty$ in the rectangle. Thus $\text{Re } \ln K_1^\dagger(\theta_1) \to -\infty$ .

If $\text{Re } \ln K_1^\dagger(\theta_1) \to -\infty$ , its derivative must be negative in the direction of increasing $\text{Im } \theta_1$ . From the Cauchy-Riemann equations it follows that the derivative of $\text{Im } \ln K_1^\dagger(\theta_1)$ must be positive in the direction of increasing $\text{Re } \theta_1$ . The contribution to (4.20) from the last side of the rectangle at $\text{Im } \theta_1 \to +\infty$ must therefore be negative. Since $\gamma_0/2\pi < 1/4$ , and this integral is also equal to $-\gamma_0/2\pi$ plus the number of zeros of $K_1^\dagger(\theta_1)$ inside the rectangle, it follows that the number of zeros is zero; $\ln K_1^\dagger(\theta_1)$ is analytic in the rectangle. By similar arguments one also concludes that $\ln K_2^\dagger(\theta_1)$ is analytic in the rectangle.

There are many ways to obtain the solution $\text{Im } \ln K_2^\dagger(\theta_1)$ of Laplace equation in a rectangular strip, but, in general, these will be in the form of infinite series or integral representations. The function we seek can also be considered as an electric potential between two parallel surfaces one of which has potential zero, the other a specified non-zero potential.

Although the exact solution may be rather tedious to compute, some properties can be seen very easily. That $\text{Im } \ln K_1^\dagger(\theta_1) \to \mp \gamma_0$ for

$\text{Im } \theta_1 \to \pm \infty$ and $\text{Re } \theta_1 = 0$ but is zero for $\text{Re } \theta_1 = \gamma$ implies that

$$\text{Im } \ln K_1^\dagger(\theta_1) \to \pm (\text{Re } \theta_1 - \gamma_1) \gamma_0/\gamma_1 \quad \text{for Im } \theta_1 \to \pm \infty \quad (4.21)$$

i.e., it varies linearly with $\text{Re } \theta_1$, at least for $0 \leq \text{Re } \theta_1 \leq \gamma_1$.

If the imaginary part of $\ln K_1^\dagger(\theta_1)$ behaves like (4.21), the real

part must have the form

$$\text{Re } \ln K_1^\dagger(\theta_1) \to \mp (\text{Im } \theta_1) \gamma_0/\gamma_1 + \ln A$$

for some real number $\ln A$, and

$$\ln K_1^\dagger(\theta_1) \to \pm i(\theta_1 - \gamma_1)\gamma_0/\gamma_1 + \ln A, \quad \text{for Im } \theta_1 \to \pm \infty$$

$$K_1^\dagger(\theta_1) \to A \exp[\pm i(\theta_1 - \gamma_1)\gamma_0/\gamma_1] \ . \quad (4.21a)$$

The unknown real number $A$, which must be positive, will eventually be

determined from the normalization of the probability density.

From (4.8) and (4.21a) we obtain

$$K_2^\dagger(\theta_1) \to \frac{(\Delta_0 + \Delta_2)^{\frac{1}{2}} (\Delta_0 + \Delta_1)^{\frac{1}{2}}}{(\Delta_1 + \Delta_2)} A \exp(\pm i\theta_1 \gamma_0/\gamma_1) \ . \quad (4.21b)$$

By mapping these into the $\lambda_1$ and $\lambda_2$ spaces through (4.1) and (4.9),

we have

$$K_1(\lambda_2) \to A' \left(\frac{\Delta_1 + \Delta_2}{\Delta_0 + \Delta_1}\right)^{\frac{1}{2}} \left[\frac{(\Delta_0 + \Delta_1)^{\frac{1}{2}}}{\lambda_2}\right]^{\gamma_0/\gamma_1} \quad (4.21c)$$

280

and

$$K_2(\lambda_1) \;\to\; A' \left(\frac{\Delta_0 + \Delta_2}{\Delta_1 + \Delta_2}\right)^{\frac{1}{2}} \left[\frac{(\Delta_1 + \Delta_2)^{\frac{1}{2}}}{\lambda_1}\right]^{\gamma_0/\gamma_1} \;, \qquad (4.21d)$$

as $\lambda_2$ and $\lambda_1$, respectively, become infinite in the right-half plane; $A'$ is some new positive constant. The main feature of this is that $K_1(\lambda_2)$ is proportional to $\lambda_2^{-\gamma_0/\gamma_1}$ and $K_2(\lambda_1)$ to $\lambda_1^{-\gamma_0/\gamma_1}$ for $\lambda_1$, $\lambda_2 \to \infty$.

For $\lambda_1$, $\lambda_2 \to \infty$, $c_1 = c_2 = \infty$, (1.13) gives

$$K(\lambda_1,\lambda_2) \;\to\; \frac{(\lambda_1 - \lambda_2)(\Delta_0 + \Delta_1)K_1(\lambda_2) + \lambda_2(\Delta_1 + \Delta_2)K_2(\lambda_1)}{\Delta_0\lambda_1^2 + \Delta_1(\lambda_1 - \lambda_2)^2 + \Delta_2\lambda_2^2} \;, \qquad (4.22)$$

whereas (1.15a), (1.16) give

$$K(0,\lambda_2) \;\to\; \frac{2(\mu_2 - \mu_0)}{(\Delta_1 + \Delta_2)\lambda_2 + 2(\mu_2 - \mu_1)} - \frac{(\Delta_0 + \Delta_1)K_1(\lambda_2)}{(\Delta_1 + \Delta_2)\,\lambda_2} \;. \qquad (4.23)$$

The behavior of $K(\lambda_1,\lambda_2)$ for $\lambda_1$, $\lambda_2 \to \infty$ determines the behavior of $g^*(\ell_1,\ell_2)$ for $\ell_1$, $\ell_2 \to 0$, and the behavior of $K(0,\lambda_2)$ for $\lambda_2 \to \infty$ determines the behavior of $g_2^*(\ell_2)$ for $\ell_2 \to 0$. Equations (4.21c,d) still contain an unspecified constant (relative to the $\lambda$'s), but the fact that (4.21c,d) and (4.22) describe $K(\lambda_1,\lambda_2)$ as a homogeneous function of degree $-1 - \gamma_0/\gamma_1$ in $\lambda_1, \lambda_2$ for $\lambda_1$, $\lambda_2 \to \infty$ implies that $g^*(\ell_1,\ell_2)$ is a homogeneous function of degree $-1 + \gamma_0/\gamma_1$ in $\ell_1$, $\ell_2$ for $\ell_1$, $\ell_2 \to 0$.

Actually (4.21c,d), (4.22) also specify the nature of this homogeneo function, i.e., the angular dependence of $g^*(\ell_1, \ell_2)$ in the $\ell_1$, $\ell_2$-space near the origin. It is not necessary to pursue this further here, however, because the behavior of $g^*(\ell_1, \ell_2)$ near the origin is identical to that described previously in Chapter III, section 6, (III 6.11).

That the second term of (4.23) is proportional to $\lambda_2^{-1+\gamma_0/\gamma_1}$ implies that $g_2^*(\ell_2)$ behaves like

$$g_2^*(\ell_2) \simeq \frac{2(\mu_2 - \mu_0)}{(\Delta_1 + \Delta_2)} \exp\left[-\frac{2(\mu_2 - \mu_1)\ell_2}{(\Delta_1 + \Delta_2)}\right] - A'' \, \ell_2^{\gamma_0/\gamma_1} \qquad (4.24)$$

with $A'' > 0$ independent of $\ell_2$ for $\ell_2 \to 0$. For $\mu_2 = \mu_1$, the first term of (4.24) is a constant and $g_2^*(\ell_1)$ has the same type of behavior as described in (III 8.3) for a system with $\mu_2 = \mu_1 = \mu_0$ but $c_1 < \infty$ ($c_2 \leq \infty$). If $\mu_2 < \mu_1$, the first term of (4.24) is an increasing exponential, which for sufficiently small $\ell_2$ would be linearly increasing. Correspondingly for $\mu_2 > \mu_1$, the first term is linearly decreasing for small $\ell_2$. The power $\gamma_0/\gamma_1$ of the second term could have any positive value but for $\gamma_0 < \gamma_1$ ($\Delta_0 < \Delta_1$), this power would be fractional and dominate over the linear behavior of the first term.

From the results of Chapters III, IV and this chapter, one would expect $g_2^*(\ell_2)$ to be very "well-behaved" over an intermediate range of $\ell_2$. If one knew the constant $A''$ in (4.24) and one knew the coefficient of the exponential in the large $\ell_2$ asymptotic behavior, one could probably make a reasonably accurate graphical interpolation and sketch a graph of $g_2^*(\ell_2)$ over all values of $\ell_2$. It seems to be generally true that the exact formulas are complicated because functions such as $g_2^*(\ell_2)$ are unusually smooth, except at the ends of the range of definition.

It was to be expected that the behavior of $g^*(\ell_1,\ell_2)$ and $g_2^*(\ell_2)$
for $\ell_1$, $\ell_2 \to 0$ with $c_1 = c_2 = \infty$ and $\mu_0 < \mu_1$, $\mu_2$ should be
similar to that described in Chapter III for $c_1$, $c_2 < \infty$, $\mu_0 = \mu_1 = $
Except for the (as yet unknown) constants $A'$, $A''$, similar behavior
should arise also for arbitrary $\mu_j$'s and $c_1$, $c_2 < \infty$; the exponent
$-1 + \gamma_0/\gamma_1$ and $\gamma_0/\gamma_1$ appearing in the small argument expansions of
$g^*(\ell_1,\ell_2)$ and $g_2^*(\ell_2)$ do not depend upon the service rates or capaciti
only the variance rates $\Delta_j$.

Mathematically, the reason that the form of $g^*(\ell_1,\ell_2)$ or $g_2^*(\ell_2)$
is independent of the $\mu_j$'s or $c_j$'s is that the boundary conditions
on $g^*(\ell_1,\ell_2)$ determine the nature of the singularity of the function
at the corner $\ell_1 = \ell_2 = 0$, and the boundary conditions depend mainly
on the $\Delta_j$'s. More intuitively, the reason is that if $Q_1$, $Q_2$ are
close to 0, the exchange of customers among servers is dominated by the
interruptions of service caused by fluctuations. The system will underg
many interruptions in a time which is too short for the system to recognize the mean arrival rates or whether the system is stable by virtue of
$\mu_0 < \mu_1$, $\mu_2$ and/or $c_1$, $c_2 < \infty$. The system sees the actual values
of $Q_1$, $Q_2$ (but not how it got there). It sees the actual arrivals of
customers but would not realize the rates or the $c_j$'s until sufficient
many customers had passed through the server for the system to make a
measurement of the arithmetic average service time of many customers, or
the state of the system had reached a full storage. Of course, the probability of $Q_1$, $Q_2$ being near zero (proportional to the $A'$) depends
upon the $\mu_j$'s and $c_j$'s; it is only the shape of the distribution near
$\ell_1$, $\ell_2 = 0$ that is independent of the $\mu_j$'s and $c_j$'s.

From the above arguments one could infer also that, for $c_1$, $c_2 <$

the nature of the singularities of $g^*(\ell_1,\ell_2)$ at all corners, as described in Chapter III, should be independent of the service rates; also the analytic properties of $g_2^*(\ell_2)$ at $\ell_2 = 0$ and $\ell_2 = c_2$. The magnitudes of $g^*(\ell_1,\ell_2)$ at the corners will depend upon the $\mu_j$'s and $c_j$'s, also the relative amplitudes at the various corners.

Other Special Cases. We saw in the last section that $\operatorname{Im} \ell n\, K_1^+(\theta_1)$ and $\operatorname{Im} \ell n\, K_2^+(\theta_1)$ satisfy Laplace's equation in a strip with known boundary conditions. Consequently, it is possible to construct formal solutions for these functions. The Cauchy-Riemann equations would then give a first order differential equation for $\operatorname{Re} \ell n\, K_1^+(\theta_1)$ and $\operatorname{Re} \ell n\, K_2^+(\theta_1)$, which would define these functions to within an arbitrary constant of integration. Thus $\ell n\, K_1^+(\theta_1)$ and $\ell n\, K_2^+(\theta_1)$ would be defined to within an additive real constant; $K_1^+(\theta_1)$ and $K_2^+(\theta_1)$ to within an arbitrary positive factor. This "arbitrary factor" would, however, be specified by the normalization.

The general solution obtained in this way is probably too complicated to be very useful. It is possible, however, to obtain "closed form" expressions for $K_1^+(\theta_1)$ and $K_2^+(\theta_1)$ if $\gamma_1/\pi$ is a rational number. These solutions will be relatively simple if $\gamma_1/\pi$ is a fraction such as $1/2$, $1/3$, -- . The reason why the value of $\gamma_1$ is so crucial is that for rational values of $\gamma_1$, the "doubly infinite" sequence of poles and zeros of $K_1^+(\theta_1)$, $K_2^+(\theta_1)$ at spacings of $2\gamma_1$ and $2\pi$, as described following (4.15), coalesce into single infinite series with some periodic structure. To illustrate this, we consider in some detail the special case $\gamma_1 = \pi/2$ $(\Delta_1 = 0)$.

For $\gamma_1 = \pi/2$, $\gamma_2 = \pi/2 - \gamma_0$, (4.15) can be written as

284

$$K_2^{\dagger}(\theta_1) = \frac{\sin\left(\dfrac{\theta_1 - \theta^* - \pi/2 - 2\gamma_0}{2}\right) \sin\left(\dfrac{\theta_1 + \theta^* - 5\pi/2}{2}\right)}{\sin\left(\dfrac{\theta_1 + \theta^* - 5\pi/2 + 2\gamma_0}{2}\right)\sin\left(\dfrac{\theta_1 - \theta^* - \pi/2}{2}\right)} K_2^{\dagger}(\theta_1 - \pi) \ .$$

$$(5.1)$$

We want a solution of this finite difference equation that is symmetric $K_2^{\dagger}(\theta_1) = K_2^{\dagger}(-\theta_1)$ , analytic, and free of zeros or poles for $-\pi/2 \leq$ Re $\theta_1 \leq \pi/2$ .

If we analytically continue $K_2^{\dagger}(\theta_1)$ in the direction of increasing Re $\theta_1$ , the function $K_2^{\dagger}(\theta_1)$ will have first order poles at

$$\pi/2 + \theta^* \ , \quad 5\pi/2 - \theta^* - 2\gamma_0 \ , \quad 3\pi/2 + \theta^* \ , \quad \text{and} \quad 7\pi/2 - \theta^* - 2\gamma_0 \ ,$$

$$(5.2a)$$

and first order zeros at

$$\pi/2 + \theta^* + 2\gamma_0 \ , \quad 5\pi/2 - \theta^* \ , \quad 3\pi/2 + \theta^* + 2\gamma_0 \ , \quad \text{and} \quad 7\pi/2 - \theta^* \ .$$

$$(5.2b)$$

The first pair of poles and zeros follow directly from (5.1) as the first points at which the coefficient in (5.1) is infinite or vanishes (while $K_2^{\dagger}(\theta_1 - \pi)$ is analytic and nonzero). The second pair is obtained from a single iteration of (5.1). Each zero or pole generates a sequence of zeros or poles at spacing $\pi$ .

In the second iteration of (5.1), the poles and zeros of $K_2^{\dagger}(\theta_1 - \pi)$ coincide with values of $\theta_1$ where the coefficients are infinite or zero again (the poles or zeros of the coefficients repeat at intervals of $2\pi$), causing second order poles or zeros for $K_2^{\dagger}(\theta_1)$ . In general, each first order pole or zero at $\theta_1$ generates an nth order pole or zero at $\theta_1 +$ $2(n - 1)\pi$ .

To determine $K_2^+(\theta_1)$ it is advantageous to consider the logarithmic derivative of (5.1),

$$2 \frac{d}{d\theta_1} \ell n \; K_2^+(\theta_1) \; - \; 2 \frac{d}{d\theta} \ell n \; K_2^+(\theta_1 - \pi) \;\; = \;\; ctn \left( \frac{\theta_1 - \theta^* - \pi/2 - 2\gamma_0}{2} \right)$$

$$+ \;\; ctn \left( \frac{\theta_1 + \theta^* - 5\pi/2}{2} \right) \; - \; ctn \left( \frac{\theta_1 + \theta^* - 5\pi/2 + 2\gamma_0}{2} \right) \; - \; ctn \left( \frac{\theta_1 - \theta^* - \pi/2}{2} \right),$$

$$(5.2)$$

interpreted as a finite difference equation for the function $d\ell n \; K_2^+(\theta_1)/d\theta_1$. Any place $K_2^+(\theta_1)$ has an nth order pole or zero, $d\ell n \; K_2^+(\theta_1)/d\theta_1$ has a simple pole with residue $-n$ or $n$, respectively; otherwise $\ell n \; K_2^+(\theta_1)$ is analytic.

The function

$$g_\pm(z) \;\; = \;\; \pm \frac{z}{4\pi} \; ctn \left( \frac{z}{2} \right) \tag{5.3}$$

has poles at $z = 2n\pi$ for nonzero integer values of $n$, with residue $\pm|n|$. It is analytic everywhere else including $z = 0$. It is also a solution of the finite difference equation

$$g_\pm(z) \;\; = \;\; \pm \frac{1}{2} \; ctn \left( \frac{z}{2} \right) \; + \; g_\pm(z - 2\pi) \;\; . \tag{5.3a}$$

By comparing (5.3a) with a single iteration of (5.2), one can easily verify that the function

$$2\pi \frac{d}{d\theta_1} \ln K_2^{\dagger}(\theta_1) = \frac{(\theta_1 - \theta^* + 3\pi/2 - 2\gamma_0)}{2} ctn\left[\frac{\theta_1 - \theta^* + 3\pi/2 - 2\gamma_0}{2}\right]$$

$$+ \frac{(\theta_1 - \theta^* + \pi/2 - 2\gamma_0)}{2} ctn\left[\frac{\theta_1 - \theta^* + \pi/2 - 2\gamma_0}{2}\right] + \frac{(\theta_1 + \theta^* - \pi/2)}{2} ctn\left[\frac{\theta_1 + \theta^* - \pi/2}{2}\right.$$

$$+ \frac{(\theta_1 + \theta^* - 3\pi/2)}{2} ctn\left[\frac{\theta_1 + \theta^* - 3\pi/2}{2}\right] - \frac{(\theta_1 + \theta^* - \pi/2 + 2\gamma_0)}{2} ctn\left[\frac{\theta_1 + \theta^* - \pi/2 + 2}{2}\right.$$

$$- \frac{(\theta_1 + \theta^* - 3\pi/2 + 2\gamma_0)}{2} ctn\left[\frac{\theta_1 + \theta^* - 3\pi/2 + 2\gamma_0}{2}\right] - \frac{(\theta_1 - \theta^* + 3\pi/2)}{2} ctn\left[\frac{\theta_1 - \theta^* +}{2}\right.$$

$$- \frac{(\theta_1 - \theta^* + \pi/2)}{2} ctn\left[\frac{\theta_1 - \theta^* + \pi/2}{2}\right] , \qquad\qquad (5.4)$$

is a solution of (5.2). It is obtained simply by superimposing eight different translations of (5.3). Each term has a simple pole of residue +1 or -1 at one of the points (5.2a) or (5.2b). The right-hand side of (5.4) is also an odd function of $\theta_1$, consistent with the requirement that $K_2^{\dagger}(\theta_1)$ be an even function of $\theta_1$.

The most general solution of (5.2) is obtained by adding to (5.4) any solution of the homogeneous equation associated with (5.2), i.e., a function which is periodic with period $\pi$. Since (5.4) already describes all the singularities of the desired solution and is odd in $\theta_1$, any new term added to (5.4) would be required to be an entire function of $\theta_1$, odd and periodic with period $\pi$. Any term of its Fourier expansion (in terms of $\sin(2j\theta_1)$, $j = 1, 2, --$), however, would not behave properly at $\theta_1 \to i\infty$ . We conclude that (5.4) itself is the desired solution, and it is unique.

An integration of (5.4) determines $K_2^\dagger(\theta_1)$ :

$$\ell n \ K_2^\dagger(\theta_1) \ = \ \frac{1}{\pi} \int_{\frac{1}{2}(\theta_1-\theta^*+3\pi/2)}^{\frac{1}{2}(\theta_1-\theta^*+3\pi/2-2\gamma_0)} dz \ z \ ctn \ z \ + \ \frac{1}{\pi} \int_{\frac{1}{2}(\theta_1-\theta^*+\pi/2)}^{\frac{1}{2}(\theta_1-\theta^*+\pi/2-2\gamma_0)} dz \ z \ ctn \ z$$

$$+ \ \frac{1}{\pi} \int_{\frac{1}{2}(\theta_1+\theta^*-\pi/2+2\gamma_0)}^{\frac{1}{2}(\theta_1+\theta^*-\pi/2)} dz \ z \ ctn \ z \ + \ \frac{1}{\pi} \int_{\frac{1}{2}(\theta_1+\theta^*-3\pi/2+2\gamma_0)}^{\frac{1}{2}(\theta_1+\theta^*-3\pi/2)} dz \ z \ ctn \ z \ + \ \ell n \ B \ ,$$

$$(5.5)$$

in which $\ell n \ B$ is an integration constant to be evaluated from the normalization condition

$$K_2^\dagger(\pi/2 - \theta^*) \ = \ K_2(0) \ = \ 2(\mu_2 - \mu_0)/\Delta_2 \ . \qquad (5.5a)$$

Despite the long formula, (5.5) is not very difficult to evaluate because the integrals are all of the same type and have a range of integration of width $\gamma_0$ .

By similar methods, one can evaluate $K_1^\dagger(\theta_1)$ from (4.15a), but it can be evaluated more easily from (4.8c) and the above formulas for $K_2^\dagger(\theta_1)$ . Although it will be necessary to use (5.5) in order to evaluate some of the factors in the limit formulas for $g^*(\ell_1,\ell_2)$ and $g_2^*(\ell_2)$ discussed in the last section, the moments of $Q_1$ , $Q_2$ can be evaluated directly in terms of the logarithmic derivative of $K_2^\dagger(\theta_1)$ , as given by (5.4).

The value of $E\{Q_2\}$ is of particular interest. From (1.15a), (1.16) and (1.16a) we obtain

$$E\{Q_2\} \;=\; -\, dK(0,\lambda_2)/d\lambda_2 \Big|_{\lambda_2=0}$$

$$=\; \frac{(\Delta_1 + \Delta_2)}{2(\mu_2 - \mu_1)} \;+\; \frac{(\mu_1 - \mu_0)}{(\mu_2 - \mu_1)} \;\frac{d}{d\lambda_2}\, \ell n\, K_1(\lambda_2) \Big|_{\lambda_2=0} \quad .$$

From (4.8c), with $\gamma_1 = \pi/2$ ,

$$\frac{d}{d\theta_1}\, \ell n\, K_1^{\dagger}(\theta_1) \;=\; \frac{d}{d\theta_1}\, \ell n\, K_2^{\dagger}(\theta_1) + \frac{1}{2}\, ctn\!\left(\frac{\theta_1 - \theta^* - \pi/2}{2}\right) - \frac{1}{2}\, ctn\!\left(\frac{\theta_1 - \theta^* - \pi/2 - 2\gamma_0}{2}\right)$$

and from (4.9)

$$\frac{d\lambda_2}{d\theta_1} \;=\; \frac{\mu_1 - \mu_0}{(\Delta_0\Delta_2)^{1/2}} \quad , \qquad \text{for } \Delta_1 = 0 \,,\; \lambda_2 = 0 \,,\; \theta_1 = \gamma_1 - \theta^* \,,$$

consequently $E\{Q_2\}$ becomes

$$E\{Q_2\} \;=\; \frac{(\Delta_1+\Delta_2)}{2(\mu_2-\mu_1)} \;+\; \frac{(\Delta_0\Delta_2)^{\frac{1}{2}}}{2(\mu_2-\mu_1)} \left\{ 2\,\frac{d}{d\theta_1}\, \ell n\, K_2^{\dagger}(\theta_1) - ctn\,\theta^* + ctn(\gamma_0+\theta^*) \right\}_{\theta_1=\frac{\pi}{2}-\theta}$$

$$(5.6)$$

Substitution of (5.4) now gives

$$E\{Q_2\} \;=\; \frac{(\Delta_0\Delta_2)^{\frac{1}{2}}}{2\pi(\mu_2-\mu_1)} \left\{ 1 - \gamma_0\,ctn\,\gamma_0 - \left(\frac{\pi}{2} + \gamma_0\right) ctn\left(\frac{\pi}{2} + \gamma_0\right) + (\theta^*+\gamma_0)\,ctn(\theta^*+\gamma_0) \right.$$

$$+ \left[\frac{\pi}{2} - \theta^* - \gamma_0\right] \text{ctn}\left[\frac{\pi}{2} - \theta^* - \gamma_0\right] - \theta^* \text{ctn}\theta^* - \left[\frac{\pi}{2} - \theta^*\right] \text{ctn}\left[\frac{\pi}{2} - \theta^*\right]\right\} .$$

$$(5.6a)$$

One can express this directly in terms of the $\Delta_j$ and $\mu_j$ through the relations (for $\gamma_1 = \pi/2$)

$$\text{ctn}\gamma_0 = \left(\frac{\Delta_0}{\Delta_2}\right)^{\frac{1}{2}} , \quad \text{ctn}\theta^* = \left(\frac{\Delta_0}{\Delta_2}\right)^{\frac{1}{2}}\left(\frac{\mu_2 - \mu_1}{\mu_1 - \mu_0}\right) , \quad \text{ctn}(\theta^* + \gamma_0) = \frac{\Delta_0(\mu_2 - \mu_1) - \Delta_2(\mu_1 - \mu_0)}{(\Delta_0\Delta_2)^{1/2}(\mu_2 - \mu_0)}$$

$$(5.6b)$$

but this does not lead to any obvious simplification of (5.6a).

The solid line curves of Fig. VI-6 show the behavior of

$$2 \, E\{Q_2\}(\mu_2 - \mu_0)/(\Delta_0 + \Delta_2) \quad \text{vs} \quad (\mu_2 - \mu_0)/(\mu_1 - \mu_0)$$

for several values of $\gamma_0$ , evaluated from (5.6a,b). The graphs describe the expected queue length at the second server relative to what it would be if there were no sever 1 (or $\mu_1 \to \infty$).

The curve $\gamma_0 = \pi/2$ (and $\gamma_1 = \pi/2$) corresponds to $\Delta_0 = 0$ (and $\Delta_1 = 0$). With a regular server at both locations 0 and 1, and with $\mu_0 < \mu_1$ , server 1 will serve customers as fast as they arrive and transfer them to server 2 at regular intervals and rate $\mu_0$ . The presence of server 1 has no effect upon the arrival process at 2 nor the queue $Q_2$. Thus the curve of Fig. VI-6 for $\gamma_0 = \pi/2$ is a horizontal line. The broken line curves of Fig. VI-6 show the sum of the two queue lengths $E\{Q_1\} + E\{Q_2\}$ in the same units, but for $\Delta_0 = \Delta_1 = 0$ , $Q_1 = 0$ ; the solid line and broken line coincide for $\gamma_0 = \gamma_1 = \pi/2$ .

At the other extreme $\gamma_0 = 0$ , $\Delta_1 = \Delta_2 = 0$ , $E\{Q_2\}$ vanishes for $\mu_1 \le \mu_2$ , i.e., $(\mu_2 - \mu_0)/(\mu_1 - \mu_0) > 1$ , because the output rate from

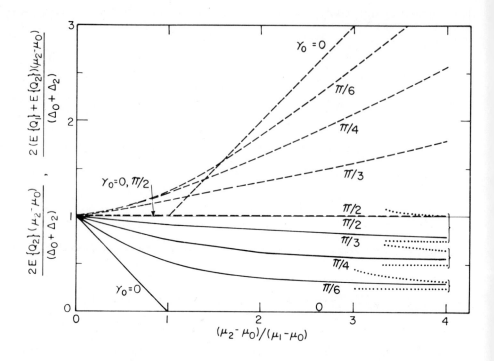

Fig. VI-6. The expected queue length $E\{Q_2\}$ (solid lines) and $E\{Q_2\} + E\{Q_1\}$ (broken lines) are shown as a function of service rates, $(\mu_2 - \mu_0)/(\mu_1 - \mu_0)$. Server 1 is a regular server ($\Delta_1 = 0$, $\gamma_1 = \pi/2$) but the values of $\gamma_0$ describe various ratios of $\Delta_0$ and $\Delta_2$.

the regular server at 1 can never exceed $\mu_1$. But with $\mu_1 \leq \mu_2$, the second server can always serve the customers as fast as they arrive. There is a queue at server 1, however, and

$$E\{Q_1\} = \frac{\Delta_0}{2(\mu_1 - \mu_0)} \quad , \quad \frac{2 E\{Q_1\}(\mu_2 - \mu_0)}{\Delta_0} = \frac{(\mu_2 - \mu_0)}{(\mu_1 - \mu_0)} \quad .$$

Thus the broken line curve for $\gamma_0 = 0$ is a straight line of slope 1 for $\mu_1 \leq \mu_2$.

For $\mu_1 \geq \mu_2$ and $\Delta_1 = \Delta_2 = 0$, $E\{Q_1\}$ is still given by the above formulas; server 2 cannot affect the behavior of $Q_1$. But since server 1 can serve faster than 2, the presence of server 1 can never cause any extra delay to a customer in going through the complete system. Any time $Q_2(t) = 0$, it is necessary that $Q_1(t)$ is also zero, therefore, $Q_1(t) + Q_2(t) = 0$. We conclude that $E\{Q_1\} + E\{Q_2\}$ is independent of $\mu_1$ for $\mu_0 \leq \mu_1 \geq \mu_2$. Thus the broken line curve of Fig. VI-6 for $\gamma_0 = 0$ is a horizontal line for $(\mu_2 - \mu_0)/(\mu_1 - \mu_0) \leq 1$. Since $E\{Q_1\}$ is known and $E\{Q_1\} + E\{Q_2\}$ is known, we can obtain $E\{Q_2\}$ by subtracting these. The solid line curve for $\gamma_0 = 0$ is linearly decreasing with slope $-1$ for $\mu_1 \geq \mu_2$.

This piecewise linear behavior of the $E\{Q_2\}$ curve of Fig. VI-6 for $\gamma_0 \to 0$ can also be deduced from (5.6a). For $\Delta_2 \to 0$ and $\mu_1 < \mu_2$, $\theta^* \to 0$, but as $\mu_2$ decreases through $\mu_1$ for any $\Delta_2 > 0$, $\theta^*$ must increase past $\pi/2$ and for $\Delta_2 \to 0$ jump to $\theta^* \to \pi$. There is a factor $\mu_2 - \mu_1$ in the denominator of (5.6a) but if one expands (5.6a) in powers of $\theta^*$ or $\pi - \theta^*$, one finds that the quantity in brackets vanishes for $\mu_2 \to \mu_1$. Except for the discontinuity in slope for $\Delta_2 \to 0$, there is no singularity in (5.6a) for $\mu_2 \to \mu_1$.

Fig. VI-6 also shows three other curves for intermediate values of $\gamma_0$ ; $\gamma_0 = \pi/3$ corresponds to $\Delta_2 = 3\Delta_0$ , $\gamma_0 = \pi/4$ to $\Delta_2 = \Delta_0$ , and $\gamma_0 = \pi/6$ to $\Delta_0 = 3\Delta_2$ . For $\gamma_0 \to 0$ , i.e., $\Delta_0 \to 0$ , the approach to the limit curve with discontinuous slope is rather slow for $\mu_2 \simeq \mu_1$ ; the value of $E\{Q_2\}$ actually decreases proportional to $\Delta_0^{1/2}$ for $\Delta_0 \to 0$ at $\mu_2 = \mu_1$ .

All the solid line curves of Fig. VI-6 lie below height 1, which means that the introduction of a regular server at location 1 decreases the value of $E\{Q_2\}$ ; also the slower the rate $\mu_1$ , the greater is the decrease in $E\{Q_2\}$ . The reason for this is that server 1 absorbs much of the variance in the output from server 0. For $\mu_1 \to \mu_0$ , i.e., $(\mu_2 - \mu_0)/(\mu_1 - \mu_0) \to \infty$ , $E\{Q_1\}$ becomes infinite and the output from server 1 is nearly regular; all the variance in the output from 0 is absorbed in the queue $Q_1$ .

For $\mu_1 > \mu_0$ , the output from server 1 actually has an average rate $\mu_0$ but the output process for $(\mu_1 - \mu_0)/\mu_0 \ll 1$ consists of rather long periods of regular service at rate $\mu_1$ interrupted by occasional idleness when $Q_1 = 0$ . One would therefore expect $E\{Q_2\}$ to be less than that which would be created by a regular server at 1 operating always at a rate $\mu_1$ (the occasional idleness of server 1 would cause a decrease in $E\{Q_2\}$) , but larger than that which would be created by a regular server at 1 operating always at rate $\mu_0$ (the fluctuations in service between rates $\mu_1$ and 0 with an average of $\mu_0$ will cause an increase in $E\{Q_2\}$). We, therefore, expect

$$\frac{\Delta_2}{\Delta_0 + \Delta_2} \leq \frac{2\,E\{Q_2\}(\mu_2 - \mu_0)}{(\Delta_0 + \Delta_2)} \leq \left(\frac{\Delta_2}{\Delta_0 + \Delta_2}\right)\frac{(\mu_2 - \mu_0)}{(\mu_2 - \mu_1)}$$

$$= \left(\frac{\Delta_2}{\Delta_0 + \Delta_2}\right) \frac{1}{1 - (\mu_1 - \mu_0)/(\mu_2 - \mu_1)} \quad .$$

The dotted line curves on the right-hand side of Fig. VI-6 show these upper and lower bounds (and confirm their validity). The bounds become tight for $\mu_1 \to \mu_0$ .

The broken line curves of Fig. VI-6 for $E\{Q_1\} + E\{Q_2\}$ show that the introduction of a regular server at 1 between servers 0 and 2 will never decrease the total queue. The variation of $E\{Q_1 + Q_2\}$ with $\gamma_0$ is not monotone; particularly for $\mu_1 > \mu_2$, the curves increase from 1 at $\gamma_0 = 0$ and return to 1 for $\gamma_0 = \pi/2$ .

The term "server" is perhaps deceptive here if one considers possible applications. A "server" is nothing more than a location at which there is some constraint on the rate at which "customers" (goods, objects, etc.) can pass. It could be a regulator in a water supply system which transfers water from one reservoir to another. If one has only a finite storage (reservoir) at 2, one may wish to introduce a regular server 1 as a "regulator," "buffer," etc., to absorb some of the fluctuations in the input and reduce the queue $Q_2$ , or at least $E\{Q_2\}$ . In effect, one transfers some of the queue that would be at 2 to another location (to $Q_1$), but if the introduction of a server 1 may on some occasions cause $Q_2$ to vanish and interrupt server 2, the combined queue $Q_1 + Q_2$ may increase.

The effect of introducing a regular server between two random servers is, in some respects, the opposite of the effect described in section 2 and Fig. VI-2 of introducing a stochastic server between two regular ones. In the latter case there would be no queue at all if server 1 were absent.

Server 1 creates two queues; the lower $\mu_1$, the larger the values of both $E\{Q_1\}$ and $E\{Q_2\}$ .

In all cases considered so far, however, the value of $2E\{Q_2\}(\mu_2 - \mu_0)$ is a smooth monotone function of $(\mu_2 - \mu_0)/(\mu_1 - \mu_0)$ which varies between known limiting values at 0 and $\infty$ ($\mu_1 = \infty$ and $\mu_1 = \mu_0$). In the former limit ($\mu_1 = \infty$) the system behaves as if server 1 were absent. The distribution of $Q_2$ should (for $\Delta_0 + \Delta_2 > 0$) be approximately exponential with $2E\{Q_2\}(\mu_2 - \mu_0) = \Delta_0 + \Delta_2$ . In the latter limit ($\mu_1 = \mu_0$), $E\{Q_1\}$ becomes infinite and server 2 behaves as if server 0 were absent. Again the distribution of $Q_2$ should be approximately exponential with $2E\{Q_2\}(\mu_2 - \mu_0) = \Delta_1 + \Delta_2$ . Furthermore, in the special case $\Delta_0 = \Delta_1$ , $2E\{Q_2\}(\mu_2 - \mu_0)$ is independent of $\mu_1$ . It seems likely that $2E\{Q_2\}(\mu_2 - \mu_0)$ is, in all cases, a monotone function of $\mu_1$ which varies between the limits $(\Delta_0 + \Delta_2)$ and $(\Delta_1 + \Delta_2)$ as $\mu_1$ goes from $\infty$ to $\mu_0$ .

The methods used above to treat the case $\gamma_1 = \pi/2$ can be generalized to give similar type solutions for $\gamma_1 = \pi/3$ , $2\pi/3$ , $\pi/4$ , -- (any rational multiple of $\pi$). The generalization of (5.6a) will simply include more translated functions of the form $\theta \, ctn \, \theta$. Although this is straightforward, the numerical evaluation of $E\{Q_2\}$ becomes more tedious as more terms are added. Rather than pursue this further here, we will turn to another class of relatively simple solutions.

The above class of solutions resulted because poles (zeros) generated from the coefficients in (4.15) or (4.15a) coalesce and form sequences of poles (zeros) of increasing order. It is also possible for some poles to coalesce with zeros and annihilate each other. If we write (4.15) in the form

$$K_2^+(\theta_1) = \frac{\sin\left(\dfrac{\theta_1 - \theta^* - 2\gamma_0 - \gamma_1}{2}\right) \sin\left(\dfrac{\theta_1 + \theta^* - \gamma_1}{2}\right)}{\sin\left(\dfrac{\theta_1 + \theta^* + 2\gamma_0 - \gamma_1}{2}\right) \sin\left(\dfrac{\theta_1 - \theta^* - \gamma_1}{2}\right)} K_2^+(\theta_1 - 2\gamma_1) \quad (5.7)$$

we see that $K_2^+(\theta_1)$ has a simple pole at $\theta_1 = \theta^* + \gamma_1$ . In general, we expect iteration of (5.7) to establish the existence of poles also at $\theta_1 = \theta^* + \gamma_1 + 2j\gamma_1$ , $j = 1, 2, --$ . We would expect $K_2^+(\theta_1)$ to have zeros at $\theta_1 = \theta^* + \gamma_1 + 2\gamma_0$ and by iteration at $\theta_1 = \theta^* + \gamma_1 + 2\gamma_0 + 2j\gamma_1$ , $j = 1, 2, --$ . If, however, the first point in the latter sequence coincides with some point in the former sequence, specifically if

$$\gamma_0 = m\,\gamma_1 \qquad \text{for some positive integer } m , \qquad (5.8)$$

then all subsequent points of the second sequence also coincide with those of the first sequence. This means that the sequence of poles at spacing $2\gamma_1$ generated by a pole in the coefficient of (5.7) terminates after $m$ poles instead of continuing indefinitely. The companion sequence of zeros disappears completely.

There are also possible poles in $K_2^+(\theta_1)$ at $\theta_1 = 2\pi - \theta^* - 2\gamma_0 + \gamma_1 + 2j\gamma_1$ , $j = 0, 1, --$ and zeros at $\theta_1 = 2\pi - \theta^* + \gamma_1 + 2j\gamma_1$ , but again, if (5.8) is true, the second series coincides with all but the first $m$ terms of the former. Since the coefficients in (5.7) are periodic, further sequences of poles are initiated at points displaced by any multiple of $2\pi$ from the above.

If (5.8) is true then an iteration of (5.7) $m - 1$ times gives

$$K_2^+(\theta_1) \prod_{j=0}^{m-1} \sin\left(\dfrac{\theta_1 + \theta^* + 2m\gamma_1 - \gamma_1 - 2j\gamma_1}{2}\right) \sin\left(\dfrac{\theta_1 - \theta^* - \gamma_1 - 2j\gamma_1}{2}\right)$$

$$= K_2^\dagger(\theta_1 - 2m\gamma_1) \prod_{j=0}^{m-1} \sin\left(\frac{\theta_1 + \theta^* - \gamma_1 - 2j\gamma_1}{2}\right) \sin\left(\frac{\theta_1 - \theta^* - 2m\gamma_1 - \gamma_1 - 2j\gamma_1}{2}\right)$$

(5.9)

If we interpret the expression on the left-hand side of (5.9) as some function $Z(\theta_1)$ , then the expression on the right-hand side is $Z(\theta_1 - 2m\gamma_1)$ , which means that $Z(\theta_1)$ is periodic with period $2m\gamma_1 = 2\gamma_0$ . The function $Z(\theta_1)$ , however, must also be entire, free of zeros, and, according to (4.21b), approach a constant for Im $\theta_1 \rightarrow \infty$ . The only function of $\theta_1$ which satisfies all these conditions is a constant. We conclude that $K_2^\dagger(\theta_1)$ must have the form

$$K_2^\dagger(\theta_1) = A \prod_{j=0}^{m-1} \left[ 2\sin\left(\frac{\theta_1 + \theta^* + (2m-2j-1)\gamma_1}{2}\right) \sin\left(\frac{-\theta_1 + \theta^* + (2j+1)\gamma_1}{2}\right) \right]^{-1}$$

(5.10)

with $A > 0$ independent of $\theta_1$ (but still a function of $\theta^*$ and the $\gamma_j$). In the product of the first factors we can reverse the order of the product; change $j$ to $m - 1 - j$ , $(2m - 2j - 1)$ to $(2j + 1)$ . The terms of the product can then be rewritten in the form

$$K_2^\dagger(\theta_1) = A \prod_{j=0}^{m-1} [\cos\theta_1 - \cos(\theta^* + (2j + 1)\gamma_1)]^{-1} \quad .$$

(5.10a)

One can apply similar arguments to (4.15a) and/or (4.8c) to show that $K_1^\dagger(\theta_1)$ has the form

$$K_1^\dagger(\theta_1) = \frac{A(\Delta_1 + \Delta_2)}{(\Delta_0+\Delta_2)^{\frac{1}{2}}(\Delta_0+\Delta_1)^{\frac{1}{2}}} \prod_{j=0}^{m-1} \left[ 2\sin\left(\frac{-\theta_1+\gamma_1+\theta^*+2(j+1)\gamma_1}{2}\right)\sin\left(\frac{\theta_1-\gamma_1+\theta^*+2(j+1)\gamma_1}{2}\right)\right]^{-1}$$

$$= \frac{A(\Delta_1 + \Delta_2)}{(\Delta_0 + \Delta_2)^{1/2}(\Delta_0 + \Delta_1)^{1/2}} \prod_{j=0}^{m-1} [\cos(\theta_1-\gamma_1) - \cos(\theta^*+2(j+1)\gamma_1)]^{-1}.$$

$$(5.11a)$$

The $K_2^\dagger(\theta_1)$ and $K_1^\dagger(\theta_1)$ have been written in the form (5.10a) and
(5.11a) to show that these functions are periodic in $\theta_1$ with period $2\pi$;
the former is necessarily symmetric to $\theta_1 \to -\theta_1$ , the latter to $\theta_1 - \gamma_1 \to$
$-(\theta_1 - \gamma_1)$ . Most important, however, is the fact that these map into
single-valued (and polynomial) solutions for $K_2(\lambda_1)$ and $K_1(\lambda_2)$ through
(4.1) and (4.9)

$$K_2(\lambda_1) = A \prod_{j=0}^{m-1} \left[ \frac{\Delta^{*3/2}\lambda_1}{\mu^\dagger(\Delta_1 + \Delta_2)^{1/2}} + 2\sin((j+1)\gamma_1)\sin(\theta^*+j\gamma_1)\right]^{-1} \qquad (5.10b)$$

$$K_1(\lambda_2) = \frac{A(\Delta_1 + \Delta_2)}{(\Delta_0+\Delta_2)^{\frac{1}{2}}(\Delta_0+\Delta_1)^{\frac{1}{2}}} \prod_{j=0}^{m-1} \left[ \frac{\Delta^{*3/2}\lambda_2}{\mu^\dagger(\Delta_0+\Delta_1)^{1/2}} + 2\sin((j+1)\gamma_1)\sin(\theta^*+(j+1)\gamma_1)\right]^{-1} .$$

$$(5.11b)$$

If we compare this with the more general result (4.21c,d), we see that
the condition (5.8) was a necessary condition to guarantee single-valued
functions for $K_2(\lambda_1)$ , $K_1(\lambda_2)$ ; any noninteger value of $\gamma_0/\gamma_1$ would
certainly have created a branch point singularity at $\lambda_1$ , $\lambda_2 \to \infty$ (and
elsewhere).

Since the value of  A  is determined by the normalization conditions
from (1.16) or (1.16a)

$$K_1(0) = \frac{2(\mu_1 - \mu_0)}{(\Delta_0 + \Delta_1)} \quad \text{or} \quad K_2(0) = \frac{2(\mu_2 - \mu_0)}{(\Delta_1 + \Delta_2)} \quad ,$$

the functions  $K_2(\lambda_1)$  and  $K_1(\lambda_2)$  are explicitly determined;  therefore
also the joint transform  $K(\lambda_1,\lambda_2)$  and the marginal transform  $K(0,\lambda_2)$  .
These are all rational functions of  $\lambda_1$  and  $\lambda_2$ ;  consequently  $g^*(\ell_1,\ell_2)$
can be written as a linear combination of finitely many products of an
exponential in  $\ell_1$  and an exponential in  $\ell_2$  (one can show that there
are actually  $2m - 1$  such terms).  The marginal distribution  $g_2^*(\ell_2)$
can be written as a linear combination of  m  exponentials in  $\ell_2$ .

The limit  $m \to \infty$  in (5.8) with  $\gamma_0 \leq \pi/2$  means that  $\gamma_1 \to 0$ ,
which, in turn, implies that  $\gamma_0$ ,  $\gamma_2 \to \pi/2$  and  $\Delta_0 \to \Delta_2 \to 0$ .  Thus
for  $m \to \infty$ ,  the limit behavior of the above formulas should produce
the results of section 2.  The more interesting results, however, are for
$m = 1, 2,$  and possibly 3.  The case  $m = 1$ ,  $\gamma_0 = \gamma_1$  corresponds to
$\Delta_0 = \Delta_1$ .  One can readily verify from the above equations that

$$K(\lambda_1,\lambda_2) = \left[1 + \frac{\lambda_2(\Delta_0 + \Delta_2)}{2(\mu_2 - \mu_0)}\right]^{-1}\left[1 + \frac{\lambda_1 \Delta_0}{\mu_1 - \mu_0}\right]^{-1} \quad \text{for } \Delta_0 = \Delta_1 \quad (5.12)$$

and therefore

$$g^*(\ell_1,\ell_2) = \left[\frac{\mu_1 - \mu_0}{\Delta_0}\right]\left[\frac{2(\mu_2 - \mu_0)}{(\Delta_0 + \Delta_2)}\right]\exp\left[\frac{-\ell_1(\mu_1 - \mu_0)}{\Delta_0}\right]\exp\left[\frac{-2\ell_2(\mu_2 - \mu_0)}{(\Delta_0 + \Delta_2)}\right] \quad .$$

$$(5.12a)$$

Thus, in this special case, the equilibrium queue lengths $Q_1$ and $Q_2$ are statistically independent and exponentially distributed, as was expected from the known results for exponentially distributed service times for servers 0 and 1.

Although the case $m = 1$ has a simple interpretation in terms of the variance coefficients ($\Delta_0 = \Delta_1$, $\Delta_2$ arbitrary) and well-known queue theory results, the interpretation of the cases $m = 2, 3, --$ is not clear. The constraint $\gamma_0/\gamma_1 = 2$, for example, describes a rather complicated relation among all three variance rates $\Delta_0$, $\Delta_1$ and $\Delta_2$, of which two interesting special cases are $\gamma_0 = \pi/2$, $\gamma_1 = \gamma_2 = \pi/4$ which corresponds to $\Delta_0 = 0$, $\Delta_1 = \Delta_2$ (for example, a regular input to consecutive exponential servers) and $\gamma_0 = \pi/3$, $\gamma_1 = \pi/6$, $\gamma_2 = \pi/2$ which corresponds to $3\Delta_0 = \Delta_1$, $\Delta_2 = 0$ (an Erlang-3 input to an exponential server to a regular server). The case $m = 3$ also includes $\gamma_0 = \pi/2$, $\gamma_1 = \pi/6$, $\gamma_2 = \pi/3$; $\Delta_0 = 0$, $\Delta_1 = 3\Delta_2$.

The case $\Delta_0 = 0$, $\Delta_2 = \Delta_1$ ($\gamma_0 = \pi/2$, $\gamma_1 = \gamma_2 = \pi/4$) is of special interest because we have already considered the cases $\Delta_0 = \Delta_2 = 0$ ($\gamma_0 = \gamma_2 = \pi/2$, $\gamma_1 = 0$) in section 2, $\Delta_0 = \Delta_1$, $\Delta_2 = 0$ ($\gamma_0 = \gamma_1 = \pi/4$, $\gamma_2 = \pi/2$) above for $m = 1$, $\Delta_0 = \Delta_1 = 0$ ($\gamma_0 = \gamma_1 = \pi/2$, $\gamma_2 = 0$) as an example of both $\gamma_1 = \pi/2$ and $m = 1$, and $\Delta_1 = \Delta_2 = 0$ ($\gamma_1 = \gamma_2 = \pi/2$, $\gamma_0 = 0$). These include all combinations corresponding to exponential and regular servers.

For $\Delta_0 = 0$, $\Delta_2 = \Delta_1$, one can show that

$$K(\lambda_1,\lambda_2) = \frac{\frac{1}{2}(\alpha_1 + \alpha_2)\alpha_1(2\alpha_1 + \alpha_2)(\lambda_1 + \lambda_2 + 2\alpha_1 + \alpha_2)}{(\lambda_1 + 2\alpha_1 + \alpha_2)(\lambda_1 + \alpha_1)(\lambda_2 + \frac{1}{2}[2\alpha_1 + \alpha_2])(\lambda_2 + \alpha_1 + \alpha_2)}$$

(5.13)

in which $\alpha_1$ and $\alpha_2$ are as defined in (2.1). This can be obtained directly by substituting the appropriate expressions for $K_2(\lambda_1)$ and $K_1(\lambda_2)$ from (5.10b), (5.11b) into (1.13), and observing that the quadratic coefficient of $K(\lambda_1,\lambda_2)$ on the left-hand side of (1.13) also factors from the right-hand side. One can also deduce (5.13) from its known algebraic properties. The function $K(\lambda_1,\lambda_2)$ can have poles only at the points in the $\lambda_1$, $\lambda_2$ spaces where $K_2(\lambda_1)$ or $K_1(\lambda_2)$ have poles as given by (5.10b), (5.11b). This determines the four factors in the denominator of (5.13). The known behavior of $K(\lambda_1,\lambda_2)$ for $\lambda_1$, $\lambda_2 \to \infty$ requires that it behave asymptotically like a homogeneous function of degree $(-3)$, consequently the numerator of (5.13) must be linear in $\lambda_1$, $\lambda_2$. If we set $\lambda_2 = 0$ to obtain $K(\lambda_1,0)$, we know that this can have only one pole at $\lambda_1 = -\alpha_1$. Thus the numerator of (5.13) must cancel the pole at $\lambda_1 = -(2\alpha_1 + \alpha_2)$ when $\lambda_2 = 0$. Finally the form of $K(\lambda_1,\lambda_2)$ requires that its Laplace inversion contain at most three exponential terms; therefore the numerator must vanish where $K(\lambda_1,\lambda_2)$ has a pole in both $\lambda_1$ and $\lambda_2$, specifically for $\lambda_1 = -\alpha_1$ and $\lambda_2 = -(\alpha_1 + \alpha_2)$.

From (5.13) we obtain the joint distribution

$$g^*(\ell_1,\ell_2) = \frac{1}{2}\alpha_1(2\alpha_1 + \alpha_2)\exp\left(\frac{-\ell_2}{2}[2\alpha_1 + \alpha_2]\right)\{\exp(-\alpha_1\ell_1) - \exp(-\ell_1[2\alpha_1+\alpha_2]$$

$$+ \alpha_1(2\alpha_1+\alpha_2)\left(1 + \frac{\alpha_1}{\alpha_2}\right)\exp(-\ell_1[2\alpha_1+\alpha_2])\left\{\exp\left(\frac{-\ell_2}{2}[2\alpha_1+\alpha_2]\right) - \exp(-\ell_2[\alpha_1+\alpha_2])\right\}$$

$$(5.14)$$

for $\alpha_2 \neq 0$. For $\alpha_2 \to 0$ $(\mu_2 \to \mu_1)$ this gives the limit behavior

$$g^*(\ell_1,\ell_2) = \alpha_1^2 \exp(-\ell_2\alpha_1)\exp(-\ell_1\alpha_1)[1 - (1 - \ell_2\alpha_1)\exp(-\ell_1\alpha_1)].\quad (5.14a$$

For the marginal distribution, (5.13) gives

$$g_2^*(\ell_2) \;=\; \frac{1}{2}\,(\alpha_1 + \alpha_2)\exp\!\left[\frac{-\ell_2}{2}[2\alpha_1 + \alpha_2]\right]\left\{1 + \frac{2\alpha_1}{\alpha_2}\left[1 - \exp\!\left(\frac{-\ell_2\alpha_2}{2}\right)\right]\right\} \qquad (5.15)$$

for $\alpha_2 \neq 0$, and for $\alpha_2 = 0$

$$g_2^*(\ell_2) \;=\; \frac{1}{2}\,\alpha_1\,(1 + \ell_2\alpha_1)\,\exp(-\ell_2\alpha_1) \;, \qquad (5.15a)$$

from which the expected queue becomes

$$E\{Q_2\} \;=\; \frac{1}{2\alpha_1 + \alpha_2} + \frac{1}{\alpha_1 + \alpha_2} \;=\; \frac{\Delta_1}{2(\mu_1 + \mu_2 - 2\mu_0)} + \frac{\Delta_1}{2(\mu_2 - \mu_0)} \;, \qquad (5.15b)$$

$$(\alpha_1 + \alpha_2)E\{Q_2\} \;=\; (2/\Delta_1)(\mu_2 - \mu_0)E\{Q_2\} \;=\; 1 + \left[1 + \frac{\mu_1 - \mu_0}{\mu_2 - \mu_0}\right]^{-1} \;. \qquad (5.15c)$$

Fig. VI-7 shows some examples of the distribution (5.15) drawn on a semi-log scale analogous to Fig. VI-2. Although there are some qualitative similarities between Figs. VI-2 and 7, the formulas are quite different for the two figures and there is little ground for direct comparison.

Fig. VI-8 shows further graphs of the type drawn in Fig. VI-6. The curve for $\Delta_0 = 0$, $\Delta_1 = \Delta_2$ is obtained from (5.15c). Also shown in Fig. VI-8 is the corresponding curve of $E\{Q_2\}$ for $3\Delta_0 = \Delta_1$, $\Delta_2 = 0$ derived from (5.11b), and a repetition of the curve from Fig. VI-2 for $\Delta_0 = \Delta_2 = 0$ $(m \to \infty)$. Actually one can easily derive equations for $E\{Q_2\}$ from (5.11b) for any values of the $\Delta_j$ for which $\gamma_0/\gamma_1 = m$ is integer but these are rather complex functions of the $\Delta_j$'s.

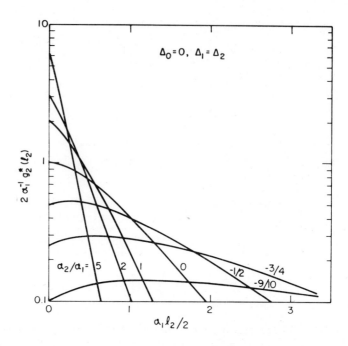

Fig. VI-7. Distribution of the queue length $Q_2$ for a regular input and $\Delta_1 = \Delta_2$, and various service rates $\alpha_2/\alpha_1$ .

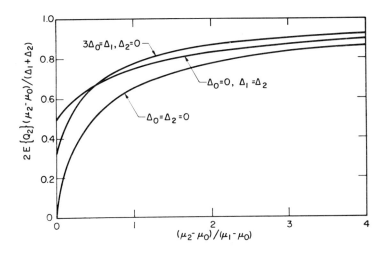

Fig. VI-8. The expected queue length $E\{Q_2\}$ as a function of service rates for special values of the $\Delta_j$.

6. <u>Interpretation</u>.  As pointed out before in section III 5, one of the main

objectives in an analytic approach, as compared with simulation or other

numerical schemes, is to expose any simple dependences of the solutions

upon the parameters.  The introduction of the diffusion approximation in

itself greatly reduced the number of parameters involved in an exact de-

scription of the servers to just the first and second moments of the ser-

vice rates, the $\mu_j$ and $\Delta_j$ .  In the previous sections we have attempte

to illustrate how the joint distribution $g^*(\ell_1,\ell_2)$ , or its marginal

distribution $g_2^*(\ell_2)$ , or just its first moment $E\{Q_2\}$ depends upon the

six parameters $\mu_0$ , $\mu_1$ , $\mu_2$ , $\Delta_0$ , $\Delta_1$ , $\Delta_2$ with $c_1 = c_2 = \infty$ .

In Chapter III we were concerned with the dependence of similar queu

properties on the six parameters $\mu_0$ $(= \mu_1 = \mu_2)$ , $\Delta_0$ , $\Delta_1$ , $\Delta_2$ , $c_1$ ,

and $c_2$ .  Actually for $\mu_0 = \mu_1 = \mu_2$ , $\mu_0$ did not enter the equations

so the queue distributions did not depend upon $\mu_0$ .  The equations were

also homogeneous in the $\Delta_j$ .  By dividing the equations by one of the

$\Delta_j$'s, one could see that the distributions depended only upon the ratios

of the $\Delta_j$ or equivalently upon the angles $\gamma_0$ , $\gamma_1$ , $\gamma_2$ with $\gamma_0 +$

$\gamma_1 + \gamma_2 = \pi$ .  Finally, one of the $c_j$'s could be chosen as the unit of

length, thus reducing the number of "basic parameters" to three, for ex-

ample, $\gamma_0$ , $\gamma_1$ , and $c_2/c_1$ .

Here also, in the choice of coordinates for drawing the graphs, we

have, in effect, reduced the number of basic parameters from six to three

First of all, the differential equation for the queues contains only dif-

ferences of the $\mu_j$ ; $(\mu_1 - \mu_0)$ and $(\mu_2 - \mu_0)$ or $(\mu_2 - \mu_1)$ ; con-

sequently the queue distributions depend only upon these differences.

The queue behavior of a system with service rates $\mu_0$ , $\mu_1$ , $\mu_2$ is

the same as for a hypothetical system with service rates $0$ , $\mu_1 - \mu_0$ ,

$\mu_2 - \mu_0$ . The latter is a little difficult to imagine, because the input server 0, serving at an average rate of zero but with a non-zero variance would have to serve with negative rate about half the time. The mathematics shows, however, that an increase of all service rates by some amount $\mu_0$ (with fixed values of the $\Delta_j$) is like sending a deterministic flow $\mu_0$ through the system. We could, of course, have given a similar interpretation in Chapter III of the fact that $\mu_0$ did not enter the equations at all and could therefore have been chosen as zero.

As in Chapter III we can further reduce the number of parameters by (1) dividing the diffusion equation by any convenient constant and (2) choosing an appropriate unit of length for $Q_1$ , $Q_2$ . If we divide the equation by one of the $\Delta_j$'s or $\Delta^*$ , the equation will contain only the ratios of the $\Delta_j$ , and the ratios of $\mu_1 - \mu_0$ and $\mu_2 - \mu_0$ to one of the $\Delta_j$'s. The ratios of the $\Delta_j$'s have again been expressed in terms of $\gamma_0$ , $\gamma_1$ , $\gamma_2$ with $\gamma_0 + \gamma_1 + \gamma_2 = \pi$ . In the graphs of the previous sections we have always used some convenient ratio of $\Delta_j$'s to $(\mu_2 - \mu_0)$ or $(\mu_1 - \mu_0)$ as a unit of length (for example $\alpha_1^{-1}$ in section 2). In most cases the three non-dimensional parameters have been chosen as $\gamma_0$ , $\gamma_1$ and $(\mu_2 - \mu_0)/(\mu_1 - \mu_0)$ .

The methods used in Chapter III to determine the queue distributions for $\mu_0 = \mu_1 = \mu_2$ ; $c_1$ , $c_2 < \infty$ , and those used in this chapter for $\mu_0 < \mu_1 \neq \mu_2$ , $c_1 = c_2 = \infty$ are so different and so specialized, it is difficult to see how either could be generalized to incorporate the other. Even if one could solve the equations for general $\mu_0$ , $\mu_1$ , $\mu_2$ and $c_1$ , $c_2 < \infty$ , the family of solutions would depend upon five irreducible parameters including "dimensionless parameters" such as $c_2(\mu_2 - \mu_0)/(\Delta_0 + \Delta_2)$, the storage capacity at server 2 compared with the average queue length

306

that would exist for $\mu_1 \to \infty$, $c_2 = \infty$, and $c_1(\mu_1 - \mu_0)/(\Delta_0 + \Delta_1)$ .

The solutions of Chapter III and those of this chapter have no over-lap (the only limiting case common to both is $\mu_0 = \mu_1 = \mu_2$, $c_1 = c_2 = \infty$ which gives infinite queues for both $Q_1$ and $Q_2$). It is, however, interesting to compare the distributions $g_2^*(\ell_2)$ and $E\{Q_2\}$ for the cases of Chapter III $\mu_0 = \mu_1 = \mu_2$, $c_1 < \infty$ and $c_2 = \infty$ with those of this chapter for $\mu_0 < \mu_1 = \mu_2$, $c_1 = \infty$ and $c_2 = \infty$. Since the former system has an overall service rate $\mu = \mu_1 - (\Delta_0 + \Delta_1)/2c_1$ (see section III 7 where, however, the common value of $\mu_0 = \mu_1 = \mu_2$ was labeled as $\mu_0$) , one might expect it to have a queue distribution comparable with the latter if $\mu_0$ is chosen so that $\mu_0 = \mu_1 - (\Delta_0 + \Delta_1)/2c_1$ .

For the above systems, it is natural to choose $c_1$ as the unit of length in the former, which we will designate below as system I. For the latter, system II, we could choose the unit of length as $\frac{1}{2}(\Delta_0 + \Delta_1)/(\mu_1 - \mu_0)$ which with our choice of $\mu_0$ would also have the value $c_1$ . Having chosen $c_2 = \infty$ for I and $\mu_1 = \mu_2$ for system II, the two systems contain only two dimensionless parameters $\gamma_0$, $\gamma_1$ or $\Delta_0/\Delta_1$, $\Delta_2/\Delta_1$ . Although we have not described the queue distributions of systems I and II for all $\gamma_0$, $\gamma_1$, most illustrations in Chapter III are for the same choice of $\gamma_0$, $\gamma_1$ as those described in this chapter for system II.

For system I, the marginal distribution of $Q_1$ is uniform for all $\gamma_0$, $\gamma_1$ with $E_I\{Q_1\} = c_1/2$ ; for system II this distribution is always exponential with $E_{II}\{Q_1\} = c_1$ . From the following examples, it would appear that $E_I\{Q_2\}$ is also less than $E_{II}\{Q_2\}$ for all values of $\gamma_0$, $\gamma_1$, although the relative values vary considerably with $\gamma_0$ and $\gamma_1$ .

For $\Delta_0 = \Delta_1$, $\gamma_0 = \gamma_1$, $g_{II_2}^*(\ell_2)$ is exponential for all values of $\Delta_2/\Delta_1$ with

$$E_{II}\{Q_2\} = \frac{(\Delta_2 + \Delta_1)}{2(\mu_2 - \mu_0)} = \left[\frac{\Delta_2 + \Delta_1}{2\Delta_1}\right] c_1 \qquad (6.1)$$

for the chosen value of $\mu_0$ . For system I, $g_{I_2}^*(\ell_2)$ has a variety of
forms. In the limiting case $\Delta_0 = \Delta_1 \to 0$ , $\gamma_0 = \gamma_1 \to \pi/2$ , $g_{I_2}^*(\ell_2)$
is also nearly exponential with $E_I\{Q_2\}$ given by (III 2.10a)

$$E_I\{Q_2\} \simeq \left[\frac{\Delta_2 + 2\Delta_1/3}{2\Delta_1}\right] c_1 \qquad . \qquad (6.1a)$$

For $(\Delta_2/\Delta_1) \gg 1$ , the leading terms of (6.1) and (6.1a) are the same,
but the next terms give

$$E_{II}\{Q_2\} - E_I\{Q_2\} \simeq c_1/6 \qquad . \qquad (6.1b)$$

For $\gamma_0 = \gamma_1 = \gamma_2 = \pi/3$ , $g_{I_2}^*(\ell_2)$ is shown in Fig. IV-1 where it
is also compared with the exponential distribution for $g_{II_2}^*(\ell_2)$ . The
former gave $E_I\{Q_2\} \simeq 0.87c_1$ , the latter gave $E_{II}\{Q_2\} = c_1$ . Figure IV-2
shows the distribution $g_{I_2}^*(\ell_2)$ at the other limit $\gamma_0 = \gamma_1 = \pi/4$ , $\gamma_2 = \pi/2$ $(\Delta_2 = 0)$ . It gives $E_I\{Q_2\} = 0.327c_1$ whereas the corresponding
II system has $E_{II}\{Q_2\} = (1/2)c_1$ . As $\gamma_2$ varies in the above sequence
from 0 to $\pi/2$ with $\gamma_0 = \gamma_1$ , the values of $E_{II}\{Q_2\}$ run from $\infty$ to
$c_1/2$ , but the difference $(E_{II}\{Q_2\} - E_I\{Q_2\})/c_1$ seems to be very stable,
having the values $1/6 = 0.167$ at $\gamma_2 \to 0$ , 0.13 at $\gamma_2 = \pi/3$ and
0.173 at $\gamma_2 = \pi/2$ .

Except for the cases with $\gamma_0 = \gamma_1$ , we have not evaluated $g_{II_2}^*(\ell_2)$
in many cases because of the difficulty of inverting the Laplace transform, but, for system II, it is relatively easy to determine $E_{II}\{Q_2\}$ .

On the other hand, the methods used in Chapters III and IV describe the shape of $g_I^*(\ell_2)$ quite well, but to evaluate $E_I\{Q_2\}$ generally requires the evaluation of some integrals numerically. For both systems, special cases with $\gamma_1 = \pi/2$ $(\Delta_1 = 0)$ have been analysed extensively.

For $\gamma_1 = \pi/2$, (5.6a) gives for $\mu_1 = \mu_2$ $(\theta^* \to 0)$

$$E_{II}\{Q_2\} = \frac{\Delta_0}{2\pi(\mu_2 - \mu_0)} \left[ \tan\gamma_0 + \frac{\pi}{2} \tan^2\gamma_0 - \text{ctn}\gamma_0 + \frac{\gamma_0}{\cos^2\gamma_0 \sin^2\gamma_0} \right] , \quad (6.2$$

a formula which can be easily evaluated but is too complicated to have a simple interpretation. At one extreme $\gamma_2 \to 0$, $\gamma_0 \to \pi/2$ $(\Delta_0 \to 0)$, this gives

$$E_{II}\{Q_2\} \to \frac{(\Delta_2 + \Delta_0)}{2(\mu_2 - \mu_0)} = \left(\frac{\Delta_2}{\Delta_0} + 1\right) c_1 \qquad (6.3)$$

whereas (III 2.10a) gives

$$E_I\{Q_2\} \to \left(\frac{\Delta_2}{\Delta_0} + \frac{1}{3}\right) c_1 \qquad . \qquad (6.3a)$$

The situation here is similar to (6.1), (6.1a) in that both deal with the limit $\Delta_0 \to 0$, $\Delta_1 \to 0$. In (6.1), (6.1a), however, we were taking the limit $\Delta_0 = \Delta_1 \to 0$ whereas here we consider the limit $\Delta_0 \to 0$ with $\Delta_1 = 0$. In both cases $E\{Q_2\}/c_1 \to \infty$, but in the latter case it is asymptotically twice as large. As in (6.1), (6.1a), the leading terms of (6.3), (6.3a), the $\Delta_2 c_1/\Delta_0$, are equal but now we have

$$E_{II}\{Q_2\} - E_I\{Q_2\} = 2c_1/3 \qquad (6.3b)$$

a value four times that in (6.1b).

The difference between (6.1b) and (6.3b) can be attributed in part to the fact that the unit of length in (6.3) is, in effect, only half as large as in (6.1). In addition, however, one notices that for both $\Delta_0 = \Delta_1 \to 0$ and $\Delta_0 \to 0$, $\Delta_1 = 0$,

$$E_{II}\{Q_2\} \to \frac{(\Delta_2 + \Delta_0)}{2(\mu_2 - \mu_0)} \quad ;$$

for system II, with its actual $c_1$ infinite, $E_{II}\{Q_2\}$ depends upon $\Delta_0$ but is insensitive to whether $\Delta_1 = 0$ or $\Delta_1 = \Delta_0$ for $\Delta_0 \to 0$. Apparently the fact that $\mu_1$ is larger than $\mu_0$ implies that server 1 can serve fast enough so as not to retard significantly the passing of customers from server 0 to 2, even though there are some fluctuations in the arrivals at server 1. One might expect, in fact, that for $\Delta_0 \to 0$, $\Delta_1 \to 0$, $E_{II}\{Q_2\}$ is independent of $\Delta_0/\Delta_1$. On the other hand, for system I with $c_1 < \infty$ and $\mu_0 = \mu_1$, servers 0 and 1 act as a unit with an effective variance rate of $(\Delta_0 + \Delta_1)/3$, as shown by (III 2.10a). Thus (6.1a) has a term $2\Delta_0/3$ whereas the corresponding term of (6.2a) is only $\Delta_0/3$.

For other cases with $\gamma_1 = \pi/2$, we obtain from (6.2)

$$E_{II}\{Q_2\} = \frac{(0.912)2\Delta_0}{(\mu_2 - \mu_0)} = 3.66\,c_1 \quad \text{for } \gamma_2 = \frac{\pi}{6},\ \gamma_0 = \frac{\pi}{3}, \qquad (6.4a)$$

$$E_{II}\{Q_2\} = \frac{(0.75)\,\Delta_0}{\mu_2 - \mu_0} = 1.50\,c_1 \quad \text{for } \gamma_2 = \gamma_0 = \frac{\pi}{4}, \qquad (6.4b)$$

and

$$E_{II}\{Q_2\} = \frac{(0.515)4\Delta_0}{3(\mu_2 - \mu_0)} = 0.69\,c_1 \quad \text{for } \gamma_2 = \frac{\pi}{3},\ \gamma_0 = \frac{\pi}{6}. \qquad (6.4c)$$

Numerical integrations from the $g^*_{I_2}(\ell_2)$ shown in figures IV-9, IV-2 and IV-8 with $c_2 = \infty$ give the values

$$E_I\{Q_2\} \;=\; 3.30\, c_1 \qquad \text{for } \gamma_2 \;=\; \pi/6 \;,\;\; \gamma_0 = \pi/3 \qquad (6.5a)$$

$$E_I\{Q_2\} \;=\; 1.24\, c_1 \qquad \text{for } \gamma_2 \;=\; \gamma_0 \;=\; \pi/4 \qquad\qquad (6.5b)$$

$$E_I\{Q_2\} \;=\; 0.52\, c_1 \qquad \text{for } \gamma_2 \;=\; \pi/3 \;,\;\; \gamma_0 = \pi/6 \;. \qquad (6.5c)$$

The differences $(E_{II}\{Q_2\} - E_I\{Q_2\})/c_1$ decrease with $\gamma_2$, having the values 0.67, 0.36, 0.26, and 0.17 for $\gamma_2 = 0$, $\pi/6$, $\pi/4$, and $\pi/3$, respectively.

For $\gamma_1 = \pi/2$ and $\gamma_2 \to \pi/2$, $\gamma_0 \to 0$ ($\Delta_2 \to 0$), (6.2) can be expanded in powers of $(\Delta_2/\Delta_0)^{1/2}$ to give

$$E_{II}\{Q_2\} \;\to\; \frac{\Delta_0}{2(\mu_2 - \mu_0)}\left\{ \frac{8}{3\pi}\left(\frac{\Delta_2}{\Delta_0}\right)^{\frac{1}{2}} + \frac{1}{2}\left(\frac{\Delta_2}{\Delta_0}\right) + --\right\} \qquad (6.6)$$

$$\simeq \; \frac{8}{3\pi}\left(\frac{\Delta_2}{\Delta_0}\right)^{\frac{1}{2}} c_1 \;\simeq\; (0.850)\left(\frac{\Delta_2}{\Delta_0}\right)^{\frac{1}{2}} c_1 \;.$$

This is to be compared with (IV 2.17) which shows that for $\Delta_2 \to 0$, $\Delta_1 = 0$

$$E_I\{Q_2\} \;\simeq\; (0.532)\,(\Delta_2/\Delta_0)^{\frac{1}{2}} c_1 \;. \qquad (6.6a)$$

Neither (6.6) nor (6.6a) is very accurate until $(\Delta_2/\Delta_0)$ is very small (so that $(\Delta_2/\Delta_0)^{1/2} \ll 1$), but they both show $E\{Q_2\}$ going to zero proportional to $(\Delta_2/\Delta_0)^{1/2}$ as $\Delta_2/\Delta_0 \to 0$. System II still has the larger queue (by a factor of about 1.6) but we again encounter this dependence upon $\Delta_2^{1/2}$ discussed after equation (III 2.17).

There are two other cases which have been analysed for both systems I and II, the cases $\Delta_0 = 0$, $\Delta_2 = 0$, $\Delta_1 > 0$ ($\gamma_0 = \gamma_2 = \pi/2$, $\gamma_1 = 0$) and $\Delta_0 = 0$, $\Delta_2 = \Delta_1 > 0$ ($\gamma_0 = \pi/2$, $\gamma_1 = \gamma_2 = \pi/4$). The former case is that discussed in section 2, for system II; in particular we are concerned with the special case $\mu_1 = \mu_2$ ($\alpha_2 = 0$) of Figs. VI-2 and 4, which is to be compared with the limit behavior of system I shown in Fig. IV-4. For system I, the distribution $g^*_{I_2}(\ell_2)$ with $\gamma_1 = 0$ is exactly rectangular with $E_I\{Q_2\} = c_1/2$. For system II, the distribution for $\alpha_2 = 0$ in Fig. VI-4 is certainly not rectangular but it is very similar in shape to what one would obtain for system I from a small value of $\alpha_1$, i.e., $g^*_{II_2}(\ell_2)$ has a shape similar to the rescaled limit distribution of Fig. IV-4. For system II

$$E_{II}\{Q_2\} = \frac{0.65 \, \Delta_1}{2(\mu_2 - \mu_0)} = 0.65 \, c_1$$

only about 30% larger than the $c_1/2$ for system I.

The case $\Delta_0 = 0$, $\Delta_2 = \Delta_1$ for system I is shown in Fig. IV-2 and for system II in Fig. VI-7 (with $\alpha_2 = 0$). Although Fig. IV-2 is drawn on a linear scale and Fig. VI-7 on a semi-log scale, it is clear that the two distributions have very similar shapes; they both decrease near $\ell_2 = 0$ like $\ell_2^2$, and like an exponential for larger $\ell_2$. Furthermore the first moments

$$E_I\{Q_2\} = 1.45\ c_1\ ,\qquad E_{II}\{Q_2\} = 1.50\ c_1$$

are nearly equal.

VII.  Equilibrium Queue Distributions; n = 2;

$$\mu_1 \; < \; \mu_0 \; , \; \; \mu_2 \; ; \; \; c_1 \; , \; \; c_2 \; \to \; \infty$$

. <u>Introduction.</u>  In Chapter VI we dealt exclusively with the queue distributions for a system with $\mu_0 < \mu_1$, $\mu_2$ and $c_1 = c_2 = \infty$.  If $\mu_2 < \mu_1$,
$\mu_0$ there is a tendency for both storages to fill.  It is natural, therefore, to consider the distribution of holes rather than customers, as
discussed in sections I 3 and III 5.  Since a system with parameters $\mu_0$,
$\Delta_0$; $c_1$, $\mu_1$, $\Delta_1$; $c_2$, $\mu_2$, $\Delta_2$ is equivalent to one with parameters
$\mu_2$, $\Delta_2$; $c_2$, $\mu_1$, $\Delta_1$; $c_1$, $\mu_0$, $\Delta_0$ but with $Q_j$ replaced by $Q_j' =$
$c_j - Q_j$, the family of queue distributions with $\mu_0 < \mu_1$, $\mu_2$ can be
mapped into a family of distributions for holes with $\mu_2 < \mu_1$, $\mu_0$.  In
particular, the queue distributions of Chapter VI for $\mu_0 < \mu_1$, $\mu_2$ and
$c_1$, $c_2$ sufficiently large that the storages hardly ever fill ($c_1$,
$c_2 \to \infty$) map into distributions of holes for a system with $\mu_2 < \mu_1$,
$\mu_0$ and $c_1$, $c_2$ sufficiently large that the storages hardly ever empty.
There is no reason to consider separately the queue distributions for
$\mu_2 < \mu_0$, $\mu_1$; they are determined easily from those with $\mu_0 < \mu_1$, $\mu_2$.

If, however, $\mu_1 < \mu_0$, $\mu_2$ there is a tendency for the storage $c_1$
to become full and $c_2$ to become empty.  If $c_1$ and $c_2$ are sufficiently
large, it would also be true that the storage $c_1$ is hardly ever empty
and $c_2$ is hardly ever full.  In the formulas of section VI 6, the limit
behavior for $c_1$, $c_2 \to \infty$ results from setting $K_1(\lambda_2) = 0$ ($Q_1$ is
almost never 0 for any $Q_2$) and $K_2^*(\lambda_1) = 0$ ($Q_2$ is almost never $c_2$
for any $Q_1$).

The marginal distributions for $Q_1$, $Q_2$ resulting from VI (1.15)
and (1.15a) give

$$(-\lambda_1 - \alpha_1) \, K(\lambda_1, 0) \;=\; \exp(-\lambda_1 c_1) \, K_1^*(0) \quad , \tag{1.1}$$

with $\qquad \alpha_1 \;=\; -2(\mu_0 - \mu_1)/(\Delta_0 + \Delta_1) \quad ,$ $\tag{1.1a}$

$$(\lambda_2 + \alpha_2) \, K(0, \lambda_2) \;=\; K_2(0) \quad , \tag{1.2}$$

with $\qquad \alpha_2 \;=\; 2(\mu_2 - \mu_1)/(\Delta_2 + \Delta_1) \quad .$ $\tag{1.2a}$

Equation (1.1) describes the distribution of $Q_1$ (actually the distribution of $Q_1' = c_1 - Q_1$ for $c_1 \to \infty$). The normalized distribution obtained from the inversion of (1.1) is

$$g_1^*(\ell_1) \;=\; (-\alpha_1) \, \exp(\alpha_1(c_1 - \ell_1)) \; , \quad \text{for } \ell_1 < c_1$$
$$\tag{1.1b}$$
$$\;=\; 0 \quad , \quad \text{for } \ell_1 > c_1$$

which describes an exponential distribution of holes with

$$E\{Q_1'\} \;=\; 1/(-\alpha_1) \quad . \tag{1.1c}$$

Equation (1.2) describes an exponential distribution for $Q_2$

$$g_2^*(\ell_2) \;=\; \alpha_2 \, \exp(-\alpha_2 \ell_2) \tag{1.2b}$$

with

$$E\{Q_2\} \;=\; 1/\alpha_2 \quad . \tag{1.2c}$$

These results were to be expected since (1.1b) is but a special case of VI (1.17); the marginal distribution of $Q_1$ is the same as it would be if server 2 were not there (for $c_2 \to \infty$). Since server 1 is the bottl neck and has a nearly infinite queue behind it, server 2 responds only to

the uninterrupted output from server 1. Thus (1.2b) is the distribution
that would exist if server 0 were absent and server 1 were the input server.

Despite this apparent "independence" of servers 0 and 2, $Q_1$ and
$Q_2$ are certainly not statistically independent; the joint distribution
for $Q_1$, $Q_2$ is not the product of the marginals because any fluctuation in the service rate of server 1 affects both $Q_1$ and $Q_2$. We expect $Q_1$ and $Q_2$ to be negatively correlated since an excess of service
at 1 will cause $Q_2$ to increase and $Q_1$ to decrease.

To determine the joint distribution of $Q_1$, $Q_2$ or actually $Q_1'$, $Q_2$,
we proceed in a manner similar to that of sections VI 2 and 3. It is convenient, however, first to convert the equations for the transforms of
the $Q_1$, $Q_2$ distributions into transforms for the $Q_1'$, $Q_2$ distributions. Let

$$\bar{K}(\lambda_1,\lambda_2) \equiv \int_0^\infty d\ell_1' \int_0^\infty d\ell_2\, g^*(c_1 - \ell_1', \ell_2)\exp(-\lambda_1\ell_1' - \lambda_2\ell_2)$$

$$\qquad\qquad\qquad (1.3)$$

$$= e^{-\lambda_1 c_1} K(-\lambda_1,\lambda_2)$$

and correspondingly

$$\bar{K}_2(\lambda_1) = \int_0^\infty d\ell_1'\, g^*(c_1 - \ell_1',0)\exp(-\lambda_1\ell_1') = e^{-\lambda_1 c_1} K_2(-\lambda_1). \quad (1.3a)$$

For $c_1$, $c_2 \to \infty$, $K_1(\lambda_2) = 0$, $K_2^*(\lambda_1) = 0$, equation VI (1.13) requires
that $\bar{K}(\lambda_1,\lambda_2)$ satisfy the equation

$$\left[ -\lambda_1(\mu_1 - \mu_0) + \lambda_2(\mu_2 - \mu_1) + \frac{\Delta_0}{2}\lambda_1^2 + \frac{\Delta_1}{2}(\lambda_1 + \lambda_2)^2 + \frac{\Delta_2}{2}\lambda_2^2 \right] \overline{K}(\lambda_1,\lambda_2)$$

$$(1.4)$$

$$= \frac{\lambda_2}{2}(\Delta_1 + \Delta_2)\,\overline{K}_2(\lambda_1) + \frac{\lambda_1}{2}(\Delta_0 + \Delta_1)\,K_1^*(\lambda_2) \ .$$

Since $\overline{K}(\lambda_1,\lambda_2)$, $\overline{K}_2(\lambda_1)$, and $K_1^*(\lambda_2)$ are Laplace transforms of non-negative functions, we again have the further requirements that these functions must be analytic at least in the right-half $\lambda_1$ and/or $\lambda_2$ spaces (Re $\lambda_1$, Re $\lambda_2 \geq 0$), and they must be real, positive and monotone non-increasing for $\lambda_1$, $\lambda_2$ real and positive. These analytic properties along with (1.4) should determine all three functions.

2. <u>Joint Distribution for $\Delta_0 = \Delta_2 = 0$</u> . It is advantageous again to treat the case $\Delta_0 = \Delta_2 = 0$ separately.

From (I 5.6) we see that $g^*(\ell_1,\ell_2;t)$ satisfies the diffusion equation

$$\frac{\partial g^*}{\partial t} = (-\mu_0 + \mu_1)\frac{\partial g^*}{\partial \ell_1} + (-\mu_1 + \mu_2)\frac{\partial g^*}{\partial \ell_2} + \frac{\Delta_1}{2}\left(\frac{\partial}{\partial \ell_1} - \frac{\partial}{\partial \ell_2}\right)^2 g^* \ .$$

$$(2.1)$$

The equation for the equilibrium distribution $(\partial g^*/\partial t = 0)$ is of parabolic type rather than elliptic type and its solutions have quite different properties than for $\Delta_j > 0$ . If we were to change coordinates to $(\ell_1 + \ell_2)$ and $(\ell_1 - \ell_2)$ , (2.1) would convert to a standard type parabolic equation like the heat conduction equation in which the variable $\ell_1 + \ell_2$ assumes the role customarily identified with the time coordinate, with a "diffusion constant" having the sign of $(\mu_0 - \mu_2)$ .

That (2.1) is of parabolic type originates from the fact that, for

$\Delta_0 = \Delta_2 = 0$ , the evolution of $Q_1(t) + Q_2(t)$ is deterministic as long as the $Q_j$ are not either 0 or $c_j$ , $j = 1, 2$; $Q_1(t) + Q_2(t)$ or $Q_2(t) - Q_1'(t)$ must increase at a rate $\mu_0 - \mu_2$ .

In Chapter IV some consequences of this were discussed for the special case $\mu_0 = \mu_1 = \mu_2$ . There it was argued that the equilibrium queue distribution for $\Delta_0 = \Delta_2 = 0$ must lie along the line $\ell_1 + \ell_2 = c_1$ and be uniform along this line. This led to the uniform marginal distributions of figure IV-4.

Generalizing the arguments of Chapter IV, we observe again that if $Q_1 = 0$ or $Q_2 = c_2$ , server 1 is interrupted. This, however, has no immediate effect upon the value of $Q_1(t) + Q_2(t)$ , the total number of customers between servers 0 and 2, which continues to increase at the rate $\mu_0 - \mu_2$ . If, however, $Q_1(t) = c_1$ $(Q_1'(t) = 0)$, server 0 is interrupted causing $Q_1(t) + Q_2(t)$ to decrease, and if $Q_2(t) = 0$ , server 2 is interrupted causing $Q_1(t) + Q_2(t)$ to increase.

If $\mu_0 \leq \mu_2$ and $Q_1(t) + Q_2(t) > c_1$ , then $Q_1(t) + Q_2(t)$ is non-increasing in time. It either decreases at a rate $-(\mu_0 - \mu_2)$ if $Q_1(t) < c_1$ or it decreases when $Q_1(t) = c_1$ and server 0 is interrupted; it is not possible to have $Q_1(t) + Q_2(t) > c_1$ and $Q_2(t) = 0$ . We conclude that states with $Q_1(t) + Q_2(t) > c_1$ are transient for $\mu_0 \leq \mu_2$ ; the equilibrium queue distribution $g^*(\ell_1, \ell_2)$ must vanish for $\ell_1 + \ell_2 > c_1$ . Equivalently, the equilibrium distribution of $Q_1'$ , $Q_2$ must vanish for $\ell_2 > \ell_1'$ . The equilibrium for $\ell_1 + \ell_2 \leq c_1$ is maintained by balancing the decrease of $Q_1(t) + Q_2(t)$ due to the difference in service rates $\mu_0 \leq \mu_2$ against the increase when $Q_2(t) = 0$ and server 2 is interrupted.

Correspondingly, if $\mu_0 \geq \mu_2$ and $Q_1(t) + Q_2(t) < c_1$ , it is impossible for $Q_1(t) + Q_2(t)$ to decrease. We conclude that the equilibrium distribution $g^*(\ell_1, \ell_2)$ vanishes for $\ell_1 + \ell_2 < c_1$ for $\mu_0 \geq \mu_2$; the equilibrium distribution for $Q_1'$, $Q_2$ vanishes for $\ell_2 < \ell_1'$.

Such arguments were used in Chapter IV to conclude that for $\mu_0 = \mu_1 = \mu_2$, $g^*(\ell_1, \ell_2)$ must vanish for both $\ell_1 + \ell_2 < c_1$ and $\ell_1 + \ell_2 > c_1$; it can be nonzero only on the line $\ell_1 + \ell_2 = c_1$. Actually this must be true also for $\mu_0 = \mu_2 \neq \mu_1$ for any $\mu_1$ and any $c_1$, $c_2$, for $\Delta_0 = \Delta_2 = 0$.

The above properties are related to the fact that the heat conduction equation has a well-defined solution only in the direction of positive "time." In the present case, the role of "time" is taken by the variable $\ell_1 + \ell_2$ if $\mu_0 > \mu_2$. The equilibrium distribution for $\mu_0 > \mu_2$ exists only for $\ell_1 + \ell_2$ larger than some value $(c_1)$, i.e., for "time" increasing from some origin. For $\mu_0 < \mu_2$, the "time" runs backwards, i.e., the solution is well-defined only for $\ell_1 + \ell_2$ decreasing from some value $(c_1)$.

It is undoubtedly possible to solve (2.1) along with the appropriate boundary conditions by some type of image methods, but we shall determine the solution from the transform of the last section. The purpose of the above discussion is merely to identify and explain some properties which will emerge also from the transform solutions but for reasons which, in terms of the transforms, seem rather abstract.

For $\Delta_0 = \Delta_2 = 0$, (1.4) simplifies to

$$[-\alpha_1 \lambda_1 + \alpha_2 \lambda_2 + (\lambda_1 + \lambda_2)^2] \, \overline{K}(\lambda_1, \lambda_2) = \lambda_2 \overline{K}_2(\lambda_1) + \lambda_1 K_1^*(\lambda_2) \tag{2.2}$$

in which

$$\alpha_1 = 2(\mu_1 - \mu_0)/\Delta_1 \quad , \quad \alpha_2 = 2(\mu_2 - \mu_1)/\Delta_1 \tag{2.2a}$$

are the same as in (VI 2.1) except now we have

$$\alpha_1 < 0 , \qquad \alpha_2 > 0$$

and $\alpha_1 + \alpha_2 = 2(\mu_2 - \mu_0)/\Delta_1$ may be either positive or negative.

As in section VI 2, it is convenient to write (2.2) in terms of the variables

$$z_1 = \lambda_1 + \lambda_2 , \qquad z_2 = \lambda_1 - \lambda_2 ,$$

(2.3)

$$\left[ \frac{(\alpha_2 - \alpha_1)}{2} z_1 - \frac{(\alpha_1 + \alpha_2)}{2} z_2 + z_1^2 \right] \overline{K} = \frac{(z_1 - z_2)}{2} \overline{K}_2 \left( \frac{z_1 + z_2}{2} \right) + \frac{(z_1 + z_2)}{2} K_1^* \left( \frac{z_1 - z_2}{2} \right) .$$

Since $\overline{K}$ is required to be analytic at least in the right-half $\lambda_1$ , and $\lambda_2$ planes, the left-hand side of (2.3) must vanish for

$$z_2 = \left[ \frac{(\alpha_2 - \alpha_1)}{2} z_1 + z_1^2 \right] \frac{2}{(\alpha_1 + \alpha_2)} , \quad \text{if } \alpha_1 + \alpha_2 \neq 0 \qquad (2.4)$$

at least for any values with Re $\lambda_1$ , Re $\lambda_2 \geq 0$ .

From the above description of the properties of $g^*(\ell_1, \ell_2)$ , we can anticipate that the solutions of (2.3) will have different forms for $\alpha_1 + \alpha_2 > 0$ , $\alpha_1 + \alpha_2 < 0$ , and $\alpha_1 + \alpha_2 = 0$ , corresponding respectively to $\mu_2 > \mu_0$ , $\mu_2 < \mu_0$ , and $\mu_2 = \mu_0$ . We will not analyse the case $\mu_2 = \mu_0$ separately, but treat it as a common limiting form of the two others.

The analogue of (VI 2.3) is the relation

$$\overline{K}_2 \left( \frac{-\left( \frac{\alpha_2}{2} \right)^2 + \left( \frac{\alpha_2}{2} + z_1 \right)^2}{\alpha_1 + \alpha_2} \right) = \left( \frac{\alpha_2 + z_1}{-\alpha_1 + z_1} \right) K_1^* \left( \frac{\left( \frac{\alpha_1}{2} \right)^2 - \left( -\frac{\alpha_1}{2} + z_1 \right)^2}{\alpha_1 + \alpha_2} \right) . \qquad (2.5)$$

For $\alpha_1 + \alpha_2 > 0$, the requirement that $\overline{K}_2(\lambda_1)$ be analytic and bounded for Re $\lambda_1 > 0$ means that $\overline{K}_2$, considered as a function of $z_1$, is analytic and bounded at least for

$$\text{Re}(z_1 + \alpha_2/2)^2 \quad > \quad (\alpha_2/2)^2 \quad , \tag{2.6a}$$

illustrated by the shaded area of Fig.VII-1a. That $K_1^*(\lambda_1)$ is analytic and bounded for Re $\lambda_2 > 0$ means that $K_1^*$, considered as a function of $z_1$, is analytic and bounded in the region

$$\text{Re}(z_1 - \alpha_1/2) \quad < \quad (-\alpha_1/2)^2 \tag{2.6b}$$

shown by the shaded area of Fig.VII-1b (note that $\alpha_1 < 0$). The function $K_1^*$ is also required to be real and positive along the broken lines of Fig.VII-1b and symmetric to reflections through $\alpha_1/2$.

The regions of Figs.VII-1a and 1b overlap. It is in this region of overlap where (2.5) must hold. If, however, we can analytically continue $\overline{K}_2$ and $K_1^*$ beyond these regions, (2.5) must hold also in the region of continuation. If we analytically continue $K_1^*$ throughout the region of Fig. VII-1a we see from (2.5) that $K_1^*$ must also be analytic and bounded in this region (because $K_2$ and the coefficient in (2.5) are analytic and bounded there). Since $K_1^*$ is symmetric to reflections through $\alpha_1/2$, it follows that $K_1^*$ is analytic and bounded throughout the entire $z_1$-plan It must, therefore, be a constant. From (1.1), the constant must be $(-\alpha_1)$

$$K_1^*(\lambda_2) \quad = \quad (-\alpha_1) \qquad \text{for } -\alpha_2 < \alpha_1 < 0 \quad . \tag{2.7}$$

From (VI 1.9), $K_1^*(\lambda_2)$ is interpreted as the Laplace transform with

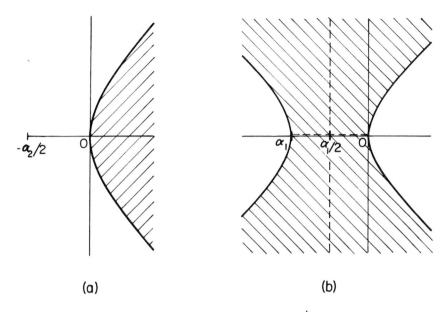

Fig. VII-1.  Regions where $\overline{K}_2$  and  $K_1^*$  are analytic.

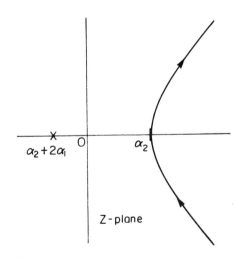

Fig. VII-2.  Path of integration in  z-plane.

322

respect to $\ell_2$ , of the joint density $g^*(c_1,\ell_2)$ evaluated along the boundary $\ell_1 = c_1$ . That this transform is a constant means that $g^*(c_1,\ell_2$ is a Dirac $\delta$-function (has a lump mass at $\ell_2 = 0$). That $g^*(c_1,\ell_2) = 0$ for $\ell_2 > 0$ is, of course, consistent with the previous conclusions that $g^*(\ell_1,\ell_2)$ should vanish for all $\ell_1$, $\ell_2$ with $\ell_1 + \ell_2 > c_1$ , if $\mu_0 \leq$ $\mu_2$ $(\alpha_1 + \alpha_2 > 0)$.

   Substitution of (2.7) into (2.5) gives

$$\overline{K}_2\left(\frac{-\left(\frac{\alpha_2}{2}\right)^2 + \left(\frac{\alpha_2}{2} + z_1\right)^2}{\alpha_1 + \alpha_2}\right) = (-\alpha_1)\frac{(\alpha_2 + z_1)}{(-\alpha_1+z_1)} \quad \text{for } -\alpha_2 < \alpha_1 < 0 . \quad (2.7a)$$

   From the symmetry between customers and holes, a system with $\mu_0 \leq \mu_2$ $(\alpha_1 + \alpha_2 \geq 0)$ is equivalent to one with $\mu_2$ and $\mu_0$ interchanged so that $\mu_2 \leq \mu_0$ $(\alpha_1 + \alpha_2 \leq 0)$, but with $Q_1'$ , $Q_2$ replaced by $Q_2'$ , $Q_1$ . In (2.5) this symmetry emerges from the fact that an interchange of $\mu_0$ and $\mu_2$ is equivalent to replacing $\alpha_1$ by $-\alpha_2$ ; $-(\alpha_1 + \alpha_2)$ by $+(\alpha_1+\alpha_2)$ This, in effect, reverses the roles of $\overline{K}_2$ and $K_1^*$ . If $\mu_0 = \mu_2$ $(\alpha_1 = -\alpha_2)$, the coefficient in (2.5) becomes 1 and (2.7a) implies that $\overline{K}_2$ is also a constant, in fact, $\overline{K}_2 = K_1^*$ . It suffices to consider only the case $\alpha_1 + \alpha_2 \geq 0$ .

   Since the marginal distributions $g_1^*(\ell_1)$ and $g_2^*(\ell_2)$ are already known from (1.1a), (1.2a), our goal here is to determine the joint distribution $g^*(\ell_1,\ell_2)$ . By substituting (2.7) and (2.7a) into (2.2), one can show that

$$\overline{K}\left(\frac{-\alpha_2^2 + z^2}{4(\alpha_1+\alpha_2)}, \lambda_2\right) = \frac{4(-\alpha_1)(\alpha_1 + \alpha_2)(z + \alpha_2)}{(z - 2\alpha_1 - \alpha_2)[4\lambda_2(\alpha_1+\alpha_2) + (z+\alpha_1+\alpha_2)^2 - \alpha_1^2]} \cdot \quad (2.8)$$

If we substitute this into the inversion formula for the Laplace transform (1.3)

$$g^*(c_1-\ell_1',\ell_2) = \frac{1}{(2\pi i)^2} \int_{-i\infty}^{+i\infty} d\lambda_1 \int_{-i\infty}^{+i\infty} d\lambda_2 \ \overline{K}(\lambda_1,\lambda_2) \ \exp(\lambda_1\ell_1' + \lambda_2\ell_2)$$

we can immediately perform the $\lambda_2$ integration since (2.8) has only a simple pole as a function of $\lambda_2$. For any imaginary value of $\lambda_1$, this pole is in the left-half $\lambda_2$-plane, consequently

$$g^*(c_1-\ell_1',\ell_2) = 0 \qquad \text{for } \ell_2 < 0 , \qquad (2.9a)$$

as it should.

For $\ell_2 > 0$, we change the variable of integration from $\lambda_1$ to z,

$$\lambda_1 = \frac{-\alpha_2^2 + z^2}{4(\alpha_1 + \alpha_2)} , \qquad (2.9b)$$

and perform the $\lambda_2$ integration to obtain

$$g^*(c_1-\ell_1',\ell_2) = \frac{(-\alpha_1)}{4\pi i(\alpha_1+\alpha_2)} \int dz \frac{z(z + \alpha_2)}{(z-2\alpha_1-\alpha_2)} \exp\left\{\ell_1'\left[\frac{-\alpha_2^2 + z^2}{4(\alpha_1+\alpha_2)}\right] + \ell_2\left[\frac{\alpha_1^2-(z+\alpha_1+\alpha_2)^2}{4(\alpha_1 + \alpha_2)}\right]\right\} ,$$

$$(2.9c)$$

in which the path of integration, $\lambda_1$ going from $-i\infty$ to $+i\infty$, maps into a hyperbolic curve crossing the real z axis at $\alpha_2$, as in Fig. VII-2 to the right of the pole singularity at $\alpha_2 + 2\alpha_1$.

The exponential factor in (2.9c) can be rearranged into the form

$$\exp\left\{\frac{(\ell_1' - \ell_2)}{4(\alpha_1 + \alpha_2)}\left[z - \frac{\ell_2(\alpha_1 + \alpha_2)}{(\ell_1' - \ell_2)}\right]^2 - \frac{(\ell_2\alpha_1 + \ell_1'\alpha_2)^2}{4(\alpha_1 + \alpha_2)(\ell_1' - \ell_2)}\right\} \ .$$

If $\ell_2 > \ell_1'$ , the integrand of (2.9c) vanishes for $z \to +\infty$ . The path of integration can be closed by a large arc in the right-half z-plane. Since the closed path encloses no singularities, the integral must vanish, i.e.,

$$g^*(c_1 - \ell_1', \ell_2) \quad = \quad 0 \qquad \text{for } \ell_2 > \ell_1' \ , \qquad (2.10)$$

again in accord with our previous conclusions.

For $\ell_2 < \ell_1'$ , the integrand of (2.9c) becomes infinite on an arc at $\infty$ in the right-half plane so we cannot close the path of integration. Instead, we deform it to a vertical contour through the point $\dfrac{\ell_2(\alpha_1 + \alpha_2)}{(\ell_1' - \ell_2)}$ ; let

$$z \quad = \quad \frac{(\alpha_1 + \alpha_2)\ell_2}{(\ell_1' - \ell_2)} \quad + \quad i\,u \quad , \quad -\infty < u < +\infty \ .$$

If by deforming the contour in this way, we move the path to the left of the singularity at $\alpha_2 + 2\alpha_1$ , we must add to the integral the residue from the pole at $\alpha_2 + 2\alpha_1$ . For

$$(\alpha_1 + \alpha_2)\ell_2/(\ell_1' - \ell_2) \quad > \quad \alpha_2 + 2\alpha_1 \qquad (2.11)$$

(2.9c) can be written in the form

$$g^*(c_1 - \ell_1', \ell_2) = \frac{(-\alpha_1)}{4\pi(\alpha_1 + \alpha_2)} \exp\left[\frac{-(\ell_2\alpha_1 + \ell_1'\alpha_2)^2}{4(\alpha_1 + \alpha_2)(\ell_1' - \ell_2)}\right]$$

$$\cdot \int_{-\infty}^{+\infty} du \exp\left[\frac{-(\ell_1' - \ell_2)u^2}{4(\alpha_1 + \alpha_2)}\right]\left[\frac{2(2\alpha_1 + \alpha_2)(\alpha_1 + \alpha_2)}{iu - 2\alpha_1 - \alpha_2 + (\alpha_1 + \alpha_2)\ell_2/(\ell_1' - \ell_2)} + \frac{(\alpha_1 + \alpha_2)(2\ell_1' - \ell_2)}{(\ell_1' - \ell_2)} + iu\right].$$

The integral from $-\infty$ to $0$ is the complex conjugate of that from $0$ to $\infty$ , so the integrand can be replaced by its real part. The first term of the integral can be evaluated in terms of the error integral; the second term is elementary, and the third term contributes nothing. The result is

$$g^*(c_1 - \ell_1', \ell_2) = \frac{(-\alpha_1)(2\ell_1' - \ell_2)(\alpha_1 + \alpha_2)^{\frac{1}{2}}}{2\pi^{1/2}(\ell_1' - \ell_2)^{3/2}} \exp\left[\frac{-(\ell_2\alpha_1 + \ell_1'\alpha_2)^2}{4(\alpha_1 + \alpha_2)(\ell_1' - \ell_2)}\right]$$

$$\text{(2.12)}$$

$$+ (-\alpha_1)(2\alpha_1 + \alpha_2)\exp[-\ell_2(2\alpha_1 + \alpha_2) + \ell_1'\alpha_1]\,\Phi\left(\frac{-[\ell_2(\alpha_1 + \alpha_2) - (\ell_1' - \ell_2)(2\alpha_1 + \alpha_2)]}{(\ell_1' - \ell_2)^{1/2}(\alpha_1 + \alpha_2)^{1/2}\sqrt{2}}\right).$$

$$\text{for } 0 \leq \ell_2 < \ell_1'$$

An evaluation of (2.9c) when (2.11) is not true, i.e., the path is deformed to the left of the singularity, shows that (2.12) is still valid.

It is possible to integrate (2.12) with respect to $\ell_1'$ or $\ell_2$ and verify that the contributions from the two terms of (2.12) conveniently combine to give the simple exponential marginal distributions for $Q_1'$ or $Q_2$ , but this does not help very much in describing the shape of (2.12).

326

The distribution (2.12) can be interpreted as a function of two dimensionless coordinates, for example, $\alpha_2 \ell_1'$ and $\alpha_2 \ell_2$, and one extra parameter such as $(\alpha_1 + \alpha_2)/\alpha_2$. It is rather difficult to show the nature of this distribution graphically, but it is possible to describe some qualitative properties for various limiting situations.

We know that for $\alpha_1 + \alpha_2 \to 0$, the distribution should behave like a one-dimensional distribution along the line $\ell_1' = \ell_2$. To describe the behavior of $g^*(c_1 - \ell_1', \ell_2)$ for $2\alpha_1 + \alpha_2 < 0$ but particularly for $\alpha_1 + \alpha_2 \ll (-\alpha_1)$, it is convenient to write (2.12) in the form

$$g^*(c_1 - \ell_1', \ell_2) = -\alpha_1 \exp[-\ell_2(\alpha_1 + \alpha_2) + (\ell_1' - \ell_2)\alpha_1]$$

$$\cdot \left\{ \frac{(2\ell_1' - \ell_2)(\alpha_1 + \alpha_2)^{1/2}}{2\pi^{1/2}(\ell_1' - \ell_2)^{3/2}} \exp\left(-\frac{w^2}{2}\right) + (2\alpha_1 + \alpha_2)\, \Phi(-w) \right\} , \qquad (2.12a)$$

with

$$w \equiv \frac{\ell_2(\alpha_1 + \alpha_2) - (\ell_1' - \ell_2)(2\alpha_1 + \alpha_2)}{(\ell_1' - \ell_2)^{1/2}(\alpha_1 + \alpha_2)^{1/2} 2^{1/2}} . \qquad (2.13)$$

For $2\alpha_1 + \alpha_2 < 0$ we can also write $w$ in the form

$$w = \left[\frac{-\ell_2(2\alpha_1 + \alpha_2)}{2}\right]^{\frac{1}{2}} \left\{ \left[\frac{\ell_2(\alpha_1 + \alpha_2)}{-(2\alpha_1 + \alpha_2)(\ell_1' - \ell_2)}\right]^{\frac{1}{2}} + \left[\frac{-(2\alpha_1 + \alpha_2)(\ell_1' - \ell_2)}{\ell_2(\alpha_1 + \alpha_2)}\right]^{\frac{1}{2}} \right\} .$$

$$\qquad (2.13a)$$

If $(\alpha_1 + \alpha_2) \ll -(2\alpha_1 + \alpha_2)$, the variation of $g^*$ with $\ell_1' - \ell_2$ is very rapid and is determined mainly by the dependence of $w$ on $\ell_1' - \ell_2$. The second factor of (2.13a) is of the form $(x + 1/x)$, which is positive for all  x  and has a minimum at  x = 1 ,  i.e.,

$$w = [-2\ell_2(2\alpha_1 + \alpha_2)]^{1/2} \tag{2.14}$$

for

$$\ell_2(\alpha_1 + \alpha_2) = -(2\alpha_1 + \alpha_2)(\ell_1' - \ell_2) . \tag{2.14a}$$

Since the marginal distributions of  $Q_1'$ , $Q_2$  are exponential with means of  $(-\alpha_1)^{-1}$  and  $\alpha_2^{-1}$ ,  respectively, we expect, for $\alpha_2 \simeq -\alpha_1$ , that most of the probability mass will lie in a range with  $-(2\alpha_1 + \alpha_2)\ell_2$ $\simeq \alpha_2\ell_2$  comparable with 1.  For a fixed value of $\alpha_2\ell_2$  comparable with 1,  w  will become larger than (2.14) by an amount comparable with 1 if $\ell_1' - \ell_2$  deviates from (2.14) by an amount such that

$$\left| \frac{\ell_2(\alpha_1 + \alpha_2)}{-(2\alpha_1 + \alpha_2)(\ell_1' - \ell_2)} - 1 \right| \tag{2.15}$$

is comparable with 1.  In view of the manner in which  w  enters (2.12a), it is clear that the important range of  $\ell_1' - \ell_2$  is confined to a narrow strip about the line (2.14a) having a width of order  $-(\alpha_1+\alpha_2)\ell_2/(2\alpha_1+\alpha_2)$ $\ll \ell_2$ ,  at least for $\alpha_2\ell_2$  comparable with 1.

In Fig. VII-3, the solid line represents (2.14a).  It has a slope only slightly different from the 45° line  $\ell_1' = \ell_2$ .  Along the line  $\ell_1' = \ell_2$ shown by the  thin  solid  line,  $g^*$  must vanish, but it also must be relatively small as  $\ell_1' - \ell_2$  deviates from the solid line by a comparable distance on the lower side.

For  $\alpha_1 + \alpha_2 \ll (-\alpha_1)$ , $\ell_1'$ , $\ell_2$  in the cone between the broken lines of Fig. VII-3 and  $\alpha_2\ell_2$  comparable with 1, the first exponential factor of (2.12a) is approximately 1 and the second term of (2.12a) is small

328

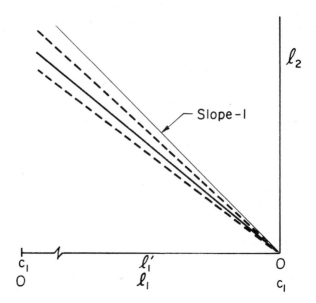

Fig. VII-3. For $\Delta_0 = \Delta_2 = 0$ and $\mu_0$ close to $\mu_2$, the joint probability density of $Q_1$, $Q_2$ is concentrated between the broken lines.

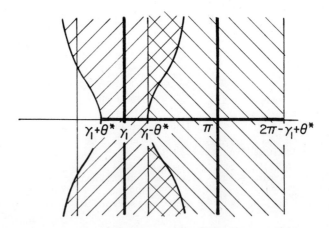

Fig. VII-4. Regions of the $\theta_1$-plane where $K_1^{*\dagger}$ and $\overline{K}_2^{\dagger}$ are analytic.

compared with the first term. We can approximate (2.12a) by the simpler

expression

$$g^*(c_1 - \ell_1', \ell_2) \simeq \frac{\alpha_2 \ell_2 (\alpha_1 + \alpha_2)^{1/2}}{2\pi^{1/2} (\ell_1' - \ell_2)^{3/2}} \exp\left\{ -\frac{\alpha_2 \ell_2}{4} \left[ \frac{\ell_2 (\alpha_1 + \alpha_2)}{\alpha_2 (\ell_1' - \ell_2)} + \frac{\alpha_2 (\ell_1' - \ell_2)}{\ell_2 (\alpha_1 + \alpha_2)} + 2 \right] \right\} .$$

$$(2.16)$$

This formula is valid also for $\alpha_2 \ell_2 \gg 1$ ; it is inaccurate only

for $\alpha_2 \ell_2 < \alpha_2 \ell_1' \lesssim (\alpha_1 + \alpha_2)/\alpha_2 \ll 1$ where the behavior of (2.12a) is

quite violent and the second term is of comparable size to the first.

Except for these small values of $\alpha_2 \ell_1'$ , $\alpha_2 \ell_2$ , the behavior of the ex-

ponential factor in (2.14a) or (2.16) is described more accurately by the

observation that, near the line (2.14a), the exponential can be expanded

in the form

$$-\frac{\alpha_2 \ell_2}{4} \left[ \frac{\ell_2 (\alpha_1 + \alpha_2)}{\alpha_2 (\ell_1' - \ell_2)} + \frac{\alpha_2 (\ell_1' - \ell_2)}{\ell_2 (\alpha_1 + \alpha_2)} + 2 \right] \simeq -\alpha_2 \ell_2 - \frac{\alpha_2 \ell_2}{4} \left[ \frac{\alpha_2 (\ell_1' - \ell_2)}{\ell_2 (\alpha_1 + \alpha_2)} - 1 \right]^2 + -- .$$

$$(2.17)$$

This shows that the distribution $g^*$ actually has an effective

width about the line (2.14a) of approximately

$$\frac{2\ell_2 (\alpha_1 + \alpha_2)}{\alpha_2 (\alpha_2 \ell_2)^{1/2}} \simeq \frac{2 (\alpha_1 + \alpha_2)}{\alpha_2} \frac{(\alpha_2 \ell_2)^{\frac{1}{2}}}{\alpha_2}$$

$$(2.18)$$

rather than a width of about $(\alpha_1 + \alpha_2)\ell_2/\alpha_2$ as described by the cone of

Fig. VII-3. These two expressions for the width are comparable if $(\alpha_2 \ell_2)$

is comparable with 1 , but for large $(\alpha_2 \ell_2)$, (2.18) shows that the width is much narrower than the cone; the width grows like $\ell_2^{1/2}$ rather than $\ell_2$ .

In the vicinity of the line

$$\ell_2(\alpha_1 + \alpha_2) \;\simeq\; \alpha_2(\ell_1' - \ell_2) \tag{2.19}$$

$$g^*(c_1 - \ell_1', \ell_2) \;\simeq\; [\alpha_2 \exp(-\alpha_2 \ell_2)] \,\frac{\alpha_2^{3/2}}{2\pi^{1/2}\ell_2^{1/2}(\alpha_1+\alpha_2)}\; \exp\left( \frac{-\alpha_2 \ell_2}{4}\left[ \frac{\alpha_2(\ell_1'-\ell_2)}{\ell_2(\alpha_1+\alpha_2)} - 1 \right]^2 \right)$$

The first factor describes the marginal distribution of $Q_1'$ or $Q_2$ , the other factors describe the narrow distribution around this line. On the line itself, $g^*$ decays like $\ell_2^{-1/2}\exp(-\alpha_2\ell_2)$ with the $\ell_2^{-1/2}$ originating from the fact that the width of the distribution increases like $\ell_2^{1/2}$.

In the limit $\alpha_1 + \alpha_2 \to 0$ , the distribution (2.19) does approach a distribution concentrated along (near) the line $\ell_1' = \ell_2$ , and, furthermore, for $\alpha_1 \to 0$ , $\alpha_2 \to 0$ , it "approaches" the uniform distribution along this line described in Chapter IV, in the sense that one would obtain a slowly decaying exponential distribution in $\ell_2$ if one integrated the distribution over its narrow (but $\ell_2$-dependent) width.

The detailed mathematical form of $g^*$ , which is given explicitly by (2.12), is not of very much practical value in itself. It is of interest mainly through the expectation that it may give some clues as to how one might solve more general cases (with $\Delta_0$ , $\Delta_2 > 0$) and what effect a finite but "large" value of $c_1$ or $c_2$ would have on the overall service rate (the blocking effect). There is one special case of (2.12), however, which is relatively simple. This is for

$$2\alpha_1 + \alpha_2 = 0 \qquad \text{i.e.,} \quad \mu_1 + \mu_2 = 2\mu_0 \; .$$

The second term of (2.12) vanishes and

$$g^*(c_1 - \ell_1', \ell_2) = \frac{(\alpha_2/2)^{3/2}(2\ell_1' - \ell_2)}{2\pi^{1/2}(\ell_1' - \ell_2)^{3/2}} \exp\left[-\frac{(2\ell_1' - \ell_2)^2(\alpha_2/2)}{4(\ell_1' - \ell_2)}\right] \; .$$

. Joint Distributions for $\Delta_0$, $\Delta_2 > 0$. To analyse the properties of $g^*(\ell_1, \ell_2)$ or $\overline{K}(\lambda_1, \lambda_2)$ for $\Delta_0$, $\Delta_2 \to 0$; $c_1$, $c_2 \to \infty$; and $\mu_1 < \mu_0$, $\mu_2$, one can mimic the methods used in Chapter VI, sections 4 and 5. We shall, therefore, only sketch the main points following the same order of presentation as before.

The transformation of variables VI (4.1), (4.2) was designed to convert the quadratic form VI (4.6) into (4.6a). The corresponding quadratic form (1.4) differs from VI (4.6) only in that $\lambda_1$ is changed to $-\lambda_1$. Consequently, we need only change the sign of $\lambda_1$ in VI (4.1) to achieve the same conversion of (1.4) into VI (4.6a). Thus we replace VI (4.1) by

$$-\lambda_1 = \mu^\dagger \Delta^{*-3/2} (\Delta_1 + \Delta_2)^{1/2} [\cos\theta_1 - \cos(\theta^* - \gamma_1)] \qquad (3.1)$$

but retain the same form for $\lambda_2$, namely VI (4.2). The definition of $\theta^*$ remains as in VI (4.4) but, with $\mu_1 < \mu_0$, $\mu_2$, $\theta^*$ is negative, and condition VI (4.4a) is replaced by

$$-\pi \leq -(\gamma_0 + \gamma_2) \leq \theta^* \leq 0 \qquad . \qquad (3.2)$$

Since, with (1.4) written in terms of $\theta_1$, $\theta_2$ as in VI (4.6a), the left-hand side of (1.4) vanishes for $\theta_1 = \theta_2$, we obtain, as the analogue of VI (4.8), a relation between $\overline{K}_2(\lambda_1)$ and $K_1^*(\lambda_2)$ when $\theta_1 =$ $\theta_2$, namely

$$(\Delta_1 + \Delta_2)^{\frac{1}{2}} [\cos(\theta_1 - \gamma_1) - \cos\theta^*] \, \overline{K}_2^{\dagger}(\theta_1) \;=\; (\Delta_0 + \Delta_1)^{\frac{1}{2}} [\cos\theta_1 - \cos(\theta^* - \gamma_1)] K_1^{*\dagger}(\theta_1)$$

$$(3.3)$$

in which

$$\overline{K}_2^{\dagger}(\theta_1) \;\equiv\; \overline{K}_2(\lambda_1(\theta_1)) \quad \text{and} \quad K_1^{*\dagger}(\theta_1) \;=\; K_1^*(\lambda_2(\theta_2))|_{\theta_1 = \theta_2}$$

and $\lambda_2(\theta_2)|_{\theta_1 = \theta_2}$ is still as in VI (4.9).

Again, as in VI (4.8), both sides of (3.3) vanish for $\theta_1 = \gamma_1 - \theta^*$ where $\lambda_1(\theta_1) = \lambda_2(\theta_1) = 0$. Since both sides of (3.3) must be analytic in some neighborhood of $\theta_1 = \gamma_1 - \theta^*$, we can factor $\sin([\theta_1 + \theta^* - \gamma_1]/2)$ from both sides and reduce (3.3) to

$$(\Delta_1 + \Delta_2)^{\frac{1}{2}} \sin\left(\frac{\theta_1 - \gamma_1 - \theta^*}{2}\right) \overline{K}_2^{\dagger}(\theta_1) \;=\; (\Delta_0 + \Delta_1)^{\frac{1}{2}} \sin\left(\frac{\theta_1 + \gamma_1 - \theta^*}{2}\right) K_1^{*\dagger}(\theta_1) \quad (3.3a)$$

the analogue of VI (4.8c).

The $K_1^{*\dagger}(\theta_1)$ and $\overline{K}_2^{\dagger}(\theta_1)$ must further satisfy the conditions that, since $K_1^*(\lambda_2)$ is analytic for $\mathrm{Re}\,\lambda_2 \geq 0$,

$$K_1^{*\dagger}(\theta_1) \quad \text{is analytic for} \quad \mathrm{Re}\,\cos(\theta_1 - \gamma_1) \geq \cos\theta^*, \qquad (3.4)$$

and, since $\overline{K}_2(\lambda_1)$ is analytic for $\mathrm{Re}\,\lambda_1 \geq 0$,

$$\overline{K}_2^{\dagger}(\theta_1) \quad \text{is analytic for} \quad \mathrm{Re}\,\cos\theta_1 \leq \cos(\gamma_1 - \theta^*) \qquad (3.5)$$

at least for $\theta_1$ in the strip of the complex $\theta_1$-plane

$$0 \leq \text{Re } \theta_1 \leq \pi$$

containing the point $\theta_1 = \gamma_1 - \theta^*$ . Condition (3.4) is the same as VI (4.13) but (3.5) is the opposite of VI (4.11) (also $\theta^*$ is now negative).

That (3.4) includes the point $\theta_1 = \gamma_1$ and $\cos(\theta_1 - \gamma_1)$ is an even function of $\theta_1 - \gamma_1$ implies that $K_1^{*\dagger}(\theta_1)$ is also an even function of $\theta_1 - \gamma_1$ , i.e.,

$$K_1^{*\dagger}(\theta_1) = K_1^{*\dagger}(2\gamma_1 - \theta_1) \tag{3.6}$$

as in VI (4.14). The $\overline{K}_2^{\dagger}(\theta_1)$ is not necessarily analytic at $\theta_1 = 0$ as was $K_2^{\dagger}(\theta_1)$ in VI (4.12), but it is analytic at $\theta_1 = \pi$ , another symmetry point of $\cos \theta_1$ . Thus $\overline{K}_2^{\dagger}(\theta_1)$ must satisfy the condition

$$\overline{K}_2^{\dagger}(\theta_1) = \overline{K}_2^{\dagger}(2\pi - \theta_1) . \tag{3.7}$$

The above relations, which may initially be true only for a restricted range of $\theta_1$ , will, by analytic continuation, be true for all values of $\theta_1$ .

Since $K_1^*(\lambda_2)$ and $\overline{K}_2(\lambda_1)$ are real, positive and monotone decreasing along the positive $\lambda_2$ or $\lambda_1$ line, $K_1^{*\dagger}(\theta_1)$ must be real and positive on $\gamma_1 + \theta^* \leq \theta_1 \leq \gamma_1 - \theta^*$ and $\text{Re } \theta_1 = \gamma_1$ ; $\overline{K}_2^{\dagger}(\theta_1)$ must be real and positive on $\gamma_1 - \theta^* \leq \theta_1 \leq 2\pi - \gamma_1 + \theta^*$ and $\text{Re } \theta_1 = \pi$ . Fig. VII-4 illustrates the regions of the $\theta_1$-plane analogous to Fig. VI-5.

From the analytic continuation of $K_1^{*\dagger}(\theta_1)$ and $\overline{K}_2^{\dagger}(\theta_1)$ , it follows that the only singularity of $\overline{K}_2^{\dagger}(\theta_1)$ in the strip $\gamma_1 + \theta^* \leq \text{Re } \theta_1 \leq \pi$ is a simple pole at $\theta_1 = \gamma_1 + \theta^*$ where the coefficient of $\overline{K}_2^{\dagger}(\theta_1)$ vanishes in (3.3a), but $K_1^{*\dagger}(\gamma_1 + \theta^*)$ is positive. The only singularity of $K_1^{*\dagger}(\theta_1)$ in the strip $\gamma_1 < \text{Re } \theta_1 < 2\pi - \gamma_1$ is a simple pole at

$\theta_1 = 2\pi - \gamma_1 + \theta^*$ where the coefficient of $K_1^{*\dagger}(\theta_1)$ vanishes in (3.3a),

but $\overline{K}_2^\dagger(2\pi - \gamma_1 + \theta^*)$ is positive. Both $K_1^{*\dagger}(\theta_1)$ and $\overline{K}_2^\dagger(\theta_1)$ are ana-

lytic in the strip $\gamma_1 \leq \text{Re } \theta_1 \leq \pi$ between the two reflection points of

(3.6) and (3.7). It follows by reflection that $\overline{K}_2^\dagger(\theta_1)$ is analytic in

the strip $\gamma_1 \leq \text{Re } \theta_1 \leq 2\pi - \gamma_1$ , and $K_1^{*\dagger}(\theta_1)$ is analytic in the strip

$-\pi + 2\gamma_1 < \text{Re } \theta_1 < \pi$ ; both strips of width $2\pi - 2\gamma_1$ .

To describe the properties of the analytic continuations of $\overline{K}_2^\dagger(\theta_1)$

and $K_1^{*\dagger}(\theta_1)$ outside the above strips of width $2\pi - 2\gamma_1$ , it is con-

venient to obtain the finite difference equations analogous to VI (4.15)

and (4.15a). If we divide (3.3a) by the same equation with $\theta_1$ replaced

by $2\gamma_1 - \theta_1$ and use (3.6), (3.7), we obtain

$$\overline{K}_2^\dagger(\theta_1) = \frac{\sin\left(\dfrac{\theta_1 + \gamma_1 - \theta^*}{2}\right)\sin\left(\dfrac{\theta_1 - \gamma_1 + \theta^*}{2}\right)}{\sin\left(\dfrac{-3\gamma_1 + \theta^* + \theta_1}{2}\right)\sin\left(\dfrac{\theta_1 - \gamma_1 - \theta^*}{2}\right)} \overline{K}_2^\dagger(2\pi - 2\gamma_1 + \theta_1) \; . \qquad (3.8)$$

Correspondingly, we obtain for $K_1^{*\dagger}(\theta_1)$ the equation

$$K_1^{*\dagger}(\theta_1) = \frac{\sin\left(\dfrac{\theta_1 - \gamma_1 - \theta^*}{2}\right)\sin\left(\dfrac{\theta_1 - \gamma_1 + \theta^*}{2}\right)}{\sin\left(\dfrac{\theta_1 + \gamma_1 + \theta^*}{2}\right)\sin\left(\dfrac{\theta_1 + \gamma_1 - \theta^*}{2}\right)} K_1^{*\dagger}(\theta_1 - 2\pi + 2\gamma_1) \; . \qquad (3.9)$$

Starting from the strip of width $2\pi - 2\gamma_1$ in which each function

is known to be analytic, the above finite difference equations in steps

of $2\pi - 2\gamma_1$ will describe the zeros and poles of each function in successive strips of width $2\pi - 2\gamma_1$ on either side. We could proceed to analyse the asymptotic properties of $\overline{K}_2^{+}(\theta_1)$ and $K_1^{*+}(\theta_1)$ analogous to the procedure of section VI 4, without actually solving the equations. These equations have much simpler properties, however, than their counterparts VI (4.15) and (4.15a), and can be solved explicitly.

If we write (3.8) in the form

$$\frac{\overline{K}_2^{+}(\theta_1)}{\sin\left(\dfrac{\theta_1+\gamma_1-\theta^*}{2}\right)\sin\left(\dfrac{\theta_1-\gamma_1+\theta^*}{2}\right)} = \frac{\overline{K}_2^{+}(2\pi-2\gamma_1+\theta_1)}{\sin\left(\dfrac{2\pi-2\gamma_1+\theta_1+\gamma_1-\theta^*}{2}\right)\sin\left(\dfrac{2\pi-2\gamma_1+\theta_1-\gamma_1+\theta^*}{2}\right)}$$

(3.10)

we see that the left-hand side is the same function of $\theta_1$ as the right-hand side except for a displacement of $\theta_1$ by $2\pi - 2\gamma_1$. It follows that (3.10) must be a periodic function of $\theta_1$ with period $2\pi - 2\gamma_1$.

Since $\overline{K}_2^{+}(\theta_1)$ is analytic in the strip $\gamma_1 \leq \mathrm{Re}\ \theta_1 \leq 2\pi - \gamma_1$; $\overline{K}_2^{+}(2\pi - 2\gamma_1 + \theta_1)$ is analytic for $-2\pi + 3\gamma_1 \leq \mathrm{Re}\ \theta_1 \leq \gamma_1$. The right-hand side of (3.10), therefore, has singularities (simple poles) only at $\theta_1 = \gamma_1 + \theta^*$ and $-2\pi + 3\gamma_1 - \theta^*$ in the strip $-2\pi + 3\gamma_1 \leq \mathrm{Re}\ \theta_1 \leq \gamma_1$. Because of the periodicity, (3.10) has simple poles at

$$\theta_1 = \gamma_1 + \theta^* + j(2\pi - 2\gamma_1) \quad \text{and} \quad \gamma_1 - \theta^* + j(2\pi - 2\gamma_1)$$

for integer values of $j$. Consequently,

$$\frac{\overline{K}_2^{+}(\theta_1)\ \sin\left(\dfrac{\theta_1-\gamma_1-\theta^*}{2(1-\gamma_1/\pi)}\right)\sin\left(\dfrac{\theta_1-\gamma_1+\theta^*}{2(1-\gamma_1/\pi)}\right)}{\sin\left(\dfrac{\theta_1+\gamma_1-\theta^*}{2}\right)\sin\left(\dfrac{\theta_1-\gamma_1+\theta^*}{2}\right)}$$

(3.11)

is analytic for all $\theta_1$ and periodic. It can be expanded in a Fourier series of period $2\pi - 2\gamma_1$ , but, by analysing the behavior of the Fourier series for $\mathrm{Im}\ \theta_1 \to \infty$ , one can show that all terms except the constant term lead to improper singularities in the probability densities. We conclude that this function is a constant (relative to $\theta_1$).

From (1.2) we know the value of $K_2(0) = \overline{K}_2(0)$

$$\overline{K}_2(0) = \overline{K}_2^\dagger(\gamma_1 - \theta^*) = 2(\mu_2 - \mu_1)/(\Delta_1 + \Delta_2) \ .$$

Consequently we can evaluate the constant value of (3.11) and determine $\overline{K}_2^\dagger(\theta_1)$ ,

$$\overline{K}_2^\dagger(\theta_1) \ = \ \frac{- 2\ \mu^\dagger\ \sin\left(\dfrac{\theta^*}{1 - \gamma_1/\pi}\right)\ \sin\left(\dfrac{\theta_1 + \gamma_1 - \theta^*}{2}\right)\ \sin\left(\dfrac{\theta_1 - \gamma_1 + \theta^*}{2}\right)}{(\Delta_1 + \Delta_2)^{1/2}\ \Delta^{*1/2}\ (1 - \gamma_1/\pi)\sin\left(\dfrac{\theta_1 - \gamma_1 - \theta^*}{2(1 - \gamma_1/\pi)}\right)\ \sin\left(\dfrac{\theta_1 - \gamma_1 + \theta^*}{2(1 - \gamma_1/\pi)}\right)}\ .$$

$$(3.12)$$

One could determine $K_1^{*\dagger}(\theta_1)$ by a similar procedure starting from (3.9), but it can also be obtained from substitution of (3.12) into (3.3a)

$$K_1^{*\dagger}(\theta_1) \ = \ \frac{- 2\ \mu^\dagger\ \sin\left(\dfrac{\theta^*}{1 - \gamma_1/\pi}\right)\ \sin\left(\dfrac{\theta_1 - \gamma_1 - \theta^*}{2}\right)\ \sin\left(\dfrac{\theta_1 - \gamma_1 + \theta^*}{2}\right)}{(\Delta_0 + \Delta_1)^{1/2}\ \Delta^{*1/2}\ (1 - \gamma_1/\pi)\ \sin\left(\dfrac{\theta_1 - \gamma_1 - \theta^*}{2(1 - \gamma_1/\pi)}\right)\ \sin\left(\dfrac{\theta_1 - \gamma_1 + \theta^*}{2(1 - \gamma_1/\pi)}\right)}\ .$$

$$(3.13)$$

From these explicit formulas for $\overline{K}_2^\dagger(\theta_1)$ and $K_1^{*\dagger}(\theta_1)$ , one can, through substitution of (3.1) and VI(4.9), evaluate $\overline{K}_2(\lambda_1)$ and $K_1^*(\lambda_2)$

and, from these and (1.4), evaluate $\bar{K}(\lambda_1,\lambda_2)$ . Moments of $Q_1'$ , $Q_2$ can be evaluated explicitly from derivatives of $\bar{K}(\lambda_1,\lambda_2)$ evaluated at $\lambda_1$ , $\lambda_2 \to 0$ . The first moments, however, are already known from (1.1b) and (1.2b) and all higher moments of $Q_1'$ or $Q_2$ alone are easily found from the marginal distributions of $Q_1'$ , $Q_2$ in (1.1a) and (1.2a). One needs $\bar{K}(\lambda_1,\lambda_2)$ only for the cross-moments , $E\{Q_1'^{\ell}Q_2^m\}$ with $\ell$, $m \geq 1$, particularly the covariance. The evaluation of these moments, even the covariance, is quite tedious however. Actually we are more interested in the analytic properties of $g^*(c_1-\ell_1',\ell_2)$ , particularly those for large or small values of $c_1 - \ell_1'$ and $\ell_2$ .

Although it is possible to write an explicit formula for $\bar{K}(\lambda_1,\lambda_2)$, the formula is quite cumbersome. The main analytic complication arises from the fact that the denominator of (3.12) or (3.13) contains

$$2 \sin\left(\frac{\theta_1 - \gamma_1 - \theta^*}{2(1 - \gamma_1/\pi)}\right) \sin\left(\frac{\theta_1 - \gamma_1 + \theta^*}{2(1 - \gamma_1/\pi)}\right) = -\cos\left(\frac{\theta_1 - \gamma_1}{1 - \gamma_1/\pi}\right) + \cos\left(\frac{\theta^*}{1 - \gamma_1/\pi}\right)$$

$$(3.14)$$

whereas the formulas relating $\theta_1$ to $\lambda_1$ and $\lambda_2$ involve $\cos\theta_1$ and $\cos(\theta_1-\gamma_1)$ , respectively. If one tried to write (3.14) as an algebraic function of $\lambda_1$ or $\lambda_2$ , it would involve the $1/(1-\gamma_1/\pi)$th power of the roots of a quadratic equation and have a variety of branch point singularities.

There is one exception. If $\gamma_1 = \pi/2$ $(\Delta_1 = 0)$, (3.14) contains $\cos 2(\theta_1-\gamma_1) = -\cos 2\theta_1 = -2\cos^2\theta_1 + 1$ which can be written as a quadratic function of $\lambda_1$ or $\lambda_2$ . One can readily verify that $\bar{K}(\lambda_1,\lambda_2)$ is not only a rational function of $\lambda_1$ , $\lambda_2$ but also a simple product of a function of $\lambda_1$ and of $\lambda_2$ . Therefore $g^*(c_1-\ell_1',\ell_2)$ is a product of the two marginal distributions (1.1a) and (1.2a) for $\Delta_1 = 0$ , i.e., $Q_1'$ and $Q_2$ are statistically independent.

This result for $\Delta_1 = 0$ is not surprising. Server 1 has an arbitrarily large queue $c_1 - Q_1'$ with $c_1 \to \infty$ and is, therefore, always busy. For $\Delta_1 = 0$ , server 1 contributes nothing to the fluctuations in $Q_1'$ or $Q_2$ . The distribution of $Q_1'$ is generated entirely from the variations in service from server 0, that of $Q_2$ entirely from the variations in service from server 2; but servers 0 and 2 behave independently. Any statistical dependence between $Q_1'$ and $Q_2$ is generated from the fact that a variation in the service rate of server 1 influences both $Q_1'$ and $Q_2$ (they are positively correlated).

From (3.12) and (3.13) we can easily see that for Im $\theta_1 \to \pm \infty$

$$\overline{K}_2^{\dagger}(\theta_1) \simeq \frac{\mu^{\dagger} \sin(-\theta^*/(1 - \gamma_1/\pi))}{(\Delta_1 + \Delta_2)^{1/2} \Delta^{*1/2} (1 - \gamma_1/\pi)} \exp[\pm i(\theta_1 - \pi)\gamma_1/(\pi-\gamma_1)] \qquad (3.15a$$

and

$$K_1^{*\dagger}(\theta_1) \simeq \frac{\mu^{\dagger} \sin(-\theta^*/(1 - \gamma_1/\pi))}{(\Delta_0 + \Delta_1)^{1/2} \Delta^{*1/2} (1 - \gamma_1/\pi)} \exp[\pm i(\theta_1 - \gamma_1)\gamma_1/(\pi-\gamma_1)] \ , \quad (3.15$$

which are analogous to VI(4.21a), (4.21b). Since from (3.1) and VI(4.9) we have

$$\exp[\mp i(\theta_1 - \pi)] \simeq \frac{2 \lambda_1 \Delta^{*3/2}}{\mu^{\dagger}(\Delta_1 + \Delta_2)^{1/2}} \ , \quad \exp[\mp i(\theta_1 - \gamma_1)] \simeq \frac{2 \lambda_2 \Delta^{*3/2}}{\mu^{\dagger}(\Delta_0 + \Delta_1)^{1/2}} \ ,$$

we can also express these in terms of $\lambda_1$ , $\lambda_2$ . For $\lambda_1$ , $\lambda_2 \to \infty$

$$\overline{K}_2(\lambda_1) \simeq \frac{2\mu^\dagger \sin(-\theta^*/(1-\gamma_1/\pi))}{(\Delta_1+\Delta_2)^{1/2}\Delta^{*1/2}(1-\gamma_1/\pi)}\left(\frac{\mu^\dagger}{2\Delta^{*3/2}}\right)^{\gamma_1/(\pi-\gamma_1)}\left(\frac{(\Delta_1+\Delta_2)^{\frac{1}{2}}}{\lambda_1}\right)^{\gamma_1/(\pi-\gamma_1)},$$

(3.16a)

$$K_1^*(\lambda_2) \simeq \frac{2\mu^\dagger \sin(-\theta^*/(1-\gamma_1/\pi))}{(\Delta_0+\Delta_1)^{1/2}\Delta^{*1/2}(1-\gamma_1/\pi)}\left(\frac{\mu^\dagger}{2\Delta^{*3/2}}\right)^{\gamma_1/(\pi-\gamma_1)}\left(\frac{(\Delta_0+\Delta_1)^{\frac{1}{2}}}{\lambda_2}\right)^{\gamma_1/(\pi-\gamma_1)}.$$

(3.16b)

This behavior of $\overline{K}_2(\lambda_1)$ , $K_1^*(\lambda_2)$ merely reconfirms what we already anticipated at the end of section VI 4. Substitution of (3.16a,b) into (1.4) shows that for $|\lambda_1|$, $|\lambda_2| \to \infty$ , $\overline{K}(\lambda_1,\lambda_2)$ becomes a homogeneous function of degree $-\pi/(\pi-\gamma_1)$ in $\lambda_1$ , $\lambda_2$ . This, in turn, implies that for $c_1 - \ell_1'$ , $\ell_2 \to 0$ , $g^*(c_1 - \ell_1', \ell_2)$ becomes a homogeneous function of degree $-(1-2\gamma_1/\pi)/(1-\gamma_1/\pi)$ in $\ell_1'$ , $\ell_2$ . This is the same type of singular behavior described by III (6.9) for $\mu_0 = \mu_1 = \mu_2$ . Equation (1.4) also describes the angular dependence of $g^*(c_1-\ell_1',\ell_2)$ near this corner; this also agrees with III (6.9).

From (3.16a,b), one can determine not only the nature of the singularity in $g^*(c_1-\ell_1', \ell_2)$ but the amplitude as well. From (1.4), we can write, for $|\lambda_1|$, $|\lambda_2| \to \infty$

$$\overline{K}(\lambda_1,\lambda_2) \simeq \frac{\lambda_2(\Delta_1+\Delta_2)\overline{K}_2(\lambda_1)+\lambda_1(\Delta_0+\Delta_1)K_1^*(\lambda_2)}{\Delta_0\lambda_1^2+\Delta_1(\lambda_1+\lambda_2)^2+\Delta_2\lambda_2^2}$$

(3.17a)

and

$$g^*(c_1-\ell_1',\ell_2) = \frac{1}{(2\pi i)^2}\int_{-i\infty}^{+i\infty}d\lambda_1\int_{-i\infty}^{+i\infty}d\lambda_2\,\overline{K}(\lambda_1,\lambda_2)\exp(\lambda_1\ell_1'+\lambda_2\ell_2).$$

(3.17b)

The $\bar{K}_2(\lambda_1)$ and $K_1^*(\lambda_2)$ have been chosen so as to guarantee that the numerator of (3.17a) vanishes whenever the denominator vanishes; consequently there is no singularity of $\bar{K}(\lambda_1,\lambda_2)$ induced by the denominator vanishing. Since, however, one term of the numerator has a branch point in $\lambda_1$ and the other a branch point in $\lambda_2$, it is convenient to separate the two terms of (3.17a) and integrate the first term initially with respect to $\lambda_2$ and the second term initially with respect to $\lambda_1$. With the two terms separated, the first term has, for any fixed $\lambda_1$, two poles in the $\lambda_2$-space; the second term has, for any fixed $\lambda_2$, two poles in the $\lambda_1$-space, both created where the denominator of (3.17a) vanishes. The denominator of (3.17a) vanishes when

$$\frac{\lambda_1}{(\Delta_1 + \Delta_2)^{1/2}} \frac{(\Delta_0 + \Delta_1)^{1/2}}{\lambda_2} = \exp(\pm i(\pi-\gamma_1)) \quad . \quad (3.18)$$

If the integrals with respect to $\lambda_1$ and $\lambda_2$ in (3.17b) both follow a path up the imaginary axis, then, for any imaginary value of $\lambda_1$, one of the roots (3.18) lies in the right-half $\lambda_2$-plane and the other in the left-half plane. Similarly, for any imaginary value of $\lambda_2$, one of the roots (3.18) lies in the right-half $\lambda_1$-plane and the other in the left-half plane. If, in evaluating the $\lambda_2$ integration of the first term of (3.17a) (or the $\lambda_1$ integration of the second term), we close the contour by a large semi-circle in the left-half $\lambda_2$-plane (or $\lambda_1$-plane), the integrand vanishes on the semi-circle (because $\ell_1'$, $\ell_2 > 0$) and the contour encloses only one of the two poles.

The first term of (3.17b) will contain an integral of the form

$$\frac{1}{2\pi i} \int_{-i\infty}^{+i\infty} d\lambda_2 \; \frac{\lambda_2 \exp(\lambda_1 \ell_1' + \lambda_2 \ell_2)}{(\lambda_2 - \lambda_2^{(-)})(\lambda_2 - \lambda_2^{(+)})} \tag{3.19}$$

in which $\lambda_2^{(-)}$ and $\lambda_2^{(+)}$ are the roots of the denominator in the left-half and right-half plane respectively.

$$\left.\begin{array}{c} \lambda_2^{(\mp)} \\ \\ \\ \lambda_2^{(\pm)} \end{array}\right\} = \lambda_1 \left[\frac{\Delta_0 + \Delta_1}{\Delta_1 + \Delta_2}\right]^{1/2} e^{\pm i(\pi - \gamma_1)} \qquad \begin{array}{l} \text{if} \quad \mathrm{Im}\, \lambda_1 > 0 \\ \\ \\ \text{if} \quad \mathrm{Im}\, \lambda_1 < 0 \quad . \end{array}$$

The value of (3.19) is

$$\frac{\lambda_2^{(-)} \exp(\lambda_1 \ell_1' + \lambda_2^{(-)} \ell_2)}{\lambda_2^{(-)} - \lambda_2^{(+)}} = \frac{\pm i e^{\mp i \gamma_1}}{2 \sin \gamma_1} \exp\left\{\lambda_1 \ell_1' + \lambda_1 \left[\frac{\Delta_0 + \Delta_1}{\Delta_1 + \Delta_2}\right]^{\frac{1}{2}} e^{\pm i(\pi - \gamma_1)} \ell_2 \right\}$$

with the upper sign for $\mathrm{Im}\, \lambda_1 > 0$ and the lower sign for $\mathrm{Im}\, \lambda_1 < 0$.

To evaluate the $\lambda_1$-integral of this, we separate the integral into the parts from $\lambda_1 = -i\infty$ to 0 and from $\lambda_1 = 0$ to $+i\infty$ and make the substitution

$$\lambda_1 \ell_1' + \lambda_1 \ell_2 \left[\frac{\Delta_0 + \Delta_1}{\Delta_1 + \Delta_2}\right]^{\frac{1}{2}} e^{\pm i(\pi - \gamma_1)} = z_1 e^{\pm i\pi} \quad .$$

As $\lambda_1$ goes from 0 to $+i\infty$ (or 0 to $-i\infty$), $z_1$ goes from 0 to a point at $\infty$ for which $\mathrm{Re}\, z_1 > 0$. Since the integrand vanishes at $\infty$ for $\mathrm{Re}\, z_1 > 0$, the integral can be displaced to the real line, 0 to $+\infty$.

An analogous procedure can be applied to the second term of (3.17b), but with the roles of $\lambda_1$ and $\lambda_2$ interchanged. The final integrals with respect to $z_1$ or $z_2$ are all identical and can be evaluated in terms of the $\Gamma$-function. The result is

$$g^*(c_1 - \ell_1', \ell_2) \simeq \frac{4 \, \Delta^* \sin(-\theta^*/(1 - \gamma_1/\pi))}{(1 - \gamma_1/\pi) \sin \gamma_1 \, \Gamma(\gamma_1/(\pi - \gamma_1))} \left[ \frac{\mu^\dagger}{2 \, \Delta^{*3/2}} \right]^{\pi/(\pi-\gamma_1)}$$

$$\cdot \text{Re} \left[ (\Delta_1 + \Delta_2)^{\frac{1}{2}} \ell_1' \exp(i(\pi - \gamma_1)/2) + (\Delta_0 + \Delta_1)^{\frac{1}{2}} \ell_2 \exp(-i(\pi - \gamma_1)/2) \right]^{-(\pi - 2\gamma_1)/(\pi - \gamma_1)}$$

$$(3.20)$$

for $\ell_1'$, $\ell_2 \to 0$ .

The dependence of $g^*(c_1 - \ell_1', \ell_2)$ upon $\ell_1'$, $\ell_2$, for $\ell_1'$, $\ell_2 \to 0$, is described by the last factor. This factor is independent of the $\mu_j$'s and agrees with the results from III (6.9). The dependence upon the $\mu_j$'s is contained in the factors $\sin(-\theta^*/(1 - \gamma_1/\pi))$ and $(\mu^\dagger)^{\pi/(\pi-\gamma_1)}$ with the $\theta^*$ and $\mu^\dagger$ defined in VI (4.3), (4.4). The explicit dependence upon the $\mu_j$'s is rather complicated, however, because of the fractional angle in $\sin(-\theta^*/(1-\gamma_1/\pi))$, except in the special case $\gamma_1 = \pi/2$ discussed above for which $g^*(c_1 - \ell_1', \ell_2)$ is a product of exponential distributions.

The factor $\Delta^*/\mu^\dagger$ has the "dimension" of length. It is, therefore, convenient to regroup the factors in (3.20) in the form

$$g^*(c_1 - \ell_1', \ell_2) \simeq \left( \frac{\mu^\dagger}{\Delta^*} \right)^2 \frac{\sin(-\theta^*/(1 - \gamma_1/\pi))}{(1 - \gamma_1/\pi) \sin \gamma_1 \, \Gamma(\gamma_1/(\pi - \gamma_1))}$$

$$(3.20a)$$

$$\cdot \text{Re} \left[ \frac{(\Delta_1 + \Delta_2)^{\frac{1}{2}}}{2 \, \Delta^{*1/2}} \left( \frac{\mu^\dagger \ell_1'}{\Delta^*} \right) \exp(i(\pi - \gamma_1)/2) + \frac{(\Delta_0 + \Delta_1)^{\frac{1}{2}}}{2 \, \Delta^{*1/2}} \left( \frac{\mu^\dagger \ell_2}{\Delta^*} \right) \exp(-i(\pi - \gamma_1)/2) \right]^{\frac{-(\pi - 2\gamma_1)}{(\pi - \gamma_1)}}$$

because now the factor $(\mu^\dagger/\Delta^*)^2$ has the dimension of (length)$^{-2}$ as appropriate for a two-dimensional density and the last factor now measures $\ell_1'$ and $\ell_2$ in units of $\Delta^*/\mu^\dagger$ .

The angle $\theta^*$ depends upon the ratios of the $\mu_j$'s and $\Delta_j$'s . For $\mu_0 = \mu_1$ , $\theta^* = 0$ ; as $(\mu_0 - \mu_1)/(\mu_2 - \mu_1)$ increases, $-\theta^*$ increases until, for $\mu_2 = \mu_1$ , it has the value $\pi - \gamma_1$ . At each extreme $\sin(-\theta^*/(1-\gamma_1/\pi))$ vanishes, as is to be expected since, for $\mu_0 = \mu_1$ , $E\{Q_1'\}$ should become infinite and, for $\mu_2 = \mu_1$ , $E\{Q_2\}$ should become infinite causing the probability density to go to zero for all $\ell_1'$ , $\ell_2$ .

For $\mu_2 = \mu_0$ , the formulas simplify somewhat because $-\theta^* = \gamma_0$ and $\mu^\dagger = \Delta^{*-1/2}(\Delta_0 + \Delta_2)^{1/2}(\mu_0 - \mu_1)$ . If, in addition, $\Delta_0 = \Delta_2$ , then $\gamma_0 = \gamma_2 = (\pi - \gamma_1)/2$ and $\sin(-\theta^*/(1-\gamma_1/\pi)) = 1$ . In the special case $\Delta_0 = \Delta_1 = \Delta_2$ , $\gamma_0 = \gamma_1 = \gamma_2 = \pi/3$ and $\mu_2 = \mu_0$ , (3.20) simplifies to

$$ g^*(c_1-\ell_1',\ell_2) \simeq 2\left(\frac{2}{3\pi}\right)^{1/2}\left(\frac{\mu_0 - \mu_1}{\Delta_0}\right)^{3/2} \text{Re}[(\ell_1'+\ell_2) + i\sqrt{3}(\ell_1'-\ell_2)]^{-1/2} . \quad (3.20b) $$

The methods described above for inverting the Laplace transform of the asymptotic form of $\overline{K}(\lambda_1,\lambda_2)$ , for $|\lambda_1|, |\lambda_2| \to \infty$ , can be generalized, in part, to the exact formulas. We are particularly interested in obtaining a representation of $g^*(c_1-\ell_1',\ell_2)$ which will describe its behavior for large $\ell_1'$ and/or $\ell_2$ .

If we substitute the exact expression for $\overline{K}(\lambda_1,\lambda_2)$ from (1.4) into (3.17b), there will still be a quadratic function of $\lambda_1$ , $\lambda_2$ in the denominator of the integrand, namely the coefficient of $\overline{K}(\lambda_1,\lambda_2)$ on the left-hand side of (1.4). The $\overline{K}_2(\lambda_1)$ and $K_1^*(\lambda_2)$ , however, have been defined so that the right-hand side of (1.4) vanishes wherever this coefficient vanishes (not only for $\lambda_1$ and $\lambda_2$ in the right-half plane where the functions are known to be analytic, but throughout the region of analytic continuation). Thus the complete integrand of (3.17b) has no singularities induced by the denominator vanishing; the only singularities are those generated from $\overline{K}_2(\lambda_1)$ and $K_1^*(\lambda_2)$ in the $\lambda_1$ and $\lambda_2$ spaces, respectively.

Although the path of integration in (3.17b) has been chosen to be up the imaginary axis for both $\lambda_1$ and $\lambda_2$ , we can translate these paths to any vertical lines in the complex plane as long as the translation does not displace the path over any singularities of $\overline{K}_2(\lambda_1)$ or $K_1^*(\lambda_2)$ , and the integrand goes to zero fast enough at the ends of the lines. Having made any appropriate translation of these paths, we can then separate the integrand into two terms, one proportional to $\overline{K}_2(\lambda_1)$ , the other to $K_1^*(\lambda_2)$ . Mimicing the procedure described above for the asymptotic forms (in which a translation of the path was not performed), we can now integrate the term proportional to $\overline{K}_2(\lambda_1)$ with respect to $\lambda_2$ and the term proportional to $K_1^*(\lambda_2)$ with respect to $\lambda_1$ . Each of these integrations is simple because the integrand of the first term contains only two poles in the $\lambda_2$-space for any fixed $\lambda_1$ , and the integrand of the second term contains only two poles in the $\lambda_1$-space for any fixed $\lambda_2$ , each induced from the denominator vanishing. Each of these integrals can be evaluated from the residues of the poles, leading to an integral representation of $g^*(c_1-\ell_1',\ell_2)$ involving only single integrals.

We would like (if possible) to choose the translated paths of integration so that the path of integration for $\lambda_2$ in the first term and for $\lambda_1$ in the second term runs between the two zeros of the denominator in the $\lambda_2$ and $\lambda_1$ spaces, respectively, for any choice of the $\lambda_1$ and $\lambda_2$.

From (3.1) it seems advantageous to send the $\lambda_1$ path of integration up the line

$$\text{Re } \lambda_1 \quad = \quad \mu^\dagger \, \Delta^{*-3/2} \, (\Delta_1 + \Delta_2)^{1/2} \, \cos(\theta^* - \gamma_1) \quad , \qquad (3.21)$$

which is the image in the $\lambda_1$-space of the vertical path $\text{Re } \theta_1 = \pi/2$ in the $\theta_1$-space. This path is indeed in a region of analyticity of $\overline{K}_2^\dagger(\theta_1)$ and consequently also of $\overline{K}_2(\lambda_1)$. With the $\lambda_1$-path chosen in this way, it would seem appropriate from VI (4.2) to choose the $\lambda_2$-path so that

$$\text{Re } \lambda_2 \quad = \quad - \, \mu^\dagger \, \Delta^{*-3/2} \, (\Delta_0 + \Delta_1)^{1/2} \, \cos \theta^* \qquad (3.22)$$

because this is the image in the $\lambda_2$-space of a vertical path $\text{Re } \theta_2 = 0$, for $\text{Re } \theta_1 = \pi/2$. This is also an acceptable path because $K_1^*(\lambda_2) = K_1^{*\dagger}(\theta_1)$ with $\lambda_2$ and $\theta_1$ related through VI (4.9); but the path (3.22) corresponds under the mapping VI (4.9) to the path $\text{Re } \theta_1 = \gamma_1 + \pi/2$ which is in the region of analyticity of $K_1^{*\dagger}(\theta_1)$. Thus the path (3.22) is in the region of analyticity of $K_1^*(\lambda_2)$.

For any given value of $\lambda_1$ on the contour (3.21) corresponding to $\text{Re } \theta_1 = \pi/2$, the zeros of the denominator in the $\lambda_2$-space correspond to points in the $\theta_1$, $\theta_2$-space where $\theta_1 = \pm\theta_2$, i.e., from VI (4.2), to values of $\lambda_2$ for which

$$\lambda_2^{(\pm)} \quad = \quad \mu^\dagger \, \Delta^{*-3/2} \, (\Delta_0 + \Delta_1)^{1/2} \, [-\cos\theta^* + \cos\gamma_1\cos\theta_1 \pm \sin\gamma_1\sin\theta_1] \, . \quad (3.23)$$

The term $\cos\gamma_1\cos\theta_1$ is imaginary for $\text{Re } \theta_1 = \pi/2$ whereas the term

$\sin\gamma_1\sin\theta_1$ is real and positive. Consequently $\lambda_2^{(-)}$ is on the left-hand side of the path (3.22) and $\lambda_2^{(+)}$ is on the right-hand side (for all $\lambda_1$ on the path (3.21)), as we wished them to be for the purpose of evaluating the $\lambda_2$-integral of the term containing $\overline{K}_2(\lambda_1)$ .

For a corresponding analysis of the other integration, we note that for any given value of $\lambda_2$ on the contour (3.22) corresponding in the $\theta_1$, $\theta_2$ space to a given value of

$$\cos\gamma_1\cos\theta_1 \;+\; \sin\gamma_1\sin\theta_2 \;=\; \text{Imag.} \quad ,$$

the two zeros of the denominator in the $\lambda_1$-space occur for $\theta_1 = \pm\theta_2$ , i.e

$$\cos(\theta_1\mp\gamma_1) \;=\; \text{Imag.} \quad , \qquad \theta_1 \;=\; \pi/2 \pm \gamma_1 + \text{Imag.}$$

$$\cos\theta_1 \;=\; \cos(\theta_1\mp\gamma_1)\cos\gamma_1 \mp \sin(\theta_1\mp\gamma_1)\sin\gamma_1$$

$$\text{Re }\cos\theta_1 \;=\; \mp \cos(\text{Imag.}) \sin\gamma_1 \quad .$$

Since

$$\lambda_1 \;=\; \mu^\dagger \Delta^{*-3/2} (\Delta_1 + \Delta_2)^{1/2} [-\cos\theta_1 + \cos(\theta^*-\gamma_1)] \qquad (3.24)$$

one of the zeros of the denominator in the $\lambda_1$-space is on the right-hand side of the line (3.21) and the other is on the left-hand side.

If we characterize the value of $\lambda_2$ on the line (3.22) by the value of $\theta_1$ such that

$$\lambda_2 \;=\; \mu^\dagger \Delta^{*-3/2} (\Delta_0 + \Delta_1)^{1/2} [\cos(\theta_1 - \gamma_1) - \cos\theta^*] \qquad (3.25)$$

as in VI (4.9), with $\theta_1$ on the line $\text{Re }\theta_1 = \gamma_1 + \pi/2$ then the two roots are at

$$\lambda_1^{(\pm)} = \mu^\dagger \Delta^{*-3/2} (\Delta_1 + \Delta_2)^{1/2} [-\cos(\theta_1 - \gamma_1 \pm \gamma_1) + \cos(\theta^* - \gamma_1)] \quad (3.26)$$

with $\lambda_1^{(+)}$ to the right of the line (3.21) and $\lambda_1^{(-)}$ to the left of (3.21).

Following the same procedure as in (3.19), we can integrate each term of (3.17b) with respect to one of the $\lambda_j$'s to give

$$g^*(c_1 - \ell_1', \ell_2) = \frac{1}{2\pi i} \int d\lambda_1 \frac{\lambda_2^{(-)} \overline{K}_2(\lambda_1) \exp(\lambda_1 \ell_1' + \lambda_2^{(-)} \ell_2)}{(\lambda_2^{(-)} - \lambda_2^{(+)})}$$

$$\quad (3.27)$$

$$+ \frac{1}{2\pi i} \int d\lambda_2 \frac{\lambda_1^{(-)} K_1^*(\lambda_2) \exp(\lambda_1^{(-)} \ell_1' + \lambda_2 \ell_2)}{(\lambda_1^{(-)} - \lambda_1^{(+)})}$$

in which the $\lambda_2^{(\pm)}$ is interpreted as a function of $\lambda_1$ and $\lambda_1^{(\pm)}$ as a function of $\lambda_2$. The integral with respect to $\lambda_1$ is up the line (3.21) and that with respect to $\lambda_2$ is up the line (3.22).

We shall not try to write these integrands explicitly in terms of $\lambda_1$ or $\lambda_2$. Since all quantities in these integrands are easily expressed as functions of $\theta_1$ through (3.24) and (3.25), it is natural that one should convert these integrals with respect to $\lambda_1$ and $\lambda_2$ into integrals with respect to $\theta_1$.

A direct substitution of $\lambda_1$, $\lambda_2$ from (3.24), (3.25); $\lambda_2^{(\pm)}$, $\lambda_1^{(\pm)}$ from (3.23), (3.26); and $\overline{K}_2^\dagger(\theta_1)$, $K_1^{*\dagger}(\theta_1)$ from (3.12), (3.13) gives

$$g^*(c_1 - \ell_1', \ell_2) = - \frac{\mu^{\dagger^2} \sin(-\theta^*/(1 - \gamma_1/\pi))}{2\pi i \, \Delta^{*2} \, (1 - \gamma_1/\pi) \sin \gamma_1}$$

$$\cdot \left\{ \int_{\pi/2 - i\infty}^{\pi/2 + i\infty} d\theta_1 \, \frac{[-\cos\theta^* + \cos(\theta_1+\gamma_1)]\sin\left(\dfrac{\theta_1+\gamma_1-\theta^*}{2}\right)\sin\left(\dfrac{\theta_1-\gamma_1+\theta^*}{2}\right)}{\sin\left(\dfrac{\theta_1 - \gamma_1 - \theta^*}{2(1 - \gamma_1/\pi)}\right)\sin\left(\dfrac{\theta_1 - \gamma_1 + \theta^*}{2(1 - \gamma_1/\pi)}\right)} \right.$$

$$\cdot \exp\left[ \ell_1' \mu^\dagger \Delta^{*-3/2} \, (\Delta_1 + \Delta_2)^{1/2} \, [-\cos\theta_1 + \cos(\theta^*-\gamma_1)] \right.$$

$$\left. + \ell_2 \mu^\dagger \Delta^{*-3/2} \, (\Delta_0 + \Delta_1)^{1/2} \, [-\cos\theta^* + \cos(\theta_1+\gamma_1)] \right]$$

$$+ \int_{\gamma_1 + \pi/2 - i\infty}^{\gamma_1 + \pi/2 + i\infty} d\theta_1 \, \frac{[-\cos(\theta_1-2\gamma_1) + \cos(\theta^*-\gamma_1)]\sin\left(\dfrac{\theta_1-\gamma_1-\theta^*}{2}\right)\sin\left(\dfrac{\theta_1-\gamma_1+\theta^*}{2}\right)}{\sin\left(\dfrac{\theta_1 - \gamma_1 - \theta^*}{2(1 - \gamma_1/\pi)}\right)\sin\left(\dfrac{\theta_1 - \gamma_1 + \theta^*}{2(1 - \gamma_1/\pi)}\right)}$$

$$\cdot \exp\left[ \ell_1' \mu^\dagger \Delta^{*-3/2} \, (\Delta_1 + \Delta_2)^{1/2} \, [-\cos(\theta_1-2\gamma_1) + \cos(\theta^*-\gamma_1)] \right.$$

$$\left. \left. + \ell_2 \mu^\dagger \Delta^{*-3/2} \, (\Delta_0 + \Delta_1)^{1/2} \, [\cos(\theta_1-\gamma_1) - \cos\theta^*] \right] \right\} \cdot$$

It is possible to combine these two integrals into a single integral. If we replace $\theta_1$ by $\theta_1 + 2\gamma_1$ in the second integral, then the exponential factor in the second integrand becomes the same as that in the first integrand. The path of integration in the second integral, however, will now go from $-\gamma_1 + \pi/2 - i\infty$ to $-\gamma_1 + \pi/2 + i\infty$ , whereas the first integral is from $\pi/2 - i\infty$ to $\pi/2 + i\infty$ . Either of these paths may be translated toward the other provided that one picks up the residue of any poles which one crosses, if any. The nearest singularity of the first integrand to the left of $\mathrm{Re}\ \theta_1 = \pi/2$ is at $\theta_1 = \gamma_1 + \theta^*$ . The nearest singularity of the second integrand to the right of $\mathrm{Re}\ \theta_1 = \pi/2 - \gamma_1$ is at $\theta_1 = 2\pi - 3\gamma_1 + \theta^*$ (in terms of the new $\theta_1$). These two singularities are separated by

$$(2\pi - 3\gamma_1 + \theta^*) - (\gamma_1 + \theta^*) = 2\pi - 4\gamma_1 \geq 0 \quad ,$$

consequently we can translate both paths of integration to a common vertical path $C$ between these poles. (The special case $\gamma_1 = \pi/2$ , for which the poles coalesce, can be treated as a limiting case for $\gamma_1 \rightarrow \pi/2$.)

Actually, for reasons of symmetry, it is more convenient to change the variable of integration to

$$\theta_1' = \theta_1 - \pi + \gamma_1 - \theta^* \qquad\qquad (3.28)$$

in the first integral, and

$$\theta_1' = \theta_1 - \pi - \gamma_1 - \theta^*$$

in the second integral so that the two singularities are symmetrically located at

$$\theta_1' = 2\gamma_1 - \pi \leq 0 \quad \text{and} \quad \theta_1' = \pi - 2\gamma_1 \geq 0$$

on either side of the $\theta_1'$ origin.

By combining the integrals as described above, one can express $g^*(c_1 - \ell_1', \ell_2)$ in the form

$$g^*(c_1 - \ell_1', \ell_2) = \frac{\mu^{\dagger 2} \sin\left(\dfrac{-\theta^*}{(1-\gamma_1/\pi)}\right) \sin\left(\dfrac{\gamma_1}{(1-\gamma_1/\pi)}\right)}{\pi\, i\, \Delta^{*2}\,(1-\gamma_1/\pi)\,\sin\gamma_1}$$

$$\cdot \int_{C'} d\theta_1' \frac{\sin\left(\dfrac{\theta_1'+\pi+2\theta^*}{2}\right) \sin\left(\dfrac{\theta_1'+\pi-2\gamma_1+2\theta^*}{2}\right) \sin^2\left(\dfrac{\theta_1'+\pi}{2}\right) \sin\left(\dfrac{\theta_1'+\theta^*}{1-\gamma_1/\pi}\right)}{\sin\left(\dfrac{\theta_1'+\pi+2\theta^*}{2(1-\gamma_1/\pi)}\right) \sin\left(\dfrac{\theta_1'+\pi-2\gamma_1+2\theta^*}{2(1-\gamma_1/\pi)}\right) \sin\left(\dfrac{\theta_1'-\pi+2\gamma_1}{2(1-\gamma_1/\pi)}\right) \sin\left(\dfrac{\theta_1'+\pi-2\gamma_1}{2(1-\gamma_1/\pi)}\right)}$$

$$\cdot \exp\left(-\ell_1'\mu^\dagger\Delta^{*-3/2}\,(\Delta_1+\Delta_2)^{1/2}\left[\cos(\theta_1'+\pi-\gamma_1+\theta^*)+\cos(\pi+\theta^*-\gamma\right.\right.$$

$$\left.\left.-\ell_2\,\mu^\dagger\,\Delta^{*-3/2}\,(\Delta_0+\Delta_1)^{1/2}\left[\cos(\theta_1'+\theta^*)+\cos\theta^*\right]\right) . \quad (3.29)$$

For $\ell_1'$, $\ell_2 > 0$, this formula, as derived, is certainly correct if the path $C$ for the $\theta_1$ integration lies in a strip $-\gamma_1 + \pi/2 <$ Re $\theta_1 < \pi/2$ where Re $\lambda_1^{(-)} < 0$ and Re $\lambda_2^{(-)} < 0$, and also lies between the two poles at $\theta_1 = \gamma_1 + \theta^*$ and $2\pi - 3\gamma_1 + \theta^*$. Correspondingly, it is valid if the path $C'$ satisfies the conditions

$$-\frac{\pi}{2} - \theta^* < \text{Re } \theta_1' < -\frac{\pi}{2} + \gamma_1 - \theta^*$$

$$(3.29a)$$

and $\qquad -\pi + 2\gamma_1 < \text{Re } \theta_1' < \pi - 2\gamma_1 .$

Regardless of how it was derived, however, the integrand can be defined outside the strip (3.29a) in the complex $\theta_1'$-plane by analytic continuation, and one can deform the path so as to run outside the strip if one wishes (taking proper account of any singularities which one may cross).

For large values of $\ell_1'$ and/or $\ell_2$, the exponential factor in (3.29) has a dominant influence on the integrand. To describe its properties, it is convenient to consider $\ell_1'(\Delta_1+\Delta_2)^{\frac{1}{2}}\Delta^{*-\frac{1}{2}}$ and $\ell_2(\Delta_0+\Delta_1)^{\frac{1}{2}}\Delta^{*-\frac{1}{2}}$ as if they were vectors making an angle $\pi - \gamma_1$, as shown in Fig. VII-5 Let $\ell^*$ be the vector sum of these two vectors having magnitude

$$\ell^* = [\ell_1'^2(\Delta_1+\Delta_2) + \ell_2^2(\Delta_0+\Delta_1) - 2\ell_1'\ell_2(\Delta_0+\Delta_1)^{\frac{1}{2}}(\Delta_1+\Delta_2)^{\frac{1}{2}}\cos\gamma_1]^{\frac{1}{2}} \Delta^{*-1/2}$$

$$= [\ell_1'^2\Delta_2 + \ell_2^2\Delta_0 + (\ell_1' - \ell_2)^2\Delta_1]^{1/2} \Delta^{*-1/2} \quad . \tag{3.30}$$

For real values of $\theta_1'$, draw a unit vector $01$ making an angle $-\theta^*$ with $\ell_2(\Delta_0 + \Delta_1)^{1/2}\Delta^{*-1/2}$ (an angle $\pi-\gamma_1+\theta^*$ with $\ell_1'(\Delta_1+\Delta_2)^{1/2}\Delta^{*-1/2}$), and a vector $02$ making an angle $\theta_1'$ with the vector $01$, as shown in Fig. VII-5. The argument of the exponential in (3.29) consists of four terms. The two terms containing $\theta_1'$ can be considered as the sum of the projections of $(-\mu^\dagger\Delta^{*-1})\ell_1'(\Delta_1+\Delta_2)^{1/2}\Delta^{*-1/2}$ and $(-\mu^\dagger\Delta^{*-1})\ell_2(\Delta_0+\Delta_1)^{1/2}\Delta^{*-1/2}$ on the line $02$; those not containing $\theta_1'$ can be considered as the corresponding sum of projections on the line $01$. We can also consider these sums of projections as the projection of the vector sum $\ell^*$ on these two lines. If we let $\phi$ be the angle which $\ell^*$ makes with the direction $01$, then the exponential factor in (3.29) can be written as

$$\exp(-[\ell^*\mu^\dagger/\Delta^*][\cos(\phi-\theta_1') + \cos\phi]) \quad . \tag{3.31}$$

This factor has a minimum with respect to values of $\theta_1'$ along the real axis at $\theta_1' = \phi$, and, consequently, a saddle-point in the complex $\theta_1'$-space. It would, therefore, seem advantageous to translate the $\theta_1'$ integration path to a vertical line $\mathrm{Re}\ \theta_1' = \phi$, particularly for large

352

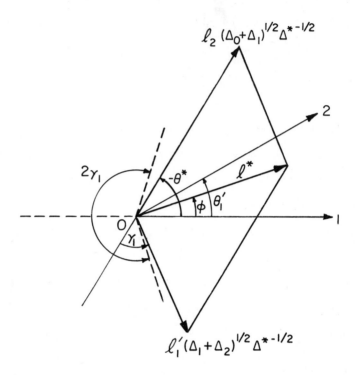

Fig. VII-5. Vector representation of coordinates.

values of $(\ell^{*}\mu^{\dagger}/\Delta^{*})$. Such a translation may or may not cross one of the

singularities of the integrand of (3.29) at $\theta_{1}' = \pm (\pi - 2\gamma_{1})$ . If it

does, i.e., if $|\phi| > \pi - 2\gamma_{1}$ , then one must pick-up the residue at

the pole one crosses. For large $\ell^{*}\mu^{\dagger}/\Delta^{*}$ , this residue will dominate

the value of (3.28), because the exponential factor (3.31) evaluated at

the singularity will be large compared with its value along the path

through the saddle-point. If the translation of the path to the saddle-

point does not cross a pole of the integrand, then, for large $\ell^{*}\mu^{\dagger}/\Delta^{*}$ ,

one can approximate the integral (3.29) by a saddle-point integration.

If, however, the saddle-point $\theta_{1}' = \phi$ lies so close to one of the sin-

gularities that the variation of the integrand near $\theta_{1}' = \phi$ is influenced

significantly by both the pole of the integrand and the exponential fac-

tor, then one must consider some approximations including both factors.

For sufficiently large $\ell^{*}$ , this last condition will apply only for a

narrow range of angles $\phi$ , describing a "transition zone" between two

relatively simple types of asymptotic behaviors.

Except for a scale of units $\mu^{\dagger^{2}}/\Delta^{*^{2}}$ for $g^{*}$ and $\Delta^{*}/\mu^{\dagger}$ for $\ell^{*}$ ,

(3.29) still contains two parameters $\gamma_{1}$ and $\theta^{*}$ , besides the "space

coordinates" $\ell_{1}'$ , $\ell_{2}$ which are represented in Fig.VII-5 through the

new coordinates $\ell^{*}$ and $\phi$ . The $\gamma_{1}$ can be interpreted as a measure

of the variance of server 1 as compared with servers 0 and 2, and can

have any value in the range $0 \le \gamma_{1} \le \pi/2$ . The value of $\theta^{*}$ is inter-

preted primarily as a measure of the relative service rates $\mu_{0} - \mu_{1}$

and $\mu_{2} - \mu_{1}$ , and can have any values in the range $0 < - \theta^{*} < \pi - \gamma_{1}$.

For given $- \theta^{*}$ and $\gamma_{1}$ , $\phi$ will span the range

$$- \pi + \gamma_{1} - \theta^{*} \le \phi \le - \theta^{*} \qquad (3.32)$$

which always includes $\phi = 0$ . As $\phi$ varies over this range, the saddle-point at $\theta_1' = \phi$ covers the same range. It will include the pole at $\theta_1' = -\pi + 2\gamma_1$ , shown in Fig. VII-5 by one of the broken radial lines, if

$$- \pi + \gamma_1 - \theta^* < - \pi + 2\gamma_1 \; ; \quad -\theta_1^* < \gamma_1 \; ; \tag{3.33a}$$

it includes the pole at $+\pi - 2\gamma_1$ if

$$\pi - 2\gamma_1 < - \theta^* \quad , \tag{3.33b}$$

and, of course, it includes both poles if

$$\pi - 2\gamma_1 < - \theta^* < \gamma_1 \quad \text{(for } \gamma_1 > \pi/3\text{)}. \tag{3.33c}$$

If (3.33a) applies and $\ell^*$ is sufficiently large, the main contribution to (3.29) for $-\pi + \gamma_1 - \theta^* < \phi < -\pi + 2\gamma_1$ comes from the residue of the pole at $\theta_1' = - \pi + 2\gamma_1$ . At this pole, one can verify from (3.23), (3.24), and (3.28) that

$$\lambda_1 = \alpha_1 \qquad \text{for} \quad \theta' = -\pi + 2\gamma_1 \tag{3.34a}$$

$$\lambda_2^{(-)} = - \alpha_2^* \equiv - \alpha_2 - \alpha_1 2\Delta_1/(\Delta_1 + \Delta_2) \quad \text{for } \theta' = -\pi + 2\gamma_1 \tag{3.34b}$$

and

$$g^*(c_1 - \ell_1', \ell_2) \simeq (-\alpha_1)(\alpha_2^*) \exp(\alpha_1 \ell_1' - \alpha_2^* \ell_2) \quad . \tag{3.34c}$$

On the other hand, if (3.33b) applies, the main contribution to (3.29), for $\pi - 2\gamma_1 < \phi < - \theta^*$ , comes from the residue of the pole at $\theta_1' = \pi - 2\gamma_1$ . At this pole

$$\lambda_2 \quad = \quad - \alpha_2 \qquad\qquad\qquad\qquad \text{for} \quad \theta' = \pi - 2\gamma_1 \quad (3.35\text{a})$$

$$\lambda_1^{(-)} \quad = \quad \alpha_1^* \quad \equiv \quad \alpha_1 + \alpha_2 2\Delta_1/(\Delta_0 + \Delta_1) \quad \text{for} \quad \theta' = \pi - 2\gamma_1 \quad (3.35\text{b})$$

and

$$g^*(c_1 - \ell_1', \ell_2) \quad \simeq \quad (-\alpha_1^*)(\alpha_2)\exp(\alpha_1^*\ell_1' - \alpha_2\ell_2) \quad . \qquad\qquad (3.35\text{c})$$

If either (3.34c) or (3.35c) were valid for all values of $\phi$ satisfying (3.32), it would describe $Q_1'$ and $Q_2$ as being statistically independent and exponentially distributed. These distributions would even be properly normalized. But (3.34c) or (3.35c) apply only for limited ranges of $\phi$ (if at all). Furthermore, for $\gamma_1 < \pi/2$ $(\Delta_1 > 0)$, the exponential distribution of $Q_2$ in (3.34c) is not the correct marginal distribution (which has parameter $\alpha_2$ instead of $\alpha_2^*$), nor is the exponential distribution in (3.35c) the correct marginal distribution of $Q_1'$ .

In the limiting case $\gamma_1 \to \pi/2$ $(\Delta_1 \to 0)$, the two poles at $\theta_1' = \pm(\pi - 2\gamma_1) \to 0$ coalesce, $\alpha_2^* \to \alpha_2$ , $\alpha_1^* \to \alpha_1$ , and both (3.34c) and (3.35c) give a joint distribution equal to the product of the marginal distributions. Furthermore, if one translates the path of integration in (3.29) over either pole before one takes the limit $\gamma_1 \to \pi/2$ , the factor $\sin(\gamma_1/(1-\gamma_1/\pi))$ of (3.29) vanishes for $\gamma_1 \to \pi/2$ . Thus the value of (3.29) is given exactly by the residue at either pole; (3.34c) or (3.35c) is exact for $\gamma_1 = \pi/2$ and all values of $\phi$ (as previously known).

The $\alpha_2^*$ in (3.34b) is proportional to $\sin(\theta^* + \gamma_1)$ . If (3.33a) is true then this is positive, as would be necessary also to guarantee that $g^* \geq 0$ in (3.34c). Since $\mu_0 > \mu_1$ and $\Delta_1 \geq 0$ , it follows that

$$0 \leq \alpha_2^* \leq \alpha_2$$

i.e., the rate of decrease of $g^*$ with $\ell_2$ in (3.34c) is slower than for the marginal distribution of $Q_2$. Similarly in (3.35b)

$$\alpha_1 \leq \alpha_1^* \leq 0$$

so that the rate of decrease of $g^*$ with $\ell_1'$ in (3.35c) is slower than for the marginal distribution of $Q_1'$. This is, of course, consistent with the property that $Q_1'$ and $Q_2$ are positively correlated for $\Delta_1 > 0$; a positive (negative) fluctuation in the service at 1 will cause both $Q_1'$ and $Q_2$ to increase (decrease).

One can readily verify that (3.34c) and (3.35c), when applicable, satisfy exactly the boundary conditions (I 5.7f) and (I 5.7a) at $\ell_2 = 0$ ($\phi = - \pi + \gamma_1 - \theta^*$) and $\ell_1' = 0$ ($\phi = - \theta^*$), respectively. Since equations (I 5.6), (I 5.7) are linear homogeneous, it follows that any correction terms to (3.34c) and (3.35c) must also satisfy the same boundary conditions.

If, particularly for $|\phi| < |\pi - 2\gamma_1|$, one translates the path $C'$ to a vertical line $\mathrm{Re}\ \theta_1' = \phi$, it is convenient to write (3.31) as

$$\exp\left(- \frac{\ell^* \mu^\dagger}{\Delta^*}[1 + \cos\phi]\right)\ \exp\left(- \frac{\ell^* \mu^\dagger}{\Delta^*} 2\left[\sinh\left(\frac{\theta_1' - \phi}{2i}\right)\right]^2\right) \tag{3.36a}$$

in which only the second factor depends upon $\theta_1'$. Along the vertical path, this factor has a maximum at $\theta_1' = \phi$ and decays very rapidly for large values of $|(\theta_1' - \phi)/2i|$. If $\ell^* \mu^\dagger/\Delta^* \gg 1$, it decays appreciably on a scale $|(\theta_1' - \phi)/2i|$ comparable with $(\Delta^*/\mu^\dagger \ell^*)^{1/2} \ll 1$, in which case one may approximate the second factor of (3.36a) by

$$
\exp\left(-\frac{\ell^{*}\mu^{\dagger}}{2\,\Delta^{*}}\left[\frac{\theta_{1}' - \phi}{2\,i}\right]^{2}\right) \,. \tag{3.36b}
$$

If $|\phi| \geq \pi - 2\gamma_1$ , the exact formula for $g^{*}(c_1-\ell_1',\ell_2)$ can be written as the sum of the residue from the pole at $\pm(\pi - 2\gamma_1)$ , as in (3.34c) or (3.35c), plus the value of the integral (3.29) up the vertical line $\mathrm{Re}\ \theta_1' = \phi$ . If $|\phi| < \pi - 2\gamma_1$ , the value of $g^{*}(c_1-\ell_1',\ell_2)$ is simply (3.29) integrated along $\mathrm{Re}\ \theta_1' = \phi$ without any residue. In any case, the main contribution to the integral (3.29) along $\mathrm{Re}\ \theta_1' = \phi$ , for $\ell^{*}\mu^{\dagger}/\Delta^{*} \gg 1$ , will come from a small range of $|\theta_1' - \phi|$ of order $(\Delta^{*}/\mu^{\dagger}\ell^{*})^{1/2}$ . Over this short range of $|\theta_1' - \phi|$ near the maximum of (3.36a), the other factors of the integrand in (3.29) will be nearly constant, provided $\phi$ is not too close to one of the singularities or zeros of the integrand, specifically if

$$
|\phi + \pi - 2\gamma_1| \quad \gg \quad (\Delta^{*}/\mu^{\dagger}\ell^{*})^{1/2} \tag{3.37a}
$$

$$
|\phi - \pi + 2\gamma_1| \quad \gg \quad (\Delta^{*}/\mu^{\dagger}\ell^{*})^{1/2} \tag{3.37b}
$$

$$
|\phi + \theta^{*}| \quad \gg \quad (\Delta^{*}/\mu^{\dagger}\ell^{*})^{1/2} \tag{3.37c}
$$

and $\quad |\phi + \theta^{*} + \pi - \gamma_1| \quad \gg \quad (\Delta^{*}/\mu^{\dagger}\ell^{*})^{1/2} \,. \tag{3.37d}$

Except for $\phi$ in one of the narrow ranges where one or more of the conditions (3.37) is violated, the integration of (3.29) with respect to $\theta_1'$ along $\mathrm{Re}\ \theta_1' = \phi$ is essentially an integration of the factor

(3.36b), which has a value $i(2\pi\Delta^*/\ell^*\mu^\dagger)^{1/2}$ . Thus,

$$g^*(c_1-\ell_1',\ell_2) \simeq \left(\frac{2}{\pi\ell^*}\right)^{\frac{1}{2}} \left(\frac{\mu^\dagger}{\Delta^*}\right)^{\frac{3}{2}} \frac{\sin\left(\dfrac{-\theta^*}{(1-\gamma_1/\pi)}\right) \sin\left(\dfrac{\gamma_1}{(1-\gamma_1/\pi)}\right)}{(1-\gamma_1/\pi)\sin\gamma_1}$$

$$\cdot \frac{\sin\left(\dfrac{\phi+\pi+2\theta^*}{2}\right) \sin\left(\dfrac{\phi+\pi-2\gamma_1+2\theta^*}{2}\right) \sin^2\left(\dfrac{\phi+\pi}{2}\right) \sin\left(\dfrac{\phi+\theta^*}{(1-\gamma_1/\pi)}\right)}{\sin\left(\dfrac{\phi+\pi+2\theta^*}{2(1-\gamma_1/\pi)}\right) \sin\left(\dfrac{\phi+\pi-2\gamma_1+2\theta^*}{2(1-\gamma_1/\pi)}\right) \sin\left(\dfrac{\phi-\pi+2\gamma_1}{2(1-\gamma_1/\pi)}\right) \sin\left(\dfrac{\phi+\pi-2\gamma_1}{2(1-\gamma_1/\pi)}\right)}$$

$$\cdot \exp(-[\ell^*\mu^\dagger/\Delta^*][1+\cos\phi]) \qquad . \qquad (3.38)$$

This formula is definitely a poor approximation for $\phi \to \pm(\pi - 2\gamma_1)$ because (3.38) becomes infinite, whereas the correct $g^*$ is finite. Also for $\phi + \theta^* \to 0$ or $-\pi + \gamma_1$ , (3.38) vanishes whereas the correct $g^*$ does not. In that part of the range $|\phi| < \pi - 2\gamma_1$ where (3.37a,b, c,d) apply, (3.38) is still a complicated function of $\phi$ and the parameters $\theta^*$ , $\gamma_1$ , but the dependence upon $\ell^*$ is always (asymptotically) of the form $\ell^{*-1/2}$ times an exponential in $\ell^*$ .

The complications in the formula (3.38) are mostly in the coefficient of the exponential, but, if (3.38a,b,c,d) are true, this coefficient is a slowly varying function of $\phi$ as compared with the exponential factor. If we were to consider the asymptotic expansion of $-\ln g^*$ , the leading term would be simply the argument of the exponential, which is proportional to $\ell^*$ ; the coefficient of the exponential would contribute terms only of order $\ln \ell^*$ or $\ell^{*0}$ . Thus

$$- \ln g^* \sim (\mu^\dagger/\Delta^*)\ell^*[1 + \cos\phi] \quad \text{for} \quad |\phi| < \pi - 2\gamma_1$$

$$\text{and} \quad -\theta^* - \pi + \gamma_1 < \phi < -\theta^* . \tag{3.39a}$$

If (3.33a) applies, the corresponding approximation for $-\ln g^*$ from (3.34) would give

$$- \ln g^* \sim (\mu^\dagger/\Delta^*)\ell^*[\cos(\phi+\pi-2\gamma_1) + \cos\phi] \tag{3.39b}$$

$$\text{for} \quad -\theta^* - \pi + \gamma_1 < \phi < -\pi + 2\gamma_1 ;$$

whereas, if (3.33b) applies, the corresponding approximation from (3.35) is

$$- \ln g^* \sim (\mu^\dagger/\Delta^*)\ell^*[\cos(\phi-\pi+2\gamma_1) + \cos\phi] \tag{3.39c}$$

$$\text{for} \quad \pi - 2\gamma_1 < \phi < -\theta^* .$$

The approximations (3.39a,b,c) are not very accurate for evaluating $g^*$ but they do describe the most important qualitative properties of $g^*$ for large $\ell^*$ .

To illustrate the dependence of (3.39a,b,c) upon the spacial coordinates $\ell^*$ , $\phi$ or $\ell_1'$ , $\ell_2$ , and the parameters $\theta^*$ , $\gamma_1$ , it is convenient to consider the curves of constant $- \ln g^*$ . For $|\phi| < \pi-2\gamma_1$, the curves

$$\ell^* [1 + \cos\phi] = C = \text{constant} \tag{3.40a}$$

are parabolas with axis along $\phi = 0$ , as illustrated in Fig. VII-6 by the two solid line curves labeled $C = 1, C = 2$ . The parabolas for other values of $C$ differ only in a scale of length; they do not depend upon either $\theta^*$ or $\gamma_1$ .

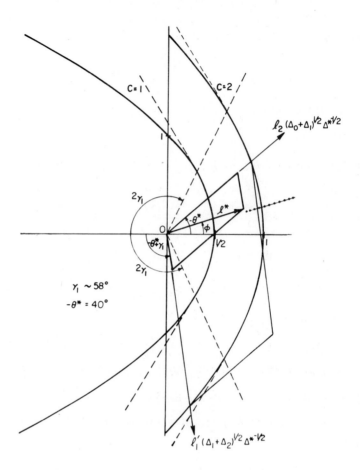

Fig. VII-6.   Approximate curves of constant
probability density in a non-
orthogonal coordinate system.

For $|\phi| > \pi - 2\gamma_1$ , the curves

$$\ell^*[\cos(|\phi| - \pi + 2\gamma_1) + \cos\phi] = C$$

$$2\ell^* \sin(\gamma_1 + |\phi|) \sin \gamma_1 = C$$

(3.40b)

are straight lines making angles $\pm \gamma_1$ with the horizontal. They are, in fact, the tangent lines to the parabola (3.40a) at $\phi = \pm |\pi - 2\gamma_1|$ as shown in Fig. VII-6 by the broken lines. Although these tangent lines depend upon $\gamma_1$ , they are still independent of $- \theta^*$ .

To describe the curves of constant $-\ell n \ g^*$ in terms of the coordinates $\ell_1'$ , $\ell_2$ , one can superimpose on Fig. VII-6 a non-orthogonal coordinate system $\ell_1'(\Delta_1 + \Delta_2)^{1/2}\Delta^{*-1/2}$ , $\ell_2(\Delta_0 + \Delta_1)^{1/2}\Delta^{*-1/2}$ with axes at $\phi = - \theta^*$ , $-\theta^* + \gamma_1 - \pi$ as in Fig. VII-5. For any choice of $\pi - \gamma_1$ (the angle between the coordinate axes) and $-\theta^*$ (the direction of one axis relative to the axis of the parabolas), one can immediately read from the graph of the family of parabolas the value of $C$ associated with any point $\ell_1'$ , $\ell_2$ .

For any given values of $\theta^*$ , $\gamma_1$ we could have drawn the graphs of constant $- \ell n \ g^*$ in a rectangular coordinate system $\ell_1'$ , $\ell_2$ . These would also have been parabolas joined to tangent lines, since any linear mapping of a parabola is another parabola. The shape and orientation of the parabolas in an $\ell_1'$ , $\ell_2$ space, however, would depend upon $\theta^*$ , $\gamma_1$ . To see how the shape of the curves of constant $- \ell n \ g^*$ depend upon $\theta^*$ and $\gamma_1$ , as well as $\ell_1'$ , $\ell_2$ , it is easier to work from Fig. VII-6 with its single family of parabolas but variable rotation and angles between coordinate axes, than to work from a figure with fixed coordinate axes $\ell_1'$ , $\ell_2$ but different families of parabolas for each $\gamma_1$ , $\theta^*$ .

Even though a constant value of $- \ln g^*$ implies a constant value of $g^*$, we have referred to the curves of Fig.VII-6 as curves of constant $- \ln g^*$ rather than $g^*$ as reminder than an approximate evaluation of $- \ln g^*$ from Fig.VII-6 cannot be used for quantitative estimates of $g^*$. The approximations (3.39) discard the coefficient of the exponential factors in (3.34), (3.35) and (3.38) which would, of course, be important in any numerical evaluation of $g^*$ itself. The purpose of Fig.VII-6 is mainly to classify types of behaviors relative to the parameters $\gamma_1$ and $- \theta^*$. For numerical evaluations, we can always go back to the formulas and compute $g^*$ to any desired accuracy.

The curves of Fig.VII-6 have the convenient feature that they are continuous and have continuous derivatives at the angles $\phi = \pm (\pi - 2\gamma_1)$ and the boundaries $\phi = -\theta^*$ and $-\theta^* - \pi + \gamma_1$ corresponding to $\ell_1' = 0$ or $\ell_2 = 0$, where even the complex formula (3.38) is inaccurate. The curves do, however, have discontinuities in the second derivative at $\phi = \pm (\pi - 2\gamma_1)$.

The exact $g^*$ is a smooth function. As is typically true of all previous calculations of distributions, the formulas are most complicated when they are merely trying to describe a smooth interpolation between relatively simple limit behaviors.

To describe an exact curve of constant $g^*$, it might be appropriate to imagine a coordinate system in which one coordinate is the family of curves of Fig.VII-6 for different $C$ values and the other coordinate is $\phi$. Since an exact curve of constant $g^*$ will stay close to a curve of Fig.VII-6 it could then be represented by a curve $C(\phi)$ in a $C, \phi$ space. The function $C(\phi)$ would be nearly constant in the sense that for large $C$, the fractional change in $C(\phi)$ is small for all $\phi$.

If the range of $\phi$ extends into $\phi < -\pi + 2\gamma_1$, the approximation (3.34) is quite accurate; thus $C(\phi)$ is indeed nearly constant for $\phi < -\pi + 2\gamma_1$. If the range of $\phi$ also extends into $\phi > \pi - 2\gamma_1$, the approximation (3.35) is quite accurate so that $C(\phi)$ is again nearly constant for $\phi > \pi - 2\gamma_1$. The nearly constant values of $C(\phi)$ for $\phi < -\pi + 2\gamma_1$ and $\phi > \pi - 2\gamma_1$ will be slightly different, however, (for $\gamma_1 < \pi/2$) because the coefficient of the exponential in (3.34) is different from that in (3.35). The two limit values for $C(\phi)$ differ, however, by an amount which is independent of $C$; therefore the fractional difference is small for large $C$.

Over the range $|\phi| < \pi - 2\gamma_1$, the value of $C(\phi)$ will vary slowly, since the coefficient in (3.29) depends upon $\phi$. Despite the fact that (3.29) becomes infinite for $\phi \to \pm (\pi - 2\gamma_1)$, the correct function will, in effect, merely give a very smooth interpolation between the $C(\phi)$ curves on either side. The interpolation is over the range of $\phi$ where (3.37a,b) fail.

If the boundaries $\ell_1' = 0$ or $\ell_2 = 0$ lie inside the range $|\phi| < \pi - 2\gamma_1$, the curves of Fig. VII-6 will not satisfy the proper boundary conditions at $\phi = -\theta^*$ or $\phi = -\theta^* - \pi + \gamma_1$. The exact curves of constant $g^*$ will show a "boundary layer effect." In the narrow range of $\phi$ where (3.37c,d) fail, the curves will bend so as to approach the boundary with the correct slope.

One can derive approximate formulas which will describe in detail any of the qualitative effects discussed above, but the variation of $C(\phi)$ is a rather complex function of $\gamma_1$ and $-\theta^*$. Except possibly for special values of $\gamma_1$ and $-\theta^*$, the details are not of much practical interest.

364

We can anticipate that our primary interest in the formulas for $g^*$ relates to their properties in the original coordinates $\ell_1'$ , $\ell_2$ . We are particularly interested in the amount of probability which lies in regions of the type $\ell_1' > c_1$ and/or $\ell_2 > c_2$ , and in the values of $g^*$ along $\ell_1' = c_1$ or $\ell_2 = c_2$ for particular choices of $c_1$ , $c_2$ , since this will give some indication of the consequences of finite (but large) storage capacities $c_1$ and/or $c_2$ (and of what is meant by "large").

On Fig. VII-6 one can see immediately from the way the lines of constant $\ell_1'$ or $\ell_2$ intersect the curves of constant $-\ell n\ g^*$ , that the variation of $-\ell n\ g^*$ along a line of constant $\ell_1'$ or $\ell_2$ may be monotone or it may show a single minimum (a maximum for $g^*$) . For the particular choice of $\gamma_1$ and $\theta^*$ $(\gamma_1 \sim 58^o$ , $-\theta^* \sim 40^o)$ in Fig. VII-6, $-\ell n\ g^*$ is monotone along the lines $\ell_1' = $ constant but has a minimum along the lines $\ell_2 = $ constant.

For large values of $\ell_1'$ or $\ell_2$ (such that $\ell^*\mu^\dagger/\Delta^* \gg 1$ for all $\phi$ , $-\theta^* - \pi + \gamma_1 < \phi < -\theta^*)$ any changes in $-\ell n\ g^*$ along lines of constant $\ell_1'$ or $\ell_2$ will be measured on a scale proportional to $\ell_1'$ or $\ell_2$ , i.e., the C values in Fig. VII-6 will change on a scale proportional to the minimum C value along the line. The density $g^*$ measured relative to its maximum value along the line will, therefore, decrease very rapidly as $\phi$ deviates from the point where $g^*$ has its maximum value, regardless of whether this maximum is at a boundary $\ell_2 = 0$ or $\ell_1' = 0$ , or an interior point.

In describing the behavior of $g^*$ along the lines of constant $\ell_1'$ or $\ell_2$ we obviously do not need to know $g^*$ accurately at points where its value is very small relative to its maximum value. Any possible consequence of a finite storage $\ell_1' = c_1$ and/or $\ell_2 = c_2$ , for example, would clearly be sensitive only to the behavior of $g^*$ in its region of maximum concentration. We are, therefore, particularly interested in the location of the maximum of $g^*$ along lines of constant $\ell_1'$ or $\ell_2$ and the behavior of $g^*$ in the vicinity of the maximum, as a function of the parameters $\gamma_1$ and $-\theta^*$ .

From (3.39a) we can evaluate the partial derivatives of $-\ell n\ g^*$ with respect to $\ell_2$ and $\ell_1'$ , for $|\phi| < \pi - 2\gamma_1$

$$\frac{\Delta^{*3/2}}{\mu^\dagger(\Delta_0 + \Delta_1)^{1/2}} \frac{\partial}{\partial\ell_2}(-\ell n\ g^*) = \cos(\theta^* + \phi) + \cos\theta^* \qquad (3.41a)$$

$$\frac{\Delta^{*3/2}}{\mu^\dagger(\Delta_1 + \Delta_2)^{1/2}} \frac{\partial}{\partial\ell_1'}(-\ell n\ g^*) = \cos(\phi+\pi+\theta^*-\gamma_1) + \cos(\pi+\theta^*-\gamma_1) . \qquad (3.41b)$$

By symmetry the right-hand side of (3.41b) can be obtained from (3.41a) by changing $\phi$ to $-\phi$ and $-\theta^*$ to $\pi + \theta^* - \gamma_1$ , so it suffices to consider only one of these in detail.

For constant $\ell_1'$, $\phi$ increases from $-\pi - \theta^* + \gamma_1$ to $-\theta^*$ as $\ell_2$ increases from 0 to $\infty$ . Thus (3.41a) is a monotone increasing function of $\ell_2$ . For $\ell_2 \to 0$ , $\phi \to -\pi - \theta^* + \gamma_1$ , (3.41a) has the value $-\cos\gamma_1$ $+ \cos(-\theta^*)$ . If $-\theta^* > \gamma_1$ , (3.41a) is negative for $\ell_2 \to 0$ (but positive for $\ell_2 \to \infty$). Thus, along a line of constant $\ell_1'$ , $g^*$ has a unique maximum approximately where (3.41a) vanishes, i.e., for

$$\phi = -\pi - 2\theta^* \qquad \text{if } -\theta^* > \gamma_1 . \qquad (3.42a)$$

Correspondingly, along a line of constant $\ell_2$ , $g^*$ has a maximum at

$$\phi = -\pi - 2\theta^* + 2\gamma_1 \qquad \text{if } \pi - 2\gamma_1 > -\theta^* . \qquad (3.42b)$$

Fig. VII-7 shows graphs of (3.42 a and b). The two parallel broken lines of slope 1 represent the range of $\phi$ for various values of $-\theta^*$ but a particular choice of $\gamma_1$ . The upper and lower solid lines represent (3.42a) and (3.42b), the (approximate) location of the maximum of $g^*$ along a line of constant $\ell_1'$ or constant $\ell_2$ respectively.

From Fig. VII-7 or equations (3.42 a or b) we see that if $g^*$ has a internal maximum along either $\ell_1'$ or $\ell_2$ constant, it is located at a value of $\phi$ between the two singularities represented by the broken line radii of Fig. VII-6 at $\phi = \pm (\pi - 2\gamma_1)$ . (Actually equations (3.42a,b) apply only in this range of $\phi$ anyway.) If in Fig. VII-6, the boundary $\ell_1' = 0$ , $\phi = -\theta^*$ has an angle $-\theta^* < \pi - 2\gamma_1$ (as shown), then $g^*$ has a maximum along the line of constant $\ell_2$ at the angle (3.42b) shown in Fig. VII-6 by the dotted radius. If $-\theta^* > \pi - 2\gamma_1$ there is no internal maximum along $\ell_2$ = constant. Correspondingly if the boundary $\ell_2 = 0$ , $\phi = -\pi + \gamma_1 - \theta^*$ has an angle $-\pi + \gamma_1 - \theta^* > -\pi + 2\gamma_1$ , then $g^*$ has a maximum along $\ell_1' = 0$ . If, however, $-\pi + \gamma_1 - \theta^* < -\pi + 2\gamma_1$ (as shown in Fig. VII-6), the maximum of $g^*$ along $\ell_1'$ = constant is on the boundary $\ell_2 = 0$ .

Depending upon the values of $-\theta^*$ and $\gamma_1$ , $g^*$ may have an internal maximum along both lines, $\ell_1'$ = constant or $\ell_2$ = constant, along one or the other, or along neither. If $\pi - 2\gamma_1 > \gamma_1$ ($\gamma_1 < \pi/3$) as illustrated in Fig. VII-7, there is a range of $-\theta^*$ , $\gamma_1 < -\theta^* < \pi - 2\gamma_1$ in which $g^*$ has an internal maximum along both the lines $\ell_1'$ = constant and $\ell_2$ = constant. For $\gamma_1 \to 0$ , this is true for all allowed values of $-\theta^*$ , $0 < -\theta^* < \pi$ . (This is consistent with the results of section 2, although it is not obvious that some of the present approximations will apply for $\gamma_1 \to 0$ because the lines of constant $\ell_1'$ and $\ell_2$ become parallel for $\gamma_1 \to 0$ .)

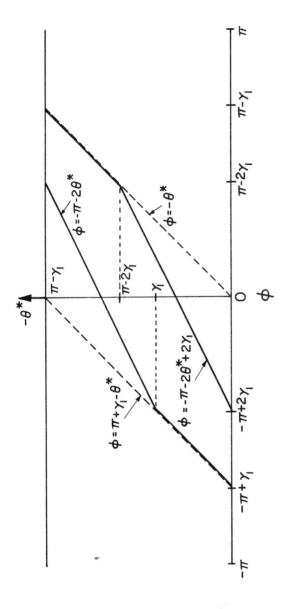

Fig. VII-7. Location of maximum conditional probability densities of $Q_1'$, $Q_2$.

If $\pi/3 < \gamma_1 < \pi/2$ , there is a range of $-\theta^*$ , $\pi - 2\gamma_1 < -\theta^* < \gamma_1$, for which there is no internal maximum of $g^*$ along either line. In particular for $\gamma_1 = \pi/2$ , there is no internal maximum for any values of $-\theta^*$ in the allowed range $0 < -\theta^* < \pi - \gamma_1 = \pi/2$ . This is, of course, consistent with the fact that $g^*$ is an exponential function of both $\ell_1'$ and $\ell_2$ for $\gamma_1 = \pi/2$ and has maxima on the boundaries $\ell_1' = 0$ or $\ell_2 = 0$ .

For $0 < -\theta^* < \gamma_1$ and constant $\ell_1'$ , $g^*$ is a monotone decreasing function of $\phi$ , i.e., $\ell_2$ , and therefore has its maximum at $\phi = -\theta^* + \gamma_1 - \pi$ , $\ell_2 = 0$ . For $-\theta^* + \gamma_1 - \pi < \phi < -\pi + 2\gamma_1$ , $g^*$ is nearly an exponential function of $\ell_2$ as described in (3.34). For $-\alpha_1 \ell_1' \gg 1$ , this formula is quite accurate, except if $-\theta^*$ is too close to $\gamma_1$ , i.e., $\alpha_2^*$ in (3.34) is too close to zero. For $-\theta^* < \gamma_1$, the formula is valid for a positive range of $\phi$ thus a range of $\ell_2$ of order $\ell_1'$ , which includes most of the distribution of $Q_2$ . Indeed (3.34) is properly normalized. Thus, for $-\theta^* < \gamma_1$ , the conditional distribution of $Q_2$ given $Q_1'$ is essentially an exponential with parameter $\alpha_2^*$ .

If, on the other hand, $-\theta^* > \gamma_1$ (but again $\theta^*$ is not too close to $\gamma_1$) , $g^*$ as a function of $\ell_2$ has a maximum value at $\phi = -\pi - 2\theta^*$ as in (3.42a). Most of the conditional distribution of $Q_2$ will lie in some neighborhood of this maximum. From (3.38) we see that, for $(\ell^* \mu^\dagger / \Delta^*) \gg 1$ , the variation of $g^*$ with $\phi$ for $\phi$ near $-\pi - 2\theta^*$ will be dominated by the behavior of the exponential factor which is a rapidly varying function of $\phi$ . The coefficient of the exponential will be essentially independent of $\phi$ over the small range of $\phi$ containing most of the distribution of $Q_2$ (except for $\phi \approx -\pi - 2\theta^* \approx -\pi + 2\gamma_1$).

To estimate $g^*$ near this maximum, we can evaluate the coefficient of the exponential at $\phi = -\pi - 2\theta^*$ and make a power series expansion of the exponent of the exponential about this maximum point, either in powers of $\phi + \pi + 2\theta^*$ or in powers of the difference between $\ell_2$ and the value of $\ell_2$, $\ell_{2m}$, at $\phi = -\pi - 2\theta^*$. The terms of the expansion which are linear in $\phi$ or $\ell_2$ will vanish because the first derivative of the exponent vanishes at the maximum point. If we keep only the constant and quadratic terms in the expansion, we obtain the form,

$$g^*(c_1 - \ell_1', \ell_2) \simeq [-\alpha_1 \exp(\ell_1'\alpha_1)] \, (2\pi\sigma_{2m})^{-1/2} \, \exp\left(-\frac{(\ell_2 - \ell_{2m})^2}{2\,\sigma_{2m}^2}\right), \quad (3.43)$$

with

$$\ell_{2m} = \ell_1' \left(\frac{\Delta_1 + \Delta_2}{\Delta_0 + \Delta_1}\right)^{\frac{1}{2}} \frac{\sin(-\gamma_1 - \theta^*)}{\sin(-\theta^*)} \,, \qquad \sigma_{2m}^2 = \frac{\ell_1' \, \Delta^{*5/2}}{(\Delta_0 + \Delta_1)^{3/2} \mu^\dagger \sin^3(-\theta^*)} \,, \quad (3.44)$$

i.e., the conditional distribution of $Q_2$ given $Q_1$ is a normal distribution. Note that (3.43) is consistent with the known fact that the marginal distribution of $Q_1$, i.e., the integral of (3.43) with respect to $\ell_2$, is an exponential in $\ell_1'$.

Neither (3.43) nor (3.34) is valid if $-\theta^* - \gamma_1$ is too close to zero. As $-\theta^* - \gamma_1 \to 0$ from above, (3.43) predicts that the distribution of $Q_2$ is normal with a mean approaching zero and a standard deviation proportional to $\ell_1'^{1/2}$, but some of this distribution must be reflected because $Q_2$ cannot be negative. As $-\theta^* - \gamma_1 \to 0$ from below, (3.34) predicts that the distribution of $Q_2$ is exponential with a parameter $\alpha_2^*$ which goes to zero. One can obtain more accurate approximations from (3.29) that will apply through the transition, but they only give a quantitative description of the obvious; that the transition is a smooth one. The details of this are not very important, particularly since they are relevant only for a narrow range of $\theta^*$ .

Any of the above comments about the behavior of $g^*$ along lines of constant $\ell_1'$ can be transformed into corresponding statements about its behavior along lines of constant $\ell_2$ . One need only interchange $\ell_1'$ and $\ell_2$ , $-\theta^*$ and $\pi - \gamma_1 + \theta^*$ , $\Delta_0$ and $\Delta_2$ , etc.

To see how the distribution $g^*$ depends upon the original parameters $\Delta_j$ and $\mu_j$ , it suffices to recall that $\gamma_1$ is essentially a measure of $\Delta_1$ relative to $\Delta_0$ and $\Delta_2$ ($\gamma_1 = \pi/2$ for $\Delta_1 = 0$ and $\gamma_1 = 0$ for $\Delta_0 = \Delta_2 = 0$), and $-\theta^*$ is primarily a measure of the relative size of $\mu_0 - \mu_1$ and $\mu_2 - \mu_1$ ($-\theta^* \to 0$ for $\mu_0 - \mu_1 \to 0$ , $-\theta^* = \gamma_0$ for $\mu_0 - \mu_1 = \mu_2 - \mu_1$ , and $-\theta^* \to \pi - \gamma_1$ for $\mu_2 - \mu_1 \to 0$). The qualitative behavior of $g^*$ (for large $\ell^*$) can now be seen directly from Fig. VII-6 in which the curves of constant $-\ell n\ g^*$ depend upon $\gamma_1$ and $-\theta^*$ in a very simple way. The parabolas of Fig. VII-6 do not depend upon either $\gamma_1$ or $-\theta^*$ . The complete curves of constant $-\ell n\ g^*$ are independent of $-\theta^*$ and depend upon $\gamma_1$ only in that the tangent lines are drawn from points at angles $\pm(\pi - 2\gamma_1)$ and have a direction at angles $\pm\gamma_1$ to the horizontal. The variation of $g^*$ with $\ell_1'$ , $\ell_2$ depends upon $\gamma_1$ and $-\theta^*$ in that the coordinates of $\ell_1'$ , $\ell_2$ in Fig. VII-6 are along the directions $-\pi + \gamma_1 - \theta^*$ and $-\theta^*$ respectively.

In the limit $\gamma_1 \to \pi/2$ , $\Delta_1 \to 0$ , the tangent lines of Fig. VII-6 are to be drawn from points at angles $\pm(\pi - 2\gamma_1) \to 0$ ; the parabolic section of the curves of constant $-\ell n\ g^*$ disappears and these curves approach vertical lines. The value of $-\theta^*$ can vary from 0 for $\mu_0 - \mu_1 = 0$ to $\pi/2$ for $\mu_2 - \mu_1 = 0$ while $-\pi + \gamma_1 - \theta^*$ goes from

$- \pi/2$ to $0$. As $\mu_0 - \mu_1 \to 0$, the direction of $\ell_1'$ approaches $-\pi/2$, nearly parallel to the lines of constant $-\ln g^*$. Thus $g^*$ becomes nearly independent of $\ell_1'$, i.e., the distribution of $Q_1'$ becomes nearly uniform and spread infinitely far, for any value of $Q_2$. (Since the curves of Fig. VII-6 or equations (3.40), do not include the normalization of the distribution $g^*$, there is no difficulty here with the fact that $g^*$ itself must go to zero if the range of $Q_1'$ becomes infinite.) Correspondingly, for $\mu_2 - \mu_1 \to 0$, the direction of $\ell_2$ becomes vertical and the distribution of $Q_2$ is spread infinitely far. For any value of $-\theta^*$, the distribution of $Q_1'$ and $Q_2$ are (exactly) exponential. Of course, all these facts were previously known. The purpose in identifying them again is to demonstrate how they are illustrated in Fig. VII-6.

As $\gamma_1$ decreases ($\Delta_1$ increases), the parabolic section of the curve of constant $-\ln g^*$ between angles $\pm(\pi - 2\gamma_1)$ increases; so does the angle $\pi - \gamma_1$ between the coordinate axes. For small values of $-\theta^*$ (small $\mu_0 - \mu_1$), the angle of the axis $\ell_1'$ approaches $-\pi + \gamma_1$ (which is less than the angle $-\pi + 2\gamma_1$ where the parabola terminates). The lines of constant $\ell_2$ again become nearly parallel to the lines of constant $-\ln g^*$, at least in the sector $-\pi + \gamma_1 < \phi < -\pi + 2\gamma_1$. Thus the distribution of $Q_1'$ again becomes very broad for $\mu_0 - \mu_1 \to 0$ (as would be expected). Most of the joint distribution of $Q_1'$, $Q_2$ lies in this sector, in a range of $\ell_1'$, $\ell_2$ where (3.34) applies; i.e., the distribution is nearly joint exponential.

For small values of $-\theta^*$, the conditional distribution of $Q_1'$ given $Q_2$ has a maximum at an angle $\phi$ slightly larger than $-\pi + 2\gamma_1$. For $-\theta^* \to 0$, however, this maximum of $g^*$ along a line of constant

372

$\ell_2$ occurs so close to the angle $-\pi + 2\gamma_1$ that the normal distribution in $\ell_1$ for $\phi > -\pi + 2\gamma_1$ (the distribution analogous to (3.43) but with the role of $\ell_1'$ and $\ell_2$ reversed) joins a very slowly decreasing exponential distribution in $\ell_1'$ almost immediately after $\ell_1$ passes the maximum point of $g^*$. Because of the positive correlation between $Q_1'$ and $Q_2$, it is relatively improbable for $Q_1'$ to lie in the range corresponding to $-\pi + 2\gamma < \phi < 0$, i.e., it is relatively improbable, for given $Q_2$, to have

$$Q_1'/Q_2 \lesssim 2\Delta_1/(\Delta_1 + \Delta_2) .$$

Since the distribution of $Q_1'$ is very broad, this exclusion of relatively small values of $Q_1'$ has little effect upon most properties of $Q_1'$.

In (3.34) we noted that the exponential parameter $\alpha_2^*$ was not the same as the parameter $\alpha_2$ of the marginal distribution of $Q_2$ (although they are nearly the same for small $\mu_0 - \mu_1$). For small $-\theta^*$, i.e., small $\mu_0 - \mu_1$, however, there is a relatively small probability associated with $-\pi + 2\gamma_1 < \phi$. Thus the marginal distribution of $Q_2$ should be approximately equal to the integral of (3.34c) with respect to $\ell_1'$ from the "boundary" $2\Delta_1\ell_2/(\Delta_1 + \Delta_2)$, corresponding to $\phi = -\pi + 2\gamma_1$, to $\ell_1' = \infty$. Such an integration of (3.34c) does, in fact, give exactly the correct marginal distribution of $Q_2$, $\alpha_2\exp(-\alpha_2\ell_2)$; i.e., along any line of constant $\ell_2$, if we approximate $g^*$ by simply truncating (3.34c) at $\phi = -\pi + 2\gamma_1$, we underestimate $g^*$ for $-\pi + 2\gamma_1 < \phi$ but overestimate it for $\phi < -\pi + 2\gamma_1$ in such a way that the integral of the error over all $\ell_1'$ is exactly zero (for any value of $-\theta^*$).

As $\mu_0 - \mu_1$ and $-\theta^*$ increase, the maximum of $g^*$ along the lines of constant $\ell_2$ at angle $-\pi + 2\gamma_1 - 2\theta^*$ moves away from the critical angle $-\pi + 2\gamma_1$. The exponential tail of the distribution for $\phi < -\pi + 2\gamma_1$ decays more rapidly and has a smaller amplitude. The bulk of the distribution becomes concentrated near the maximum of $g^*$. As shown in Fig. VII-7, the maximum of $g^*$ continues to move to larger values of $\phi$ as $-\theta^*$ increases until it reaches the other critical angle at $\pi - 2\gamma_1$. As $-\theta^*$ passes $\pi - 2\gamma_1$ the normal distribution for $Q_1'$ given $Q_2$ switches back to another exponential distribution.

By symmetry, one obtains an analogous behavior for the distribution of $Q_2$ given $Q_1$ as $\mu_2 - \mu_1$ and $\pi - \gamma_1 + \theta^*$ increase from 0.

4. **Service Rate for Large But Finite $c_1, c_2$.** An evaluation of the joint distribution $g^*$ or its transform $K(\lambda_1,\lambda_2)$ from VI(1.13) when $c_1$ and/or $c_2$ are finite appears to be hopelessly difficult. The most important practical questions concerning finite storages, however, relate to consequences of "large" but finite values of $c_1$ and $c_2$. The simplest question is: how large must $c_1$ and $c_2$ be in order that they have a negligible effect upon the queue distributions and particularly the overall service rate $\mu$? Secondly one might wish to obtain some quantitative "first order" estimates of the decrease in $\mu$ caused by finite but large $c_1$ and/or $c_2$. One can use the solutions for $c_1$ and $c_2 = \infty$ described in Chapters VI and VII, along with some of the previous results from Chapters III and IV for $\mu_0 = \mu_1 = \mu_2$ to obtain answers to these questions without actually evaluating the $g^*$ explicitly.

We could make some estimates of the effect of finite $c_1$, $c_2$ in the case $\mu_0 < \mu_1$, $\mu_2$ or $\mu_2 < \mu_0$, $\mu_1$ but the solutions for $c_1$,

374

$c_2 = \infty$ in Chapter VI are more complex than those for $\mu_1 < \mu_0$, $\mu_2$
described in this chapter. It also seems more likely in practical applications that one would be interested in the latter. If one had a sequence of servers with service rates $\mu_j$ and finite (but large) storage
capacities $c_j$, one would first identify the smallest of the $\mu_j$'s
(the bottleneck). One might then further identify that pair of servers
and intermediate storage which gives a smallest $\mu$, as discussed in
section III 1. In most practical problems it is likely to be the server
with the smallest $\mu_j$ which limits the overall service rate, rather
than some faster server which is more severely constrained by storage.
The objective in designing the storage generally is to provide enough
storage both upstream and downstream of the slowest server so that it is
seldom blocked.

Whereas the results of Chapter VI could be used to assess the consequences of finite storages between the bottleneck and two other servers on the same side, either upstream or downstream of the bottleneck,
the results of the present chapter relate to the case of finite storages
between the bottleneck and two servers on opposite sides of the bottleneck. We will consider here only the latter.

We already know that, if $c_1 = \infty$, the marginal distribution for
$Q_2$ behaves as if it were the queue for a single server system fed by
the output from server 1. The overall service rate for such a system
is known for any finite $c_2$ from section II 3. Specifically, from
(II 3.2)

$$\mu = \frac{(\mu_2 + \mu_1)}{2} - \frac{(\mu_2 - \mu_1)}{2} \, \text{ctnh}\left(\frac{\alpha_2 c_2}{2}\right) \, .$$

If $\alpha_2 c_2$ is sufficiently large, we can expand $\mathrm{ctnh}(\alpha_2 c_2/2)$ in powers of $\exp(-\alpha_2 c_2)$ and obtain

$$\mu \simeq \mu_1 - (\mu_2 - \mu_1)\exp(-\alpha_2 c_2)[1 + 0(\exp(-\alpha_2 c_2))] \ . \tag{4.1}$$

Thus the blocking effect decreases proportional to $\exp(-\alpha_2 c_2)$ . Similarly, for $c_2 = \infty$ , the marginal distribution of $Q_1$ behaves as if it were the queue for a single server system fed by server 0. The corresponding service rate is

$$\mu = \frac{(\mu_0 + \mu_1)}{2} - \frac{(\mu_0 - \mu_1)}{2} \mathrm{ctnh}\left(-\frac{\alpha_1 c_1}{2}\right)$$

$$\simeq \mu_1 - (\mu_0 - \mu_1)\exp(\alpha_1 c_1)[1 + 0(\exp(\alpha_1 c_1))] \tag{4.2}$$

$$\text{for} \quad \exp(\alpha_1 c_1) \ll 1 \ .$$

Since a finite value of $c_1$ will certainly cause a smaller value of $\mu$ than $c_1 = \infty$ for any value of $c_2$ , and a finite $c_2$ will cause a smaller $\mu$ than $c_2 = \infty$ for any finite $c_1$ , it follows that

$$\mu_1 - \mu \geq \max\{(\mu_2 - \mu_1)\exp(-\alpha_2 c_2) \ , \ (\mu_0 - \mu_1)\exp(\alpha_1 c_1)\} \tag{4.3}$$

$$\text{for} \quad \exp(-\alpha_2 c_2) \ll 1 \ , \quad \exp(\alpha_1 c_1) \ll 1 \ .$$

But a finite value of $c_1$ will also cause server 1 to be interrupted occasionally thereby reducing the input to server 2. This, in turn, will reduce the queue length $Q_2$ as compared with $c_1 = \infty$ , and therefore decrease the probability that $Q_2$ will be large enough to cause server 1 to be blocked by a finite storage $c_2$ . We conclude from this and (I 7.8) that the combined reduction in service rate due to $c_1 < \infty$

and $c_2 < \infty$ can be no greater than the sum of the reductions due to $c_1 < \infty$, $c_2 = \infty$, and $c_1 = \infty$, $c_2 < \infty$. Therefore

$$\mu_1 - \mu \leq (\mu_2 - \mu_1)\exp(-\alpha_2 c_2) + (\mu_0 - \mu_1)\exp(\alpha_1 c_1) \qquad (4.4)$$

$$\text{for } \exp(-\alpha_2 c_2) \ll 1 \text{ and } \exp(\alpha_1 c_1) \ll 1 .$$

Similar types of bounds were used previously in section V 5. Together (4.3) and (4.4) determine $\mu_1 - \mu$ at least within a factor of 2 even when the two terms of (4.3) or (4.4) are equal. If either term is large compared with the other, the upper and lower bounds are nearly equal. The only problem now is to obtain better estimates of $\mu$ when the two terms of (4.3) or (4.4) are of comparable size.

A finite value of $c_1$ will not only truncate the distribution of $Q_1'$ for $Q_1' > c_1$, it will also distort the distribution $g^*(c_1 - \ell_1', \ell_2)$ for $\ell_1'$ close to $c_1$, because $g^*$ must satisfy certain boundary conditions along $\ell_1' = c_1$. For $c_2 < \infty$, $g^*$ must also satisfy certain boundary conditions for $\ell_2 = c_2$; and, for $c_1 < \infty$ and $c_2 < \infty$, it must vanish at the corner $\ell_1' = c_1$, $\ell_2 = c_2$.

Despite this distortion, we know that the marginal distribution of $Q_1'$ for $c_2 = \infty$ and the marginal distribution of $Q_2$ for $c_1 = \infty$ are simply truncated exponential distributions. Thus, for $c_2 = \infty$, any distortion of the joint distribution near the line $\ell_1' = c_1$ has essentially no effect upon the integral of the joint distribution with respect to $\ell_2$ along a line of constant $\ell_1'$ except that the truncated exponential distribution of $Q_1'$ must be renormalized (but this contributes an effect of second order in $\exp(\alpha_1 c_1)$ to the value of $\mu$). This is true for $c_2 = \infty$, but we now ask what effect a finite value of $c_2$ would

have on the integral of the joint distribution along the line $\ell_1' = c_1$
(i.e., on the contribution to $\mu$ from $Q_1' = c_1$)?

If $Q_2$ should reach $c_2$, this interrupts server 1 which causes
a decrease in $Q_1'$. Thus any probability which is reflected off the
boundary $Q_2 = c_2$ tends, on the average, to drift toward both smaller
$Q_2$ and $Q_1'$ (although fluctuations may cause them to increase temporarily). The point here is that this probability becomes dispersed over
the whole range of $\ell_1'$, $\ell_2$; it does not tend to go directly toward
the other boundary $\ell_1' = c_1$. The only place where there is a strong
local interaction between the two boundaries is near the corner $\ell_1' = c_1$,
$\ell_2 = c_2$. Any path of $Q_1'(t)$, $Q_2(t)$ which goes near this corner is
reflected very quickly ($g^*$ vanishes at the corner). We expect, therefore, that the presence of a second boundary at $\ell_2 = c_2$ will have
little effect upon the joint distribution near $\ell_1' = c_1$ except that it
causes $g^*$ to vanish at the corner $\ell_1' = c_1$, $\ell_2 = c_2$ and for $\ell_2 > c_2$.
It will also cause a slight change in the amplitude of $g^*$ everywhere
due to a renormalization of the probability, but this is again a second
order effect near the boundaries. If the integral of $g^*(c_1-\ell_1',\ell_2)$
along $\ell_1' = c_1$ for $c_2 = \infty$ were to receive a negligible contribution
from the range of $\ell_2$, $\ell_2 > c_2$, one would not expect the finite storage $c_2$ to have much effect upon the marginal distribution of $Q_1'$ at
$\ell_1' = c_1$.

To describe the effect of finite values for both $c_1$ and $c_2$ upon
$\mu_1 - \mu$, we return again to Fig.VII- 6 and 7 for preliminary estimates
of the integrals of $g^*(c_1-\ell_1',\ell_2)$ along the two boundaries $\ell_1' = c_1$
and $\ell_2 = c_2$, i.e., the marginal distributions of $Q_1'$ at $c_1$ and $Q_2$
at $c_2$ required in (I 7.8). We will show that, except in certain limiting

cases, the value of $\mu_1 - \mu$ is much closer to the bound (4.4) than (4.3) whenever these are appreciably different.

From (3.41a,b) we see that $-\ln g^*$ is decreasing in $\ell_1'$ for $\phi < -\pi - 2\theta^*$ (if $-\theta^* > \gamma_1$) and it is decreasing in $\ell_2$ for $\phi > -\pi - 2\theta^* + 2\gamma_1$ (if $\pi - 2\gamma_1 > -\theta^*$). It is not possible for both to be true for the same $\phi$, i.e., at the same values of $\ell_1'$, $\ell_2$, except possibly if $\gamma_1 = 0$ and $\phi = -\pi - 2\theta^*$. In particular, at $\ell_1' = c_1$, $\ell_2 = c_2$, $-\ln g^*$ must be increasing (and $g^*$ decreasing) in the direction of either $\ell_1'$ or $\ell_2$ or both. Since the main contribution to the integrals of $g^*$ along $\ell_1' = c_1$ or $\ell_2 = c_2$ comes from some neighborhood of the maximum points along these lines, to truncate an integral at a point where $g^*$ is already decreasing will have little effect upon the value of $\mu_1 - \mu$. Thus a truncation of both integrals along $\ell_1' = c_1$ and $\ell_2 = c_2$ can at most have a significant effect upon only one of the two terms of (I 7.8) or (4.4).

In order for the two terms of (4.3) or (4.4) to be of comparable size, however, it is necessary that the minimum value of $-\ln g^*$ (maximum value of $g^*$) along $\ell_1' = c_1$ be approximately the same as the minimum value of $-\ln g^*$ along $\ell_2 = c_2$, for otherwise the exponents of the two terms in (4.3) or (4.4) would not match (for large $-\alpha_1 c_1$ and $\alpha_2 c_2$). If $-\ln g^*$ is decreasing ($g^*$ increasing) with $\ell_1'$ for $\ell_1' < c_1$ along the line $\ell_2 = c_2$ so that its minimum on $\ell_1' < c_1$ is at $\ell_1' = c_1$ (so that the truncation of the integral of $g^*$ along $\ell_2 = c_2$ might have a significant effect upon its value), then it is also true that, without any truncation, the minimum value of $-\ln g^*$ along $\ell_2 = c_2$ is less than the minimum of $-\ln g^*$ along the line $\ell_1' = c_1$. The blocking effect due to $Q_2 = c_2$ is therefore small compared with that due to $Q_1 = c_1$.

Correspondingly, if $-\ln g^*$ is decreasing with $\ell_2$ for $\ell_2 < c_1$ along the line $\ell_1 = c_1$, the blocking effect due to $Q_1 = c_1$ is small compared with that due to $Q_1 = c_2$. In any other case, $-\ln g^*$ is increasing in $\ell_1'$ and $\ell_2$ along $\ell_2 = c_2$ and $\ell_1' = c_1$ respectively for $\ell_1'$, $\ell_2$ near $c_1$, $c_2$, and the truncation of either integral will have a small effect upon the value of $\mu_1 - \mu$.

We conclude from this that the bound (4.4) is actually an approximate equality (except possibly for very small values of $\gamma_1$). Any time one of the terms of (4.4) gives an inaccurate estimate of the appropriate term in (I 7.8), this term is small compared with the other term anyway.

Although some of the approximations of section 3 are of questionable accuracy for small $\gamma_1$, the exact $g^*$ for $\gamma_1 = 0$ is described in section 2. One can show from (2.12) that the curves of constant $-\ln g^*$ are still either straight lines or parabolas similar to Fig. VII-6. The only difference is that certain asymptotic properties vary like $\ell^{*1/2}$ instead of $\ell^*$. It is also true, even for $\gamma_1 = 0$, that (4.4) is nearly an equality for $\alpha_2 > 0$, $\alpha_1 < 0$ except in the limiting case $\mu_0 \to \mu_2$ $(\alpha_1 + \alpha_2 \to 0)$ for which the distribution $g^*$ lies (nearly) along the line $\ell_1' = \ell_2$ as discussed in section 2. Thus the cases for which (4.3) is more accurate than (4.4), when they are appreciably different, are quite exceptional.

In comparing the results here with those of section IV 5, we see that, in some respects at least, the qualitative properties of $g^*$ are simpler for $\alpha_2 > 0$, $\alpha_1 < 0$ than for $\alpha_1 = \alpha_2 = 0$ $(\mu_0 = \mu_1 = \mu_2)$. Whereas for $\alpha_2 > 0$, $\alpha_1 < 0$ any probability reflected off a boundary $\ell_1' = c_1$ or $\ell_2 = c_2$ tends to drift away from both boundaries; for $\mu_0 = \mu_1 = \mu_2$, the probability follows a free diffusion and has a non-negligible probability of hitting any boundary after any reflection. Thus in section IV 5, we found a much more complex dependence of $\mu$ upon $c_1$ and $c_2$ than here.

## VIII.  Epilogue

. <u>What Was the Question?</u>  This analysis of tandem queues ends here not because "the problem" has been solved nor because one can go no further,
but because the author, after about three years of rather concentrated
effort, has lost some of his enthusiasm.  Each new chapter, which began
with the expectation that the analysis would be straightforward, has led
to some subtle complications which required that the chapter be reorgan-
ized and rewritten three or four times.  Nothing was easy and it seems
unlikely that any further analysis will be easy either.  Furthermore,
if one were to continue by treating systems with three or more storages,
the number of parameters and special cases gets out of hand.  If there
were some <u>specific</u> problem that one wished to pursue, there is a good
chance that it could be analysed, but, at the moment, no problem stands
out as being singularly more important than others.

We will conclude this study by summarizing some of the principal
results, commenting further on the advantages and limitations of some
of the mathematical techniques, and speculating on what directions one
could (or could not) pursue with a reasonable likelihood of success.

There are two motivations behind this investigation, one was to test
the power of some mathematical techniques, and the other was to find approximate solutions to some practical problems.  An attempt to do both
at the same time perhaps means that one can do neither very well.  If
the motivation were only the former, one would feel obliged to give rigorous proofs or accurate estimates of errors and to avoid reckless con-
jectures.  Certain parts of the analysis described here would have been
deleted as incomplete and others would have been described in twice the
detail so as to prove the obvious.  If the motivation were only the latter,

much of the mathematical analysis would have been eliminated entirely; only the simple techniques would be described in detail and the complex results would be reduced to charts and graphs or "it can be shown that --.

There were, in fact, some specific problems that motivated this study. Tandem queues arise in a host of specific transportation systems, but the particular problem that triggered the present study was that of determining the effect of a finite block length on the overall service rate of a sequence of traffic signals along a highway. It began with an attempt to analyse the behavior of a sequence of _identical_ servers (traffic intersections), i.e., parts of Chapters I and III, but, as it turns out, this special case of identical servers, instead of being a simple special case, was a complicated special case. Needless to say, the solution of this particular problem does not justify the effort expended in the present study (the original question was only partly answered and has long since been forgotten), but, since any highway can be considered as a sequence of service points with finite storage capacity, the phenomena of a queue behind one server blocking another is rather basic to the analysis of traffic flow generally.

Although similar types of problems exist in the analysis of telephone switching networks, no attempt has been made to orient the analysis toward the special types of problems encountered in this area, despite the fact that the service systems in telephone networks handle exceptionally large arrival rates for which the approximation techniques used here are particularly well suited.

Certainly the motivation for this study was not to develop mathematical methods for their own sake. The motivation was to develop techniques and describe phenomena relevant to the initial design of transportation systems, or, perhaps more important, to the prediction of the

consequences of modifications in an existing system (widening a highway,
increasing the spacing between traffic signals, moving a service point
so as to shift storage space from one side of a server to the other, etc).
To analyse a real (and complex) system one does not wish to waste time
analysing parts of the system which cause no problems; to collect accurate data is expensive and tedious. One wants to identify the critical
points of the system; one wants simple tools for simple problems and to
recognize when a problem is not simple.

One common type of problem for an existing tandem queueing system
is that it has a "bottleneck." One need not measure all the service
rates and storages to calculate where it is. One knows where it is from
observation; it is where the queue usually forms. The question is:
what will be the consequences of increasing the service rate or storage
capacities of selected servers? One can also usually identify from ob-
servations if the storage capacity may be limiting the flow. The characteristic feature of this is that the server which usually causes a long
queue is sometimes idle for lack of customers upstream or lack of storage
downstream. If one has the ability to increase the service rate or the
storage at the bottleneck so as to relieve the bottleneck, one must look
to see where the new bottleneck will be. The likely candidates are the
servers with service rates closest to that of the original bottleneck.
If one does not know for sure which one it will be, one typically would
at least know the most probable candidates so that one need make measure-
ments of the service rates and capacities at only a few key locations.

Another common problem occurs if, in the schematic representation
of figure I-1, the "bottleneck" is server 0. In this case server 0 would
usually be interpreted as an artificial generator of some given stationary
arrival process with arrival rate $\mu_0$ less than the effective service

rate of the system consisting of servers 1, 2, --, n.  Except possibly
for "lost call" models in telephone traffic, one would ordinarily assume
that the storage to the first server  $c_1$  is effectively infinite.  For
such a system one would typically be interested in the average total
number of customers in the storages  $c_1, \ldots, c_n$ ,  i.e.,

$$E\left\{\sum_{j=1}^{n} Q_j(t)\right\} = \sum_{j=1}^{n} E\{Q_j(t)\} , \tag{1.1}$$

in particular the equilibrium value.  Equivalently, one is interested
in the expected transit time of a customer through the system, which, by
virtue of the relation  "L = λW,"  is simply  $\mu_0^{-1}$  times (1.1).

For the above type of system, there is again usually some particular
server which causes most of the delay;  it is likely to be the one with
the smallest  $\mu_j$   (j ≠ 0).  For an existing system one can see which servers are causing most of the delays but one would like to know the consequences of making appropriate improvements in the service rates or storages at critical locations.

Most real tandem queueing systems can be changed in many ways, i.e.,
there are many parameters associated with the description of the system.
An analytic approach has an advantage over a simulation in that it can
often describe, at least qualitatively, what parameters are important
and the consequences of changes in certain parameters.  In effect, it
should reduce the dimensionality of the parameter space.  If it cannot
actually give the solution to a particular problem to a desired accuracy,
it should greatly aid in the search for a solution if one must resort to
a simulation.

2. Graphical Representations. The simplest tools for making a preliminary analysis of a queueing system are described already in the first few sections of Chapter I. If one can disregard irregularities in the service rates (stochastic behavior) of the servers, one can easily describe the complete time-dependent (transient) behavior of the system in terms of the service rates $\mu_j$ and storages $c_j$. Although the discussion in Chapter I is limited to the case of time-independent service rates, the graphical solutions of figure I-3 or the analytic solution (I 2.3) can easily be generalized to time-dependent rates particularly a time-dependent input $\mu_0$.

The graphical solution clearly shows the obvious fact that the bottleneck (the server with the smallest $\mu_j$) will eventually cause a queue to form upstream filling all storages upstream, and cause all queues downstream to vanish. Although the queue $Q_j(t)$ behind the jth server was defined as $D_{j-1}(t) - D_j(t) \le c_j$, it is also useful to recognize that, if $Q_j(t) = c_j$, the "queue" behind the jth server could alternatively have been defined as the number of consecutive filled storage spaces behind the jth server. If $\mu_{j-1}$ is significantly larger than $\mu_j$, it has essentially no effect upon the overall behavior of the system. If this server were removed, the storage behind the jth server would be reinterpreted as $c_{j-1} + c_j$. Actually this removal of unessential servers is, in effect, implied in the modeling of most physical systems. On a highway, for example, one could consider every point along the highway as a "server" with a specified service rate (and a very small storage space), but in idealizing the system one only considers certain critical points as "service points" (for example, the highway junctions).

This removal of unessential servers seems to be one of the most troublesome features of any rigorous mathematical treatment of stochastic queues. One of the advantages of dealing with the cumulative counts $D_j(t)$ rather than with the queue lengths $Q_j(t)$ is that $D_j(t)$ has the simple interpretation of being the cumulative count of customers that an observer would see if he watched customers pass the jth server. To ob-serve the counts $D_j(t)$ , one need not also observe the counts $D_{j-1}(t)$. Although one might not be able to remove the server $j - 1$ , one can remove the observer.

Of course, the purpose of a theory is to predict the behavior of $D_j(t)$ from certain other descriptions of the system parameters (service rates, storages, etc.). The critical question is whether or not the presence of a server $j - 1$ affects the predicted behavior of $D_j(t)$ . If it does not, then one must also ask whether or not, for any purpose, one really wanted to know the behavior of $D_{j-1}(t)$ . The answer to the latter is usually negative. In most cases, one is interested only in the input $D_0(t)$ and the output $D_n(t)$ . From these one can evaluate the number of customers in the system $D_0(t) - D_n(t)$ and, if customers are served FIFO, the time which the jth customer spends in the system $D_n^{-1}(j) - D_0^{-1}(j)$. If one chooses to analyse the system by studying the behavior of the $Q_j(t)$ , one is already committed to an investigation of the behavior of each server, even though the final question may not require that one know the individual queue lengths.

Indeed, the most complicated mathematical aspects of most queueing systems occur when there is hardly any queue at some server and one worries about whether the queue is 0 or 1; or when a storage is nearly full and one worries about whether there is 0 or 1 empty spaces. But if there is a sizeable queue somewhere in the system and one is concerned with the

total delay or service rate of the system as a whole, it really does not
make much difference whether some particular queue is 0 or 1. Furthermore when a queue changes from 1 to 0, the customer who has been served
merely joins another queue leaving the sum of the $Q_j(t)$ constant. It
is such service points that one would disregard in the idealization of
a real physical system since they have little effect upon the remaining
$D_j(t)$ .

3. **Diffusion Approximations.** Unfortunately, the deterministic approximations do not, by themselves, define their own limitations. Even if·sto-
chastic effects are negligible, one at least must make some order of
magnitude estimates to verify that they can be neglected. If they are
not negligible, one would, of course, wish to obtain some quantitative
estimates of their effect.

Stochastic effects are of practical significance primarily in two
respects. First, and most important, the combined effect of stochastic
fluctuations and finite storages can cause a reduction in the overall
service rate of the system. Particularly if there are finite storages
either upstream or downstream of a bottleneck, it is possible that the
bottleneck server will occasionally be idle because the upstream server
temporarily served at a low rate causing the bottleneck server to serve
all customers in the upstream storage, or the downstream server temporarily served at a low rate causing the downstream storage to become full
and block the bottleneck server. In effect, due to fluctuations, some
server other than the one with the smallest $\mu_j$ may act as if it were
the bottleneck, indeed for a sufficiently long period of time that the
storages cannot absorb the fluctuations in queues.

Even if the storages are sufficiently large that the blocking effects are negligible, the second significant consequence of fluctuations is that positive queues will, on the average, form behind every server. Although most of these queues may be small compared with the one behind the bottleneck, the total delay from all such servers may have an important effect upon the time required for a customer to pass through the entire system. It will, in fact, be the main issue if the "bottleneck" is the (artificial) input server.

The purpose of the diffusion approximations introduced in Chapter I is to obtain quantitative estimates of those queues which, on the average, are large compared with 1. In most practical applications there is at least one queue which is large, and those which are not are unimportant anyway. If queues are large compared with 1, the diffusion approximation typically gives quite accurate estimates for the number of customers in the queue. It does not usually make a distinction between the number of customers in the queue excluding the server and the number in the queue including the server. Indeed the diffusion approximation usually overestimates the former and underestimates the latter (it is usually closer to the latter), but, in any case, typically estimates either to within one customer.

The diffusion equation does not contain a detailed description of the service time distribution, only its first and second moments. In essence, it exploits the robustness of the behavior of the system induced by the fact that sums of independent random variables are nearly normally distributed even under conditions where rigorous application of the central limit theorem is questionable.

The answer to the commonly posed question "how accurate is the solution of the diffusion equation?" is that it is usually much more accurate than anyone would need.  If it is not accurate enough, one must have had

such a detailed description of the properties of the system in question

that one could have done a simulation.  In fact, in most applications,

one is lucky if one has a good estimate of the service rates $\mu_j$ (to

within 5% say);  the variance rates $\Delta_j$ are often known only to within

a factor of 2 seldom to within an accuracy of 20%.

Whereas most studies of stochastic queues deal only with the queue

lengths themselves, there are certain advantages to analysing the more

general properties of the cumulative number of customers to pass server

j, $D_j(t)$;  other than reasons given in section 2.  The joint probability

density of either the $D_j(t)$ or the $Q_j(t)$ satisfy diffusion type equa-

tions (I 4.3) or (I 5.3);  the former has a more symmetrical form but one

extra dimension.

If it were not for the fact that queue lengths are bounded $0 < Q_j(t)$

$\leq c_j$ , the solution of the diffusion equations would be trivial for any

number of servers.  As long as the queues stay away from the boundaries

0 or $c_j$ , changes in the $D_j(t)$ or $Q_j(t)$ during any time interval

are joint normally distributed (I 4.2).

The diffusion equation is valid for any states not on (or near) the

boundary, but, to define a "well-posed" problem, the solution must also

satisfy certain boundary conditions which describe the fact that some

service is interrupted at a boundary.  Unfortunately, these boundary

conditions are not of the same type as occur in classical physics (heat

conduction, diffusion, etc.) and cause some complications not only in

the explicit solution of the equations but even in the more abstract

formulation.  The boundary conditions along the surfaces on which only

one of the queues is either 0 or $c_j$ are well-defined (I 4.7) and (I 4.8), but these are not generally sufficient to define a unique solution. One must also specify boundary conditions (for $n \geq 2$) along edges where two or more of these surfaces intersect (for example, $Q_j(t) = 0$ and $Q_{j+1}(t) = c_{j+1}$). Along some edges the probability density must vanish but along others it must become infinite (in some special way).

To analyse the conditions along or near edges, it was necessary to imagine that each server was like a multiple channel server which would, in effect, allow $Q_j(t)$ to be negative or larger than $c_j$. When $Q_j(t) < 0$ or $Q_{j+1}(t) > c_{j+1}$, however, the service rate of server j would decrease (be partially blocked). Thus the "hard boundary" at $Q_j(t) = 0$ or $Q_{j+1}(t) = c_{j+1}$ was replaced by a "soft boundary." Now, by letting the service rate decrease very rapidly as $Q_j(t)$ went below zero or $Q_{j+1}(t)$ became greater than $c_{j+1}$, one could generate a "well-posed" problem. The limiting solution, however, for a hard boundary has singularities at the edges. The nature of these singularities was not fully explored and is still somewhat of a problem.

Although no explicit solutions of the diffusion equation with soft boundaries have been obtained here, the device of introducing a soft boundary and then taking a limit as the boundary becomes hard was used in several places to derive "global properties" of the hard boundary solutions. These properties were then exploited to define unique solutions in those cases where explicit solutions were obtained in later chapters.

Section I 7, for example, dealing with the moments of $D_k(t)$ was based upon limits of soft boundaries. This led to an equation (I 7.8) describing the long time average service rates of all servers in terms of the boundary values of the probability density. The fact that these rates must be equal for an equilibrium was imposed as a subsidiary condition in order to obtain unique solutions for the queue distributions in Chapter IV. Again in Chapter VI, the limits of soft boundaries were used to derive properties of the Laplace transforms of the probability densities. Some effects of edges were implied by these equations and were necessary to define the solutions of Chapters VI and VII.

Despite the fact that unique solutions were obtained for some special problems, no general scheme for treating (time-dependent) edge effects has been developed. Although it would seem that there should be some "local conditions" near the edges, any analysis of this has been by-passed here through conversion of these conditions into other properties. Since our goal has been to obtain answers to specific problems by whatever means we could, we leave this as a problem for someone more inclined toward the abstract theory than the solutions.

4. A Single Server. Chapters II - VII deal mostly with the analysis of special systems for which one can obtain exact solutions of the diffusion equation; but since the behavior of a multi-server system is usually dominated by the behavior of one or two critical servers, the analysis of certain one and two server systems will tell us a good deal about the behavior of some larger systems.

Since the number of parameters and the general complexity of the diffusion equation increases rapidly with the number of servers, it is natural that one should first analyse the single server in some detail before trying to study more complex systems. Of course the "single server" need not be the only server in the system. If there are infinite (or sufficiently large) storages downstream from server 1, the flow of customers past server 1 will be independent of the behavior of servers 2,

392

3, --. Since servers 2, 3, --, are fed by the output from server 1, it
may be useful to obtain some qualitative properties of the output from
server 1 preliminary to investigating the queueing downstream.

It is possible to obtain explicitly the complete time-dependent
solution of the diffusion equation for the joint distribution of the input $D_0(t)$ and output $D_1(t)$. The solution, however, would, generally,
be in the form of an infinite series or an integral. It is more useful,
for future applications, to determine only some of the special properties
that are particularly relevant to the output process.

For a single server, the edge effects discussed above do not exist
because the boundaries for $D_0(t)$, $D_1(t)$, namely $D_0(t) - D_1(t) = 0$
or $c_1$ are simply parallel lines in a two-dimensional space. One does
not encounter the edge effects until one has more than one queue. As
compared with the more conventional approach to the analysis of queues in
which one treats only the queue lengths, Chapter II illustrates further
advantages of dealing with the cumulative counts. Aside from the fact
that one can draw some convenient illustrations of the evolution of realizations of the vector $D_0(t)$, $D_1(t)$, one will obtain automatically the
properties of the output process $D_1(t)$.

The exact properties of the probability distributions for $D_1(t)$
are quite complex, particularly over "short times." However, from an
analysis of the distribution for queue lengths $Q_1(t)$, which satisfies
a diffusion equation in only one-dimension, one can establish a "relaxation time" (II 2.8). This is approximately the time it takes for the
distribution of $Q_1(t)$ to reach an equilibrium, starting from any initial state with queue lengths of size comparable with the equilibrium
mean queue length. This is also the time it takes for the mean departure

rate to become approximately the equilibrium value $\mu$ , (II 3.2).

If one knows that the queues downstream from server 1 will be fairly large and slowly varying, then they can be studied on a coarse time scale, measured by the time it takes these queues to make significant fractional changes. If, in particular, the natural time scale for investigating these downstream queues is large compared with the relaxation time (II 2.8) for $Q_1(t)$ , then on such a coarse time scale the process $D_1(t)$ behaves very much like a diffusion process. To describe the coarse properties of $D_1(t)$ as seen by the sluggish downstream queues, it suffices to specify the coarse-time mean rate $\mu$ , (II 3.2), and variance rate $\Delta$ , (II 5.3) of $D_1(t)$ .

The value of $\Delta$ described by (II 5.3) was evaluated from some asymptotic properties of the probability densities for large times evaluated by some special type of perturbation methods directly from the diffusion equation, rather than from the exact solution. No attempt was made in later chapters to extend for $n > 1$ some of the methods used in section II 4. Most of this calculation leading to the $\Delta$ depended upon knowledge of equilibrium distribution of $Q_1$ . There is a possibility that one could use the equilibrium distributions of $Q_1$ , $Q_2$ obtained in later chapters to determine the long-time variance rate of the output from certain systems with two queues. This would then be useful for the analysis of the queueing downstream from a subsystem with $n = 2$ .

If, on the other hand, the queues downstream form and disappear in a time which is short compared with the relaxation time (II 2.8), the output process $D_1(t)$ can be considered, most of the time, to be the uninterrupted output from server 1, but with occasional periods of lower output when $Q_1(t)$ is close to 0. The queues downstream will, most of the time, be like those created by a diffusion process input with rates $\mu_1$, $\Delta_1$. Occasionally (when $Q_1(t) = 0$), however, the queues downstream will have smaller values because the arrival rate drops, but these periods of shorter queues will not contribute much to the long time average.

To understand the time-dependent behavior of the distributions for $D_j(t)$ and $Q_j(t)$ is not just a challenging mathematical exercise; it is the key to the solution of many practical problems, including some approximate methods for determining equilibrium queue distributions (as suggested, in part, by the above comments regarding time scales). It is obvious that many of the properties of systems with time-dependent (but slowly varying) inputs $\mu_0(t)$ could be determined if one knew how the system recovers from disturbances. Anything that one can determine about transient behavior of queues has potential applications to the analysis of "rush hours." The lack of much literature on this subject is not because it is unimportant but because the techniques of analysis are limited.

By drawing possible realizations of the $D_j(t)$ as in figures I-3, I-4, one clearly sees that a $D_j(t)$ may stay close to one boundary for a while, then wander clear of any boundaries and later hit another boundary. Hitting a boundary interrupts one server. We can analyse the temporary consequences of this by disregarding the other boundaries and analysing what happens while the queue is near that boundary. We can also analyse how long it takes the queue to move free of the boundary. If the $c_j$ are large compared with 1, it takes a considerable time for a queue to wander from one boundary to another. One can understand certain properties even of the equilibrium queues by recognizing that expected behavior of any property of $Q_j(t)$ is the same as the long-time average behavior (i.e., the system is ergodic). The temporal behavior of $Q_j(t)$ , however, shows that a queue cannot jump from a value 0 to $c_j$ and that the time spent in one state depends upon the time spent in neighboring states.

The image solution of section II 6 for $n = 1$, $c_1 = \infty$ describes some basic features of time-dependent behavior which are also relevant to the analysis of systems with $n > 1$ and $c_j < \infty$ , because it shows in some detail what happens to the queues and service rates when any one queue is close to 0 or $c_j$ . (Note that because of the symmetry between customers and holes, anything that is said about queues near 0 can be translated into a statement about storages nearly full.)

Although subsequent chapters concentrate on exact solutions of equilibrium queue distributions, the interpretation of the results (particularly limiting cases) often hinges upon descriptions of the dynamic properties. For example, if servers 0 and 1 are both nearly regular, the output $D_1(t)$ must be nearly regular and therefore $Q_2(t)$ must behave like a single server queue with regular input. It seems likely that successful further extensions of the theory will emerge more from exploitation of rather intuitive consequences of occasional interruption of various servers and the geometry of realizations of the cumulative curves $D_j(t)$, than from further attempts to find general and exact solutions. For example, one should be able to exploit equation (II 7.10) which shows the effect upon $D_j(t)$ of "accidentally" hitting a boundary even though the average drift is away from the boundary.

5. Joint Probability Density for $Q_1, Q_2$ . Despite the very tedious analysis of Chapters III, IV, VI, and VII, the general solution of the queue distribution for arbitrary service rates $\mu_0$ , $\mu_1$ , $\mu_2$ and storages $c_1$, $c_2$ for $n = 2$ was not obtained. Yet one could infer, from the behavior

of special cases, at least the qualitative properties of the joint queue distribution for any $\mu_j$'s or $c_j$'s . Whereas Chapters III and IV deal with $\mu_0 = \mu_1 = \mu_2$ and $c_1$ , $c_2 < \infty$ , Chapters VI and VII deal with $\mu_0 \neq \mu_1 \neq \mu_2$ but $c_1 = c_2 = \infty$ . The former cases emphasize the properties of the distribution near corners of the rectangle $0 < Q_1 < c_1$ , $0 < Q_2 < c_2$ ; the latter emphasize the decay of the distributions due to unequal service rates. The behavior of the distribution near corners is not sensitive to the $\mu_j$'s , however, so it is easy to see qualitatively how one must distort the solutions with unequal $\mu_j$'s and $c_j = \infty$ to satisfy boundary conditions with $c_j < \infty$ . To obtain accurate numerical results is generally another matter, however.

The conformal mapping techniques used in Chapters III and IV are very specialized; they apply only for $\mu_0 = \mu_1 = \mu_2$ and for $n = 2$ . There is no possibility of generalizing these methods to $n > 2$ or unequal $\mu_j$'s . It is not even clear how one could use these solutions to develop a "perturbation" scheme for small differences in the $\mu_j$'s . The solutions can be used, however, to obtain various bounds particularly on the service rate $\mu$ for more complex systems, as discussed in section III 1. With $\mu_0 = \mu_1 = \mu_2$ there are limited possibilities of finding approximations of the type suggested above in section 4, because one cannot single out any particular server as the "bottleneck." These cases, in a sense, describe the most complex interactions between the queues.

The solutions of Chapters III and IV show that the probability density has analytic singularities at all corners of the space $0 < Q_1 < c_1$, $0 < Q_2 < c_2$ , except for very special values of the $\Delta_j$'s . The density is either zero or infinite at most corners but always vanishes at the corner $Q_1 = 0$ , $Q_2 = c_2$ . One can imagine how confusing it would be if someone were to try to classify properties of the joint queue distributions from exact solutions of discrete systems with some special service distributions (even exponential) or from simulations. One would collect masses of numerical solutions before recognizing that there were some analytic approximations. Indeed one probably never would discover these things unless one could first recognize some similarities in solutions with different parameters, i.e., one could reduce the parameter space through such scaling transformations as described in section III 5.

Despite the complexity of the analytic properties of the joint density near boundaries or corners, the system does show some simple global properties. If $c_1 < \infty$ and $c_2 = \infty$, servers 0 and 1 together determine the service rate $\mu$ and $\mu < \mu_2$ $(= \mu_0 = \mu_1)$. Thus we can think of the pair of servers 0 and 1 with finite storage as a bottleneck which generates the input to server 2.

From IV (2.10) we saw that for $(\Delta_0 + \Delta_1)/\Delta_2 \ll 1$ (even for a value of about 1), the distribution of $Q_2$ was very similar to that of a system fed by a diffusion input of rate $\mu$ and variance rate $\Delta = (\Delta_0 + \Delta_1)/3$ (the long time variance rate of the output from server 1). On the other hand one could not establish (for $\mu_0 = \mu_1 = \mu_2$) anything analogous to having a short relaxation time of $Q_2$ as compared with $Q_1$. For $(\Delta_1 + \Delta_2)/\Delta_0 \ll 1$ we found in III (2.17) that the queue $Q_2$ was proportional to $[(\Delta_1 + \Delta_2)/\Delta_0]^{1/2}$, which had no obvious interpretation. Also for $(\Delta_0 + \Delta_2)/\Delta_1 \ll 1$ we obtained some unusual results; the distribution of $Q_2$ was nearly rectangular.

The analysis in Chapters III and IV for $\mu_0 = \mu_1 = \mu_2$ is fairly complete. A detailed study is rather tedious, however, because the system still has three dimensionless parameters $\Delta_0/\Delta_1$, $\Delta_2/\Delta_1$, and $c_1/c_2$.

One cannot very well describe the joint distribution for all parameter values but there is a well-defined procedure for evaluating the distribution for any specified parameter values and one can describe the behavior of all limiting cases. Some fairly simple approximations were also obtained for the service rate $\mu$ as a function of $c_1$ and $c_2$. One could thus obtain some illustrations of the combined "blocking effect" of two finite storages.

The use of Laplace transforms in Chapters VI and VII was initiated with great reluctance and modest hopes. Although there are some powerful mathematical methods derived from transforms, one loses most of one's "physical intuition." As long as one works directly with the probability densities one can generate a mental picture of a fluid moving around and bouncing off boundaries. One can visualize the decay of functions in various directions and the truncation of these functions at boundaries. In the transform space, these local properties in the physical space are translated into conditions that certain functions must be analytic in appropriate parts of the complex plane; conditions which may be useful in the mathematical analysis but which do not generate a clear "physical picture." On the other hand, the transform methods handled very easily the problem of edge conditions which caused difficulties in the physical space.

Chapter VI deals with the case $\mu_0 < \mu_1$, $\mu_2$ for which server 0 is the bottleneck (equivalently we have a given undersaturated input to servers 1 and 2). For $c_1$, $c_2 = \infty$, the behavior of $Q_1$ is, of course, known because it is not affected by the behavior of server 2. The main goal in this chapter was to determine the marginal distribution of $Q_2$ (or its transform) and particularly $E\{Q_2\}$, but to do so one needed to evaluate the Laplace transform of the joint distribution.

We did not succeed in obtaining useful formulas for arbitrary values of the $\Delta_j$'s but we could at least verify the nature of the singularity of the joint density for $Q_1$, $Q_2 \to 0$ and the asymptotic behavior for large $Q_1$ and/or $Q_2$. We did obtain usable formulas for a number of specific choices of the $\Delta_j$'s : $\Delta_0 = \Delta_2 = 0$ and $\Delta_1 > 0$ ; $\Delta_1 = 0$ and $\Delta_0$, $\Delta_2 > 0$ ; $\Delta_0 = \Delta_1 > 0$ and $\Delta_2 > 0$ ; and several others. Although the detailed properties of the queue distributions are quite complex, all special cases showed that $2E\{Q_2\}(\mu_2 - \mu_0)$ is a monotone function of $\mu_1$ which varies between the limits $(\Delta_0 + \Delta_2)$ and $(\Delta_1 + \Delta_2)$ as $\mu_1$ goes from $\infty$ to $\mu_0$. Since, for most systems, one would not expect $(\Delta_0 + \Delta_2)$ and $(\Delta_1 + \Delta_2)$ to differ greatly one should have no difficulty in making a crude guess (to within 20%, say) of the value of $E\{Q_2\}$.

There is little discussion in Chapter VI of the properties of the joint distribution of $Q_1$, $Q_2$, except for the special case $\Delta_0 = \Delta_2 = 0$ in section 2. This omission is not because one can do nothing but because, for $\mu_0 < \mu_1$, $\mu_2$ and $c_1 = c_2 = \infty$, this is of limited practical interest. Most practical questions would relate to the wait $E\{Q_2\}$ and the rate of decay of the queue distribution. The latter is of interest so that one can estimate how large $c_2$ need be in order that it seldom causes an interruption of server 1.

There is a lengthy discussion in Chapter VII of the approximate inversion of the Laplace transforms to obtain estimates of the joint distributions of $Q_1$, $Q_2$ for the case $\mu_1 < \mu_0$, $\mu_2$. No doubt similar methods could be developed for $\mu_0 < \mu_1$, $\mu_2$, at least in those cases for which the Laplace transforms were determined in Chapter VI. This might be useful for the purpose of developing an approximate description

400

of the effects of finite but "large" $c_1$, $c_2$.

It is quite clear that the evaluation of the transforms of the joint density, for $c_1$, $c_2 < \infty$, is not very encouraging. It was not easy even for $c_1$, $c_2 = \infty$. If, however, one were to take the solutions for $c_1$, $c_2 = \infty$ and invert them back to the "physical space" of $Q_1$, $Q_2$, one could develop some crude approximations for large $c_1$, $c_2$ by simply truncating the distributions. The solutions for $c_1$, $c_2 \to \infty$ would at least show what one must cut off for $c_1$, $c_2 < \infty$.

For $c_1 < \infty$, $c_2 = \infty$, the blocking effect would cause $\mu$, given by II (3.2), to be less than $\mu_0$ and further restrict the input to server 2 (and decrease $E\{Q_2\}$). The comparisons of $E\{Q_2\}$ in section VI 6 for $\mu_0 = \mu_1$, $c_1 < \infty$ and $\mu_0 < \mu_1$, $c_1 = \infty$ suggest that one could guess (by interpolation) an approximate value of $E\{Q_2\}$ by choosing a value between that for a hypothetical system with $\mu_0 = \mu_1$ and a modified value of $c_1$ which gives the correct $\mu$, and a hypothetical system with $c_1 = \infty$ but a $\mu_0$ modified so as to give the correct $\mu$. Although a precise calculation of $E\{Q_2\}$ may be very tedious, there should not be much question as to its approximate value (to within 20% or so). This is probably as accurate as anyone would need anyway in any practical application.

The most troublesome cases would be those for which $c_2$ is finite having a value such that the $\mu$ value determined by servers 1 and 2 with storage $c_2$ is approximately equal to $\mu_0$, or the value of $\mu$ associated with just servers 0 and 1 with storage $c_1$. It is, of course, situations analogous to this which caused the difficult numerical computations of $\mu$ in Chapter III for $\mu_0 = \mu_1 = \mu_2$. Even here one could possibly use some of the results of Chapter III as a guide to guessing at a value of $\mu$ resulting from the combined blocking effects of $c_1 < \infty$

and $c_2 < \infty$ .

It is worth noting here also that the value of $\mu$ for $c_1$ , $c_2 < \infty$

must be less than for a hypothetical system consisting only of servers

0 and 2 with storage $c_1 + c_2$ . Indeed, if $\mu_1$ is sufficiently larger

than $\mu_0$ and $\mu_2$ , the system should behave approximately like one with

no server 1 (or $\mu_1 \to \infty$). One can see from figures VI 4 and VI 7 that

the shape of the marginal distribution of $Q_2$ for $\mu_2 > \mu_1$ $(\alpha_2/\alpha_1 > 0)$

are quite different from those for $\mu_2 < \mu_1$ $(\alpha_2/\alpha_1 < 0)$. In the latter

cases it might be advantageous to analyse the marginal distribution of

$Q_1 + Q_2$ instead of $Q_2$ since this presumably will show properties sim-

ilar to that of a system without a server 1. In any case, it would be

worthwhile to make a more detailed study of the joint distribution of

$Q_1$ and $Q_2$ for $\mu_0 < \mu_1$ , $\mu_2$ , perhaps in a manner similar to that

of Chapter VII for $\mu_1 < \mu_0$ , $\mu_2$ .

The main conclusion of Chapter VII is that for $\mu_1 < \mu_0$ , $\mu_2$ and

$c_1$ , $c_2$ large but finite, the reduction in $\mu$ due to both $c_1 < \infty$

and $c_2 < \infty$ is, in nearly all cases, approximately the sum of that for

$c_1 < \infty$ , $c_2 = \infty$ and $c_1 = \infty$ , $c_2 < \infty$ . Although an exact evaluation

of $\mu$ may be very complex, there should be no difficulty in estimating

$\mu - \mu_1$ to within 10 or 20%.

Although the exact formula for the joint probability density of $Q_1'$,

$Q_2$ was quite difficult to derive and even more difficult to evaluate,

the main features of the asymptotic solution for large $\ell_1'$ , $\ell_2$ were

relatively simple. In retrospect, at least, one can see that many of

the features illustrated in figure VIII - 6 could have been derived

without knowing the exact solution explicitly. It would suffice to know the location of two singularities of the transform $\overline{K}(\lambda_1, \lambda_2)$ in the complex plane to specify the two possible critical directions of $\ell_1'$, $\ell_2$ where the asymptotic form of $g^*$ changes. Between these critical directions the form of $g^*$ is determined by the form of the diffusion equation and is nearly independent of the boundary conditions. Outside of this region the form of $g^*$ is nearly exponential in $\ell_1'$, $\ell_2$, and strongly dependent on the boundary conditions.

It would seem that, in more complex problems which cannot be easily solved explicitly, that one might now be in a position to look for certain types of properties which one might not otherwise have expected. It was certainly not obvious to the author before doing the analysis of Chapter VII that one should look for different types of analytic forms of $g^*$ in different regions of the $\ell_1'$, $\ell_2$ space. It is also encouraging that the solutions in certain regions are insensitive to boundary conditions.

Perhaps the final conclusion of this study is that any hope of one finding simple and general solutions to queueing systems problems has been shattered. Many problems can be solved, but most solutions are not simple, even qualitatively. On the other hand, there is a vast literature on methods for solving partial differential equations of the type encountered here. Not all of the known techniques of analysis have been exploited yet.

# Notation

| | | Page | Reference |
|---|---|---|---|
| $a$ | a real number | 256 | (VI 3.8) |
| $A$ | integration constant | 47<br>106<br>279<br>296 | (II 2.7)<br>(III 3.1)<br>(VI 4.21a)<br>(VI 5.10) |
| $A'$ | integration constant | 279 | (VI 4.21c) |
| $A''$ | integration constant | 281 | (VI 4.24) |
| $A(x_0;t)$ | integration constant | 51 | (II 4.1b) |
| $A^\dagger(\xi_0;\tau)$ | transformation of $A(x_0;t)$ | 53 | (II 4.5) |
| $B_+^{(k)}$, $B_-^{(k)}$ | boundary terms | 18 | (I 4.6a,b) |
| $B_+^{(k,k+1)}$, $B_-^{(k,k+1)}$ | boundary terms | 23 | (I 4.11) |
| $B$ | a positive number | 115<br>287 | (III 4.5)<br>(VI 5.5) |
| $B'$ | a positive number | 137 | (III 7.7) |
| $B_.(\cdot,\cdot)$ | incomplete beta-function | 180 | (IV 4.2) |
| $c_j$ | storage capacity before server j | 2 | Fig. I 1 |
| $c_j^*$ | rescaled values of the $c_j$ | 97 | (III 2.5) |
| $\cos z$ | cosine of $z$ | | |
| $\cosh z$ | hyperbolic cosine of z | | |
| $\cos^{-1} z$ | inverse cos = arccos | | |
| $\cosh^{-1} z$ | inverse cosh = arccosh | | |
| $cn(\cdot)$ | elliptic function | 213 | (IV 6.31) |
| $ctn\ z$ | cotangent z | | |
| $ctnh\ z$ | hyperbolic cotangent z | | |
| $C(z_2)$ | unknown function | 245 | (VI 2.6) |
| $C$ | a constant<br>a boundary<br>path of integration | 247<br>277<br>349 | (VI 2.8)<br>(VI 4.20) |

404

|  |  | Page | Reference |
|---|---|---|---|
| $g_k^*(\ell_k)$ | equilibrium probability density of $Q_k$ | 38<br>94 | (I 7.6)<br>(III 2.4) |
| $g^\dagger; g^\dagger(\xi_0,\ell_1;\tau)$ | transformation of $g(x_0,\ell;t)$ | 51 | (I 4.2) |
| $\overline{g}(k_0,\ell_1,s)$ | transform of $g(x_0,\ell_1;t)$ | 87 | (II 8.1) |
| $g^{**}(\ell_1^*,\ell_2^*)$ | probability density of $Q_1^*$, $Q_2^*$ | 98 | (III 2.7) |
| $g_k^{**}(\ell_k^*)$ | probability density of $Q_k^*$ | 99 | (III 2.11) |
| $g_{\pm}(z)$ | known function | 285 | (IV 5.3) |
| $G^*(\ell_1;t)$ | distribution function of $Q_1(t)$ | 45 | (II 2.1) |
| $G^*(\ell_1)$ | equilibrium distribution function of $Q_1(t)$ | 46 | (II 2.6) |
| $G$ | a complex variable | 96 | Fig. III 1 |
| $G(\zeta)$ | an analytic function | 104 | (III 2.18) |
| $G$ | general service distribution in queue classification D/G/1 | 158 | |
| $h(x_0,x_1;t)$ | a linear mapping of $f(x_0,x_1;t)$ | 71 | (II 6.3) |
| $H(w)$ | an analytic function | 104 | (III 2.19) |
| $i$ | $\sqrt{-1}$ | | |
| Im | imaginary part of | | |
| $j$ | integer index | 3 | |
| $j_1$ | server with smallest $\mu_k$ | 9 | |
| $j_2$ | server with second smallest $\mu_k$ | 10 | |
| $k$ | integer index | 7 | (I 2.3) |
| $k_0$ | transform variable | 87 | (II 8.1) |
| $K(\cdot),\ K'(\cdot)$ | complete elliptic integrals | 117 | (IV 3.8) |
| $K(\lambda_0,\lambda_1,\lambda_2;t)$ | Laplace Transform of $f(x_0,x_1,x_2;t)$ | 231 | (VI 1.1) |

| | | Page | Reference |
|---|---|---|---|
| $K(\lambda_1,\lambda_2;t)$ | Laplace Transform of $g^*(\ell_1,\ell_2;t)$, $K(0,\lambda_1,\lambda_2;t)$ | 236 | (IV 1.12) |
| $K(\lambda_1,\lambda_2)$ | $K(\lambda_1,\lambda_2;\infty)$ | 237 | (VI 1.13) |
| $K_1(\lambda_0,\lambda_2;t)$ | Laplace Transform of $g(x_0,0,\ell_2;t)$ | 233 | (VI 1.3) |
| $K_1(\lambda_2;t)$ | $K_1(0,\lambda_2;t)$ | 236 | (VI 1.12) |
| $K_1(\lambda_2)$ | $K_1(\lambda_2;\infty)$ | 237 | (VI 1.13) |
| $K_2(\lambda_0,\lambda_1;t)$ | Laplace Transform of $g(x_0,\ell_1,0;t)$ | 234 | (VI 1.7) |
| $K_2(\lambda_1;t)$ | $K_2(0,\lambda_1;t)$ | 236 | (VI 1.12) |
| $K_2(\lambda_1)$ | $K_2(\lambda_1;\infty)$ | 237 | (VI 1.13) |
| $K_1^*(\lambda_0,\lambda_2;t)$ | Laplace Transform of $g(x_0,c_1,\ell_2;t)$ | 234 | (VI 1.9) |
| $K_1^*(\lambda_2;t)$ | $K_1^*(0,\lambda_2;t)$ | 236 | (VI 1.12) |
| $K_1^*(\lambda_2)$ | $K_1^*(\lambda_2;\infty)$ | 237 | (VI 1.13) |
| $K_2^*(\lambda_0,\lambda_1;t)$ | Laplace Transform of $g(x_0,\ell_1,c_2;t)$ | 235 | (VI 1.9a) |
| $K_2^*(\lambda_1;t)$ | $K_2^*(0,\lambda_1;t)$ | 236 | (VI 1.12) |
| $K_2^*(\lambda_1)$ | $K_2^*(\lambda_1;\infty)$ | 237 | (VI 1.13) |
| $K_1^\dagger(\theta_1)$ | coordinate change of $K_1(\lambda_2)$ | 265 | (VI 4.8b) |
| $K_2^\dagger(\theta_1)$ | coordinate change of $K_2(\lambda_1)$ | 264 | (VI 4.8a) |
| $\overline{K}(\lambda_1,\lambda_2)$ | Laplace Transform of $g^*(c_1-\ell_1',\ell_2)$ | 315 | (VII 1.3) |
| $\overline{K}_2(\lambda_1)$ | Laplace Transform of $g^*(c_1-\ell_1',0)$ | 315 | (VII 1.3a) |
| $K_1^{*\dagger}(\theta_1)$ | coordinate change of $K_1^*(\lambda_2)$ | 332 | (VII 3.3) |
| $\overline{K}_2^{\dagger}(\theta_1)$ | coordinate change of $\overline{K}_2(\lambda_1)$ | 332 | (VII 3.3) |
| $\ell_j$ | coordinate for queue length $Q_j(t)$ | 27 | |
| $\ell_j^*$ | rescaled queue lengths | 97 | (III 2.5) |

|  |  | Page | Reference |
|---|---|---|---|
| $\ell$ | an integer index | 102 | |
| $\ell'_j$ | rescaled queue lengths | 121 | |
| $\ell^*$ | a vector length | 351 | (VII 3.30) |
| $\ell_{2m}$ | mean queue length | 369 | (VII 3.44) |
| $\ln z$ | natural logarithm | | |
| L | length scale parameter | 51 | (II 4.2) |
| m | integer index | 7<br>295 | (I 2.3)<br>(VI 5.8) |
| n | number of servers | 3 | |
| $n_j$ | number of channels for server j | 32 | |
| $O(\cdot)$ | order of $(\cdot)$ | | |
| $P\{\cdot\}$ | probability of $\{\cdot\}$ | 4 | (I 1.6) |
| $q(\cdot)$ | the nome | 177 | (IV 3.9) |
| $Q_j(t)$ | customer queue waiting for server j at time t | 3 | Fig. I 2 |
| $Q'_j(t)$ | number of empty positions in $c_j$ at time t | 11 | (I 3.1) |
| $Q_j$ | equilibrium queue length for server j | | |
| $Q^*_j$ | rescaled queue lengths | 97 | (III 2.5b) |
| Re | real part of | | |
| s | transform variable | 87 | (II 8.1) |
| $\sin z$ | sine of z | | |
| $\sinh z$ | hyperbolic sine of z | | |
| $\sin^{-1}z$ | inverse sine = arcsine | | |
| $\sinh^{-1}z$ | inverse sinh = arcsinh | | |
| $sn(\cdot)$ | elliptic function | 213 | (IV 6.4) |
| t | time | 3 | |

|  |  | Page | Reference |
|---|---|---|---|
| $t_0$ | initial time | 6 | |
| tan z | tangent z | | |
| tanh z | hyperbolic tangent | | |
| $\tan^{-1} z$ | inverse tangent | | |
| $\tanh^{-1} z$ | inverse hyperbolic tangent | | |
| T | time scale parameter | 51 | (II 4.2) |
| u | argument of elliptic function | 213 | (IV 6.3) |
| | integration variable | 324 | |
| w | a complex variable | 96 | Fig. III 1 |
| | a parameter | 326 | (VII 2.13) |
| $w_1$, $w_3$ | singular points in w-plane | 106 | (III 3.1) |
| $x_j$ | coordinate for customer count at server j | 4 | (I 1.6) |
| $x_0^*$ | displacement of coordinate $x_0$ | 55 | |
| $x_0'$, $x_1'$ | linear transformation of $x_0$, $x_1$ | 68 | (II 6.2) |
| x | integration variable (real) | 107 | (III 3.5) |
| $y_j$ | initial customer count $D_j(t_0)$ | 6 | (I 2.1) |
| $y_j'$ | initial count of holes $D_j'(t_0)$ | 14 | |
| z | integration variable (complex) | 106 | (III 3.2) |
| $z_1$, $z_2$ | complex variables | 241 | |
| | | 319 | (VII 2.3) |
| $Z(x_0, x_1, \cdots, x_n)$ | an arbitrary function | 37 | (I 7.1) |
| $Z(\theta_1)$ | a periodic function | 296 | (VI 5.9) |
| $\alpha_1$ | parameter | 45 | (II 2.5) |
| $\alpha_1$, $\alpha_2$ | parameters | 241 | (VI 2.1) |
| | | 314 | (VII 1.1a) |
| | | 314 | (VII 1.2a) |
| $\alpha_1^*$ | parameter | 355 | (VII 3.35b) |
| $\alpha_2^*$ | parameter | 354 | (VII 3.34b) |

|  |  | <u>Page</u> | Reference |
|---|---|---|---|
| $\lambda_1^{(\pm)}$ | roots of equation | 347 | (VII 3.26) |
| $\mu_j$ | service rate of server j | 4 | (I 1.4) |
| $\mu_j^*; \mu_j^*(x_{j-1}, x_j, x_{j+1})$ | service rate of multiple channel server | 33 | (I 6.3) |
| $\mu$ | equilibrium service rate of the system | 39 | (I 7.7) |
| $\mu_{max}$ | maximum $\mu$ for $c_1 + c_2$ fixed | 194 | (IV 5.5) |
| $\mu^\dagger$ | a service rate parameter | 263 | (VI 4.3) |
| $\tau$ | time interval<br>rescaled time variable | 3<br>51 | (II 4.2) |
| $\pi$ | 3.14-- | | |
| $\sigma_{2m}$ | standard deviation of queue length | 369 | (VII 3.44) |
| $\phi_4$ | angle in the complex $\zeta$-plane | 130 | |
| $\phi_0$ | angle in the complex $\zeta$-plane | 133 | (III 6.13) |
| $\phi$ | angle of $\ell^*$ | 351 | (VII 3.31) |
| $\Phi\{\cdot\}$ | normal distribution function | | |
| $\psi(\cdot)$ | digamma function | 136 | (III 7.4) |